A Watermark Learning Publication

PMI-PBA®
CERTIFICATION
STUDY GUIDE

Praise for *Watermark Learning Study Guides*

"I wrote and passed the CBAP exam on June 28. It was a tough one. Thank you very much for your study guide and online study exam. **I wouldn't have passed without them!**"
Sandra Koehler, CBAP, PMP

"I wanted to say thank you - just wrote (and passed) the CBAP this afternoon, and your study guide was a **key factor** in this."
Sean Adams, CBAP, PMP

"I had very little time to prepare the CBAP exam, more precisely 5 weeks. Although a seasoned practitioner, I realized that passing the exam takes a lot more, as the PMP exam taught me years ago. After browsing the Internet for a couple of hours, I selected your tools to help me prepare the exam in such a short time. **Your Study Guide & online Study Exam were my secret weapons** that helped me be successful from the first attempt!"
Maria Lutz, PMP, CBAP

"I took the CBAP exam today and cleared it! Your book definitely helped me with many of the questions directly and indirectly, and most importantly putting me in the right frame of mind for the exam."
Chetan Mehta, CBAP

"I am delighted to inform you that I successfully certified as CBAP yesterday at Mumbai, India. **Thanks for your study material and support**. Without your study guide, Online Exams, simulations, drill exams etc., it would not have been possible for me get certified. Watermark Learning's material, content and quality was just **perfect to give a real feel of the actual CBAP exam** and was of the same level. I strongly recommend your study/preparatory material for clearing the CBAP Exam."
Suneet Garg, CBAP, PMP, CSCP

"I wanted to say how very helpful your CBAP study guide and online exam prep was in passing the CBAP exam. The book **provided excellent learning techniques,** including the types of questions and pitfalls to expect on the exam, test-taking strategies, and key points to remember. The online exam prep **provided the ability for a user to focus in on 'problem' areas for deeper study**, with the flexibility of a simulated exam, or instant feedback after each question (including an explanation for the answer, and where to reference in the BABOK**). I passed the exam on the first try**, and your exam prep definitely assists in thinking about how to answer the questions on the exam.
Eve M. McGivern, CBAP

"Today, I passed the CBAP examination (first attempt)! The Watermark Learning Certification Study Guide, the On-Line Simulator, and the Flash Cards **played a major role** in preparing me for the CBAP examination."
Mark Viola, CBAP

ENHANCED PERFORMANCE, ENDURING RESULTS,

7301 Ohms Lane, Suite 360
Minneapolis, MN 55439
Telephone: 800-646-9362

A Watermark Learning Publication

PMI-PBA®
CERTIFICATION
STUDY GUIDE

ELIZABETH LARSON, PMI-PBA & RICHARD LARSON, PMI-PBA

Dedication

To business analysts and project managers everywhere
who are committed to our profession, and want to
achieve their PMI-PBA® certification.

ISBN: 978-0-578-15547-0

Version 1.2

Cover Design
AdVanced Design, Inc.
www.advanceddesign-online.com

Watermark Learning Publications
7301 Ohms Lane, Suite 360
Minneapolis, MN, 55439 USA
Telephone: 800-646-9362
             +1 952-921-0900

Visit our website at **www.WatermarkLearning.com** for information on training programs certification preparation or other Business Analysis and Project Management training courses.

You Have the Right Book to Help You Become Certified!

The *PMI-PBA Certification Study Guide* has been used by our class attendees, PMI® study groups, and individuals doing self-study. Our Guide, as we call it for short, is a comprehensive book to help you understand and structure the PMI-PBA examination content. Our Guide is entirely focused on helping you pass the PMI-PBA exam, and so we chose to emphasize the PMI-PBA® exam content rather than "real life." Here are some other reasons why this book will help.

Online Exam Questions

Your purchase of this book entitles you to a complimentary subscription to the Watermark Learning PMI-PBA Online Study Exam. This unique tool provides guided practice through all stages of preparation for the PMI-PBA exam. The exam includes:

1) **Warm-up** questions as you get started,
2) **Drills** to practice answering questions in specific Domains, and
3) **Exam Simulator** to practice taking 200-question tests like the actual exam.

The PMI-PBA study exam has over **800 questions** to give you extensive practice. Registration instructions are listed on the front cover of the book. Our research of successful certification candidates indicated that taking practice exam questions was vital to their passing the exam. Start practicing today! Paid subscriptions can be renewed at a discounted rate.

Updates and Resources

We continually update this book to make corrections and add additional information of value. If we discover typos or other errors, we post them to an errata document on our website. Check out the **errata document** for a list of corrections to this book at **www.WatermarkLearning.com/PBA-Study-Guide**. You will find other useful PMI-PBA related information and resources there.

To receive notices of PMI-PBA news and information, such as webinars and articles, please register as a Watermark Learning member at **www.WatermarkLearning.com/Register**. Make sure you subscribe to our ProjectBrief eNewsletter so you will receive the update notices. Plus, watch the ProjectBrief for additional resources that can help you prepare for the PMI-PBA exam and enhance your business analysis and project management skills.

Feedback

We value your opinion and need your feedback. Please visit our web site at **www.WatermarkLearning.com/Feedback** to provide feedback or comments about this book. There is a page designed for easy submission. Or, if you prefer, send your comments by email to **info@watermarklearning.com**.

Development Team

The authors gratefully thank the following people for their contribution to the development of this book.

Andrea Brockmeier, PMP, CSM, PMI-ACP
Project manager

Chris Anderson
Production manager

Dayle Beyer, PMP, CBAP, PMI-RMP, PMI-PBA
Content editor

Deb McCormick, CBAP
Content and copy editor

Jeanne Gibbs
Format editor

Mercy Ehrler
Book cover design

Vicki James, PMP, CBAP
Contributing author

Other Resources to Help You Become a PMI-PBA

We designed our *PMI-PBA Certification Study Guide* to be a comprehensive resource for your preparation for the PMI-PBA exam. If you want additional materials to complement this Guide, we have you well-covered.

All the Tools You Need to Pass the PMI_PBA Exam

PMI-PBA® Certification Preparation Classes
Our comprehensive workshops will prepare you for the PMI-PBA® exam and help you make the most of the limited study time you have. Both traditional classroom and virtual editions of this class are available.

PMI-PBA® Version 1.0 Study Guide
This comprehensive study guide is what you are reading. It helps you readily master all pertinent knowledge areas of the PMBOK® Guide plus other relevant resources and helps you focus your study time.

PMI-PBA® Online Study Exam
This self-paced program adapts as you progress in your exam preparation. It contains warm-up exams to get started, a drill section to concentrate on one PMI-PBA® domain area at a time, and a full PMI-PBA® exam simulator. Detailed feedback and summary results are provided. Your purchase of this Guide entitles you to a trial subscription.

PMI-PBA® Study Tables
Our PMI-PBA® Study Tables give you an overview of the PMI-PBA® exam content in a comprehensive and detailed, yet highly visual package. If you are studying for the PMI-PBA® exam, these study tables are a must. These colorful robust tables are designed for independent study or for use with study groups or training classes. They also are a valuable aid on the job as a quick-reference resource.

For more information, visit **www.WatermarkLearning.com/pba**. We also have a number of links to free resources on this page to help you in your preparation efforts.

OUR STORY

Today, employers are looking for more than just job expertise. They need problem solvers—highly-performing professionals with the practical know-how to create enduring results.

Since 1992, Watermark Learning has been cultivating today's problem solvers and tomorrow's leaders through business analysis, project management, and business process management training. Our clients receive skill development that enables both organizations and individuals to define, analyze, and deliver products and services that produce bottom-line results.

We maximize learning because our training is focused, immediately applicable, and engaging. Experience our unique combination of best practices, practical approach, and engaging delivery and you'll discover why organizations prefer the Watermark Learning portfolio of training services.

TRAINING SERVICES

Live Training: Our instructor-led courses cover today's most relevant topics to help you keep pace in today's demanding business environment. Classes are offered in a traditional classroom setting or through virtual delivery using the internet.

Private Classes: Minimize scheduling hassles and travel expenses by inviting a Watermark Learning expert to your site. Your project team will benefit from lower per-student cost and personalized curriculum that incorporates your organization's particular methods and corporate culture.

Public Classes: When you need to train one person or a few people, our open-enrollment classes provide you flexibility. We offer several iterations of core classes throughout the year. You can "sample" our training before committing to an onsite class.

Courseware Licensing: Jump-start your own training programs by licensing our high-quality course materials. Teach classes with your own instructors, customize them to your needs, or contract with us for a turnkey solution. Available in select markets.

Mentoring/Consultative Training: Our mentoring services tackle your unique needs while helping you keep projects on track. It reinforces classroom learning and enhances job performance.

Certification Programs: If you want a skill-based Business Analysis or Project Management program, obtain a Masters Certificate from Auburn University and expand your career horizons. If you desire an industry certification from PMI® or IIBA®, we offer best-in-class PMP®, PMI-PBA® and CBAP®/CCBA® programs.

> " Course materials were clear and concise and the exercises were excellent—make sense in my real world. Instructor was also very, very good—shared knowledge and experiences with us without making that the central point. Every minute was valuable. Thanks! "
>
> | MICHELLE WEBB, ALLIANZ LIFE INSURANCE

7301 Ohms Lane, Suite 360
Minneapolis, MN 55439
Tel +1 952-921-0900 ♦ 800-646-9362
www.WatermarkLearning.com

 Endorsed Education Provider™

BUSINESS ANALYSIS | PROJECT MANAGEMENT | BUSINESS PROCESS MANAGEMENT

COURSES

Agile Bootcamp Using Scrum
3 days—21 PDUs/CDUs | 2.1 CEUs

Agile Business Analysis
2 days—14 PDUs/CDUs | 1.4 CEUs

Agile Planning and Estimating
2 days—14 PDUs/CDUs | 1.4 CEUs

Avoiding Troubled Projects
2 days—14 PDUs | 1.4 CEUs

Bulletproof Business Cases
2 days—14 PDUs/CDUs | 1.4 CEUs

Business Analysis Fundamentals
3 days—21 PDUs/CDUs | 2.1 CEUs

Business Intelligence Requirements Analysis
2 days—14 PDUs/CDUs | 1.4 CEUs

Business Process Improvement
2 days—14 PDUs/CDUs | 1.4 CEUs

Business Process Management Foundations
1 day—7 PDUs/CDUs | .7 CEUs

Business Process Modeling
2 days—14 PDUs/CDUs | 1.4 CEUs

CBAP®/CCBA® Certification Preparation
3 days—21 CDUs | 2.1 CEUs

Certified ScrumMaster (CSM)
2 days—14 PDUs | 1.4 CEUs

Conflict Management
2 days—14 PDUs/CDUs | 1.4 CEUs

Consulting Skills to Solve Business Problems
2 days—14 PDUs/CDUs | 1.4 CEUs

Critical Thinking Skills
2 days—14 PDUs/CDUs | 1.4 CEUs

Data Modeling
2 days—14 PDUs/CDUs | 1.4 CEUs

Eliciting Business Requirements
2 days—14 PDUs/CDUs | 1.4 CEUs

Facilitation Skills Workshop
2 days—14 PDUs/CDUs | 1.4 CEUs

Getting Started in Business Analysis
2 days—14 PDUs | 1.4 CEUs

Getting Started in Project Management
1 day—7 PDUs | .7 CEUs

Influencing Without Authority
2 days—14 PDUs/CDUs | 1.4 CEUs

Organizational Change Management
2 days—14 PDUs | 1.4 CEUs

PMI-ACP® Certification Preparation
2 days—14 PDUs | 1.4 CEUs

PMI-PBA® Certification Bootcamp
4 days—35 PDUs | 3.5 CEUs

PMP® Certification Bootcamp
4 days—35 PDUs | 3.5 CEUs

Planning and Managing Requirements
2 days—14 PDUs/CDUs | 1.4 CEUs

Program Management Fundamentals
2 days—14 PDUs | 1.4 CEUs

Project Management Fundamentals
3 days—21 PDUs | 2.1 CEUs

Project Quality Management
1 days—7 PDUs | .7 CEUs

Project R.E.A.L. Live Simulation
3 days—21 PDUs/CDUs | 2.1 CEUs

Project Risk Management
2 days—14 PDUs | 1.4 CEUs

Project Sponsor Workshop
1/2 day—3.5 PDUs | .35 CEUs

Requirements Modeling Essentials
2 days – 14 PDUs/CDUs | 1.4 CEUs

Software Testing Fundamentals
2 days—14 PDUs | 1.4 CEUs

Use Case Essentials
1 day—7 PDUs/CDUs | .7 CEUs

Use Case Modeling
2 days—14 PDUs/CDUs | 1.4 CEUs

Virtual Teams
2 days—14 PDUs/CDUs | 1.4 CEUs

" The overall training provided by Watermark was very well done, with excellent training materials and case exercises... We have a high level of confidence in our skills and our process as we move forward with our project."

| RICHELLE FLEISCHER,
RIVERSIDE HEALTH SYSTEM

AUBURN UNIVERSITY
SAMUEL GINN
COLLEGE OF ENGINEERING

Masters and Associate
Certificate Programs offered
through Auburn University

Contents at a Glance

1. PMI-PBA Foundations   1

2. Needs Assessment   33

3. Planning   95

4. Analysis   147

5. Traceability and Monitoring   253

6. Evaluation   289

7. Competencies   335

8. Final Tips   359

9. Appendix A – Glossary Terms   373

10. Appendix B: Exam Simulation   387

11. Index   439

Table of Contents

1.   PMI-PBA Foundations   1

Part 1: Introduction to PMI-PBA   1
  Overview   1
  The PMI-PBA Exam   6
  Organization of this Guide   11
  What This Guide is Not   12
  What This Guide Is   13

Part 2: PMI-PBA Examination Content Overview   14
  Preparation Overview   14
  Domains   15
  Terminology "Eye Opener"   18
  Basic Terminology   19
  Adaptive Life Cycle   19
  Business Analysis   19
  Business Analyst   19
  Solution   19
  Requirement   19
  Requirements Classification (*PMBOK® Guide*)   20
  Predictive Life Cycle   21
  Project   21
  Tasks   21
  Techniques   22
  Tools   22
  Stakeholders   22
  Guide to Tools and Techniques   22
  Guide to Project Life Cycle Approaches   23

PMI-PBA Exercises   24

PMI-PBA Practice Exam   25

Exercise Answers   27

PMI-PBA Practice Exam Answers   28

Summary   32

2.   Needs Assessment   33

Overview   33
  Task Inputs, Tools and Techniques, and Outputs   36

Part 1 – Needs Assessment Tasks   38
  Task 1 – Define Business Need   38
  Task 2 – Determine Value Proposition   42
  Task 3 – Develop Project Goals   44
  Needs Assessment – Exercise 1   47
  Task 4 – Identify Stakeholders   49
  Task 5 – Determine Stakeholder Values   54

    Needs Assessment – Exercise 2   57

    Needs Assessment – Exercise 3   58

   Part 2 – Techniques for Needs Assessment   59

    Problem Solving and Opportunity Identification Tools and Techniques   60

    Root Cause Analysis Tools and Techniques   64

    Scope Models Tools and Techniques   67

    Stakeholder Analysis Tools and Techniques   70

    Valuation Tools and Techniques   73

    Needs Assessment – Exercise 4   80

   PMI-PBA Practice Exam   83

   Exercise Answers   86

   Summary   93

3. Planning   95

   Overview   95

    Task Inputs and Outputs   98

   Part 1 – Planning Tasks   100

    Task 1 – Determine Project Context   100

    Task 2 – Plan Requirements Traceability   105

    Task 3 – Plan Requirements Management   109

    Planning – Exercise 1   115

    Task 4 – Plan Requirements Change Control   115

    Needs Assessment Review – Exercise 2   120

    Task 5 – Plan Document Control   121

    Task 6 – Define Project Expected Outcomes   123

    Planning – Exercise 3   126

   Part 2 – Techniques for Planning   127

    Contingency Planning Tools and Techniques   128

    Document Management Tools and Techniques   128

    Estimation Tools and Techniques   129

    Scheduling Tools and Techniques   133

    Planning – Exercise 4   134

    Planning – Exercise 5   135

   PMI-PBA Practice Exam   136

   Exercise Answers   138

   PMI-PBA Practice Exam Answers   141

   Summary   145

4. Analysis   147

   Overview   147

    Task Inputs and Outputs   150

   Part 1 – Analysis Tasks   153

    Task 1 – Elicit Requirements   153

Task 2 – Analyze, Decompose, and Elaborate Requirements   159
Analysis – Exercise 1   165
Task 3 – Evaluate Product Options and Capabilities   165
Task 4 – Allocate Requirements   168
Analysis – Exercise 2   172
Analysis – Exercise 3   173
Task 5 – Get Requirements Sign-off   173
Task 6 – Write Requirements Specifications   175
Analysis – Exercise 4   178
Task 7 - Validate Requirements   179
Task 8 – Elaborate and Specify Acceptance Criteria   181
Analysis – Exercise 5   184

PMI-PBA Practice Exam (Part 1)   185

Part 2 – Techniques for Analysis   187
Analytic Tools and Techniques   189
Business Rule Analysis Tools and Techniques   193
Data Analysis Tools and Techniques   194
Decision Making Tools and Techniques   202
Analysis – Exercise 6   204
Elicitation Tools and Techniques   204
Analysis – Exercise 7   213
Interface Analysis Tools and Techniques   214
Measurement Tools and Techniques   218
Prioritization Tools and Techniques   220
Process Analysis Tools and Techniques   221
Analysis – Exercise 8   232

PMI-PBA Practice Exam (Part 2)   234

Exercise Answers   236

PMI-PBA Practice Exam Answers (Part 1)   242

PMI-PBA Practice Exam Answers (Part 2)   247

Summary   251

5.   Traceability and Monitoring   253

Overview   253
Task Inputs, Tools and Techniques, and Outputs   256

Part 1 – Traceability and Monitoring Tasks   258
Task 1 – Trace Requirements   258
Task 2 – Monitor Requirement Status   262
Task 3 – Update Requirement Status   264
Task 4 - Communicate Requirements Status   267
Task 5 – Manage Changes to Requirements   271
Traceability and Monitoring – Exercise 1   275

Part 2 – Techniques for Traceability and Monitoring   276
Change Control Tools and Techniques   276
Traceability Tools and Techniques   277

Version Control Tools and Techniques 279
Traceability and Monitoring – Exercise 2 280

PMI-PBA Practice Exam 281

Exercise Answers 283

PMI-PBA Practice Exam Answers 284

Summary 288

6. Evaluation 289

Overview 289
Task, Tools, Techniques, and Outputs 291

Part 1 – Evaluation Tasks 293
Task 1 – Validate Test Results 293
Task 2 – Analyze Solution Gaps 297
Task 3 – Get Solution Sign-off 301
Task 4 – Evaluate Solution Results 303

Evaluation – Exercise 1 306

Evaluation – Exercise 2 307

Part 2 – Techniques for Evaluation 308
Evaluation Tools and Techniques 310
Quality Management Tools and Techniques 312
Validation Tools and Techniques 319
Verification Tools and Techniques 320

Evaluation – Exercise 3 325

PMI-PBA Practice Exam 326

Exercise Answers 328

PBA-PBA® Practice Exam Answers 330

Summary 334

7. Competencies 335

Overview 335

Competencies Skills and Knowledge 337
Collaboration 337
Communication 338
Conflict Management 342
Negotiation 343
Facilitation 343
Leadership 345
Political / Cultural Awareness 347
Systems Thinking 348

Competencies – Exercise 349

PMI-PBA Practice Exam   350

Exercise Answers   352

PMI-PBA Practice Exam Answers   353

Summary   357

8. Final Tips   **359**

Overview   359

Preparing to Succeed   360
    Test Preparation Roadmap   360
    Final Tips – Exercise   364
    Practice Exams   366
    During the Exam   367

Summary   371

9. Appendix A – Glossary Terms   **373**

10. Appendix B: Exam Simulation   **387**

Simulated Exam Questions   388

Simulated Exam Answers   407

11. Index   **439**

Table of Figures

Figure 1-1: PMI-PBA® Certification Requirements 3

Figure 1-2: PMI-PBA Exam-Taking Tactics 8

Figure 1-3: PMI-PBA Exam Question Types 9

Figure 1-4: PMI-PBA Themes 10

Figure 1-5: PMI-PBA Preparation Roadmap 15

Figure 1-6: Percent of Questions on PMI-PBA 16

Figure 1-7: Requirements Classifications 21

Figure 1-8: Predictive and Adaptive Life Cycle Approaches 23

Figure 2-1: PMI-PBA Themes relating to Needs Assessment 34

Figure 2-2: Needs Assessment Domain 34

Figure 2-3: Needs Assessment ITTOs 37

Figure 2-4: Define Business Need ITO 38

Figure 2-5: Problem Statement Components 39

Figure 2-6: Determine Value Proposition ITO 42

Figure 2-7: Develop Project Goals ITO 44

Figure 2-8: SMART Objectives 45

Figure 2-9: Identify Stakeholders ITO 49

Figure 2-10: RACI Matrix 51

Figure 2-11: Attitude Assessment Factors 52

Figure 2-12: Influence Assessment Factors 53

Figure 2-13: Identify Stakeholder Requirements ITO 55

Figure 2-14: Tools and Techniques for Needs Assessment 60

Figure 2-15: Benchmarking Technique 61

Figure 2-16: Competitive Analysis Worksheet Sample 61

Figure 2-17: User Journey Map Example 62

Figure 2-18: Value Engineering Overview 63

Figure 2-19: Fishbone / Ishikawa Overview 64

Figure 2-20: Fishbone Diagram Example 65

Figure 2-21: Five Whys Overview 65

Figure 2-22: Interrelationship Diagram 66

Figure 2-23: Process Model Example 67

Figure 2-24: Context Diagram Overview 68

Figure 2-25: Context Diagram Example 68

Figure 2-26: Use Case Diagram Overview 69

Figure 2-27: Use Case Diagram Example 70

Figure 2-28: Organizational Chart Overview 71

Figure 2-29: Organizational Chart Example 71

Figure 2-30: RACI Matrix Overview 72

Figure 2-31: Sample RACI Chart, focused on Project Phase 72

Figure 2-32: Sample RACI Chart, focused on Stakeholders 73

Figure 2-33: Cost-Benefit Analysis Overview 74

Figure 2-34: Force Field Analysis Overview 75

Figure 2-35: Force Field Analysis Example 75

Figure 2-36: Kano Model Example 76

Figure 2-37: Net Promoter Score 77

Figure 2-38: Purpose Alignment Model 77

Figure 2-39: SWOT Analysis Overview 78

Figure 2-40: SWOT Diagram Example 79

Figure 2-41: Value Stream Map Example 79

Figure 3-1: Themes applicable to Planning 96

Figure 3-2: Planning Domain 96
Figure 3-3: Planning ITTOs 99
Figure 3-4: Determine Project Context ITO 100
Figure 3-5: Project Management Life Cycle vs. Project Life Cycle 101
Figure 3-6: Project Lifecycle Approach Overview 102
Figure 3-7: Predictive Life Cycle 102
Figure 3-8: Adaptive Life Cycle 103
Figure 3-9: Incremental Approach 104
Figure 3-10: Iterative Approach 104
Figure 3-11: Plan Requirements Traceability ITO 106
Figure 3-12: Considerations for Traceability 106
Figure 3-13: Requirements Traceability Matrix 108
Figure 3-14: Plan Requirements Management ITO 110
Figure 3-15: Work Breakdown Structure for BA Activities 111
Figure 3-16: Business Analysis Activities Schedule 112
Figure 3-17: Project Management Plan 113
Figure 3-18: Components of the Requirements Management Plan 114
Figure 3-19: Requirements Change Management ITO 116
Figure 3-20: Change Request Form 117
Figure 3-21: Plan Document Control ITO 121
Figure 3-22: Microsoft Office Backstage View (Version Control) 122
Figure 3-23: Define Project Expected Outcomes ITO 123
Figure 3-24: Techniques for Planning 128
Figure 4-1: PMI-PBA Exam Themes Applicable to Analysis 148
Figure 4-2: Analysis Domain 149
Figure 4-3: Analysis ITTOs 152
Figure 4-4: Elicit Requirements ITO 153
Figure 4-5: Iterative Elicitation Process 154
Figure 4-6: Preparation Notes Example 155
Figure 4-7: Elicitation Documentation Types 157
Figure 4-8: Analyze, Decompose, and Elaborate Requirement ITO 160
Figure 4-9: Text Requirement Guidelines 161
Figure 4-10: Opportunity Areas to Consider 162
Figure 4-11: Compare Requirements to Product Scope ITO 166
Figure 4-12: Allocate Requirements ITO 168
Figure 4-13: Requirements Prioritization Criteria 169
Figure 4-14: Get Requirements Sign-off ITO 174
Figure 4-15: Write Requirements Specifications ITO 176
Figure 4-16: Validate Requirements ITO 179
Figure 4-17: Specify Acceptance Criteria ITO 182
Figure 4-18: Tools and Techniques for Analysis 189
Figure 4-19: Decomposition Overview 190
Figure 4-20: Example of a Work Breakdown Structure (WBS) used to decompose solution scope 191
Figure 4-21: Requirements Relationships 191
Figure 4-22: Data Dictionary and Glossary Overview 195
Figure 4-23: Data Flow Diagrams Overview 196
Figure 4-24: Data Flow Diagram Example 196
Figure 4-25: Data Model Overview 198
Figure 4-26: Entity Relationship Diagram Example 198
Figure 4-27: Class Model Example 199
Figure 4-28: State Diagrams Overview 201
Figure 4-29: State Diagram Example 201
Figure 4-30: State Table Example 201
Figure 4-31: Weighted Criteria Overview 203

Figure 4-32: Weighted Criteria Example 204
Figure 4-33: Brainstorming Overview 205
Figure 4-34: Document Analysis Overview 206
Figure 4-35: Facilited Workshop Overview 207
Figure 4-36: Focus Group Overview 207
Figure 4-37: Interview Overview 208
Figure 4-38: Non-functional Requirements Analysis Overview 210
Figure 4-39: Observation Overview 211
Figure 4-40: Survey/Questionnaire Overview 212
Figure 4-41: Prototypes Overview 215
Figure 4-42: Wireframe Example 217
Figure 4-43: Display-Action-Response Model 217
Figure 4-44: Key Performance Indicators (KPI's) Overview 218
Figure 4-45: Service Level Agreement (SLA) Overview 220
Figure 4-46: Process Model Overview 223
Figure 4-47: Activity Diagram Example 224
Figure 4-48: Activity Diagram with Fork and Join Example 224
Figure 4-49: Swimlane Flowchart Example 225
Figure 4-50: Sequence Diagrams Overview 226
Figure 4-51: Sequence Diagram Example 227
Figure 4-52: Scenario and Use Case Overview 228
Figure 4-53: Use Case Diagram Example 228
Figure 4-54: Use Case Description Example 229
Figure 4-55: User Stories Overview 230
Figure 4-56: User Story Example 231
Figure 5-1: PMI-PBA Themes Related to Traceability and Monitoring 254
Figure 5-2: Traceability and Monitoring Domain 254
Figure 5-3: Traceability and Monitoring ITTOs 257
Figure 5-4: Need for Requirements Relationships 259
Figure 5-5: Trace Requirements ITO 260
Figure 5-6: Requirements Relationships 260
Figure 5-7: Monitor Requirements ITO 262
Figure 5-8: Update Requirements Status ITO 264
Figure 5-9: Example Traceability Matrix 265
Figure 5-10: Example of a Requirements Life Cycle Diagram 266
Figure 5-11: Communicate Requirements Status ITO 267
Figure 5-12: Requirements Communication Strategy Example 269
Figure 5-13: Common project roles with requirements needs 269
Figure 5-14: Manage Changes to Requirements ITO 271
Figure 5-15: Change Control RACI 272
Figure 5-16: Tools and Techniques for Traceability and Monitoring 276
Figure 6-1: PMI-PBA Themes applicable to the Evaluation domain 290
Figure 6-2: Evaluation Domain 290
Figure 6-3: Evaluation Monitoring ITTOs 292
Figure 6-4: Validate Test Results ITO 293
Figure 6-5: Quality Assurance Activities RACI 294
Figure 6-6: Cost of Quality (COQ) 295
Figure 6-7: Analyze Solution Gaps ITO 298
Figure 6-8: Defect Probability and Impact Matrix 298
Figure 6-9: Get Solution Sign-off ITO 301
Figure 6-10: Evaluate Solution Results ITO 304
Figure 6-11: Tools and Techniques for Needs Assessment 309
Figure 6-12: Lessons Learned Overview 310
Figure 6-13: Retrospectives Overview 311

Figure 6-14: Checksheet Example 313
Figure 6-15: Control Chart Example 314
Figure 6-16: Design of Experiments Cartoon 315
Figure 6-17: Flowchart Example... 316
Figure 6-18: Histogram Example 316
Figure 6-19: Pareto Diagram Example 317
Figure 6-20: Scatter Diagram Example... 318
Figure 6-21: Walk-through Overview.. 321
Figure 6-22: Structured Walk-through Process.. 322
Figure 6-23: Roles in Structured Walkthroughs 323
Figure 7-1: Tuckman Model Graphic.. 338
Figure 7-2: Dimensions of Communication 339
Figure 7-3: Basic Communication Model 340
Figure 7-4: Communications Complexity Illustrated.. 341
Figure 7-5: Conflict Resolution Strategies 342
Figure 7-6: Tools and Techniques for Facilitation 344
Figure 7-7: Leadership Success Factors.. 345
Figure 7-8: Maslow's Hierarchy of Needs 346
Figure 8-1: Insights Learning Strategies: 360
Figure 8-2: eReads and Reference Home Page 362
Figure 8-3: PMI-PBA Study Roadmap... 364
Figure 8-4: Top 10 Exam Taking Tips 369
Figure 8-5: PMI-PBA Exam Question Types... 370

1. PMI-PBA Foundations

Part 1: Introduction to PMI-PBA

Overview

The Project Management Institute (PMI)® was founded to promote the growth and professionalism in project management. In recent years it has recognized the value of having business analysis expertise involved in projects to elicit and manage requirements. Poor requirements have long been cited as a factor for project challenges and project success. The PMI Professional in Business Analysis (PMI-PBA)® was launched in 2014. "The PMI-PBA certification recognizes an individual's expertise in business analysis, and using these tools and techniques to improve the overall success of projects." (PMI-PBA Handbook).

This chapter provides an overview of the PMI-PBA including information on PMI, and several strategies and tips to prepare for and pass the exam.

When you are finished with this chapter, you will know:

- The role and function of PMI and its PMI-PBA certifications.
- How to locate the PMI-PBA certification requirements.
- What the PMI-PBA test experience is like.
- How the *PMBOK® Guide* defines some core terms.

PMI Mission and Background

The Project Management Institute (PMI) was founded in 1969. It is the world's largest not-for-profit association for the project management profession. Its contributions to the profession of project management include:

- Certification
- Global Standards
- Chapters & Communities of Practice
- Training & Education
- Research

PMI expanded its focus from solely project management to include business analysis. It started with the *Requirements Management Knowledge Center of Excellence* and in 2014 expanded to include:

- April 2014 – Announced the Project Management Institute's Professional in Business Analysis (PMI-PBA) Credential Program
- August 2014 – Released *PMI's Pulse of the Profession: Requirements Management - Core Competency for Project and Program Success*
- November 2014 – Awarded the first PMI-PBA certifications to 180 pilot participants

There are two major factors cited for PMI offering this new certification. The first is recognizing the role that requirements play in project success. The 2014 *PMI's Pulse of the Profession°: Requirements Management - Core Competency for Project and Program Success* cites that "47% of unsuccessful projects fail to meet goals due to poor requirements management." It recognizes that skilled project management practices alone will not lead to project success. Skilled business analysis is also needed to ensure that the requirements support the goals of the project and meet the needs of the project team to support satisfying those requirements.

Increased Demand!
The number of business analysis jobs is predicted to increase 19 percent by 2022, according to the U.S. Bureau of Labor Statistics. **http://www.bls.gov/oo h/business-and-financial/management-analysts.html**

The other factor is recognizing an increase in demand for skilled business analysts.

PMI-PBA Overview

PMI-PBA program was launched in 2014. It started as a pilot with 180 participants achieving the certification, having taken the exam between May and August. The certification is the result of a Role Delineation Study to understand tasks, tools, techniques, knowledge, and skills required in analyzing and managing project requirements. The Role Delineation Study results are the basis for the Examination Content Outline for the PMI-PBA Exam. The Examination Content Outline is organized into five domains (needs assessment, planning, analysis, traceability and monitoring, and evaluation) and the tasks within each domain. It additionally provides information on the skills and knowledge needed by business analysts (BAs). From that, a committee of experts developed exam questions to test the business analysis knowledge and its application by BAs. Along with a rigorous application process, that exam is used today for assessing and certifying experienced and knowledgeable BA practitioners.

PMI made the PMI-PBA application process a rigorous one to screen out underqualified and less experienced BAs. While not as rigorous as the competition's (IIBA®) application process, it does require applicants to provide information on the business analysis tasks they have done by initiative and must include some of the time on project teams. The PMI-PBA certification program is targeted primarily at intermediate and senior-level business analysts. The basic qualifications are shown in *Figure 1-1, PMI-PBA Certification Requirements*. The PMI website has a comprehensive Frequently Asked Questions document about the PMI-PBA process. Visit **www.pmi.org** and search under "certifications" for more information.

	Secondary degree (High school diploma, associate's degree or global equivalent)	Bachelor's degree or higher degree (or global equivalent)
Business Analysis Experience	7,500 hours (5 years) working as a business analysis practitioner. This experience must have been earned in the last 8 years.	4,500 hours (3 years) working as a business analysis practitioner. This experience must have been earned in the last 8 years.
General Project Experience	*2,000 hours working on project teams. This project experience can be inclusive of the 7,500 hours of business analysis experience listed. Any business analysis experience that occurred within the context of a project can be included. This experience must have been earned in the last 8 years.	*2,000 hours working on project teams. This project experience can be inclusive of the 4,500 hours of business analysis experience listed. Any business analysis experience that occurred within the context of a project can be included. This experience must have been earned in the last 8 years.
Training in Business Analysis	35 contact hours. Hours must have been earned in business analysis practices.	35 contact hours. Hours must have been earned in business analysis practices.

*Note: Active PMP® and/or PgMP® credential holders will be accepted as fulfilling the general project experience requirements.

Figure 1-1: PMI-PBA® Certification Requirements

PMI-PBA Applications

Many previous candidates have found their experience with the application difficult and challenging. It is not something to treat lightly, and we advise you to consider the application process as a small project.

Examinees must have their application approved by PMI® before applying to take the exam. You also need to complete your professional development hours before submitting the application. Make sure you can verify your education hours with a certificate or other written proof. Have your high school or college transcript available in case you get audited.

We suggest you get your education hours completed and your PMI-PBA application approved before you begin your final preparation.

Tips on Completing the PMI-PBA Application

- Your application must be approved before scheduling the exam. Wait for approval before your final prep.
- Use a worksheet to record all your project hours before completing the PMI-PBA® application.
- Make sure you have a certificate or similar documentation to validate professional development hours.

PMI-PBA Application Steps

The following is a seven-step process for successfully applying for the PMI-PBA exam. Please note that it is current as of the publication date, and the PMI® can change its process without notice. Nonetheless, it gives you a good idea of the steps you'll need to follow. Refer to **www.pmi.org** and download the most current PMI-PBA Handbook for exact application details when you apply.

1. Visit the PMI-PBA page and bookmark it for use when applying for the exam. It has links to the online application and other useful information. Download the PMI-PBA Handbook to read an overview of the process. The PMI-PBA page has a link to get to the handbook.

2. Download the *PMI-PBA Examination Content Outline* from the PMI-PBA page. Read through this to get familiar with the content and structure for the exam.

3. Begin the application. You will need to login or register to access the online application. Once logged in, follow the instructions on the screen to start the PMI-PBA application.

4. Enter information as requested for your **contact information** and **education** level.

More Tips on the PMI-PBA Application
If you would like a free copy of a template to use for recording project hours, visit **http://www.watermarklearning.com/pba** and download PMI-PBA Application Worksheet (Excel spreadsheet - requires free member registration)

5. The **Requirements** section of the application is the most extensive and most time consuming section to complete. This includes adding detail on your business analysis experience and education.

   - **Before you start**, create an electronic record of your projects so you can copy and paste into the online application. Your session may time out if you are interrupted, and you may lose what you entered (there is no intermediate save function). If you would like a free template you can use, visit **http://www.watermarklearning.com/pba.**

   - **Business Analysis Experience:** You need a minimum of 4,500 hours of unique, non-overlapping experience accrued within the last eight years. This means that each month you worked on multiple, overlapping activities (projects that ran simultaneously) counts as one month toward the total requirement.

   - **General Project Experience:** You need a minimum of 2,000 hours of unique, non-overlapping experience accrued within the last eight years. This means that each month you worked on multiple, overlapping projects (projects that ran simultaneously) counts as one month toward the total requirement.

TIME IN MONTHS

- Recording of this experience is waived if you already hold the PMP® or PgMP® certification.

- You need to list the projects on which you performed business analysis activities. Your job title or project role is not as critical as the time spent doing business analysis activities.

- The experience included as part of the business analysis experience requirement can count towards the general project experience as long as this experience occurred within the context of a project.

- You will need to indicate the number of hours spent doing business analysis activities within each of the five domains.

- For each project listed, you will need to type a 300–550 character summary of the business analysis tasks you performed. There isn't a lot of space so be concise and use the task descriptions from the *PMI-PBA Examination Content Outline* to help compose the experience.

6. There is also a discounted exam fee of **$405 USD** for PMI® members, or $555 USD for non-members. PMI® will collect the application fee online when you apply. PMI® will send an electronic notification to you requesting payment once the application has been determined to be complete.

7. You will need to agree to the **PMI Code of Conduct** during the application process.

> **Even More Tips on the PMI-PBA Application**
>
> Save money on your application by becoming a PMI® member. There are many other benefits to joining, including a free download of the *PMBOK® Guide*. There is also an extensive list of resources including access to a 24/7 eRead & References library online containing hundreds of unabridged books, including all books recommended on the PMI-PBA page reference list.

Benefits of PMI-PBA Certification

Given the strict requirements and rigorous application process, one would assume the certification is worthwhile, right? Well, as a matter of fact it is. There are a number of benefits PMI® has identified to organizations to certify their BAs...and we agree!

- **Recognition and Endorsement** – PMI® certifications recognize your knowledge, skills, and abilities. PMI® serves as an unbiased endorsement of your expertise and professional experience on a global level.

- **Increased Earnings** – PMI® certifications can lead to greater earnings. They differentiate you in the marketplace and give you a competitive advantage in the job market. Many credential holders experience salary increases because of their certification status.

- **Career Advancement** – PMI® certifications can lead to career opportunities and career advancement. PMI certification identifies you as a practitioner who has demonstrated competency and knowledge in project management processes and specialty areas of practice based on industry standards.

- **Up-to-Date Skills** – PMI® continually conducts in-depth studies to ensure that its certifications actually reflect the current skills, knowledge, and best practices you need to succeed.

- **Encourage Professional Growth** – You never have to worry about a PMI® certification becoming obsolete. The PMI® Continuing Certification Requirements (CCR) Program ensures that you to continually develop your skills and stay current as the profession changes.

- **World Renowned** – Part of that marketability comes from the prestige of PMI®'s certifications. They have provided project management certifications for over 25 years.

The PMI-PBA Exam

Hopefully, you can see that you and others at your organization can benefit from BA certification. To help you get started, here is some high-level information about the exam and tips for passing it.

PMI-PBA Exam Experience

The PMI-PBA exam is a 200 multiple-choice question exam based on the five domains, tasks within the domains, and identified knowledge and skills needed to complete these tasks. Of the 200 questions, 25 are considered pre-test questions. Pre-test questions do not affect the score and are used in examinations as an effective and legitimate way to test the validity of future questions. All questions are randomly placed throughout the exam.

The exam is generally administered as computer-based testing and proctored by Prometric (in North America). Paper-based testing is available for those who are 300 km (186.5 miles) from a Prometric test site or for employers who wish to administer the exam internally. This guide focuses on the computer based test experience.

Four hours are provided in which to complete the exam and you may find that you need most or all of that time.

There are **no scheduled breaks** during the exam, although you are allowed to take a break if needed. If you take a break during the exam, your exam clock continues to count down.

The exam is **preceded by a tutorial and followed by a survey,** both of which are optional and can take up to 15 minutes to complete. The time used to complete the tutorial and survey is not included in the exam time of four hours.

General Exam-Taking Tactics

Like any major exam, there is a bit of tension and stress associated with it. Throughout this guide we provide tips to reduce anxiety and focus on your preparation. Like many BA practitioners, it probably has been a while since you have taken a major exam. If you've recently been in an MBA or similar program, or if you have taken the PMP® exam, you will have a slight advantage. Most people, though, need some practice in taking a long multiple-choice exam. If this applies to you, the practice exams built into the guide will help a great deal. The following tactics will also help you to prepare mentally.

Some examinees have reported a feeling that the exam got easier as they progressed through it. This feeling may be because the questions are easier at the end, may be from reduced test anxiety after 3+ hours, or may be from both. Whatever the reason, we recommend a few key tactics to help reduce your test anxiety and improve your testing performance. They are listed in the following table.

Top Ten PMI-PBA Exam-Taking Tactics

Tactic	Notes
1. Rest	Get plenty of rest the night before you take the exam. Part of successful test-taking involves problem-solving and logical elimination, so a well-rested mind and body will help you much more than last-minute, anxiety-laced cramming.
2. "Brain Dump"	Because of the length, some people find it useful to start the exam by noting a few key mnemonics and definitions. If nothing else, this "brain dump" helps alleviate a little test anxiety that many people feel in a high-stakes exam.
3. Read Each Question Carefully	A common reason people fail an exam is due to not reading each question thoroughly enough. There may be one word or phrase that affects the entire answer and it will be easy to miss those if you read the question too quickly.
4. Don't Dwell	Don't dwell on questions that seem difficult or complicated. Leave them blank and go on to the next question. Chances are it will seem easier later in the exam. You will also save time and energy

Tactic	Notes
	this way. You can go back any time to review and answer past unanswered questions.
5. 1st Pass: Skip Hard Questions	Skip hard questions until you get one you feel confident about. By first answering as many of the 200 questions as you can, you will increase your confidence, learn how the question-makers think, and may even discover hints in one question that help you in another. One of the authors found this to be true for more than one question and benefited from it.
6. 2nd Pass: Review Skipped Questions	After your first pass, go back to the beginning and review questions you skipped. You may have learned from other questions, or even answers, that may trigger a thought that leads to the correct answer. If you are unsure of any question, skip it as described previously and do a 3rd pass through the questions.
7. Don't Second-Guess Yourself!	DO NOT SECOND-GUESS questions you have already answered. Chances are you will second-guess a correct answer into an incorrect one! If you're unsure, don't answer it.
8. Get down to two viable answers	For tough questions on exams, there are generally two weaker possible answers and two that are stronger. Start by eliminating the weaker answers, then work on determining the correct one from the pair remaining.
9. Watch for "distracters"	Wrong answers are known as "distracters" and are meant to distract you from the correct one. They may have an oxymoronic term, such as "requirements design," or may have a term that clearly doesn't belong in a "list of lists" (see that topic later in this section).
10. Guess if you must	If time is short and you have unanswered questions, you have one of two options. 1) Make your best guess or 2) Mark down answer "B" for each unanswered question. We don't necessarily recommend the latter, but enough urban legends exist about this being the most common answer on exams that it's worth considering. You are not downgraded for wrong answers, so an educated guess is better than a random one.

Figure 1-2: PMI-PBA Exam-Taking Tactics

Types of Exam Questions

The PMI-PBA exam questions are fairly straightforward, and the types of questions tend to fall into these four broad types. All questions have four multiple choice possible answers, and some are very close choices.

Type	Explanation	Example	Strategy
Definitions	You are expected to know key business analysis definitions, so be prepared to answer several of these.	You might see a question like "a model that depicts domain information is…" with a correct answer of "Use Case Diagram."	These are pretty straight forward. Rule out any terms or definitions that you don't recognize as they are likely distractors.

Type	Explanation	Example	Strategy
Sequences	To test your knowledge of the order of tasks, not just their content, these questions can be challenging. We cover sequences and orders of tasks in the individual chapters of this book.	In general, be prepared for questions that start with "what is the first thing you do…"	Look at the possible answers and determine their sequence process. Now review the question and determine the next step.
Scenarios	These are included to test your application of BA knowledge and skills. A project-related situation is presented and you are asked to solve a problem, synthesize variables, interpret a diagram, etc.	For example, "given a situation in which stakeholders are spread out over a wide geographic area, and are not coming to consensus about their requirements, which of the following would you do:" with a possible answer of "hold a requirements workshop."	These questions will often have extraneous information. Re-read the question to determine what the question is really asking. Now determine what information in the question is relevant. Remember soft skills when you see these types of questions as they may hold a clue to the correct answer.
List of Lists	To test your knowledge of terms and groupings of details, there are several questions to choose the correct grouping of like terms.	You may be asked, "Which group of tools for modeling is used to document business processes?" and the correct answer might be "Flowcharts, Process Maps, and Activity Diagrams." These questions are tricky, in that an alternative incorrect answer might be "Flowcharts, Sequence Maps, and Activity Diagrams."	Review each answer's list independently and determine if there is an item in the list that is not like the others. It may be a list of tools with a task thrown in, or perhaps a new nonsensical term. Rule these answers out. Compare the lists of the remaining lists to determine which best fits the question.

Figure 1-3: PMI-PBA Exam Question Types

PMI-PBA Themes

Another helpful strategy to prepare for your exam is to concentrate on key themes that run throughout the exam. One way to use these themes is when you must decide between two close answers, and the theme suggests one over the other. The common themes to watch for are as follows:

PMI-PBA Prep Tip
Start with understanding the recurring themes before you try to memorize all the tasks and techniques. There are too many items to memorize everything, and remembering the themes will help your comprehension.

Theme	Comments
Understand Stakeholders	Defining good requirements requires us to understand our stakeholders and adjust to their needs. For instance, the choice of tools or techniques may need to be modified based on the stakeholders involved.
Be Flexible and Adaptable	A related theme is to be flexible and adaptable to the audience (such as for elicitation, presentations, reporting, etc.). Remember, there is no "correct" answer when dealing with people.
Control Scope	Control scope of the solution and get approval for all changes. A recurring theme on the exam is: • Use a **Traceability Matrix** and trace requirements back to business objectives and forward to a solution.
Elicitation Keys	For effective elicitation, consider these points as keys to success: • A skilled facilitator is needed to effectively elicit requirements. • When facilitating, rely on ground rules and agendas. This is especially helpful when conflicts arise. • Interviewing knowledge and skills is critical to eliciting good requirements.

Figure 1-4: PMI-PBA Themes

Organization of this Guide

This study guide provides information, context, and examples organized by domain and tasks. Tools and techniques are fully explained in the domain in which they are predominantly used.

Mnemonic Tip
Select tips are shown in boxes like this.

- **Text** – Presented details about business analysis and requirements, the exam, tasks, techniques, etc.

- **Tips** – Add side-notes to the text, to call out special attention to certain items.

- **Terminology Tips** – Focus on select terms that are important for preparing for the exam. Refer also to the extensive Terminology Summary in the appendix.

Project
A temporary endeavor undertaken to create a unique product or service.

- **Starred items** – Like "starred" sites in a travel book, our starred items are "not to be missed." Pay special attention to these terms, tasks, and techniques.

- **Inputs, Tools and Techniques, Outputs Overviews** – The PMI-PBA exam does not follow a specific "Body of Knowledge" in terms of identifying *inputs, tools and techniques, and outputs* (ITTOs) for each of the tasks. The study guide describes some standard concepts in inputs, tools and techniques, and outputs for each task in order to provide context and greater understanding. The PMI-PBA exam will not test specifically on these ITTOs. ITTOs may be present in test questions as a means to test your understanding of the task.

- **ITOs** – For each Task, we show a high-level diagram of the major *inputs* and *outputs*, plus a brief *task* description for each domain. Again, these are provided only for context as PMI-PBA® does not provide formal reference guidance on the inputs and outputs of each task.

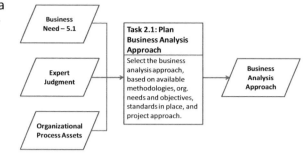

Example ITO Diagram

Other Resources Contained in this Study Guide

- **Exercises** – Primarily matching, and fill-in-the-blank exercises are spread throughout the course to help you practice and reinforce the material. Sometimes you'll see a mnemonic hint and other times not.

Needs Assessment Tasks		Mnemonic
1. Define		
2. Determine		
3. Develop		
4. Identify		
5. Elicit		

- **Practice exams** – At the end of each chapter, you'll find a series of practice questions and answers. These questions are indicative of the types of questions you'll encounter on the PMI-PBA exam. In some cases, we structure the questions to help you learn and memorize a concept or term. We do this even if the type of question may not be on the exam.

- **Appendices** – Included are appendices on terminology, domains, and more practice exam questions and answers. There are 200 questions to let you practice taking a simulated exam. Your purchase of this book also gives you access to hundreds of exam questions in the PMI-PBA Online Study Exam.

- **Overall Design** – The book is organized to allow you to pick it up and study a Domain independent of the others. It certainly allows you to read sequentially if you are starting your preparation, or by jumping to a section or task where you need the most help. Use this guide the way you learn and study best.

What This Guide is Not

- This guide is not an "exam cram" book. It's designed to help you learn and master the material, not cram for an exam only to forget all you know the next day.

- This guide is not an introduction to project management or business analysis. If you are an intermediate to senior-level BA practitioner, it will be the right level for you.

- This guide is not meant for skill development. Unlike Watermark Learning's skill-based courses, this book is knowledge-based and not skill-based. You could (and we feel should) apply the knowledge in this book to your job.

- Because this guide is focused on helping you pass the PMI-PBA exam, we do not cover how to apply the concepts to "real life." Those are completely different things and trying to do that would double the size of this book and not serve you well. We do offer select and brief examples to help relate the concepts to real life.

What This Guide Is

- Our guiding principle in writing this book is to help you structure and break down the PMI-PBA exam content so that it makes sense in your mind. That is the best preparation for you to take the exam. It is also the best way to help you retain the most information after the exam.

- Our philosophy in assembling this book is to help you learn how to learn. We don't intend for you to memorize the contents, but to use it to develop your own structures and ways to master the material, and ultimately pass the exam.

- The book is also designed so you can read and study each domain in order. But, you can also pick and choose the sections you need and read through it in any order you wish.

Part 2: PMI-PBA Examination Content Overview

Preparation Overview

When you are finished with this section, you will understand:

- The structure and context of the *PMI-PBA Examination Content Outline* and how it applies to preparing for and taking the exam.
- How the PMI® defines some core terms.

The PMI-PBA exam is based solely on the *PMI-PBA Examination Content Outline*. This is different from other certifications that align with a Body of Knowledge as the main source of content. The exam content contains five domains with tasks (discussed further below). In addition to the domains and tasks are knowledge and skills. The tools and techniques outlined in the Knowledge and Skills section generally fit within one or two domains. Each concept contained in the *PMI-PBA Examination Content Outline* will be discussed within this guide, organized by domain.

Many of the domains and tasks align with the *Project Management Body of Knowledge (PMBOK®) Guide*. Reference to the *PMBOK® Guide* section will be provided as appropriate. You are encouraged to review these referenced sections of the *PMBOK® Guide*.

PMI® has provided a PMI-PBA reference list on their website. You can access the referenced books through the 24/7 eRead & References library online if you are PMI® member. The *Practitioner's Guide to Requirements Management*, 2nd Edition, by Richard Larson and Elizabeth Larson (available at **www.watermarklearning.com** or on Amazon) will provide additional practical advice on business analysis relevant to the exam.

In addition to this guide, Watermark Learning offers a PMI-PBA Certification Preparation Course, a collection of Study Tables, and finally an Online Study Exam (simulated exam) to support you in your preparation process.

We recommend that you work through this guide one domain at a time. Review the referenced *PMBOK® Guide* sections for each domain and then test your knowledge with the chapter practice exams provided. An exam simulation covering all domains is provided in the appendices for your "final" preparation test. Subscribe to our online study exam for additional practice.

Here is a generic roadmap for preparation that could span from 2-6 months.

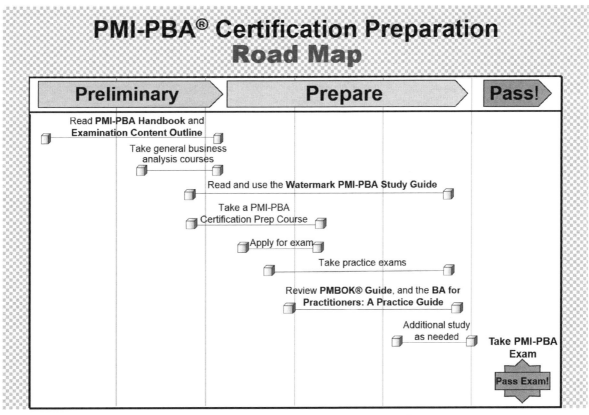

Figure 1-5: PMI-PBA Preparation Roadmap

Domains

There are five core domains in the *PMI-PBA Examination Content Outline*. This guide is organized by the domains and we'll introduce them in order in this section.

- Needs Assessment
- Planning
- Analysis
- Traceability & Monitoring
- Evaluation

The *PMI-PBA Examination Content Outline* provides an exam blueprint for the percentage of questions to expect by domain.

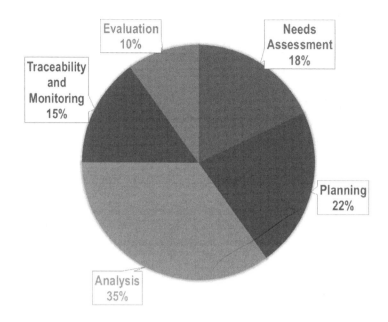

Figure 1-6: Percent of Questions on PMI-PBA
by domain. Source: PMI

As you can see by the above pie chart, the number of exam questions is not equally distributed. Most people have a limited amount of time to devote to studying the domains. Our suggestion is to study in proportion to the number of questions per domain as well as your prior knowledge (or lack thereof) of each. Also study most on topics you score the least on in your practice drills and exams. Let's preview the domains in the order they are listed in the *PMI-PBA Examination Content Outline* and the order we cover them.

Study Tip
Spend time studying in proportion to the percentages of questions on the exam, and your own knowledge of each domain.

Needs Assessment

Needs Assessment tasks relate to identifying and articulating the purpose and goals of the project, as well as identifying and understanding the project stakeholders. The activities here contribute to the development of the business case and subsequent charter for the project. Even if a business analyst is not yet assigned, the analyst should review this information to determine that the purpose, goals, and objectives are clear prior to proceeding with planning.

Goal: Fully articulate the purpose and goals for developing an effective solution.

Planning

Planning focuses both on the deliverables and activities led by the business analyst as well as the processes that will be used by the project team to support the business analysis work. This includes planning for requirements elicitation, management, approval, communications, and version control. The business analysis plans are inputs to the project management plans. In some cases the business analysis activities may be shared with the project manager, with the business analyst leading the activities related to solution scope and requirements.

Goal: Plan the activities to be completed and the business analysis processes that the project will utilize.

Analysis

Analysis is the largest domain of the exam with eight tasks and 35 percent of the questions on the exam. This domain should be your highest priority in learning the tasks and the supporting tools and techniques since it will have the largest impact on your overall test score. Tasks range from elicitation, analysis, decomposition, approval, specification, and validation of requirements. All of these tasks are conducted as outlined within the Planning domain and will be tracked in the Traceability and Monitoring domain.

Goal: Use appropriate techniques to elicit and analyze complete and accurate requirements.

Traceability and Monitoring

The Traceability and Monitoring domain includes the tasks related to managing requirements throughout the project, and includes communicating requirements status to stakeholders. Much of this domain was discussed within the Planning domain with this domain focusing on the execution of those plans.

Goal: Manage requirements throughout the project lifecycle.

Evaluation

The Evaluation domain includes the tasks along with tools and techniques in order to evaluate that the delivered solution will meet the requirements and the business need. This evaluation includes artifacts that contribute to the solution development and obtaining stakeholder sign-off that the solution is ready for deployment. This domain extends beyond the project lifecycle with task 4 being to evaluate the "deployed" solution.

Goal: Evaluate the deliverables and solution to ensure it will meet the business need.

Competencies

While not formally a domain, competencies (soft skills) are an important part of the PMI-PBA exam as outlined by the knowledge and skills needed in the *PMI-PBA Examination Content Outline*. Competencies are covered in detail in Chapter 7 of this guide. Questions relating to competencies will appear in all domains as an element of the overall situation.

Goal: Utilize soft skill competencies in order to work effectively with others.

Domain Mnemonic

As you learn the PMI-PBA domains, it may be helpful to use a mnemonic device to help you remember them. You will find mnemonics throughout this guide designed to help you learn and memorize the material of the *PMI-PBA Examination Content Outline*. Please feel free to develop your own mnemonics if the ones we created do not resonate with you.

NA – **N**eeds **A**ssessment

P – **P**lanning

A – **A**nalysis

TM – **T**raceability and **M**onitoring

E – **E**valuation

> **Domains Mnemonic**
>
> NAP-A-TME
>
> It's time for a nap!
>
> *Not you! You're studying.*

Terminology "Eye Opener"

One of the challenges in preparing for the PMI-PBA exam is understanding terminology that is not universally used by practitioners. For instance, you may create a Statement of Work for a project, whereas the next person builds a Business Case. The creators of the *PMBOK® Guide* sought out the generally accepted terms for inclusion in the guide. The *PMBOK® Guide* will be the source of reference for the PMI-PBA exam for items covered in the publication.

As you prepare for the exam, bear in mind that it will test you on terminology from the *PMBOK® Guide*. So, be sure to use that guide's terms, even if you think they are "wrong" or you disagree with them. We have heard anecdotes about study groups who have spent hours arguing about *PMBOK® Guide* terms. Don't fall into this trap! It won't help you prepare for the exam, and only leads to frustration.

> **Terminology Tips:**
>
> - Use *PMBOK® Guide* terms, even if they are different from your personal experience.
> - Start by memorizing the domains
> - Memorize tasks within the domains.
> - Pick domains with only a few tasks to start with (e.g., E-Evaluation)

- As you set out to prepare for your exam, start by memorizing all the domains. This might seem simplistic, but it's not. You need a firm foundation to build on and it starts with knowing the domains.

- Next, start memorizing the tasks within the domains. If you're bad at memorizing, use our mnemonic tips for each domain to help you.

- After you feel confident about the tasks, then work on memorizing tools and techniques used within each task.

  o Remember tools and techniques classification used in each task.

  o Memorize specific tools and techniques within classification.

                PMI-PBA Certification Study Guide

Basic Terminology

This guide presents important terminology throughout these pages, and summarizes them in *Appendix A: Terminology Summary.*

Adaptive Life Cycle

"A project lifecycle, also known as change-driven or agile methods, that is intended to facilitate change and require a high degree of ongoing stakeholder involvement." Source: *PMBOK® Guide - Fifth Edition*, Glossary (See more in Guide to Project Life Cycle Approaches).

Business Analysis

"The set of activities performed to identify business needs; recommend relevant solutions; and elicit, document, and manage requirements." Source: *PMBOK® Guide – Fifth Edition.*

Business Analyst

A business analyst is the person who performs the set of activities to identify business needs; recommend relevant solutions; and elicit, document, and manage requirements.

Solution

A Solution solves a problem or takes advantage of an opportunity to meet a business need, and results in product(s), service(s), or end result(s) of a project or program.

Requirement

"A condition or capability that is required to be present in a product, service, or result to satisfy a contract or other formally imposed specification." Source: *PMBOK® Guide – Fifth Edition*, Glossary.

Requirements Classification (*PMBOK® Guide*)

The *PMBOK® Guide* outlines various types of requirements you need to know. It is not enough to understand the definition of a "business requirement." In fact, there are six main classifications as shown below in *Figure 1-7*.

Requirement Type	Description	Example
Business Requirements	"...describe the higher-level needs of the organization as a whole, such as the business issue or opportunities, and reasons why a project has been undertaken."	Currently, customers are unable to manage their accounts without calling customer service, resulting in: • Increased customer complaints • Unnecessary calls to customer service
Stakeholder Requirements	"...describe the needs of the stakeholder or stakeholder group."	The customer needs to retrieve a forgotten user id and/or password.
Solution Requirements	"...describe features, functions, and characteristics of the product, service, or result that will meet the business and stakeholder requirements."	*(See below, Functional and Nonfunctional Requirements.)*
Solution requirements are subdivided into Functional and Nonfunctional Requirements		
• *Functional Requirements*	"...describe the behaviors of the product."	The system shall provide a tool that allows users to reset their password in the event they have forgotten.
• *Nonfunctional Requirements*	"...describe the environmental conditions or qualities required for the product to be effective."	The system shall send an email response with forgotten user id or password reset instructions within 2 minutes of the user selecting the option.
Transition Requirements	"...describe temporary capabilities such as data conversion, and training requirements needed to transition from the current "as-is" state to the future "to-be" state.	The system shall convert user ids and passwords to the new system without interruption of service to end-users.
Project Requirements	"...describe the actions, processes, or other conditions the project needs to meet."	A focus group will be used to conduct user acceptance testing and to obtain formal sign-off prior to release.

Requirement Type	Description	Example
Quality Requirements	"...capture any condition or criteria needed to validate the successful completion of a project deliverable or fulfillment of other project requirements."	The solution must be free of all Critical and Level 1 defects prior to release.

Figure 1-7: Requirements Classifications
(source: *PMBOK® Guide-Fifth Edition*)

A mnemonic way of remembering requirement types in their proper order is BSFNT PQ (Powerful Quarterbacks). Think what kind of "Bus font" you will need for your powerful quarterback. A colleague of ours uses "Buy Some Fun New Treats for Powerful Quarterbacks," so use whatever works for you.

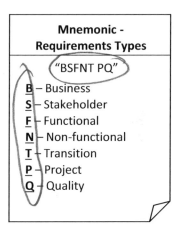

> **Mnemonic -**
> **Requirements Types**
> "BSFNT PQ"
> **B** – Business
> **S** – Stakeholder
> **F** – Functional
> **N** – Non-functional
> **T** – Transition
> **P** – Project
> **Q** – Quality

Predictive Life Cycle

"A form for project life cycle in which the project scope and the time and cost required to deliver that scope, are determined as early in the life cycle as possible." source: *PMBOK® Guide – Fifth Edition*, Glossary (See more in Guide to Project Life Cycle Approaches).

Project

"A temporary endeavor undertaken to create a unique product, service or result." Source: *PMBOK® Guide – Fifth Edition*, Glossary.

Tasks

Tasks are discrete pieces of work to perform business analysis. Generally, each task is performed one or more times during a project and functions much like a process. Tasks have specific boundaries and produce outputs.

Techniques

Techniques are disciplines or methods for carrying out a task. Examples include all the models and elicitation methods, decision analysis, estimation, SWOT analysis, etc. Some techniques apply to multiple tasks and these are called "general" techniques. Our guide presents the techniques in the domain in which they are most applicable. We feel this will aid understanding of the purpose better. (See more in Guide to Tools and Techniques.)

> **Study Tip**
>
> Study the techniques in the context of the tasks they are most closely associated with. Our guide describes techniques within domains for better understanding.

Tools

Tools are used in performing an activity and aid in completing a task given a specific technique. In some cases, a class of technique is listed without any specific tool examples.

Stakeholders

"An individual, group, or organization who may affect, be affected by, or perceive itself to be affected by a decision, activity, or outcome of a project." Source: *PMBOK® Guide – Fifth Edition*, Glossary.

> **Study Tip**
>
> See *Appendix A: "Terminology Summary"* for a comprehensive list of *PMBOK® Guide* terms and definitions.

Guide to Tools and Techniques

Each domain utilizes multiple techniques. The tasks within each domain typically cite a specific classification of technique (e.g., "using elicitation techniques"). Techniques describe different ways that a task can be performed. Tools are used in performing an activity and aid in completing a task given a specific technique. Tools and techniques are listed in the Knowledge and Skills section of the *PMI-PBA Examination Content Outline* within each classification. In some cases, a class of technique is listed without any specific tool examples.

Tools and techniques were included in this guide as a result of appearing in the following documents as they are inputs to the PMI-PBA Examination:

- *PMI-PBA Examination Content Outline*
- Business Analysis for Practitioners – A Practice Guide
- PMI's *PMBOK® Guide – Fifth Edition*

Tools and techniques are categorized based on structure provided in the *PMI-PBA Examination Content Outline* Skills and Knowledge (p. 9-10.) Here is how we have organized the tools and techniques:

- Tools and techniques belong to one primary category.

- A tool or technique that may apply to other categories is referenced within the secondary categories with information on the primary category.
- All tools and techniques are fully described by category within the domain where the category of tools and techniques is primarily used.
- Each tool and technique includes a "priority" rating of low, moderate, or high.
  - Low – These items may or may not appear on the exam. A general definition is provided.
  - Moderate – There may be a question or two on these. You should have some general familiarity but detailed questions are not expected.
  - High – These will be on the exam. You should have a good understanding of the tool or technique, how it is used, what advantages it brings to analysis, and be able to answer questions that demonstrate ability to apply the tool in business analysis work.

Guide to Project Life Cycle Approaches

PMI-PBA examinees will be expected to understand the differences in "adaptive" vs. "predictive" project life cycle approaches and the differences in techniques to fulfill the tasks of the *PMI-PBA Examination Content Outline*. The "predictive" approach generally applies to most tasks and is the first focus of this study guide. Alternatives to accommodate "adaptive" approaches are called out separately within each task as appropriate. In general, "adaptive" equates to agile and "predictive" equates to waterfall project approaches. Use *Figure 1-8* below for more information on the differences between these approaches.

Waterfall (predictive)	Agile (adaptive)
▪ Usually sequential phases (requirements and then design) ▪ Documentation and approvals tend to be more formal ▪ Can be done incrementally ▪ Often used on global projects or with geographically dispersed teams ▪ Often used on complex projects with a complex interfaces	▪ Focuses on collaboration ▪ Can be SCRUM with daily standup meetings ▪ Prioritize features ▪ Can document with user stories ▪ Best with co-located teams ▪ Iterative (evolve and improve) ▪ Does not mean no documentation!
⬅ Incremental / Iterative ➡	
▪ Increments are like small releases ▪ Both Waterfall and Agile can be incremental ▪ Add features with each increment	▪ Time-boxed ▪ Multiple phases ▪ Incremental development may or may not be iterative (including rework)

Figure 1-8: Predictive and Adaptive Life Cycle Approaches

PMI-PBA Exercises

Quiz 1a

Write your answers to the following recall exercises in the blanks provided. Check your answers at the end of the chapter. List the names of all the PMI-PBA domains in the blanks below. Do you recall the mnemonic? That may help get your started.

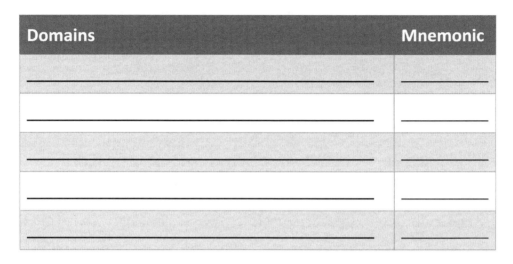

Domains	Mnemonic
_____	_____
_____	_____
_____	_____
_____	_____
_____	_____

Hint: You may take a nap after one more mnemonic quiz and a 10-question practice exam!

Quiz 1b

Write the requirements classifications that are contained in the *PMBOK® Guide*, preferably in the order presented.

Requirement Types	Mnemonic
_____	_____
_____	_____
_____	_____
_____	_____
_____	_____
_____	_____
_____	_____

PMI-PBA Practice Exam

Throughout this guide, you will have several chances to practice taking exams that test your knowledge of the PMI-PBA content. They are the ultimate "exercise" in any test preparation strategy. The questions in each chapter help you learn the concepts that you will be tested on. Explanations are given for both correct and incorrect answers, plus selected reference to help your study.

To get started, here are some questions on basic terminology. Answers are listed at the end of the chapter.

1. Which is a true statement regarding the role of a business analyst?
   a. The business analyst is the team member responsible for documenting requirements.
   b. The business analyst selects the projects that meet the organization's strategic initiatives.
   c. The role of the business analyst can be performed by anyone doing the work of business analysis.
   d. The role of the business analyst can only be fulfilled by a single person who is dedicated full-time to the work of business analysis.

2. Business analysis is:
   a. A subplan of the project management plan that includes information regarding business analysis planning decisions.
   b. The set of activities performed to identify business needs; recommend relevant solutions; and elicit, document, and manage requirements.
   c. A collection of pre-project or early project activities and approaches for capturing the necessary view of the business to provide context to requirements and functional design work for a given initiative and/or for long term planning.
   d. A set of stakeholder needs that are analyzed, structured, and specific for use in the design or implementation of a solution.

3. What are the different types of requirements?
   a. Business, stakeholder, functional, non-functional, and transition.
   b. Business, stakeholder, solution requirements, transition, project, and quality.
   c. Optional, important, critical.
   d. Sponsor, stakeholder, functional, non-functional, transition, project, and quality.

4. Who completes the business case?
   a. Project manager.
   b. Project sponsor.
   c. Business analyst.
   d. The person who requests the project.

5. Most solutions:

    a. Are systems of interacting solution components, each of which are potentially solutions in their own right.

    b. Contain only one solution component.

    c. Contain software and a process component.

    d. Are systems of interacting business applications, each one of which is unique.

6. The following is what type of requirement? "All data that is less than 3 years old should be migrated to the new system."

    a. Solution.

    b. Functional.

    c. Non-functional.

    d. Transition.

7. Requirements are defined:

    a. From a high- to low-level of detail.

    b. To the lowest possible level of detail.

    c. To the level dictated by the sponsor.

    d. To whatever detail is needed to achieve action and understanding.

8. Business analysis is performed:

    a. Sequentially and in order.

    b. According to logical relationships (dependencies).

    c. Iteratively.

    d. Iteratively after Enterprise Analysis is complete.

9. Which of the following is a stakeholder requirement?

    a. Company policy states that all transactions be posted real-time.

    b. I need to be able to see all transactions in the ledger as they occur.

    c. The system shall post all transactions within .5 seconds of a user save.

    d. The system shall have all transactions from the past year available with the original date/time posted.

10. Which statement about techniques is the most correct?

    a. They are required for all tasks.

    b. They are prescribed by the *PMBOK® Guide.*

    c. They describe different ways a task can be performed.

    d. They provide supplemental information about one and only one task.

Exercise Answers

Quiz 1a

Domains	Mnemonic
Needs Assessment	NA
Planning	P
Analysis	A
Traceability & Monitoring	TM
Evaluation	E

Quiz 1b

Requirement Types	Mnemonic
Business	B
Stakeholder	S
Functional	F
Non-Functional	N
Transition	T
Project	P
Quality	Q

PMI-PBA Practice Exam Answers

1. Which is a true statement regarding the role of a business analyst?

   a. The business analyst is the team member responsible for documenting requirements.

   Documentation is one aspect of business analysis, but it does not define the role.

   b. The business analyst selects the projects that meet the organization's strategic initiatives.

   The executive team selects the projects the organization will work on to meet the strategic objectives. Whoever is doing the work of business analysis may provide input information and make recommendations to the selection, but they do not make the selection.

   c. **The role of the business analyst can be performed by anyone doing the work of business analysis.**

   Correct!

   d. The role of business analyst can only be fulfilled by a single person who is dedicated full-time to the work of business analysis.

   The role may be filled by a single, dedicated resource, but not necessarily.

2. Business analysis is:

   a. A subplan of the project management plan that includes information regarding business analysis planning decisions.

   This is a definition of a business analysis plan.

   b. **The set of activities performed to identify business needs; recommend relevant solutions; and elicit, document, and manage requirements.**

   Correct! Definition from *Business Analysis for Practitioners: A Practice Guide*, Glossary, page 184.

   c. A collection of pre-project or early project activities and approaches for capturing the necessary view of the business to provide context to requirements and functional design work for a given initiative and/or for long term planning.

   This is only one aspect of business analysis.

   d. A set of stakeholder needs that are analyzed, structured and specific for use in the design or implementation of a solution.

   This answer is designed to sound good, but is misleading because of the focus on design and implementation.

3. What are the different types of requirements?

    a. Business, stakeholder, solution, security, and transition.

        Security is a type of solution (non-functional) requirement.

    b. Business, stakeholder, solution requirements, transition, project, and quality.

        Correct! Per PMBOK® Guide-5th Ed, Collect Requirements. Solution requirements include Functional and Nonfunctional.

    c. Optional, important, critical.

        These represent potential priorities

    d. Sponsor, stakeholder, functional, non-functional, transition, project, and quality.

        Sponsor is not a classification of requirement. Functional and non-functional requirements are included in Solution requirements.

4. Who completes the business case?

    a. Project Manager.

        There is no project and therefore no project manager at the time the business case is being developed.

    b. Project Sponsor.

        The project sponsor will need to own the business case and help shepherd it through the project request process, they may even be the original requestor. See answer D for more.

    c. Business Analyst.

        Correct! PMBOK® Guide, 4.1.1.2.

    d. The person who requests the project.

        A business analyst will need to complete the business case. They may work with the original project requestor to help articulate the information needed to support a strong business case.

5. Most solutions:

    a. Are systems of interacting solution components, each of which are potentially solutions in their own right.

        Correct!

    b. Contain only one solution component.

        This type of answer is too restrictive.

    c. Contain software and a process component.

        Solutions might, but might not, contain this.

    d. Are systems of interacting business applications, each one of which is unique.

        The word 'application' is too restrictive, since a solution can contain more than software.

6. The following is what type of requirement? "All data that is less than 3 years old should be migrated to the new system"

a.	Solution.	This does not describe a functional or non-functional requirement.
b.	Functional.	This does not describe how a system behaves.
c.	Non-functional.	This is a temporary requirement to aid with transition, not a characteristic of the system.
d.	**Transition.**	**Correct! This is an example of temporary requirement that aids in transitioning operations to a new system.**

7. Requirements are defined:

a.	From a high- to low-level of detail.	Usually, yes, but not always. There may not be a compelling reason to take them to a low-level of detail.
b.	To the lowest possible level of detail.	Not necessarily defined to lowest level.
c.	To the level dictated by the sponsor.	No. Multiple stakeholders may be involved.
d.	**To whatever detail is needed to achieve action and understanding.**	**Correct!**

8. Business analysis is performed:

a.	Sequentially and in order.	Logic would dictate this is not true.
b.	According to logical relationships (dependencies).	Too narrow an answer.
c.	**Iteratively.**	**Correct!**
d.	Iteratively after Enterprise Analysis is complete.	No such restriction. Iteratively, yes, but Enterprise Analysis is not a requirement.

9. Which of the following is a stakeholder requirement?

a.	Company policy states that all transactions be posted real-time.	This is a business requirement.
b.	**I need to be able to see all transactions in the ledger as they occur.**	**Correct! This is a stakeholder requirement.**
c.	The system shall post all transactions within .5 seconds of a user save.	This is a functional requirement.
d.	The system shall have all transactions from the past year available with the original date/time posted.	This is a transition requirement.

10. Which statement about techniques is the most correct?

    a.   They are required for all tasks.   Not all tasks require techniques.

    b.   They are prescribed by the *PMBOK®*   They are **not** prescribed.
        Guide.

    c.   **They describe different ways a task can**   **Correct!**
        be performed.

    d.   They provide supplemental information   Techniques can apply to multiple tasks.
        about one and only one task.

Summary

This chapter was provided to give a foundation of knowledge needed to better understand the domains and tasks of the PMI-PBA exam. You should now have a good understanding of the certification and the process for achieving it.

It will be important that you understand and can identify the different types of requirements:

- Business
- Stakeholder
- Solution
  - Functional
  - Non-Functional
- Transition
- Project
- Quality

Pay special attention to the terms of "adaptive" and "predictive." These describe the two major categories of project life cycle approaches that show up throughout the exam. Adaptive relates to "agile" whereas predictive the more traditional "waterfall" approach.

Adaptive = Agile
Predictive = Waterfall

2. Needs Assessment

Overview

The Needs Assessment domain includes the tasks necessary to fully understand a project. This includes defining the business problem or opportunity the project is intended to support, including the project's relationship to organization goals and objectives in order to support project goals and objectives. This domain includes understanding the value the project will bring to the organization. Part of this understanding comes from understanding the project stakeholders. Stakeholder identification and analysis is critical to ensuring the project has the right inputs and information for developing recommendations and getting project scope and requirement approvals.

 Needs Assessment Goal: Understand a business problem or opportunity and evaluate various inputs to help develop an effective solution.

When you are finished with this chapter, you will know:

- How to define Needs Assessment

- The five tasks contained in Needs Assessment

- The major areas of emphasis in Needs Assessment, including problem definition, goals and objectives, and stakeholder identification and analysis

> **Needs Assessment**
>
> The tasks for understanding the business problem or opportunity as well as to identify and evaluate inputs needed to develop an effective solution.

Domain Themes

The PMI®-PBA® exam includes several reoccurring themes. One useful way to use these themes is when you narrow down an exam question to two close answers. If one of the themes suggests one over the other, then go with the theme. The common themes to watch for in Needs Assessment are as follows:

Theme	Comments
Understand Stakeholders	Defining good requirements requires us to understand our stakeholders and adjust to their needs. For instance, the choice of tools or techniques may need to be modified based on the stakeholders involved.
Value Proposition	Valuation tools and techniques describe different ways to determine and articulate the value an organization may expect as a result of a project.
Goals and Objectives	The project should have goals and objectives that align with the organization's goals and objectives. Identifying and articulating these will provide context and scope for the project. This will further be used in Traceability and Monitoring.

Figure 2-1: PMI-PBA Themes relating to Needs Assessment

The questions for Needs Assessment represent 18 percent of all the exam questions. While this is not the largest domain in terms of number of questions, it is an important domain as it sets the stage for the project. See *Figure 2-2* below.

Domain	Percentage of Items on Test	Approximate number of questions
Domain 1: Needs Assessment	18%	36
Domain 2: Planning	22%	44
Domain 3: Analysis	35%	70
Domain 4: Traceability and Monitoring	15%	30
Domain 5: Evaluation	10%	20

Figure 2-2: Needs Assessment Domain
Source: PMI

                                       PMI-PBA Certification Study Guide

Needs Assessment: High-Level View

Listed below are the five tasks in the Needs Assessment domain. The tasks in the domain may not be performed sequentially, but it is helpful to learn the tasks and their order as a way to remember what each of them does. PMI® does not provide task titles for each task, but rather a detailed description. See the table below for the tasks as defined by PMI® with a task title developed for this study guide in order to aid in learning and remembering the tasks.

Task 1
Define Business Need

Define or review a business problem or opportunity using problem and opportunity analysis techniques in order to develop a solution scope statement and/or to provide input to create a business case.

Task 2
Determine Value Proposition

Collect and analyze information from a variety of sources using valuation tools and techniques to contribute to determining the value proposition of the initiative.

Task 3
Develop Project Goals

Collaborate in the development of project goals and objectives by providing clarification of business needs and solution scope in order to align the product with the organization's goals and objectives.

Task 4
Identify Stakeholders

Identify stakeholders by reviewing goals, objectives, and requirements in order that the appropriate parties are represented, informed, and involved.

Task 5
Determine Stakeholder Values

Determine stakeholder values regarding the product, using elicitation techniques in order to provide a baseline for prioritizing requirements.

Mnemonic Tip
BVGIV: "Bold **V**endors **G**et **S**ome **V**alue"
B   Define **B**usiness Need
V   Determine **V**alue Proposition
G   Develop Project **G**oals
S   Identify **S**takeholders
V   Determine Stakeholder **V**alues

To help you remember the tasks, use a mnemonic of "Bold Vendors Get Some Value." This nonsense acronym captures the tasks within Needs Assessment in their given order. The first letter of the mnemonic is highlighted to help you memorize it.

This chapter presents each of the tasks along with more information on the task descriptions, and tools and techniques used to perform each task.

Task Inputs, Tools and Techniques, and Outputs

The PMI-PBA exam does not follow a specific "Body of Knowledge" in terms of identifying inputs, tools and techniques, and outputs (ITTOs) for each of the tasks. The table below describes some standard concepts in inputs, tools and techniques, and outputs for each task in order to provide context and greater understanding. The PMI-PBA examination will not test specifically on these ITTOs. ITTOs may be present in test questions in this Study Guide as a means to test your understanding of the task.

Input	Task	Tools and Techniques	Output
Business problem or opportunity	1. Define or review a business problem or opportunity using problem and opportunity analysis techniques in order to develop a solution scope statement and/or to provide input to create a business case.	Problem Solving and Opportunity Identification

Root Cause Analysis | Solution scope statement |
| Solution scope statement | 2. Collect and analyze information from a variety of sources using valuation tools and techniques to contribute to determining the value proposition of the initiative. | Valuation | Value proposition (Business case) |
| Organization goals & objectives

Value proposition (Business case) | 3. Collaborate in the development of project goals and objectives by providing clarification of business needs and solution scope in order to align the product with the organization's goals and objectives. | Scope Models | Solution scope (updated)

Project goals and objectives |

           PMI-PBA Certification Study Guide

Input	Task	Tools and Techniques	Output
Business case Solution scope Project goals and objectives	4. Identify stakeholders by reviewing goals, objectives, and requirements in order that the appropriate parties are represented, informed, and involved.	Stakeholder Analysis	Stakeholder register
Solution scope Project goals and objectives Stakeholder register	5. Determine stakeholder values regarding the product, using elicitation techniques in order to provide a baseline for prioritizing requirements.	Elicitation	Stakeholder values Product scope baseline

Figure 2-3: Needs Assessment ITTOs

Part 1 – Needs Assessment Tasks

Task 1 – Define Business Need

Define or review a business problem or opportunity using problem and opportunity analysis techniques in order to develop a solution scope statement and/or to provide input to create a business case.

BVGSV

Before there is a project there is a need for a project. This task is about understanding that need in order to develop a solution scope statement for use in a business case. The business case is used to request funds to invest in the recommended solution and precedes a formal project. A business case that is funded then becomes a project with the business case providing input to the project charter.

The business analyst may be involved in the development of the business case before there is a project or they may be brought into the project after the project has been initiated. This task highlights the need to review and understand the original business problem and opportunity along with solution scope even after a business case has been approved. This is an essential element in order to provide context, structure, and limits for solution requirements that will support the original business problem or opportunity. The business analyst should push to ensure the business problem or opportunity is clearly articulated along with the solution scope statement.

More information on the business case can be found in the *PMBOK® Guide* section 4.1 – Develop Project Charter.

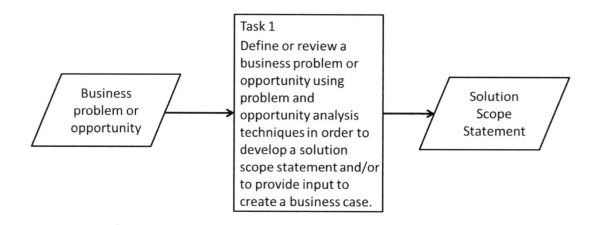

Figure 2-4: Define Business Need ITO

Considerations for Defining the Business Need

Identify Stakeholders

Stakeholder identification is critical to do during the needs assessment to understand which stakeholders will be impacted by the area undergoing analysis.

A number of tools can be used to identify stakeholders, such as RACI, which is further explained in Task 4

Problem and Opportunity Analysis

Rarely is the originally identified problem or opportunity the one that should be pursued. It is critical that analysis is done to understand the root cause problem or most beneficial opportunity for the organization.

Business Problem

The business problem describes a situation that is hindering a business from achieving maximum value. The business problem should clearly articulate the issue in factual terms that cannot be refuted and include facts about the effects and impacts of the problem to the organization. It is important that the business problem state the true root cause of the issue and not simply identify a symptom. It is by articulating and addressing the root cause that the organization will gain the most value from the eventual solution.

Problem Statement Components	
The problem of	Define the problem/situation.
Affects	Who is affected by the problem?
The impact of which is	How the problem impacts each category of stakeholder.
A successful solution would	Provide the key benefits produced by solving the problem.

Example:
We do not have a central listing of customers available for CSR use. Each time a query regarding our customer base is made, excessive staff time is spent researching the request and validating the information from various sources. It is estimated that this costs us $250,000 per year in staff time and missed revenue opportunities. Solving this problem would free up this time and money to invest in future opportunities and expansion.

Stakeholder Approval

Be sure to obtain stakeholder approval for the business problem/business opportunity statement before moving forward.

Figure 2-5: Problem Statement Components

Business Opportunity

The business opportunity describes an opportunity that will add value to the business. The opportunity should be consistent with the goals and objectives of the organization and directly support achieving stated objectives. The opportunity statement should include the specific opportunity and the impact and effect it will have in helping the organization reach its goals.

Example: *The company has invested in a new Enterprise System that includes a customer management system (CRM) module. We can leverage this module to improve our customer information and reporting capabilities saving staff time to respond to inquiries and investigations.*

Project Drivers

There may be many external factors that motivate an organization to invest in a new project.

These include:

Market demand

Organizational need

Customer request

Technological advance

Legal requirement

Ecological impacts

Social need

Tools and Techniques

There are several tools and techniques that can help in understanding the business problem or opportunity in order to create the solution scope statement and business case. These tools and techniques fall into two categories -- Problem Solving and Opportunity Identification, and Root Cause Analysis. These tools and techniques work to develop a deeper understanding of the true problem or real opportunity in order to focus on the aspects of the business need that will bring the most value to the organization. A summary of the categories are provided below. Details on each tool and technique will follow in the final section of the Needs Assessment chapter.

Techniques – *Define Business Need*

Problem Solving and Opportunity Identification Tools and Techniques Tools and techniques used to better understand the reason and source for a problem or identify a potential opportunity.	**Includes:** - Benchmarking - Gap Analysis - Scenario Analysis - User Journey Maps - Value Engineering
Root Cause Analysis Tools and Techniques A structured examination to determine the underlying source of a problem. This helps to ensure that current business thinking and processes are challenged, and that the efforts can be focused where greater benefit can be gained.	**Includes:** - Cause & Effect (Fishbone/Ishikawa Diagram) - Five Whys - Interrelationship Diagrams - Process Models

Outputs

Output: *Solution Scope Statement*

The solution scope statement includes the deliverables and new capabilities to be provided as part of a solution, and the effect on the business and its operations. Sometimes called "product scope," it is a subset of the project scope. This will be included in the business case.

Solution Scope Statement

A description of the solution scope, major deliverables, assumptions, and constraints.

PMBOK® Guide References

More information on the Business Case can be found in the *PMBOK® Guide*:

- Section 4.1 – Develop Project Charter.

Task 2 – Determine Value Proposition

Collect and analyze information from a variety of sources using valuation tools and techniques to contribute to determining the value proposition of the initiative.

B<u>V</u>GSV

Another essential piece of the decision to invest in a project is an understanding of the value that the project will bring to the organization. The business case is not complete without information on the future benefits of the project. There are many tools and techniques available to determine and state the value that a solution will bring to an organization. In some cases, multiple tools and techniques may be used to get an understanding of the value from different perspectives.

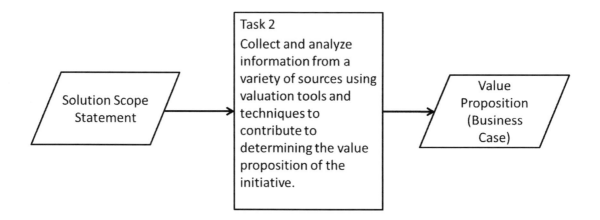

Figure 2-6: Determine Value Proposition ITO

Considerations for Determining the Value Proposition

Determine Value Proposition

Determining the value proposition is an analysis of the value an organization can expect to achieve as a result of the recommended solution. Value is often stated as the financial benefits the organization can expect to achieve. Models such as Kano Model and Net Promoter Score are ways to state benefit in overall customer satisfaction.

Techniques – *Determine Value Proposition*	
Valuation Tools and Techniques Tools and techniques used to determine the value of the potential solution to the organization.	**Includes:** - Cost-Benefit Analysis - Feasibility Analysis - Force Field Analysis - Kano Model - Net Promoter Score - Purpose Alignment Model - SWOT Analysis - Value Stream Map

Outputs

Output: *Value Proposition (Business Case)*
An important element of the business case is the statement of value that the proposed solution is expected to bring to an organization. This is a critical element in determining the benefit of the investment. Often value is stated in financial terms with cost-benefit stated in terms of: 1) payback period, 2) return on investment, 3) weighted average cost of capital, 4) net present value, 5) internal rate of return, 6) average rate of return, or 7) discounted cash flow. Models to determine and state value in terms of customer satisfaction, such as Kano Model or Net Promoter Score, may also be used to provide a different perspective to the expected value.

PMBOK® Guide References

More information on defining project value can be found can be found in the *PMBOK® Guide*:

- Section 1.6 – Business Value

- Section 4.1.1.2 – Business Case

Task 3 – Develop Project Goals

Collaborate in the development of project goals and objectives by providing clarification of business needs and solution scope in order to align the product with the organization's goals and objectives.

BV<u>G</u>SV

Project goals and objectives help provide context, boundaries, and direction for the project. The project goals and objectives should directly tie into the organization's goals and objectives. Why would the organization invest in a project that doesn't support the strategic direction? The project goals and objectives provide a framework on which to base the product scope and requirements. Fully articulated project goals and objectives can be traced to each requirement (and vice versa) to help ensure that the requirement is in scope and brings value to the project and the organization which helps to avoid scope creep.

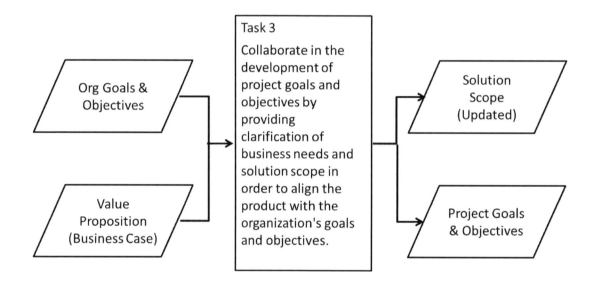

Figure 2-7: Develop Project Goals ITO

Considerations for Developing Project Goals

Project Goals and Objectives

Business targets are set by organizations for achieving new aims, and for maintaining things of value. Goals are ways that strategies can be broken down into actionable and measurable statements. They typically pertain to increased revenue and market share, increased customer satisfaction, reduced costs and expenses, etc.

Goal
Something broad that a business aims for to support its strategy and vision.

For example, a **business goal** for a company might be to "Be a recognized provider of premier customer service." A **project goal** might be developed from that business goal such as "To increase customer satisfaction levels with the ordering process." One possible **project objective** to achieve that project goal might be "To reduce customer complaints on late deliveries over the next year by 20 percent."

To be viable, objectives should be constructed along certain guidelines in order to know when the objective has been met. These are generally referred to as **SMART objectives.** SMART stands for:

> **Objective**
>
> A specific target that an organization aims for to support its goals.

S	Specific	Clear, concise, and observable outcomes are needed
M	Measurable	The outcome should be testable and measurable
A	Achievable	The outcome should be realistic and resources devoted so it can be achieved
R	Relevant	Outcomes should be aligned with the organization's mission, vision, and strategies
T	Time-bounded	A specific time period should be attached to the outcome, in line with the business need

Figure 2-8: SMART Objectives

Alignment with Organization's Goals and Objectives

We have to ask "why are we doing this project?" if the project's goals and objectives do not directly relate to the goals and objectives of the organization. "Traceability" allows us to reference the project's goals and objectives to those of the organization. This helps to demonstrate the value and importance of the project given the strategic direction the organization is taking.

Solution Scope

Scope, in general, applies to both the *project* (work to be done) as well as the *solution/product* to be produced (or delivered). You should be aware of the *project* scope considerations, but concentrate your study on the *solution (product)* scope details. As described in PMI's *Business Analysis for Practitioners: A Practice Guide (4.11),* the packaged set of requirements that addresses a business problem or opportunity defines the "solution scope."

The following contribute to defining the solution scope:

- **Major features and functions** of the solution, both in-scope and out-of-scope (*also known as "product scope"*)
- **Interactions** of the solution with people and other systems
- **Project boundaries** as defined by business units impacted, business processes affected, and IT systems involved with the solution

For example, a loan application might include a web interface for applying for loans, and for instant credit evaluations, including an interface to credit scoring services. The credit department is a major stakeholder group and business unit impacted by the solution. IT would need to provide secure application and credit scoring interfaces. Exception processes would be affected, such as processing borderline applicants. Scope models allow for presenting solution scope visually and can aid in solution scope discussions with stakeholders.

Techniques – *Develop Project Goals*	
Scope Models Tool and Techniques To describe the scope of analysis or the scope of a solution.	**Includes:** - Context Diagram - Ecosystem Map - Feature Model - Goal Model and Business Objective Model - Use Case Diagram

Outputs

Output: *Project Goals and Objectives*
The project goals and objectives clearly articulated. This includes SMART objectives, meaning objectives that are specific, measurable, achievable, relevant, and time-bounded.

Output: *Solution Scope (updated)*
The set of capabilities a solution must deliver in order to meet the business need.

PMBOK® Guide References

More information on project goals can be found can be found in:

PMBOK® Guide:

- Section 1.5 – Relationship Between Project Management, Operations Management, and Organizational Strategy

Needs Assessment – Exercise 1

How many words related to Needs Assessment can you find in the word search below? There are 10 words from the first three tasks of Needs Assessment below. See the end of this chapter for the solution.

Needs Assessment

```
B   V   E   Y   P   Y   V   I   K   Z   L   S   S   M   E

V   G   C   V   L   W   R   N   F   M   T   C   C   U   A

P   A   N   L   I   M   G   R   Z   A   O   L   A   Y   Q

N   U   L   I   A   T   U   Q   K   P   Y   F   F   K   O

Y   T   E   U   N   U   C   E   E   G   U   I   N   N   I

Z   T   L   X   E   P   H   E   E   W   T   T   X   Y   J

C   R   L   W   X   O   S   J   J   N   J   W   I   B   V

E   T   G   C   L   A   S   Z   E   B   F   W   P   S   O

H   N   J   D   D   Y   T   D   J   G   O   P   B   S   T

S   W   E   O   L   U   I   Y   N   G   Q   R   M   E   N

U   R   Y   T   I   N   U   T   R   O   P   P   O   N   X

S   P   R   O   B   L   E   M   W   A   M   T   L   I   G

T   R   A   M   S   R   M   T   I   L   V   G   D   S   C

S   F   O   Z   Y   C   H   A   C   S   Y   G   S   U   Q

R   G   O   V   E   T   I   G   H   Q   F   W   O   B   O
```

Write each word found in the form below and complete a definition of each on the following page.

Word	Definition
1.	
2.	
3.	
4.	
5.	
6.	
7.	
8.	
9.	
10.	

Hint: Words are BUSINESS, GOALS, IDENTIFY, OBJECTIVE, OPPORTUNITY, PROBLEM, SCOPE, SMART, STAKEHOLDERS, and VALUE.

Task 4 – Identify Stakeholders

Identify stakeholders by reviewing goals, objectives, and requirements in order that the appropriate parties are represented, informed, and involved.

BVGSV

This task identifies stakeholders for a given initiative or who share a common business need, and defines stakeholder influence and authority for approving project deliverables. It is performed early in a project and continues throughout business analysis. Activities include:

1. Identify stakeholders affected by a solution to a business need.

2. Group stakeholders into categories reflecting their involvement in a project.

3. Define roles, responsibilities, and authority levels for individual stakeholders or groups. For example, the project sponsor may be an individual, but the Customer Service Department is a group stakeholder.

4. Analyze stakeholders to assess their influence and attitude regarding the project, especially for negative attitudes or behavior which may adversely affect the project.

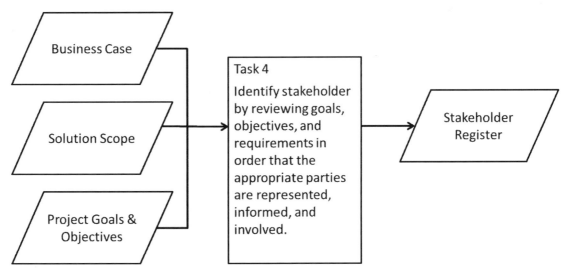

Figure 2-9: Identify Stakeholders ITO

Considerations for Identifying Stakeholders

Identify or refine stakeholder analysis

Successful projects rely on iteratively identifying relevant stakeholders, and assessing the impact on them as well as their authority to influence outcomes. It is the basis for understanding their needs, and ultimately their requirements. Missing stakeholders for an initiative usually results in missed requirements or defining incorrect requirements.

> **Stakeholder**
>
> Any individual or group who is affected by a change or project, or has influence over its outcome.

In theory, adaptive versus predictive approaches can mitigate the risk associated with missed stakeholders, but they don't eliminate it. The same effect of missed or incorrect requirements can happen with either approach.

The participants in requirements activities will vary among projects, organizations, and with methodologies. For example, some projects may have quality assurance analysts attend requirements workshops to bring a QA perspective to defining requirements or their acceptance criteria.

The RACI Matrix

One means to identify stakeholders is to determine and define their roles within the organization and the project. RACI is a technique often used to document this role definition and is called out in the *PMI-PBA Examination Content Outline* as the predominant tool.

A RACI matrix helps with assigning and documenting roles and responsibilities. It is widely used and focuses on the major task and decision-making roles for projects. RACI stands for the following:

Responsible - does the work

Accountable - approves the work

Consult With - provides knowledge, information, expertise

Inform - needs to know the result of the task/process

Process/ Phase	R	A	C	I
Identify problem/opportunity	Business Analyst	Sponsor	Subject Matter Experts (SMEs), Team	Team, Stakeholders
Assess current state of organization	Business Analyst	Sponsor	SMEs, Team	Product Manager
Recommend action	Business Analyst	Product Manager	SMEs, Team, Project Manager	Sponsor
Prepare Business Case	Business Analyst	Product Manager	SMEs	Sponsor, Project Manager, Team

Figure 2-10: RACI Matrix

Figure 2-10 provides a format useful during a needs assessment.

This diagram lists processes or phases down the left column and R, A, C, or I roles across the top. At the intersection of process and RACI, it indicates who fulfills the role/responsibility.

1. Executing the process or documenting the results is completed by **Responsible.**

2. Responsible analyzes and/or plans the process or phase listed, and identifies knowledgeable parties (**Consulted**) and asks for their help in planning or defining tasks, information needed, etc., and then communicates and recommends items for approval.

3. Responsible presents plans or requirements to **Accountable**, who approves the work.

4. Responsible then notifies **Informed** of the outcome of the decision/approval.

Complexity of Stakeholder Group

Factors to consider regarding the complexity of a stakeholder group include:

1. The number of stakeholders

2. The diversity of their needs

3. The business processes likely to be impacted by a project

4. The degree of uniformity across the processes impacted

5. The number of business units touched by stakeholders

6. The number of IT and/or external systems stakeholders work across

Attitude and Influence

This describes assessing stakeholder attitudes regarding a project or change and the relative influence they may have over it. The following table summarizes the factors that may be considered.

Attitude Factors
Attitude toward the business goals, objectives, and solution approach
Do they believe that the solution will benefit the organization?
Will the benefits affect them directly?
Will the benefits be accrued elsewhere?
Are the possible negative effects of the initiative on this stakeholder greater than the rewards?
Do they believe that the project team can successfully deliver the solution?
Attitude toward business analysis
Do they see value in defining their requirements?
Do they present solutions and expect the requirements to be contained in that solution, and believe that this will enable them to avoid requirements definition?
Attitude toward collaboration
Have they had success on previous collaborative efforts?
Does the organization reward collaboration?
Is the organization hierarchical in nature, rather than team-based?
Are personal agendas the norm?
Attitude toward the sponsor
On cross-functional efforts, do all the SMEs support the sponsor?
Are there SMEs who would prefer another sponsor?
Attitude toward team members
Have key members of the project team (including but not limited to the business analyst) built trusting relationships, or have there been prior failed projects or project phases involving those people?

Figure 2-11: Attitude Assessment Factors

Determining the influence patterns and finding individuals with influence in an organization can improve project success. It helps when building relationships and trust, which in turn increases buy-in and collaboration. These outcomes can help teams work through conflict and solve problems when they arise on projects. Influence includes:

> **Influence**
>
> To be a compelling force on or produce effects from others. Proactively shift thinking, actions, and even emotional states of other people.

Influence Factors
Influence on the project
How much influence does the stakeholder have on the project?
Which stakeholders make approvals and obtain funding?
Influence in the organization
What is the stakeholder's official title and position?
What informal influence does the individual have in the organization?
Influence needed for the good of the project
How much and what type of influence is needed to help the project succeed?
Is there a mismatch between a sponsor's influence and how much is needed? (Are risk plans needed to mitigate the mismatch?)
Influence with other stakeholders
What are the informal influence "channels"?
Who might exert negative influence and sabotage the project?

Figure 2-12: Influence Assessment Factors

Authority Levels for Business Analysis Work

In order to determine who can approve BA deliverables, the proper authority levels need to be identified. Examples of authority that stakeholders can exert over business analysis work include:

- Approve business analysis deliverables
- Inspect and approve requirements
- Request and approve changes
- Approve processes involving requirements
- Review and approve the traceability structure to be used
- Veto proposed requirements or solutions

Techniques – *Identifying Stakeholders*

Stakeholder Analysis Tools and Techniques	Includes:
Analyzing stakeholder needs and preferences in order to best determine how to engage with and manage the stakeholder for maximum project support.	- Job Analysis - Organizational Chart - Personas - Role Definition (RACI) - Skills Assessment

Output: *Stakeholder Register*

The Stakeholder Register may include any of the items below as needed to effectively plan and manage stakeholder engagement.

Roles	Required roles
Names	Names and titles of stakeholders
Categories	Categories of stakeholders
Numbers	Number of individuals in each stakeholder role
Locations	Location of stakeholders
Needs	Special needs and concerns
Influence	Description or mapping of stakeholder influence and interest
Authority	Documented stakeholder authority levels

PMBOK® Guide References

More information on stakeholders can be found can be found in the *PMBOK® Guide*:

- Section 13.1 – Identify Stakeholders

- Section 13.2 – Plan Stakeholder Management

Task 5 – Determine Stakeholder Values

Determine stakeholder values regarding the product, using elicitation techniques in order to provide a baseline for prioritizing requirements.

BVGS<u>V</u>

This task provides a further analysis of identified stakeholders' requirements in order "to provide a baseline for prioritizing requirements."

> **Baseline**
>
> The approved version of a work product that can be changed only through change control procedures and is used for a basis of comparison.

The output of Task 5 is a "product scope baseline" via elicitation techniques. Elicitation and the related techniques are discussed in greater detail in Task 1 of the Analysis domain.

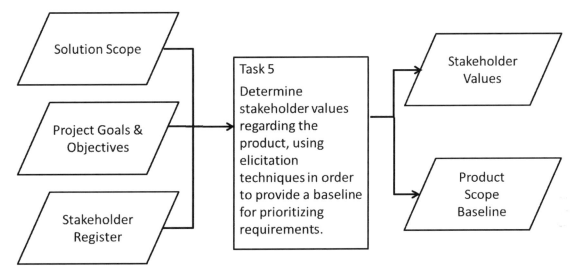

Figure 2-13: Identify Stakeholder Requirements ITO

Considerations for Determining Stakeholder Values

Stakeholder Values

The stakeholder analysis of the previous task helps to form and articulate the product scope that will satisfy the business and the stakeholder needs.

Product Scope Baseline

Provide a product scope baseline that clarifies the deliverables of the solution that will be delivered to the business and end users. The product scope that is accepted and approved by the appropriate stakeholder serves as a baseline and provides boundaries for the product requirements. Any changes to product scope after the baseline is set is subject to change control processes. This will be discussed in more detail in the Planning and Traceability and Monitoring domains.

Techniques – *Determining Stakeholder Values*	
Elicitation Tools and Techniques Tools and techniques used to draw out requirements and assumptions from stakeholders through individual and group settings and from existing documentation.	Includes: - Brainstorming - Document Analysis - Facilitated Workshops - Focus Groups - Interviews - Non-Functional Requirements Analysis - Observation - Prototypes - Research - Surveys & Questionnaires

Output: Product Scope Baseline
The approved deliverables of the product that need to be satisfied in order for the solution to be considered a project success. This product scope will serve as the basis for stakeholder requirements and solution requirements discovered through Analysis and tracked in Traceability and Monitoring.

PMBOK® Guide References

More information on stakeholder values can be found can be found in the PMBOK® Guide:

- Section 5.2 – Collect Requirements

- Section 13.3 – Manage Stakeholder Engagement

- Section 13.4 – Control Stakeholder Engagement

PMI-PBA Certification Study Guide

Needs Assessment – Exercise 2

Use the clues to complete the crossword puzzle below.

Needs Assessment

www.CrosswordWeaver.com

ACROSS

2 Ability to shift thinking or actions
5 A hinderance
8 Something to exploit
9 May be expressed as dollars or customer satisfaction
10 Good objectives are _____

DOWN

1 A condition or capability needed
3 Has a vested interest in the project
4 Specific outcomes desired
6 Describes the boundaries of a solution
7 Broad statements of expectation

See the end of this chapter for the answers.

Needs Assessment – Exercise 3

Write the mnemonic letters for the five tasks of Needs Assessment, and then complete the missing words for each task in the blanks provided below.

Needs Assessment Tasks	Mnemonic
1. Define _____ _____	_____
2. Determine _____ _____	_____
3. Develop _____ _____	_____
4. Identify_____	_____
5. Determine _____ _____	_____

Part 2 – Techniques for Needs Assessment

The tools and techniques below are those that may be most helpful in the Needs Assessment domain. Importantly, the tools and techniques are not domain or task specific; they may be used for more than one task and in more than one domain. It will be necessary for the person doing the business analysis work to determine which tools to use and when.

Category	Technique
Elicitation Tools and Techniques *(covered in Analysis domain)*	
	Brainstorming
	Document Analysis
	Facilitated Workshops
	Focus Groups
	Interviews
	Non-functional Requirements Analysis
	Observation
	Prototypes
	Research
	Survey / Questionnaire
Problem Solving and Opportunity Identification Tools and Techniques *Tools and techniques used to better understand the reason and source for a problem or identify a potential opportunity.*	
	Benchmarking
	Gap Analysis *(covered in Analysis domain)*
	Scenario Analysis
	User Journey Maps
	Value Engineering
Root Cause Analysis Tools and Techniques *A structured examination to determine the underlying source of a problem. This helps to ensure that current business thinking and processes are challenged and that the efforts can be focused where greater benefit can be gained.*	
	Cause and Effect Diagram (Fishbone or Ishikawa diagram)
	Five Whys
	Interrelationship Diagrams
	Process Models
Scope Models Tool and Techniques *To describe the scope of analysis or the scope of a solution.*	
	Context Diagram
	Ecosystem Map
	Feature Model
	Goal Model and Business Objective Model
	Use Case Diagram

Category	Technique
Stakeholder Analysis Tools and Techniques *Analyzing stakeholder needs and preferences in order to best determine how to engage with and manage the stakeholders for maximum project support*	
	Job Analysis
	Organizational Chart
	Personas
	Role Definition (RACI)
	Skills Assessment
Valuation Tools and Techniques *Tools and techniques used to determine the value of the potential solution to the organization.*	
	Cost-Benefit Analysis
	Feasibility Analysis
	Force Field Analysis
	Kano Model
	Net Promoter Score
	Purpose Alignment Model
	SWOT Analysis
	Value Stream Map

Figure 2-14: Tools and Techniques for Needs Assessment

The following pages provide additional details about the tools and techniques that may be most helpful in this domain. (Details for some techniques may be covered in a different domain as noted above.) Not all tools and techniques will be discussed at a great level of detail. The amount of information provided relates to the priority of the tool or technique on the exam. Each technique has been rated with a priority level of low, moderate, or high to help in prioritizing study. Items marked as low may appear in your certification exam; items marked moderate are likely to show up in one or two questions, and items marked high may have multiple questions relating to their use.

Problem Solving and Opportunity Identification Tools and Techniques

Tools and techniques used to better understand the reason and source for a problem or identify a potential opportunity.

Problem Solving and Opportunity Identification Tools and Techniques
Benchmarking
Gap Analysis (covered in Analysis domain)
Scenario Analysis
User Journey Maps
Value Engineering

Problem Solving Mnemonic
Billy **G**oats ride in **S U Vs**

 PMI-PBA Certification Study Guide

Benchmarking   **Priority: High**

Benchmarking is a technique for learning from key competitors and from an industry as a whole. Benchmarking aims to discover industry best practices, and to recommend which ones to adopt.

Benchmarking provides useful insights into how others are dealing with same challenges. It also provides ideas on how to approach something that the organization might not have come up with on their own or would have had to expend time discovering.

Benchmarking	
Description	Analyze an organization's methods against its key competitors, find out how competitors may achieve superior results, and uncover changes needed to meet or exceed the competition. Typically focused on things like strategies, operations, and processes.
Characteristics	Three types: • Casual review of corporate documents, e.g., web pages or reports • Study of major aspects of a product or "secret shopping" • Disassembling and/or reproducing a product (reverse engineering) to analyze it and understanding how it is built and its capabilities
Practical Example	An organization would do benchmarking when launching a new product, for example a new personal communication device. By studying and benchmarking competitive products, the new device can be launched with the same features to be competitive.

Figure 2-15: Benchmarking Technique

Competitive analysis is one form of benchmarking. It focuses on comparing an organization's own characteristics against features and functions that key competitors have, to determine changes needed to meet or exceed the competition. Below is a sample competitive analysis template that could be used to guide a benchmarking study.

COMPETITIVE ANALYSIS

FACTOR	MY BUSINESS	STRENGTH	WEAKNESS	COMPETITOR A	...	COMPETITOR N	IMPORTANCE TO CUSTOMER
Products							
Price							
Quality							
Selection							
Service							
Reliability							
Stability							
etc.							

Courtesy of SCORE; Service Corps of Retired Executives (SCORE®)

Figure 2-16: Competitive Analysis Worksheet Sample

Scenario Analysis   **Priority: High**

Scenario in this context is a way to describe a specific situation in terms of users (people or other systems) of a solution and the interactions with the solution. Scenario analysis looks to explore the current situation from the perspective of the users and interacting systems in order to better understand a problem or identify the opportunities that may be leveraged. Scenarios can play an important role in requirements later on by setting the stage for Use Cases or User Stories (discussed in the Analysis domain).

User Journey Maps   **Priority: High**

A User Journey Map describes the journey of a user through the lifecycle of a process in a visual format. The journey is described from the perspective of the user. User journey maps should always be developed in collaboration with actual users of a system and not solely rely on the business analyst's assumptions of the journey. There is no standard for developing user journey maps although review of many examples portray a timeline of events described in phases, such as in the example below. User journey maps may be very sophisticated, like the example, or simple with stick figures and smiley faces.

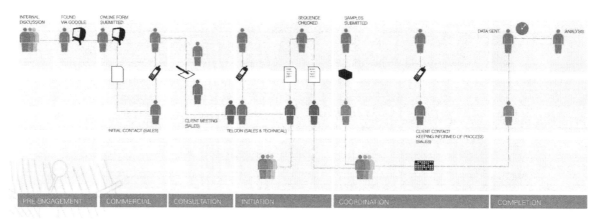

Figure 2-17: User Journey Map Example
(source: http://www.servicedesigntools.org/tools/8)

                                         PMI-PBA Certification Study Guide

Value Engineering   **Priority: High**

Value Engineering is a powerful methodology for solving problems and/or reducing costs while maintaining or improving performance and quality requirements. It describes a cyclical process in which to identify and analyze opportunities to increase value. Each step of the process is described in the overview below. Value engineering analysis explores each step with questions designed to get a deeper understanding of the opportunity. With this deeper understanding comes the ability to better articulate the benefits in terms of value.

Value Engineering	
Description	An approach used to optimize project life cycle costs, save time, increase profits, improve quality, expand market share, solve problems, and/or use resources more effectively.

Characteristics	Value = Function/Cost
	
	Gather information
	    • What is being done now?
	    • Who is doing it?
	    • What could it do?
	    • What must it not do?
	Measure
	    • How will the alternatives be measured?
	    • What are the alternate ways of meeting requirements?
	    • What else can perform the desired function?
	Analyze
	    • What must be done?
	    • What does it cost?
	Generate
	    • What else will do the job?
	Evaluate
	    • Which ideas are the best?
	Develop and expand ideas
	    • What are the impacts?
	    • What is the cost?
	    • What is the performance?
	Present ideas
	    • Sell alternatives.

Figure 2-18: Value Engineering Overview

Root Cause Analysis Tools and Techniques

Tools and techniques used to understand the underlying causes of a situation. Root cause analysis is critical to ensuring that the right problem is being addressed, rather than a symptom of the problem.

Root Cause Analysis Tools and Techniques
Cause & Effect Diagram (Fishbone / Ishikawa Diagram)
Five Whys
Interrelationship Diagram
Process Model

Root Cause Mnemonic
Cook **F**ancy **I**talian food **P**lease

Cause and Effect Diagram (Fishbone / Ishikawa Diagram)   Priority: High

Kaoru Ishikawa created this diagram in 1968 as a means to further explore a problem to find the root cause. This diagram has many names including fishbone diagram, Ishikawa diagram, and cause and effect diagram. Use of the diagram provides a structured method to identify the root causes, ensuring complete understanding. It is useful in promoting a conversation to explore factors by category and find emerging trends in underlying (or root) causes.

The diagram is developed by identifying a problem at the head of the diagram. Categories are then used to explore the various aspects of the problem. Many industries and organizations have standard categories to use but these are often suggestions that may be adjusted as necessary. The discussion then looks to explore the specific factors in each category that contribute to the overall problem. The Five Whys technique (described next) can be used in conjunction with the fishbone diagram to fully explore the problem.

Cause and Effect Diagram	
Description	A type of flowchart that helps organize thinking about a problem and diagnose cause and effect to discover root cause. Can be used in conjunction with the "Five Whys" technique.
Characteristics	The problem under consideration is at the head of the "fish." Then the rib bones are drawn to represent the categories of potential causes of the problem. Any categories can be used, but typical categories are often represented.

Figure 2-19: Fishbone / Ishikawa Overview

PMI-PBA Certification Study Guide

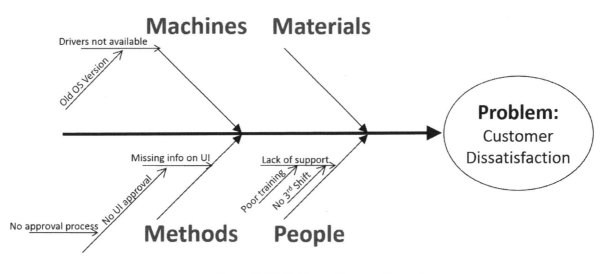

Figure 2-20: Fishbone Diagram Example

Five Whys   **Priority: High**

Five Whys is technique where the analyst asks "why" about five times. In actuality, it may be three times or even seven. The idea is to keep asking "why" until no new information is presented. At this point you are at the root of the issue or process. Business analysts need to be careful in use of this technique to not literally ask "why" five times or risk sounding irritating. A seasoned analyst will ask a question that gets to "why" without overusing the actual word. Five Whys can be combined with other techniques, such as fishbone diagram, to further understand a problem, or process maps to gain a better understanding of the process.

Five Whys	
Description	The "Five Whys" technique is one way to begin analysis and is more a guideline than a true technique. It is an integral part of other analysis tools like the fishbone diagram. It reminds us that to get to the root cause of a problem, we need to ask "why is the problem occurring" up to five times to get to the root cause.
Characteristics	Be sure to ask "why" diplomatically, such as "Help me understand why this problem is occurring," or "Tell me more about why that happens."

Figure 2-21: Five Whys Overview

Interrelationship Diagram   Priority: Low

The Interrelationship Diagram is a root-cause analysis tool that helps to explore contributing factors (causes) and effects of each factor (e.g., "late to work," "traffic," "unreliable alarm"). In the Interrelationship Diagram, factors are represented in circles in a circular format. Each factor is analyzed in relationship to every other factor (one relationship at a time) with arrows noting where one factor is a cause to another factor. The analysis continues until all relationship pairs have been analyzed by noting on each factor the number of causes that are inputs and the number of effects. The result is a quantified indicator of what factor is the biggest contributing factor to the others.

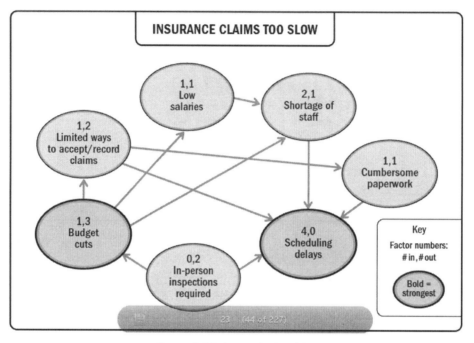

Figure 2-22: Interrelationship Diagram
From *Business Analysis for Practitioners: A Practice Guide*, p. 23, PMI

Process Model   Priority: High

A Process model identifies high-level steps in the business process and theories of problem causes within each step along the business process. It satisfies some team members' preference for sequential thinking and helps identify when process intervention may be most helpful. It also helps identify steps that may be overlooked as sources of possible causes of problems.

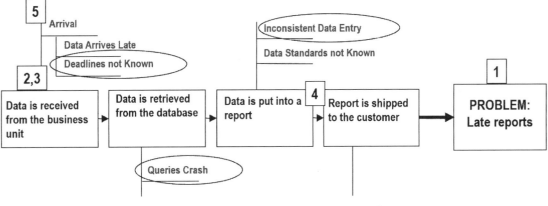

Figure 2-23: Process Model Example

Scope Models Tools and Techniques

Scope models describe tools and techniques that aid in developing and communicating solution scope. It provides a visual representation of the processes and external entities that are included in the solution scope. This is very useful in confirming scope with the project sponsor or other decision makers, and in communicating the scope to other stakeholders, including team members.

Scope Models Tool and Techniques
Context Diagram
Ecosystem Map
Feature Model
Goal Model and Business Objective Model
Use Case Diagram

Scope Models Mnemonic
Crystals **E**voke **F**unky **G**host **U**nicorns

Context Diagram   Priority: High

A Context Diagram provides a visual representation of solution scope by focusing on external agents that will be interacting with the solution and details on the processes and data used in the interactions.

Context Diagram	
Description	A context diagram allows the business analyst to clearly show the boundary of the system, the users (both human and other systems), and the high-level data provided by and to the system. A context diagram is only a high-level view, but when supported by detailed data definitions, it is an excellent tool for communicating part of the project scope to stakeholders.
Characteristics	**Context Diagram.** A visual depiction of a solution's scope, showing: • A **System**, whose scope is represented by the diagram • **External agents** (people, other systems, or events) that interact with it, and • **Data flows** that show data moving between processes, data stores, and external agents

Figure 2-24: Context Diagram Overview

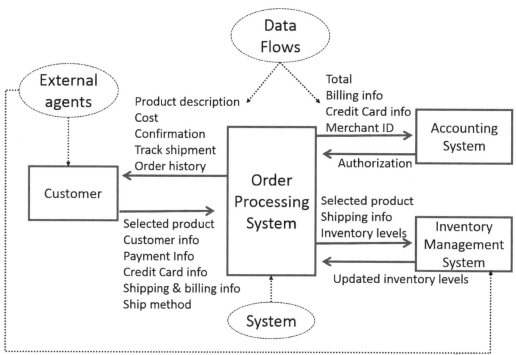

Figure 2-25: Context Diagram Example

Ecosystem Map   **Priority: Low**

An Ecosystem Map is a diagram showing relevant systems, the relationship between them, and any data passed between the systems. A relevant system is a system that may be affected by or that will impact the systems that are within the scope of the project.

Feature Model   Priority: Low

A Feature Model provides a view of the features of a solution in a tree or hierarchical structure. A major feature makes up the major branch of the tree with lower level (decomposed) features represented as sub branches.

Goal Model and Business Objective Model   Priority: Low

Goal models and business objective models are diagrams for organizing and depicting the relationships between business problems or opportunities, business objectives, success metrics, and high-level features as a chain.

Use Case Diagram   Priority: High

Use cases describe how "actors" interact with a "system" to accomplish a business goal or respond to events. Use cases contain "scenarios," which are primary and alternate paths through the use case for accomplishing the desired goal. The use case diagram is typically easy to read and understand, and it provides a visual representation of a system by focusing on the actors who will interact with the system and their goals in the interaction.

Use Case Diagram	
Description	The boundary box shows the "scope" of the system in question. It becomes the basis for describing what's in and out of the system's scope. The use cases inside the box are "in scope" and the actors outside the box are considered "out of scope". Actors are always outside of the boundary. Lines connect each actor to the processes with which they interact. Actors without a connection to any process may indicate there are processes missing, while processes without a connection to any actors may indicate missing actors or out of scope processes. Since the purpose of use cases is to identify and describe processes, focus on finding all the processes.
Characteristics	• **System (boundary Box):** everything the project has control over, usually automated. (See 3 in *Figure 2-27*.) • **Actors (stick figures, rectangle):** people, systems, or events that communicate with the system. (See 1 in *Figure 2-27*.) • **Use Case (oval):** description of what an actor wants done and what the system does in response to that request. (See 4 in *Figure 2-27*.) • **Interfaces (solid line):** a universal translator that enables the conversation between an actor and the system. (See 2 in *Figure 2-27*.)

Figure 2-26: Use Case Diagram Overview

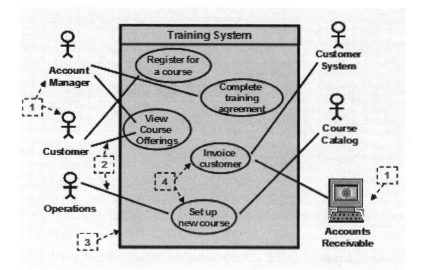

Figure 2-27: Use Case Diagram Example

Stakeholder Analysis Tools and Techniques

Tools and techniques used to identify and analyze project stakeholders. The purpose is to determine the best plan for engaging and managing stakeholder engagement to ensure the project and project requirements receive the support needed to be successful.

Stakeholder Analysis Tools and Techniques
Job Analysis
Organizational Chart
Personas
Role Definition (RACI)
Skills Assessment

Stakeholder Analysis Mnemonic
Jane **O**rganizes **P**ersonal **R**ings **S**lowly

Job Analysis   Priority: High

Job Analysis is reviewing job information for potential stakeholders in order to understand how the stakeholder's roles and responsibilities fit within the organization in order to develop stakeholder management plans.

Organizational Chart   Priority: High

Like its name implies, an organizational chart helps to depict the structure of an organization, its functions, and its people. It shows the "scope" of organization units, the relationships between people of that unit, their roles, and how they interface with other units. Overall, the goal of using organizational charts is to identify all stakeholders who may have requirements for the product or service being delivered.

Organizational Chart	
Description	Defines roles, responsibilities, and reporting relationships in an organization or parts of an organization. They can be used to help identify project stakeholders and the reporting relationships among those stakeholders.
Characteristics	May be used as a starting point or created from scratch. Developed through discussion with department managers. May identify groups or individuals, depending on intended use. Important to remember that roles may vary across the organization and the same stakeholder types may vary in their use of a product or service.
Practical Example	For the automated sales commission project, an organizational chart is obtained and perhaps needs updating. During stakeholder analysis, the team documents/updates the roles that exist within the functional unit the project is serving, such as the A/P Department.

Figure 2-28: Organizational Chart Overview

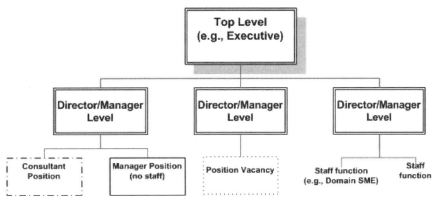

Figure 2-29: Organizational Chart Example

Personas   Priority: High

Personas are a tool used to understand the different user groups of a potential solution by assigning each role a "persona." The persona tells a story about the users of that class including information such as goals, behaviors, motivations, environment, demographics, and skills.

Role Definition (RACI)   Priority: High

One means to analyze stakeholders is to determine and define their roles with the organization and the project. RACI is a technique often used to document this role definition in a RACI matrix and is called out in the *PMI-PBA Examination Content Outline* as the predominant tool.

A RACI matrix helps with assigning and documenting roles and responsibilities. It is widely used, and focuses on the major task and decision-making roles for projects. RACI stands for the following:

- **R**esponsible - does the work.
- **A**ccountable - approves the work.
- **C**onsult With - provides knowledge, information, expertise.
- **I**nform - needs to know the result of the task/process.

> **RACI Matrix**
>
> A matrix that captures major stakeholder roles and responsibilities.
> R – Responsible
> A – Accountable
> C – Consult With
> I – Inform

Role Definition (RACI Matrix)	
Description	A matrix that captures major stakeholder roles and responsibilities.
Characteristics	**Responsible** does the work. **Accountable** approves the work. **Consult with** provides knowledge, information, expertise. **Inform** needs to know the result of the task or process.

Figure 2-30: RACI Matrix Overview

Below are two sample RACI charts. *Figure 2-31* shows a RACI matrix based on project phase, and the R, A, C, and I listed across the top. This format is useful when the initial people aren't known on a project or if they change frequently. *Figure 2-32* focuses on the typical stakeholders on projects and the phases across the top. This second format places the R, A, C, and I into the cells where the people cross-reference the phases. Both are commonly used in the industry.

Process/Phase	R	A	C	I
Plan Project	Project Manager	Sponsor	Subject Matter Experts (SMEs)	Team, Stakeholders
Plan Requirements	Business Analyst	Project Manager	SMEs	Sponsor, Quality Assurance
Analyze Requirements	Business Analyst	Business Analyst	SMEs, End-Users, Developers	Project Manager
Test Product	Quality Assurance	Project Manager	Business Analyst, Developers	Sponsor, Team

Figure 2-31: Sample RACI Chart, focused on Project Phase

                                       PMI-PBA Certification Study Guide

Process/ Phase Person	Plan Project	Plan Requirements	Analyze Requirements	Test Product
Executive Sponsor	A	I	C	I
Project Manager	R	A	A	A
Valuation Tools and Techniques	I	R	R	C
SMEs/End Users	C	C	C	C,I
Developers	I		C,I	C,I
Quality Assurance	I	I	C,I	R

Figure 2-32: Sample RACI Chart, focused on Stakeholders

Skills Assessment   Priority: High

Skills assessment looks at the skills and competencies of project stakeholders to allow for stakeholder management plans that leverages strengths and can accommodate weaknesses.

Valuation Tools and Techniques

Tools and techniques used to better understand the reason and source for a problem or identify a potential opportunity.

Valuation Tools and Techniques
Cost-Benefit Analysis
Feasibility Analysis
Force Field Analysis
Kano Model
Net Promoter Score
Purpose Alignment Model
SWOT Analysis
Value Stream Map

Valuation Techniques Mnemonic

Cool Friends Find Kind Neanderthals Playing on Silly Vines

Cost-Benefit Analysis   Priority: High

Cost-Benefit Analysis is the financial analysis of the cost of a solution compared to the benefits the solution will bring to the organization. There are many financial models available for determining cost benefit but they all have the same effect -- to put a dollar value on the expected benefits from the project. You should be familiar with the various models (detailed in the overview below) for the exam but it is unlikely you will need to do calculations.

Cost-Benefit Analysis	
Description	Cost-benefit analysis is the study of the cost versus the benefits that an organization will receive for a particular solution. This is useful in selecting projects for investments that will yield the greatest financial benefit for the organization.
Characteristics	Financial tools used for cost-benefit analysis include: **Pay Back Period**: length of time for an investment to pay for itself, usually expressed in months or years **Net Present Value**: future value a project might bring, less its calculated value today **Internal Rate of Return**: hypothetical annual yield of an investment **Discounted Cash Flow**: future value on cash flows, discounted to a present value

Figure 2-33: Cost-Benefit Analysis Overview

Feasibility Analysis   Priority: High

For smaller and simpler situations, individual or small-group analysis often is appropriate to determine a feasible approach. For larger efforts, a feasibility study is often performed. A feasibility study is an initial study to determine whether a project/solution provides the expected benefit to accomplish a business need.

The intent of this technique is to understand the business drivers behind an initiative. Informally, we often call this "what problem are we trying to solve?" Ideally, the team working on the initiative will document concise, measurable objectives for the proposed solution to meet. These objectives can form the basis for evaluating recommendations to meet the business need.

> **Feasibility Study**
>
> An initial study to determine whether a solution is viable to accomplish a desired outcome, whether it's to solve a problem or seize an opportunity.

For example, a business need might be to process loan applications in hours instead of days. An obvious objective in this case would be to lower the time a proposed solution would take to process applications. If possible, defining business benefits from a solution (e.g., money saved or increased customer satisfaction) would be useful for evaluating possible solutions.

In many cases, the feasibility study is a project in itself. Feasibility analysis is used for major business initiatives, such as adding new lines of business, performing acquisitions, new product development, etc. Shorter studies are appropriate for lower-investment situations.

Force Field Analysis   **Priority: High**

Force Field Analysis is the process of analyzing the forces for and against a change, to help form a decision and communicate the reasoning behind the decision. The analysis focuses on listing and giving weight to the force "for" change versus the forces "against" change. The overall forces "for" can be compared to the overall forces "against" to determine the net acceptance.

Force Field Analysis	
Description	An initial study to determine whether a solution is viable to accomplish a desired outcome, whether it's to solve a problem or seize an opportunity. May be used to compare multiple options to determine the most feasible.
Characteristics	Statement of Change List of forces for change with score List of forces against change with score Sum of forces for versus forces against

Figure 2-34: Force Field Analysis Overview

Force Field Analysis

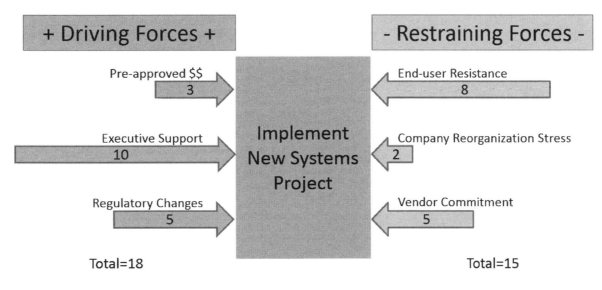

Figure 2-35: Force Field Analysis Example

Kano Model   Priority: High

A Kano Model is used to describe what it takes to positively impact customer satisfaction. The model explores customer satisfaction as it relates to what they expect, what is normal, and what they find exciting.

Effect on Customer Satisfaction

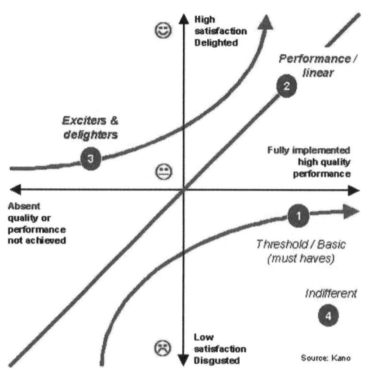

Figure 2-36: Kano Model Example

Net Promoter Score   Priority: High

The Net Promoter Score, or NPS®, is a tool for measuring customer loyalty that helps a company understand how to encourage business growth and discourage defection to competitors. To determine a company's NPS, customers score themselves in response to a question about how likely they would be to recommend a product or service to someone else. Using a scale of 1-10 in which 1=Not at all likely, and 10=Extremely likely, customers who score a 9 or 10 are identified as *Promoters* who are enthusiastic advocates of the company's products or services. Those who score 7 or 8 are the *Passives* who are satisfied, but not enthusiastic and could be easily persuaded to go to the competition. Those who score 0-6 are the *Detractors* who are not satisfied with the product or service and are unhappy with the company. To calculate the NPS, subtract the percentage of Detractors from the percentage of Promoters.

The idea of valuation is to deliver solutions that will increase the organization's NPS.

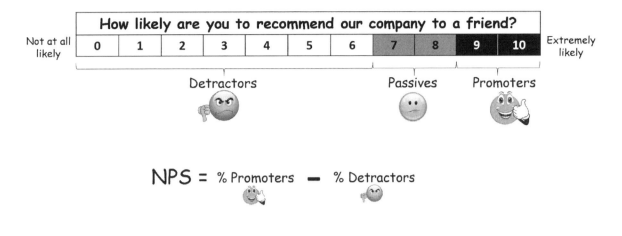

$$NPS = \%\ Promoters - \%\ Detractors$$

Figure 2-37: Net Promoter Score

Purpose Alignment Model   Priority: High

The Purpose Alignment Model is a quadrant analysis tool used for aligning business decisions, processes, and feature designs around purpose. The quadrant is created with axes for "Mission Critical" and "Market Differentiator." The proposed solution is then plotted along these axes to find the quadrant. The four quadrants are Partner, Differentiating, Who Cares, and Parity.

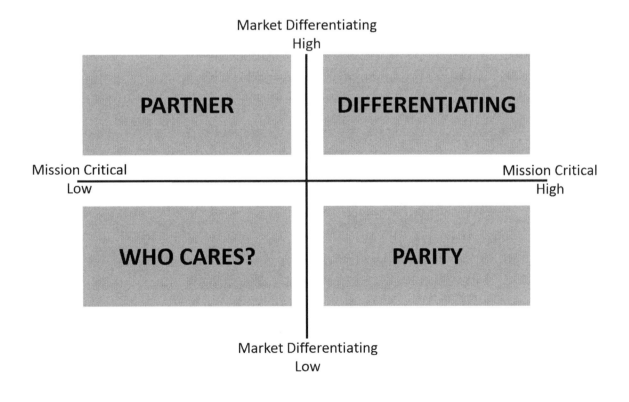

Figure 2-38: Purpose Alignment Model

SWOT Analysis   **Priority: High**

Typically used as a strategic planning tool, SWOT analysis is used to explore the current state of an organization using four key strategic variables. SWOT stands for Strengths, Weaknesses, Opportunities, and Threats. Applied to enterprise analysis, SWOT can also be used to help perform opportunity analysis (using the O or opportunity) and competitive analysis (using the T or Threat). SWOT is a quick way to uncover major variables surrounding a problem or the current state of an organization. It is very high-level, however, and typically is followed up with more detailed analysis.

SWOT Analysis	
Description	A strategic planning tool to brainstorm and examine 4 major variables of an enterprise. It is often used to help manage change in an organization, and to uncover missed opportunities and threats.
Characteristics	SWOT analysis can be used and scaled in several ways. It can be framed for an entire organization, or down to a division, department, etc. Using a grid as shown in *Figure 2-40* below, place the problem statement on top and complete the quadrants using the following guidelines: **S: Strengths.** Strengths of the organization regarding the business need at hand. These are internal to the organization. **W: Weaknesses.** Weaknesses of the organization regarding the business need. These are internal. **O: Opportunities.** List the opportunities available to solve the problem or seize the opportunity. These are external to the organization. **T: Threats.** List threats to the organization or competitor opportunities created by the problem, which would harm the organization. These are external.

Figure 2-39: SWOT Analysis Overview

                      PMI-PBA Certification Study Guide

PROBLEM		SWOT Analysis
Mortgage applications are taking too long to process		A strategic planning tool that can be applied to problem solving.

STRENGTHS	WEAKNESSES
• Experienced mortgage sales people • Organization is responsive and nimble	• Mostly manual processes or using Office apps or PDFs • IT infrastructure is not strong for processing mortgages (mostly financial applications)
OPPORTUNITIES	THREATS
• Client base is web-savvy • COTS packages available for loan applications and processing	• Competition already processing loans online

SWOT Analysis

A strategic planning tool that can be applied to problem solving.

S Strengths
W Weaknesses
O Opportunities
T Threats

Figure 2-40: SWOT Diagram Example

Value Stream Map   Priority: High

A Value Stream Map is a lean management method for analyzing the current state and designing a future state for the series of events that take a product or service from its beginning through to the customer. This is analyzed to identify opportunities for improvement and then used to develop a "future-state" map.

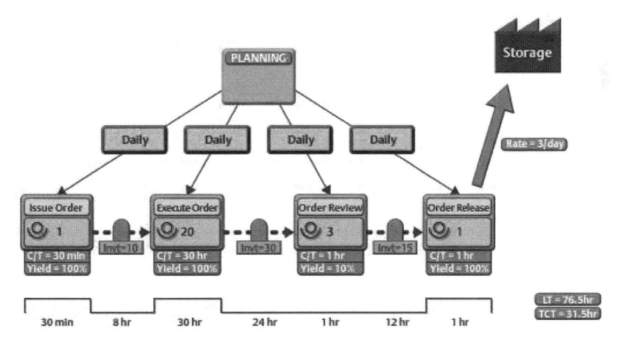

Figure 2-41: Value Stream Map Example

Needs Assessment – Exercise 4

Write the mnemonic and name for each of the **PROBLEM SOLVING AND OPPORTUNITY IDENTIFICATION** tools and techniques in the spaces below.

Mnemonic	Tools and Techniques

Write the mnemonic and name for each of the **ROOT CAUSE ANALYSIS** tools and techniques in the spaces below.

Mnemonic	Tools and Techniques

Write the mnemonic and name for each of the **SCOPE MODELS** tools and techniques in the spaces below.

Mnemonic	Tools and Techniques

Write the mnemonic and name for each of the **STAKEHOLDER ANALYSIS** tools and techniques in the spaces below.

Mnemonic	Tools and Techniques

Write the mnemonic and name for each of the **VALUATION** tools and techniques in the spaces below.

Mnemonic	Tools and Techniques

              PMI-PBA Certification Study Guide

PMI-PBA Practice Exam

Here are sample questions on Needs Assessment to help you practice taking PMI-PBA exam questions. Answers are listed at the end of the chapter.

1. Determining business value is not needed for the following type of project:
   a. Non-profit organization.
   b. Large retail chain point of sale upgrade.
   c. Government project.
   d. It is always needed.

2. Ideally, when is a business analyst assigned to a project?
   a. During project initiation.
   b. Prior to project initiation.
   c. During project planning.
   d. As soon as the charter is signed.

3. In dealing with the customer, the business analyst should:
   a. Be honest to the extent that the project organization is protected from litigation.
   b. Strive to develop a friendly, honest and open relationship.
   c. Try to maximize profits by encouraging scope creep.
   d. Do whatever it takes to satisfy the customer.

4. Which of the following statements is the best example of a business problem statement?
   a. We need to speed up the query search time in the problem database.
   b. To increase productivity in the Help Desk, we need to speed up the query search time in the Problem database.
   c. Speeding up the problem database search time will save the company approximately $300,000 per year and prevent increases in staff.
   d. Help Desk staff wait an average of 30 seconds per query, resulting in an average of 10% longer calls than the industry average.

5. As the BA you are called upon to participate in a Feasibility Study prior to launching a project initiative. Which of the following statements is the MOST true:

    a. The BA is expected to possess all of the skills required to plan and execute the study.

    b. The BA will facilitate this study, but does not have decision-making authority.

    c. The BA must enlist a team of experts with skills including: research and information analysis skills, technical writing skills, leadership and organization skills, change management skills.

    d. The Executive Team is responsible for the Feasibility Study in the pre-project phase, while the BA is responsible for feasibility after the elicitation has begun.

6. Which type of requirements best states the needs of a particular stakeholder or class of stakeholders, and how that stakeholder will interact with a solution?

    a. Business Requirements.

    b. Stakeholder Requirements.

    c. Functional Requirements.

    d. User Requirements.

7. You are in a meeting with key executives from around the company discussing long term, ongoing conditions the organization is striving to achieve. What is being discussed at this meeting?

    a. Strategic plan.

    b. Business synergy.

    c. Business values.

    d. Business measurements.

8. Joseph is working on a small project and it seems that the requirements and subsequent solution could be obvious. However, Joseph really wants to challenge his stakeholders to ensure that the current business thinking and processes are in line with the requirements and subsequent solution. What is Joseph trying to do?

    a. Decision analysis.

    b. Problem analysis.

    c. Solution scope analysis.

    d. Root cause analysis.

9. The quantifiable criteria established early in the project and upon which the project is measured are the project:

    a. Benefits.

    b. Objectives.

    c. Justification.

    d. Goals.

 PMI-PBA Certification Study Guide

10. The CFO has asked you to lead the requirements effort for a new project to implement SAP to support the organization's accounting functions. What question should you ask the sponsor first?

    a.   Who is the project manager?

    b.   When does the project need to be done?

    c.   What is the statement of work?

    d.   What business problem are you trying to solve?

Exercise Answers

Exercise 1

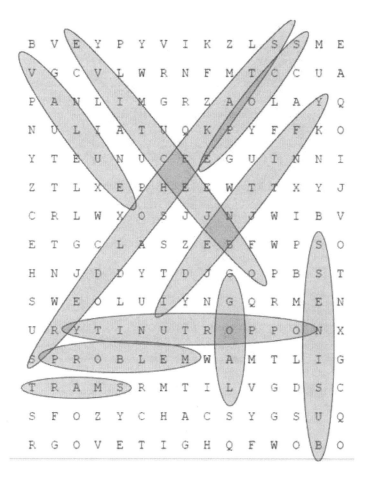

                          PMI-PBA Certification Study Guide

Exercise 2

Needs Assessment

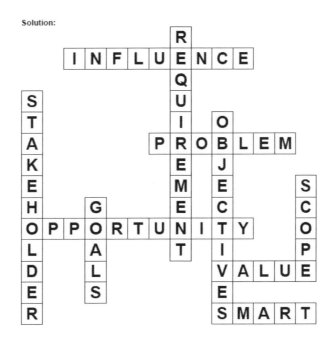

Exercise 3

Needs Assessment Tasks	Mnemonic
1. Define __Business__ __Need__	B
2. Determine __Value__ __Proposition__	V
3. Develop __Project__ __Goals__	G
4. Identify __Stakeholders__	S
5. Elicit __Stakeholder__ __Values__	V

Exercise 4

Problem Solving and Opportunity Identification Tools and Techniques
Benchmarking
Gap **Analysis**
Scenario Analysis
User Journey Maps
Value Engineering
Mnemonic: **B**illy **G**oats ride in **S U Vs**

Root Cause Analysis Tools and Techniques
Cause and Effect Diagram (Fishbone or Ishikawa diagram)
Five Whys
Interrelationship Diagrams
Process Model
Mnemonic: **C**ook **F**ancy **I**talian food **P**lease

Scope Models Tool and Techniques
Context Diagram
Ecosystem Map
Feature Model
Goal Model and Business Objective Model
Use Case Diagram
Mnemonic: **C**rystals **E**voke **F**unky **G**host **U**nicorns

Stakeholder Analysis Tools and Techniques
Job Analysis
Organizational Chart
Personas
Role Definition (RACI)
Skills Assessment
Mnemonic: **J**ane **O**rganizes **P**ersonal **R**ings **S**lowly

Valuation Tools and Techniques
Cost-Benefit Analysis
Feasibility Analysis
Force Field Analysis
Kano Model
Net Promoter Score
Purpose Alignment Model
SWOT Analysis
Value Stream Map
Mnemonic: **C**ool **F**riends **F**ind **K**ind **N**eanderthals **P**laying on **S**illy **V**ines

                 PMI-PBA Certification Study Guide

PMI-PBA Practice Exam Answers

1.   Determining business value is not needed for the following type of project:

   a. Non-profit organization.   Non-profits need to ensure value from projects to ensure they are getting the most of the donated dollar.

   b. Large retail chain point-of-sale upgrade.   A point of sale system should result in increased profits through efficiencies in the sales process.

   c. Government project.   Governments have a responsibility to ensure the tax payers' money is being spent on value added projects.

   d. It is always needed.   **Correct!** *PMBOK® Guide* **1.6 Business Value.**

2.   Ideally, when is a business analyst assigned to a project?

   a. During project initiation.   Actually, they should be assigned prior to initiation since they are involved in writing the business case.

   b. Prior to project initiation.   **Correct! The business analyst is involved in writing the business case for the project. Although this is included as an input to the project charter, it is written earlier and includes business justification to begin the project.**

   c. During project planning.   This is too late. They should be involved prior to initiation in order to be involved in writing the business case.

   d. As soon as the charter is signed.   The business case is an input into the charter and the BA helps write the business case, so this would be too late.

3.   In dealing with the customer, the business analyst should:

   a. Be honest to the extent that the project organization is protected from litigation.   This is a cynical answer that is not consistent with the PMI® Code of Ethics and Professional Conduct.

   b. Strive to develop a friendly, honest and open relationship.   **Correct! That also applies to all stakeholders, not just the customer.**

   c. Try to maximize profits by encouraging scope creep.   This is a cynical answer that is not consistent with the PMI® Code of Ethics and Professional Conduct.

   d. Do whatever it takes to satisfy the customer.   Satisfied customers are important, but not at expense of sound, ethical project management practices, so there are boundaries as to what is appropriate in satisfying stakeholders.

4. Which of the following statements is the best example of a business problem statement?

   a. We need to speed up the query search time in the problem database.

      No, this is solving a non-functional issue.

   b. To increase productivity in the Help Desk, we need to speed up the query search time in the Problem database.

      Contains some detail, but still not a problem statement.

   c. Speeding up the problem database search time will save the company approximately $300,000 per year and prevent increases in staff.

      A benefit statement to support why the objective should be met. It also describes a solution.

   d. **Help Desk staff wait an average of 30 seconds per query, resulting in an average of 10% longer calls than the industry average.**

      Correct! This problem statement gets into the business 'pain' (what is happening and the measurable impact) and states a problem needing a solution (and not a solution).

5. As the BA you are called upon to participate in a Feasibility Study prior to launching a project initiative. Which of the following statements is the MOST true:

   a. The BA is expected to possess all of the skills required to plan and execute the study.

      Wide range of techniques involved, so the BA is not expected to be skilled in everything.

   b. **The BA will facilitate this study, but does not have decision-making authority.**

      Correct! The role of the business analyst is to recommend solutions.

   c. The BA must enlist a team of experts including: research and information analysis skills, technical writing skills, leadership and organization skills, change management skills.

      The BA works with a variety of resources to ensure the right people are involved. The BA is not solely responsible for this task. Nor is it inevitable that all these skills will be needed on any given feasibility study. Finally the BA does not do the enlisting.

   d. The Executive Team is responsible for the Feasibility Study in the pre-project phase, while the BA is responsible for feasibility after elicitation has begun.

      The BA can perform a vital role by coordinating various resources and experts as a part of Needs Assessment, even before a project has been proposed.

6.   Which type of requirements best states the needs of a particular stakeholder or class of stakeholders, and how that stakeholder will interact with a solution.

   a.   Business Requirements.

These are high-level requirements concerned with goals, objectives, or needs, and are independent of a group of stakeholders.

   b.   **Stakeholder Requirements.**

Correct! *PMBOK® Guide* 5.2 Collect Requirements.

   c.   Functional Requirements.

These requirements are more detailed than user requirements and they describe the behavior of the solution or system. These are a type of solution requirement.

   d.   User Requirements.

No such category.

7.   You are in a meeting with key executives from around the company discussing long term, ongoing conditions the organization is striving to achieve. What is being discussed at this meeting?

   a.   **Strategic plan.**

Correct! *PMBOK® Guide* 4.1.

   b.   Business synergy.

Synergy is groups working together.

   c.   Business values.

Ongoing conditions or goals are more specific than business value statements.

   d.   Business measurements.

Measurements are not goals.

8. Joseph is working on a small project and it seems that the requirements and subsequent solution could be obvious. However, Joseph really wants to challenge his stakeholders to ensure that the current business thinking and processes are in line with the requirements and subsequent solution. What is Joseph trying to do?

    a. Decision analysis.

    > Supports decision-making when dealing with complex, difficult, or uncertain situations, not for small projects with an obvious solution.

    b. Problem analysis.

    > Problem analysis doesn't get to the reason of the current state to support the business need.

    c. Solution scope analysis.

    > Solution scope analysis is not a technique to understanding the business need.

    d. Root cause analysis.

    > **Correct! Joseph is trying to get to the true cause of the current state to better understand the business need.**

9. The quantifiable criteria established early in the project and upon which the project is measured are the project:

    a. Benefits.

    > These are the quantified expected outputs or results of the project.

    b. Objectives.

    > **Correct! Objectives are specific, measurable, tangible, precise, and can be validated, which is what makes it possible to measure against them.**

    c. Justification.

    > This is the purpose of the project or reason for investing organizational resources. Projects are not measured against the justification.

    d. Goals.

    > Goals are general, intangible, and can't be validated and, therefore, the project cannot be measured against them.

10. The CFO has asked you to lead the requirements effort for a new project to implement SAP to support the organization's accounting functions. What question should you ask the sponsor first?

    a. Who is the project manager?

    > Incorrect.

    b. When does the project need to be done?

    > Incorrect.

    c. What is the statement of work?

    > Incorrect.

    d. What business problem are you trying to solve?

    > **Correct! You cannot begin to understand the requirements and purpose of the project without first understanding the business need.**

Summary

The Needs Assessment domain includes the tasks necessary to fully understand a project. This includes defining the business problem or opportunity the project is intended to support, including the project's relationship to organization goals and objectives in order to support project goals and objectives. This domain includes understanding the value the project will bring to the organization. Part of this understanding comes from understanding the project stakeholders. Stakeholder identification and analysis is critical to ensuring the project has the right inputs and information for developing recommendations and getting project scope and requirement approvals.

Here are the themes covered that you should internalize:

- Understand Stakeholders

- Determine Value Proposition

- Articulate Goals and Objectives

There are five tasks in Needs Assessment. To help you remember the tasks, use a mnemonic of "Bold Vendor Get Its Value."

 Needs Assessment Goal: Understand a business problem or opportunity and evaluate various inputs to help develop an effective solution.

Notes

        PMI-PBA Certification Study Guide

3. Planning

Overview

The Planning domain includes the tasks, tools, and techniques in order to effectively plan for the deliverables and activities needed to deliver quality requirements. In addition to planning the business analysis activities, the business analyst will plan for the tools and processes to be used in order to collect, manage, communicate, and change requirements and other artifacts throughout the requirements life cycle.

 Planning Domain Goal: Prepare to effectively manage business analysis activities and requirements life cycle management.

When you are finished with this chapter, you will know:

- How to define Planning.

- The six tasks contained in Planning .

- The major areas of emphasis in Planning, including planning processes that will be used throughout the requirements activities, and estimating, communication, the Requirements Traceability Matrix, and solution acceptance criteria.

> **Planning**
>
> The tasks and outputs for planning and organizing requirements activities and for monitoring business analysis work to ensure it produces desired outcomes.

Domain Themes

The PMI-PBA exam includes several reoccurring themes. One useful way to use these themes is when you narrow down an exam question to two close answers. If one of the themes suggests one over the other, then go with the theme. The common themes to watch for in Planning are as follows:

Theme	Comments
Understand Stakeholders	Defining good requirements requires you to understand your stakeholders and adjust to their needs. For instance, the choice of tools or techniques may need to be modified based on the stakeholders involved.
Control Change	Managing changes is a significant theme throughout the exam. Business analysis planning will thoroughly consider how changes will be analyzed and accommodated, including the mechanics of business analysis documentation.
Requirements Traceability	Planning for business analysis includes determining the requirements traceability plan. What will be traced? What tool will be used? Who will have access? All aspects of traceability need to be addressed in planning and then used throughout the requirements life cycle.

Figure 3-1: Themes applicable to Planning

The questions for Planning represent 22 percent of all the exam questions. See *Figure 3-2* below.

Domain	Percentage of Items on Test	Approximate number of questions
Domain 1: Needs Assessment	18%	36
Domain 2: Planning	22%	44
Domain 3: Analysis	35%	70
Domain 4: Traceability and Monitoring	15%	30
Domain 5: Evaluation	10%	20

Figure 3-2: Planning Domain
Source: PMI

PMI-PBA Certification Study Guide

Planning: High-Level View

The six tasks in Planning are listed below. The tasks in the domain may not be performed sequentially, but it is helpful to learn the tasks and their order as a way to remember what each of them does. PMI® does not provide task titles for each task, but rather a detailed description. See the table below for the tasks as defined by PMI® with a task title developed for this guide in order to aid learning and remember the tasks.

Task 1
Determine Project Context

Review the Business Case, and the project goals and objectives, in order to provide context for business analysis activities.

Task 2
Plan Requirements Traceability

Define strategy for requirements traceability using traceability tools and techniques in order to establish the level of traceability necessary to monitor and validate the requirements.

Task 3
Plan Requirements Management

Develop a Requirements Management Plan by identifying stakeholders, roles and responsibilities, communication protocols, and methods for eliciting, analyzing, documenting, managing, and approving requirements in order to establish a roadmap for delivering the expected solution.

Task 4
Plan Requirements Change Control

Select methods for requirements change control by identifying channels for communicating requests and processes for managing changes in order to establish standard protocols for incorporation into the change management plan.

Task 5
Plan Document Control

Select methods for document control by using documentation management tools and techniques in order to establish a standard for requirements traceability and versioning.

Task 6
Define Project Expected Outcomes

Define business metrics and acceptance criteria by collaborating with stakeholders for use in evaluating when the solution meets the requirements.

Mnemonic Tip

PTMCDE: "Part Time Mechanics Can't Do Everything"

P Determine **P**roject Context
T Plan Requirements **T**raceability
M Plan Requirements **M**anagement
C Plan Requirements **C**hange
D Plan **D**ocument Control
E Define Project **E**xpected Outcomes

This chapter presents each of the tasks along with more information on the task descriptions and tools and techniques used to perform each task.

Task Inputs and Outputs

Some of the main areas addressed include planning for stakeholder needs, business analysis work, business analysis communication, and requirements management. A related task is the identification of solution acceptance criteria. The table below is a high-level view of the main inputs and outputs of this domain and the six tasks involved.

Input	Task	Tools and Techniques	Output
Business Case Project Goals and Objectives	1. Review the Business Case, and the project goals and objectives, in order to provide context for business analysis activities.	*<None>*	Business Case (Reviewed)
Business Case (Reviewed)	2. Define strategy for requirements traceability tools and techniques in order to establish the level of traceability necessary to monitor and validate the requirements.	Traceability *(covered in Traceability and Monitoring domain)*	Requirements Traceability Plan
Stakeholder Register Requirements Traceability Plan	3. Develop Requirements Management Plan by identifying stakeholders, roles and responsibilities, communication protocols, and methods for eliciting, analyzing, documenting, managing, and approving requirements in order to establish a roadmap for delivering the expected solution.	Estimation Contingency Planning Scheduling	Requirements Management Plan

Input	Task	Tools and Techniques	Output
Stakeholder Register Requirements Traceability Plan Requirements Management Plan	4. Select methods for requirements change control by identifying channels for communicating requests and processes for managing changes in order to establish standard protocols for incorporation into the change management plan.	Change Control Version Control	Change Management Plan
Requirements Management Plan Change Management Plan	5. Select methods for document control by using documentation management tools and techniques in order to establish a standard for requirements traceability and versioning.	Document Management Version Control	Document Control Plan
Stakeholder Register Business Case (Reviewed)	6. Define business metrics and acceptance criteria by collaborating with stakeholders for use in evaluating when the solution meets the requirements.	Measurement *(covered in Evaluation domain)*	Acceptance Criteria Key Performance Indicators

Figure 3-3: Planning ITTOs

Part 1 – Planning Tasks

Task 1 – Determine Project Context

Review the Business Case, and the project goals and objectives, in order to provide context for business analysis activities.

PTMCDE

You must review the available background information in order to effectively plan for the solution development activities. This task is simply a way to bridge Needs Assessment and Planning as a business analyst is often not brought into a project until the project is initiated and planning has begun. This task will be critical if the business analyst does not have first-hand knowledge of the project background as outlined in the Needs Assessment domain.

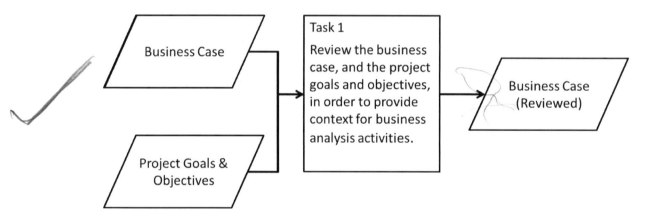

Figure 3-4: Determine Project Context ITO

Considerations for Determining Project Context

Understanding the project context is just as important as understanding the business context (business goals and objectives, project goals and objectives, problem or opportunity statement, and solution scope). Project context provides business analysts with an understanding of the project boundaries (scope) within which the requirements must align.

Business Case

The *PMBOK® Guide* defines the Business Case as "a documented economic feasibility study used to establish validity of the benefits of a selected component lacking sufficient definition and that is used as a basis for the authorization of further project management activities." Included in the Business Case are:

- Business Need
- Cost-Benefit Analysis
- Solution Scope
- Risk Assessment

Considerations for How the Project Life Cycle Influences Planning Decisions

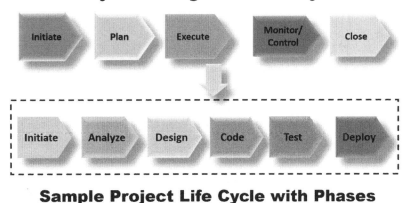

Figure 3-5: Project Management Life Cycle vs. Project Life Cycle

It is critical that the business analyst understand the particular life cycle approach that will be used on the project. The approach selected will determine the tasks that need to be done and the sequence of those tasks.

Project Management Life Cycle

We apply project management discipline, from initiating to closing, to each project phase.

Project Life Cycle

A project life cycle is a collection of phases/events that are needed to complete the project. It focuses on the process of managing the project. A generic project life cycle is shown above.

The project approach often determines the business analyst's approach. Each approach can have different processes, activities, and deliverables which will impact the business analysis work and requirements management efforts. For example, a business analyst will apply most of their work effort at the beginning of the project when using a **predictive** (plan-driven, waterfall approach), while an **adaptive** (change-driven, agile approach) spreads out the business analysis work throughout the project. The project approach can also require the use of different requirements templates, deliverables, artifacts, and elicitation and modeling techniques. It may also affect the level of requirements communication, documentation, and management processes.

.

Project Lifecycle Approaches

Predictive (Waterfall)	Adaptive (Agile)
• Usually sequential phases (requirements and then design) • Documentation and approval tend to be more formal • Can be done incrementally • Often used on global projects or with geographically dispersed teams • Often used on complex projects with complex interfaces	• Focuses on collaboration • Can be SCRUM with daily standup meetings • Prioritize features • Can document with user stories • Best with co-located teams • Iterative (evolve and improve) • Does not mean no documentation!
⬅ Incremental / Iterative ➡	
• Increments are like small releases • Both waterfall and agile can be incremental • Add features with each increment	• Time-boxed • Multiple phases • Incremental development may or may not be iterative (including rework)

Figure 3-6: Project Lifecycle Approach Overview

Predictive

A **predictive life cycle** is more formal than an adaptive life cycle. The activities are usually more detailed and planned. A predictive approach implies that each project phase is completed, documented, and approved before the next project phase is started. With a

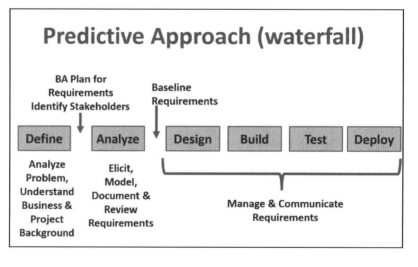

Figure 3-7: Predictive Life Cycle

predictive approach, most of the business analysis work occurs during the "analysis" project phase at the beginning of the project.

When using a formal predictive approach, all requirements are usually gathered before design begins. Most of the requirements effort (elicitation, modeling, and documentation) is spent at the beginning of the project, with traceability and change management happening throughout the rest of the project.

Key Features
- Emphasis is on minimizing uncertainty.
- The business analyst endeavors to capture all the requirements at the beginning of the project.
- Additional requirements found later in the life cycle are managed through change control processes.
- The approach is one-directional and phased (as each phase is completed, the requirements work is then handed off).
- Most of the business analysis effort occurs at the beginning of the project.

Adaptive

With the **adaptive life cycle**, three levels of planning are done with only detailed tasks and estimates for the current iteration. A backlog of requirements (user stories) are captured which will be analyzed and developed iteratively. Prior to each iteration, a business analyst helps the product owner "groom" the product backlog to ensure each user story is thoroughly understood. Therefore, business analysis occurs iteratively throughout the project. Requirement changes are documented and added as new user stories to the product backlog.

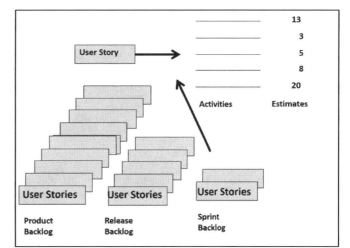

Figure 3-8: Adaptive Life Cycle

Key Features
- Business value is emphasized, minimizing uncertainty
- Evolutionary, adds new features in each iteration
- Builds deployable software features
- Delivered in short time frames (weeks vs. months)
- Works well with smaller projects
- Uses both incremental and iterative methodologies

Incremental Approach

An **incremental approach** divides the product deliverable into smaller components or increments. Each increment produces a small deliverable component of the entire solution. Thus, after a very short period of time, you have a working deliverable, even though the final product is not complete.

Mini reviews are set after each increment has been completed. Dividing a project into incremental components must take into consideration the strategy of designing, constructing, testing, and deploying the deliverable. Increments can be divided by functionality or be time-boxed, delivering the functionality that will fit into that time box.

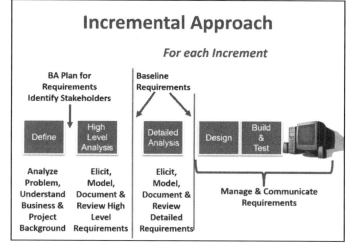

Figure 3-9: Incremental Approach

Iterative Approach

An **iterative approach** develops limited results in short timeframes. Only a fraction of the project is developed in an iteration. Rather than the stepped approach of waterfall, iterative development occurs in a circular manner. In iterative development, the overall life cycle is composed of several iterations in sequence. Each iteration is a self-contained mini-project composed of activities such as requirements analysis, design, development, and test.

Iterative Approach

Figure 3-10: Iterative Approach

Iterative development is often confused with incremental development. Iterative development is about planned rework. You create something, review it, and then improve upon it based on the feedback. Each iteration should be better than the one you had before, even if you don't add features. Incremental development only develops new functionality in an iteration.

[handwritten margin note: Each next iteration than better not. necessarily add new features.]

Techniques – *Determine Project Context*	
<None>	

Outputs

Output: *Business Case (Reviewed)*
The business analyst should now have a full background and understanding of the project and the expected outcomes. This will serve as a basis for all future business analysis work on the project.

PMBOK® Guide References

More information on Determining Project Context can be found can be found in the *PMBOK® Guide:*

- 4.1.1.2 – Business Case

- 4.1.3.1 – Project Charter

More information on Project Life Cycles can be found in the *PMBOK® Guide*:

- 2.4.2.2 - Predictive Life Cycles

- 2.4.2.3 - Iterative and Incremental Life Cycles

- 2.4.2.4 - Adaptive Life Cycles

Task 2 – Plan Requirements Traceability

Define strategy for requirements traceability using traceability tools and techniques in order to establish the level of traceability necessary to monitor and validate the requirements.

P**T**MCDE

The Requirements Traceability Matrix is one of the important deliverables of business analysis. Thorough planning for the Traceability Matrix early will make requirements elicitation, analysis, management, and communication much easier throughout the requirements life cycle. Planning ahead allows for input from stakeholders, especially the project team, and begins to set expectations.

The Requirements Traceability Matrix (RTM) may be captured in a word table, spreadsheet, database, or management tracking tool which allows the business analyst to sort by any of the organizational components. Regardless of the form, the RTM serves the same purpose – to trace requirements back to the project and organization's objectives, and forward to the project team deliverables that support the requirements. The RTM further provides value in allowing for the recording of additional requirements information (or attributes) to further aid in the management and communication of requirements.

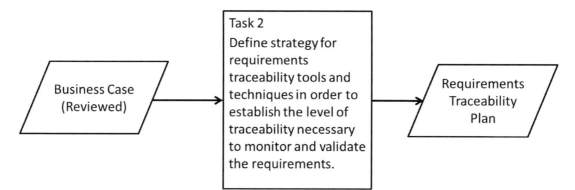

Figure 3-11: Plan Requirements Traceability ITO

Considerations for Plan Requirements Traceability

Planning for the Requirements Traceability Matrix

Elements of the matrix that must be defined in planning include:
- What tool will be used?
- Where will it be stored?
- Who has access to it?
- What requirements attributes do we need to capture?
- Is any training needed for project staff so they can find and use the RTM?
- How will problems with requirements be tracked and resolved?

Traceability Components	Attributes	Management Components
■ Related requirements (dependencies) ■ External interfaces ■ Business rules ■ Business objective ■ Design reference ■ Test reference	■ Absolute Reference/ ID ■ Author ■ Complexity ■ Ownership ■ Priority ■ Risks ■ Source ■ Stability ■ Status ■ Urgency	■ Requirement type ■ Logical sequence ■ Version/release ■ Approval ■ Date completed ■ Comments ■ Process ■ Functions ■ Use Cases

Figure 3-12: Considerations for Traceability

Traceability Components: Includes any related requirements, external interfaces, business rules, the business objective the requirements satisfies, where it can be found in the design document, and the related test reference numbers.

Mnemonic Tip
C.A.R.A.'S S.O.U.P.S.
Complexity **A**bsolute reference **R**isks **A**uthor **S**ource **S**tatus **O**wnership **U**rgency **P**riority **S**tability

Attributes: Each requirement should be uniquely identified and will have supporting "attributes" or information about itself. Attributes often comprise the columns on an RTM and may include:

- **Complexity** - how hard the requirement will be to implement.

- **Absolute reference** - unique identifier, not to be altered or re-used if the requirement is moved, changed or deleted.

- **Risks** associated with meeting or not meeting the requirement.

- **Author** of the requirement. If the requirement is later found to be ambiguous, the author may be consulted for clarification.

- **Source** of the requirement. Every requirement needs a source with authority to specify and approve requirements. Consult the source if the requirement changes, or if more information regarding the requirement has to be gathered.

- **Status** of the requirement currently; typically indicating whether it is proposed, accepted, verified with the users, or implemented.

- **Ownership** - individual or group needing the requirement or will be the business owner after the project is released.

- **Urgency** – when a given requirement is needed; i.e., how urgent it is. Only necessary to specify separately from Priority when an implementation deadline exists.

- **Priority** - which requirements need to be implemented first.

- **Stability** - how mature the requirement is. Used to determine whether the requirement is firm enough to start work on.

Unique ID	Abbreviated Requirements Statement	Dependency	Business Rules	Priority	Source	Status	Objective Refs.	Design Refs.	Test Case Refs.

Figure 3-13: Requirements Traceability Matrix

Management Components: Includes elements that can help the business analyst manage the requirement. For example, what version or release the requirement will be implemented in, who approved the requirement, the date it was implemented into the system, and a comments section (allows you to capture why the requirement was deleted or rejected, by whom, and when). The business analyst may also add additional categories that will help to manage and organize the requirements such as tracing requirements to processes, functions, or use cases, etc.

Project Approach

A formal, detailed Requirements Traceability Matrix is most applicable to predictive (waterfall) projects. Adaptive (agile) projects will rely on user stories and a product backlog to serve the same purpose with less formality and detail.

User stories represent stakeholder requirements. The product backlog is a prioritized list of user stories. User stories are taken from the product backlog and moved to a sprint backlog where they are assigned to the current iteration. Once assigned to a current iteration, the agile team will further decompose and determine the detail requirements needed to support the user story. The process and tools for tracking these detailed requirements will vary by team depending on the determination of what is needed to successfully develop, test, and implement the user story.

Techniques – *Plan Requirements Traceability*	
Traceability Tools and Techniques *(covered in Traceability and Monitoring domain)* Tools and techniques to identify and document the lineage of each requirement and to make connections within and between requirements and other project elements.	**Includes:** - Backlog Management - Issues (Problem) Tracking - Requirements Traceability Matrix

Output: *Requirements Traceability Plan*

The requirements traceability plan should address each of the questions listed above (page 106) as elements of the RTM. The plan should be communicated to the project team as appropriate so that they have the information needed to find and use the RTM. There may be some additional planning items identified as a result of the requirements traceability plan such as provisioning for requirements tools or training for business analysts and other project staff. The overall project management plan should reflect all of the tasks and needs of the requirements traceability plan.

PMBOK® Guide References

More information on Planning Requirements Traceability can be found in the *PMBOK® Guide*:

- 5.1.3.2 – Requirements Management Plan

- 5.2.3.2 – Requirements Traceability Matrix

Task 3 – Plan Requirements Management

Develop Requirements Management Plan by identifying stakeholders, roles and responsibilities, communication protocols, and methods for eliciting, analyzing, documenting, managing, and approving requirements in order to establish a roadmap for delivering the expected solution.

PT**M**CDE

This is the largest task of the Planning domain and is a broad-reaching planning task. It really is the center of all business analysis planning with the exception of traceability, change control, and document control that are called out as separate tasks. That leaves plenty of requirements work that is planned within this task.

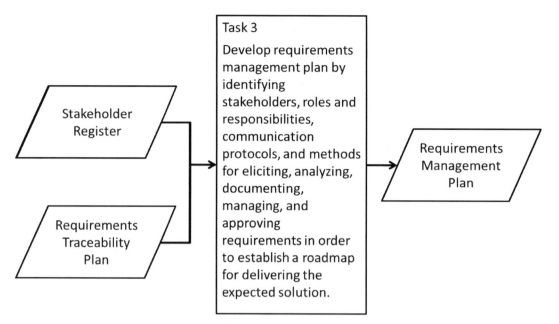

Figure 3-14: Plan Requirements Management ITO

Considerations for Plan Requirements Management

Leverage Past Experiences When Planning

- **Lessons Learned (Predictive):** This technique is done by project teams and key stakeholders to reflect on and capture project successes and areas that could be improved for the future. There is no standard way of conducting a lessons learned session, and the stakeholders' preferences often dictate how they are run. When celebrations are done in conjunction with a lessons learned session, it can encourage participation and emphasize the positive outcomes from a project or project phase/iteration.

- **Retrospectives (Adaptive):** Retrospectives are more than just a fancy way of saying "lessons learned." There are many differences. In particular, lessons learned sessions typically happen at the end of a project or major project phase. This means the review happens long after the project action. In contrast, a retrospective occurs at the end of each iteration. Agile iterations are typically one to four weeks. This means that the team is never more than four weeks away from the work of the iteration being reviewed. The retrospective identifies what is working well, what needs to be improved, and what should be discontinued in order for the team to be most effective. When this review happens at regular, short intervals, the team can do away with bad practices and increase productivity quickly.

Refine Stakeholders Analysis

A key to successful planning is addressing the needs of the stakeholders in the plans. What we know about our stakeholders should influence the development of the Requirements Management Plan. The stakeholders should also have an opportunity to review plans and provide feedback to plans that will impact their engagement with the project. Finally, stakeholders may have a direct role in the management of the requirements as outlined in Roles and Responsibilities using a RACI Matrix (see Stakeholder Analysis Tools and Techniques in the Needs Assessment chapter).

Business Analysis Activities
What will the BA create and deliver to support the project?

A large part of the Requirements Management Plan that is hidden in the intent of this task is the identifying and detailed planning for the deliverables that the business analysts must deliver, and the activities required to do so. A Work Breakdown Structure (WBS) can aid in decomposing large deliverables into more manageable pieces that are easier to plan and estimate. For example, deliverables may include planning meetings or reports necessary to create the deliverables. The related activities may include coordinating and facilitating the meetings, or writing the reports.

> **WBS**
>
> **Work Breakdown Structure**. A project planning technique that hierarchically breaks down deliverables of a project into manageable pieces.

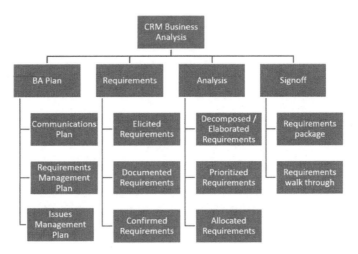

Figure 3-15: Work Breakdown Structure for BA Activities

Business Analysis Activities Schedule

The results of this business analysis planning will feed the overall project management plan including project schedule and budget.

ID		Task Name	Duration	Start	'11 S	W	May 15, '11 S T M	F	May 29, '11 T S W	Jun 12, '11 S T M	F	Jun 26, T
2		**BA Plan**	15.25 days	Wed 5/11/11								
3		**Communications**	10.5 days	Wed 5/11/11								
4	✓	Stakeholders	1 day	Wed 5/11/11	Project Manager							
5	✓	Org Culture/Expectations	1 day	Wed 5/11/11	Business Analyst,Project Manager							
6		**Communications Plan**	5.5 days	Wed 5/18/11								
7	▦ ▯	Develop Communications Plan	2 days	Wed 5/18/11			Business Analyst					
8	▯	Team Review / Approval	3 days	Fri 5/20/11			Project Manager,Business Analyst					
9		Update Communication Plan	0.5 days	Wed 5/25/11			Business Analyst					
10		**Requirements Management**	15.25 days	Wed 5/11/11								
11	✓	Proof of Concept	0.5 days	Wed 5/11/11	Business Analyst							
12	✓	Team Approval	1.14 days	Tue 5/17/11		Project Manager						
13	✓	Requirements Management Plan	0.25 days?	Wed 5/18/11		Business Analyst						
14	✓	Develop Requirements Plan	0.5 days?	Wed 5/18/11		Business Analyst						
15	▦ ▯	Team Review / Approval	1 day	Wed 6/1/11						Project Manager		
16		Update Requirements Plan	0.25 days?	Thu 6/2/11						Business Analyst		
17		**Issues/Risk Management**	9.49 days?	Wed 5/18/11								

Figure 3-16: Business Analysis Activities Schedule

A project management rule of estimating is that the person completing the work needs to estimate the work. This is true for business analysis just as it is true for development and quality assurance. A great plan of business analysis work serves to make the case to provide the time and resources needed for project success. "You have three weeks to get requirements" is not a plan.

Risk Planning

Risks to the product scope or requirements fall under the responsibility of the business analyst. Plans to identify, monitor, and manage requirements risks should be included in the Requirements Management Plan. As with other plans, this may be a subset of the project risk management plan rather than an independent plan. This includes contingency planning.

Contingency Planning is the outcome of analyzing the risks to a product and the planned response if the risk becomes a reality. Contingency planning may also result in schedule and budget reserves by determining the likelihood and impact of a risk occurring. The likelihood (%) is multiplied by the impact ($) to determine an appropriate reserve amount.

Cost of Risk ($) * Likelihood (%) = $ Contingency Reserve

Prioritization

The methods for prioritizing requirements, including stakeholders involved, should also be considered in the Requirements Management Plan. (See Prioritization tools and techniques in Analysis chapter.)

Project Management Plan

The Requirements Management Plan feeds the project management plan. Elements of the requirements plan may be accounted for in project management artifacts. For example, there may be only one communication plan, however, the business analyst is responsible for leading the planning and activities related to communicating product scope and requirements. The Requirements Management Plan should clearly identify where business analysis planning is captured in project management plans in order to reduce duplication and confusion.

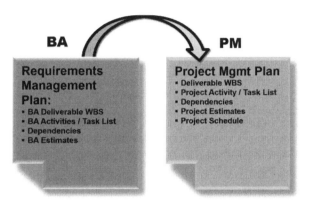

Figure 3-17: Project Management Plan

Project Approach

An adaptive (agile) project will require some requirements management planning. This may take on a different flavor using tools and techniques specific to agile such as user stories and the product backlog with stack-ranked stories to indicate priority. However, planning cannot be overlooked to identify, document, and communicate how things such as risks, communications, traceability, and stakeholder engagement will be managed throughout the project.

Techniques – *Plan Requirements Management*	
Estimation Tools and Techniques Tools and techniques used to estimate cost and effort to complete a task or project.	**Includes:** - Analogous - Averaging - Bottom Up - Estimation Poker - Parametric
Scheduling Tools and Techniques Tools and techniques used to develop and track schedules.	**Includes:** - Precedence Diagram Method
Contingency Planning Tools and Techniques Tools and techniques for identifying and planning contingencies of time and cost.	*<None>*

Outputs

Output: *Requirements Management Plan*

The Requirements Management Plan may be a single plan, include subsidiary plans, be encompassed in project management plans, or any combination of these. What is important is that all of the information needed to understand what business analysis deliverables and activities will be completed, the processes and tools to be used, and where to find needed information is clearly articulated and stakeholders have an opportunity to provide feedback. (This plan is called the Business Analysis Plan in PMI's Business Analysis for Practitioners: A Practice Guide.)

Figure 3-18: Components of the Requirements Management Plan

PMBOK® Guide References

More information on Planning Requirements Management can be found in the *PMBOK® Guide*:

- 5.1.3.2 – Requirements Management Plan
- 6.2 – Define Activities
- 6.3 – Sequence Activities
- 6.4 – Estimate Activity Resources
- 6.5 – Estimate Activity Durations

Planning – Exercise 1

Write the mnemonic letters for the six tasks of Planning, and then complete the missing words for each task in the blanks provided.

Planning Tasks		Mnemonic
1. Determine _____ _____		_____
2. Plan _____ _____		_____
3. Plan _____ _____		_____
4. Plan _____ _____ _____		_____
5. Plan _____ _____		_____
6. Define _____ _____ _____		_____

Task 4 – Plan Requirements Change Control

Select methods for requirements change control by identifying channels for communicating requests and processes for managing changes in order to establish standard protocols for incorporation into the change management plan.

PTM<u>C</u>DE

Change control is an essential element of project management and business analysis. Change control is what allows the project to adapt for needed changes to project baselines (including requirements baseline) in a systematic, thoughtful way. With good change control we avoid "scope creep" and project overruns. The project manager is responsible for ensuring changes to the project are controlled and managed. The business analyst is responsible for managing changes to the product scope and requirements. Requirements change control may be captured in the overall project change control plan or a separate, complementary plan. As with the Requirement Management Plan, the important piece is that the plan is developed and shared with stakeholders so they have an opportunity to provide feedback, approve, and understand the processes involved in requesting changes.

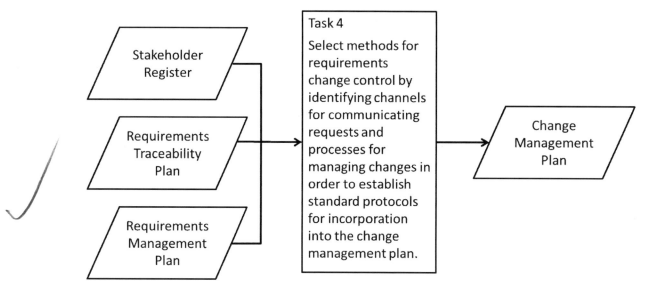

Figure 3-19: Requirements Change Control ITO

Considerations for Plan Requirements Change Control

Change Request

One element of planning for change control is to define and communicate the process and tools that stakeholders will use to request changes to the product scope or requirements. This should include the media and format for requesting changes, information on how changes will be analyzed for impact, how change requests are approved or denied, and how change request decisions will be communicated.

A Change Request Form may be developed for project use as part of this planning. The form should contain the following elements in order to collect the detailed information needed for thorough analysis, decision making, and tracking of the request status.

Information	Completed by
Identifying information	
• Project name	Requestor
• Requestor name	Requestor
• Date of request	Requestor
• Unique identifier	Business analyst
Request Information	
• Description of request	Requestor
• Justification	Requestor
• Impacts if not approved	Requestor
• Alternatives considered	Requestor
• Additional information	Requestor
Impact Analysis	
• Identified product / requirement impacts	Business analyst
• Impact on cost	Project manager

 PMI-PBA Certification Study Guide

Information	Completed by
• Impact on schedule	Project manager
• Value of change	Business analyst
• Recommendation	Project manager / business analyst
Approval	
• Final decision	Approver
• Approved by	Approver
• Date approved	Approver
• Comments / instructions	Approver
Tracking	
• Requirements baseline updated	Business analyst
• Project schedule and budget baselines updated	Project manager
• Change communicated	Business analyst

Figure 3-20: Change Request Form

Change Control Approvals

For a predictive approach, a Change Control Board (CCB) is a group that has been given the responsibility to review and approve all project change requests. In many organizations, the project sponsor will need to approve of the Change Control Board participants and may serve as the chair. The project governance may dictate that the project sponsor is the sole decision maker for change requests.

Other variations to this may occur depending on organizational culture and PMO processes. Documenting approval authorities is a critical piece of the Requirements Change Management planning.

In an adaptive approach, change is managed through the product backlog. The product backlog may be modified at any time with new stories, changes in priority, or changes to existing stories at any time prior to the user story being selected for the current iteration. The product owner is the keeper of the product backlog and has the authority to make these changes without escalating to the project sponsor or a CCB.

Baselining Requirements

According to the *PMBOK® Guide*, a baseline is "the approved version of a work product that can be changed only through formal change control procedures and is used as a basis for comparison."

For a predictive approach, projects requirements are usually baselined after the business analysis phase. New requirements and changes are usually run through a change control process in which new requirements may be requested, associated costs and benefits are determined, and the requirement is approved or rejected. If approved, the requirements are then re-baselined.

For an adaptive approach, new features cannot be added to the current iteration (called a sprint if using Scrum) since the number of days in the iteration or sprint is fixed. The product owner, with the help of the business analyst, turns the feature into a user story which is put into the overall product backlog.

Configuration Management System

The *Business Analysis for Practitioners: A Practice Guide* defines Configuration Management as "a collection of formal documented processes, templates, and documentation used to apply governance to changes to the product, service, results, or subcomponent being developed." A configuration management system is the formal tools, processes, and procedures that are used to manage these changes. The system may be largely manual with updates to documents that are recorded in a separate log, or may involve use of an automated configuration management system.

Many automated configuration management tools are available on the market (e.g., Visual SourceSafe, Rational Clear Case, and Source Anywhere). Configuration management tools that are developed specifically for managing requirements are called Requirements Management Tools (e.g., Blue Print Systems, CaseComplete, and Jama). These tools greatly streamline the work of the business analyst by allowing the easy collection, management, and communication of requirements in a centralized tool.

Techniques – *Plan Requirements Change Control*

Change Control Tools and Techniques *(covered in Traceability and Monitoring domain)* Tools and techniques that facilitate modifications to documents, deliverables, or baselines associated with the project are identified, documented, approved, or rejected. There are many automated tools on the market to facilitate change control, however, the system may also be a manual process or set of processes.	Includes: - Configuration Management System (CMS)
Version Control Tools and Techniques *(covered in Traceability and Monitoring domain)* Tools and techniques used to manage and control versions of a work product, including revisions. There are many automated tools on the market to facilitate this, however, the system may also be a manual process or set of processes.	Includes: - Version Control System (VCS)

Outputs

Output: *Requirements Change Management Plan*

The Requirements Change Management Plan may be included in the overall project Change Control Plan or stand alone as a separate planning document. What is important is that all of the information needed to understand how to request, approve, and track change requests is readily available to stakeholders and the project team. It should include information on how to submit a request, who has authority for approving change requests, and what tools are used to track requests and subsequent changes to requirements.

PMBOK® Guide References

More information on Planning Requirements Change Control can be found can be found in the *PMBOK® Guide*:

- 4.5 – Perform Integrated Change Control

- 5.1 – Plan Scope Management

- 5.6 – Control Scope

Business Analysis for Practitioners: A Practice Guide References

5.8.2.1 – Configuration Management System (CMS)

Needs Assessment Review – Exercise 2

Do you recall the tasks from Needs Assessment? Write the mnemonic letters for the five tasks of Needs Assessment, and then complete the missing words for each task in the blanks provided below.

Needs Assessment Tasks	Mnemonic
1. Define _____ _____	_____
2. Determine _____ _____	_____
3. Develop _____ _____	_____
4. Identify_____	_____
5. Determine _____ _____	_____

                   PMI-PBA Certification Study Guide

Task 5 – Plan Document Control

Select methods for document control by using documentation management tools and techniques in order to establish a standard for requirements traceability and versioning.

PTMC**D**E

Have you ever been to a meeting to review a document and found that not everyone in the room had the same version of the document? Most people find that to be very frustrating, not to mention a waste of time. This task ensures there is a solid plan in place to avoid this problem. Recipients and readers of our documents should have assurance that they are looking at the latest version and are able to understand the differences between versions. Tools may be as simple as a table in the document that contains information on each version, or as sophisticated as a document control system.

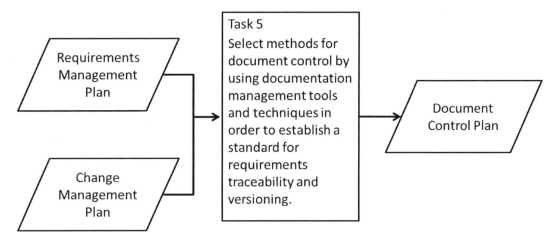

Figure 3-21: Plan Document Control ITO

Considerations for Plan Document Control

Version Control System

Version control tracks the history of revisions. It speaks specifically to document controls including processes for making updates, controlling access, and archiving previous versions. The system may be a manual system of logging changes to documents or may include using a version control tool (e.g., Visual SourceSafe, SharePoint, and Vault). Many software tools today have some versioning controls built into them. *Figure 3-22* is an example of Microsoft Office 2013 built-in version control.

Adaptive (Agile) Approach to Document Control

One of the Agile Manifesto values is "Working software over comprehensive documentation," which suggests documenting only what the team needs to be successful, and at the time when it is needed. Thus, document management and version control will likely be less formal on adaptive or agile projects.

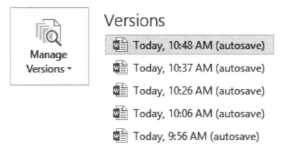

Versions

- Today, 10:48 AM (autosave)
- Today, 10:37 AM (autosave)
- Today, 10:26 AM (autosave)
- Today, 10:06 AM (autosave)
- Today, 9:56 AM (autosave)

Figure 3-22: Microsoft Office Backstage View (Version Control)

Techniques – *Plan Document Control*	
Document Management Tools and Techniques Tools and techniques that facilitate modifications to documents, deliverables, or baselines associated with the project are identified, documented, approved, or rejected. There are many automated tools on the market to facilitate change control, however, the system may also be a manual process or set of processes.	*<None>*
Version Control Tools and Techniques *(covered in Traceability and Monitoring domain)* Tools and techniques used to manage and control versions of a work product, including revisions. There are many automated tools on the market to facilitate this, however, the system may also be a manual process or set of processes.	**Includes:** - Version Control System (VCS)

Outputs

Output: *Document Control Plan*
The Document Control Plan may be included in the overall project Change Control Plan or stand alone as a separate planning document. What is important is that all of the information needed to understand how to find and update documents, including versioning and archival, is available and understood by team members. The plan should include the tools, location, and access permissions for document changes.

5.8.2.2 – Version Control System (VCS)

Task 6 – Define Project Expected Outcomes

Define business metrics and acceptance criteria by collaborating with stakeholders for use in evaluating when the solution meets the requirements.

PTMCD<u>E</u>

The final step of planning is to make sure we know how project success will be evaluated. This evaluation will take place in the final task of the Evaluation domain but planning for the measure of the success will enable the business analyst and project team to make decisions that will support the expected outcomes of the project. It is important to note that this final evaluation happens after a solution has been deployed and the users have had time to adapt and use the solution effectively.

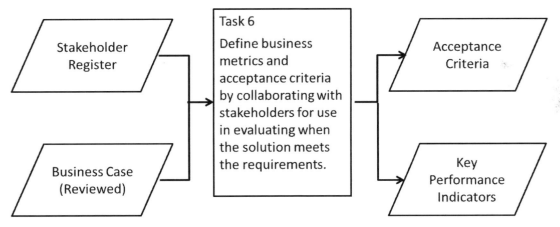

Figure 3-23: Define Project Expected Outcomes ITO

Considerations for Define Project Expected Outcomes

Define the Solution Evaluation Process

Solution evaluation planning involves defining:

- Evaluation criteria and acceptance levels

- Qualitative and quantitative evaluation activities to be performed

- When and how often evaluation will be performed

- Evaluation techniques

It is important to understand that this task is about selecting the metrics that will measure the effectiveness of the solution, not about measuring the project progress. This evaluation will happen long after the project has been closed and the project team has moved on to new projects. The focus should be on evaluating the benefits and effectiveness of the solution in achieving business value. Sample metrics for a process may include:

- Time to process

- Customers per hour

- Increased sales

- Increased profit

Techniques – *Define Project Expected Outcomes*	
Measurement Tools and Techniques *(covered in Analysis domain)* Tools and techniques used to measure solution performance after implementation.	**Includes:** - Metrics such as Key Performance Indicators (KPIs) - Service Level Agreement (SLA) - Planguage

Outputs

Output: *Acceptance Criteria / Key Performance Indicators*

Acceptance Criteria

A set of conditions that is required to be met before deliverables are accepted. Acceptance criteria are:

- ▶ Written from the perspective of the end-user or customer

- ▶ Not technical requirements (test cases are written from acceptance criteria)

- ▶ Written using S.M.A.R.T.

- ▶ Owned by the project sponsor (product owner in adaptive approach)

Key Performance Indicators

Measures and metrics that will be used to evaluate the effectiveness of the solution. Considerations for measures include: customer metrics, sales and marketing metrics, operational metrics and assessments, and functionality.

PMBOK® Guide References

The *PMBOK® Guide* touches on project expected outcomes in the following section.

- 4.1.3.1 – Project Charter

- 5.3.3.1 – Project Scope Statement

Planning – Exercise 3

Use the clues below to complete the crossword puzzle.

Planning

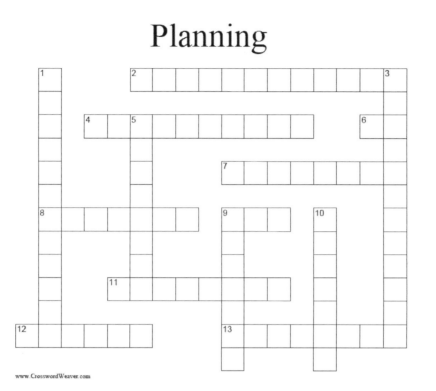

www.CrosswordWeaver.com

ACROSS

2   These must be identified before activities can be identified

4   Business analysis plans are often _____ to project management plans

6   Person responsible for estimating the business analysis work (abbr.)

7   Assess how well the solution met the project objectives

8   Features, requirements, or user stories that have not yet been implemented

9   Group that reviews and approves change requests (abbr.)

11   This is used to keep track of stakeholders and engagement plans

12   Set of processes, procedures, and tools working together as a whole

13   Expected results of solution implementation

DOWN

1   Being able to track product requirements from their origin to the deliverables and back.

3   Has opportunity to review and provide feedback to business analysis plans

5   The approved version

9   The most important thing to do with change

10   Group or person providing resources for the project and accountable for project success

---

                   PMI-PBA Certification Study Guide

Part 2 – Techniques for Planning

The tools and techniques below are those that may be most helpful in the Planning domain. Importantly, the tools and techniques are not domain or task specific; they may be used for more than one task and in more than one domain. It will be necessary for the person doing the business analysis work to determine which tools to use and when.

Category	Techniques
Change Control Tools and Techniques *(covered in Traceability and Monitoring domain)*	
	Configuration Management System
Contingency Planning Tools and Techniques *Tools and techniques for identifying and planning contingencies of time and cost.*	
	No specific tools
Document Management Tools and Techniques *Tools and techniques used to facilitate modifications to documents, deliverables, or baselines associated with the project.*	
	No specific tools
Estimation Tools and Techniques *Tools and techniques used to estimate cost and effort to complete a task or project.*	
	Analogous
	Averaging
	Bottom-up
	Estimation Poker
	Parametric
Measurement Tools and Techniques *(covered in Analysis domain)*	
	Metrics such as Key Performance Indicators (KPIs)
	Service Level Agreement (SLA)
	Planguage
Prioritization Tools and Techniques *(covered in Analysis domain)*	
	High, Medium, Low
	MoSCoW
	Voting
	Weighted Criteria
Scheduling Tools and Techniques *Tools and techniques used to develop and track schedules.*	
	Precedence Diagramming Method
Traceability Tools and Techniques *(covered in Traceability and Monitoring domain)*	
	Backlog Management
	Issue (Problem) Tracking
	Requirements Traceability Matrix
Validation Tools and Techniques *(covered in Evaluation domain)*	
	Day-in-the Life (DITL) Testing
	Exploratory Testing
	Given-Then-When
	Integration Testing

Category	Techniques
	User Acceptance Testing
Version Control Tools and Techniques *(covered in Traceability and Monitoring domain)*	
	Version Control System (VCS)

Figure 3-24: Techniques for Planning

The following pages provide additional details about the tools and techniques that may be most helpful in this domain. (Details for some techniques may be covered in a different domain as noted above.) Not all tools and techniques will be discussed at a great level of detail. The amount of information provided relates to the priority of the tool or technique on the exam. Each technique has been rated with a priority level of low, moderate, or high to help in prioritizing study. Items marked as low may appear in your certification exam; items marked moderate are likely to show up in one or two questions, and items marked high may have multiple questions relating to their use.

Contingency Planning Tools and Techniques

Contingency planning may include allocation of time and/or money in the plan to account for mitigating or accepting identified risks. Quantitative risk analysis tools and techniques may be used to define a contingency reserve amount to be applied as a percentage of estimated activity duration for individual activities, a fixed number of work periods, or at higher levels of aggregated work.

Contingency Planning Tools and Techniques
No specific tools

Document Management Tools and Techniques

Tools and techniques that facilitate modifications to documents, deliverables, or baselines associated with the project are identified, documented, approved, or rejected. There are many automated tools on the market to facilitate change control, however, the system may also be a manual process or set of processes.

Document Management Tools and Techniques
No specific tools

         PMI-PBA Certification Study Guide

Estimation Tools and Techniques

Tools and techniques used to estimate cost and effort to complete a task or project.

Estimation Tools and Techniques
Analogous
Averaging (Three-Point Estimation)
Bottom-up
Estimation Poker
Parametric

Estimating Mnemonic
"**A**lways **A**nswer **B**efore **E**liminating **P**ossibilities"

Analogous	Priority: High

Otherwise known as a "Rough Order of Magnitude" or "SWAG," this is the quickest to develop yet least accurate of the estimating techniques. The analogous estimate is generally used early in a project when little detail is known. Other estimating techniques are preferred as more information becomes available.

Analogous	
Description	Analogous estimating is a technique using similar past projects to forecast hours and/or costs. It is typically used in the early stages of a project when there may not be a great deal of information available. It leverages similar past projects to forecast a new one, usually at a high level, or what is called a ROM (Rough Order of Magnitude). Example: Management has requested an estimate for a Project Charter. The project is for a new back office billing module. We did a back office registration module last year and it cost us about $65,000. We are using the same application platform and vendor and the functionality change is about the same magnitude. Therefore, we expect it to cost us about $65,000 this time as well.
Advantages	Can get an estimate quickly.
Disadvantages	Analogous estimates may not reflect the true needs of the project. Can often be taken as a "firm" estimate. Best when stated as a range (e.g., $1-3m)

Averaging (Three-Point Estimation)   Priority: Moderate

Averaging allows for estimates that have basis in reality yet allow for some uncertainty (risk). The estimator will identify estimates for the most likely scenario, the worst case (or pessimistic) scenario, and best case (optimistic) scenario. An average of the three is calculated and used for the plan.

Averaging (Three-Point Estimation)	
Description	A simple average of three estimates (optimistic, most likely, pessimistic) can be used to provide an estimate that reveals the range of uncertainty about activity duration or cost. The 3-point formula used depends on what the distribution of the values might be. For a triangular distribution, the 3-point average is used. Variables: • Most Likely (ML) (Sometimes called Realistic, R) • Pessimistic (P) • Optimistic (O) 3-Point (Average) = (ML+P+O) / 3
Advantages	Factors in a range of scenarios.
Disadvantages	Uses historical data which could be outdated or incorrect.

Bottom-Up   Priority: Moderate

Bottom-up estimating is the most precise of the techniques available. It is reliant on full information for project deliverables being available on which to base an estimate. Bottom-up estimating will be done at a very granular level of detail. The right level of detail is an estimate where progress can be measured and reported with sufficient time to determine variances that will impact the overall project schedule. For example, estimates between four and 40 hours work well for tracking on a daily and weekly basis. Here are two rules of thumb when looking at bottom-up estimates:

- It should not take longer to complete the estimate than it will to do the work being estimated.
- The only accurate estimate is for work that has already been completed. Until then, it is just an estimate.

                     PMI-PBA Certification Study Guide

Bottom-Up	
Description	Bottom-up estimating is completed through a process known as decomposition. Each activity on the Activity List is decomposed, or broken down into subsequently smaller and smaller pieces, to the lowest-level activities. You will know you are at the lowest level when you are comfortable with the estimate. If you feel that you are pulling the estimate from thin air, you are at too high a level. Decompose further. Think of as many components as possible that comprise the activity, until it becomes apparent and obvious how much time it will take. Can use 3-point estimates to accommodate for risk.
Advantages	It is the most precise estimate available. Is developed by the resources doing the work.
Disadvantages	Takes a lot of time to get to the estimate. Team members may be reluctant to commit to an estimate.

Estimation Poker   **Priority: Moderate**

Estimation poker is a tool used to estimate deliverables (typically user stories) relative to each other, without specific time periods attached. Agile teams using estimation poker will track the team "velocity" over time and adjust the amount of work the team can take on for any given iteration (or sprint). This way, if more team members are added to the team, velocity can be increased which allows the team to take on more work for each iteration without requiring new estimates.

Estimation can be a fun team activity. Many tools are available to support estimation poker, from decks of cards with T-shirt sizing to web and mobile phone applications that teams can use to vote on story size.

Estimation Poker (aka Planning Poker)	
Description	Estimation poker is a technique primarily used by agile teams to estimate the effort for each user story. User stories are estimated in relation to each other and not assigned a time estimate. With estimation poker, a user story is read, team members may ask questions, and then they "vote" on the size of the story. Team members discuss differences when votes are not the same and revote. The process continues until all team

Estimation Poker (aka Planning Poker)	
	members agree on the size of the story. This is an example of a Delphi decision-making technique applied to estimation. Examples: • T-shirt Sizing (S, M, L, and XL) • Fibonacci sequence (0, 1, 2, 3, 5, 8, 13, and 20) • Dog breeds
Advantages	Allows for thorough discussion and understanding of a user story before committing to a "size." Relies on the expertise of the team members doing the work.
Disadvantages	Team members may try to assign time values to the stories either directly or through the voting mechanism selected.

Parametric   **Priority: Moderate**

Parametric estimating works well for projects where historical averages can be compiled on some aspect of the project. For example, there are published guidelines for commercial contracting that provide industry standards on things such as cost per square foot of warehouse space or average cost per lane of interstate highway. This information is used to determine an estimate based on the current project given similar factors.

Parametric	
Description	Parametric estimating uses historical data to determine parameters to be in formulas or algorithms to extrapolate an estimate for a small amount of work to a large amount of work. For example, if one activity (or series of activities) can be estimated in detail, an algorithm can be developed to determine the total effort for all work involving that activity or series of activities. It's basically using mathematical models to predict time or cost. One example of parametric estimating is the use of function points. Another example would be to estimate how long it will take to update all the laptops in an organization by determining how long it takes to update one laptop and then multiplying that amount of time by the total number of laptops to be updated.
Advantages	Estimates can be developed with some precision relatively quickly.
Disadvantages	Requires some experience or data on a comparable project.

Example

Jill has found from her past projects that it generally takes her two weeks to fully elicit the requirements for each major function and interface of the solutions she has analyzed in the past. The current project has 6 functions and 3 interfaces identified. She estimates it will take her 18 weeks (2 weeks * 9 function/interface) to fully elicit the requirements for the solution.

Scheduling Tools and Techniques

Scheduling Tools and Techniques
Precedence Diagramming Method

Precedence Diagramming Method (PDM)   Priority: Low

A technique used for constructing a schedule model in which activities are represented by nodes and are graphically linked by one or more logical relationships to show the sequence in which the activities are to be performed. (*PMBOK® Guide*, Glossary)

Planning – Exercise 4

Write the mnemonic letters for the six tasks of Planning. Fill in the blanks to complete the task name for each task within Planning. This time you get to write in the full phrase.

Planning Tasks	Mnemonic
1. _____ _____ _____	_____
2. _____ _____ _____	_____
3. _____ _____ _____	_____
4. _____ _____ _____ _____	_____
5. _____ _____ _____	_____
6. _____ _____ _____ _____	_____

Planning – Exercise 5

How many tools and techniques can you find in the word search below? Hint -- words may be across, down, diagonal, or backwards. There are a total of 15 words. Challenge yourself to recall the description and use of the technique as it applies to planning as you find each word. Additional space has been provided for you to take notes.

Planning

```
N  O  I  T  A  M  I  T  S  E  W  A  P  V  T
P  J  P  C  D  Z  A  E  Z  G  E  A  M  X  R
Z  C  F  V  Y  Y  I  T  N  L  R  V  S  N  A
J  J  O  P  H  V  N  I  S  A  N  E  U  B  C
G  W  H  N  O  G  G  I  M  S  A  R  O  Q  E
H  C  A  T  F  A  N  E  F  X  O  S  G  D  A
P  R  I  O  R  I  T  I  Z  A  T  I  O  N  B
T  N  A  E  B  R  G  E  L  C  U  O  L  C  I
G  H  V  N  I  Y  A  U  G  U  P  N  A  O  L
X  A  S  C  K  U  K  J  R  N  D  M  N  F  I
T  R  A  C  K  I  N  G  E  A  A  E  A  E  T
W  O  C  S  O  M  N  D  K  M  T  H  H  R  Y
O  R  S  N  R  V  K  G  O  I  T  I  C  C  I
U  T  W  Z  Z  U  G  Y  P  G  Y  D  O  C  S
J  E  B  Y  L  M  W  O  T  G  N  W  C  N  O
```

NOTES

_____

_____

_____

_____

_____

_____

_____

_____

_____

PMI-PBA Practice Exam

Here are sample questions on Planning to help you practice taking PMI-PBA exam questions. Answers with detailed explanations are listed at the end of the chapter.

1. What should be included in the Requirements Management Plan?
    a. Requirements analysis activities, configuration management process, requirements prioritization process, traceability structure
    b. Requirements analysis activities, project schedule, project team RACI
    c. A Requirements Management Plan is not needed
    d. How activities will be planned, tracked, and reported

2. What are valid elements to include in a Requirements Traceability Matrix?
    a. Priority, status, owner, complexity
    b. Business needs, project scope, product development, test scenarios
    c. Project team progress
    d. Changes to requirements

3. Which of the following best describes planning on an adaptive project?
    a. The degree of formality depends on the needs of the sponsor.
    b. It may be informal if the project manager has sufficient experience with the approach.
    c. There is one level of planning that includes very detailed activities.
    d. It includes multiple levels of planning with details developed iteratively.

4. Which of the following can be said about a configuration management system?
    a. It includes the configuration control system, which is focused on the specification of the requirements, as well as the change control system, which is focused on identifying, documenting, and controlling changes to the stakeholders' needs.
    b. It includes the configuration control system, which is focused on the delivery mechanism for the products, as well as the change control system, which is focused on identifying, documenting, and controlling changes to the project and product baselines.
    c. It includes the configuration control system, which is focused on the specification of both the deliverables and the processes, as well as the change control system, which is focused on identifying, documenting, and controlling changes to the project and product baselines.
    d. It includes the traceability management system which is focused on the specification of both the deliverables and the processes, as well as the change control system which is focused on identifying, documenting, and controlling changes to the requirements.

5. You are making a case for using a traceability matrix. Which of the following is included in your presentation?
    a. It provides metrics for quantifying the business value of each requirement.
    b. It provides a method for confirming cross-functional value of project and product requirements.
    c. It provides the method for communicating requirements to stakeholders to manage product expectations.
    d. It helps validate the business value of each requirement.

6. Organizations may have informal and formal standards for business analysis work, including how they fit into a project. Which of the following statements is the most correct?
    a. The approach should be tailored to the needs of a specific initiative.
    b. A standard approach must be followed exactly for every project.
    c. Review the organization standards and dictate to the stakeholders the best approach.
    d. Organizations don't really have standards and it's always best to follow what all other projects are doing.

7. Which statement best describes how to plan business analysis activities?
    a. Determine the activities that must be performed, the deliverables that must be produced, and estimate the effort required to perform that work.
    b. Determine the activities that must be performed to ensure compliance with stakeholder expectations.
    c. Identify management tools required to measure the progress of business analysis work.
    d. Build the requirements estimates.

8. Which of the following is an important tool in defining the scope of work and in developing estimates?
    a. WBS
    b. RBS
    c. OBS
    d. TBS

9. Lydia is planning her business analysis communications with stakeholders on a major new project. Which stakeholder type would she spend the most time with in creating the plan?
    a. Domain SME/End user
    b. Others on the BA team
    c. Sponsor
    d. Project manager

10. Which of the following approaches is most likely to use a formal requirements change management system?
    a. Agile
    b. Scrum
    c. Waterfall
    d. Extreme programming

Exercise Answers

Planning – Exercise 1

Needs Assessment Tasks	Mnemonic
1. Determine _Project_ _Context_	P
2. Plan _Requirements_ _Traceability_	T
3. Plan _Requirements_ _Management_	M
4. Plan _Requirements Change Control_	C
5. Plan _Document_ _Control_	D
6. Define _Project Expected Outcomes_	E

Needs Assessment Review – Exercise 2

Needs Assessment Tasks	Mnemonic
1. Define _Business_ _Need_	B
2. Determine _Value_ _Proposition_	V
3. Develop _Project_ _Goals_	G
4. Identify _Stakeholders_	S
5. Elicit _Stakeholder_ _Values_	V

     PMI-PBA Certification Study Guide

Planning – Exercise 3

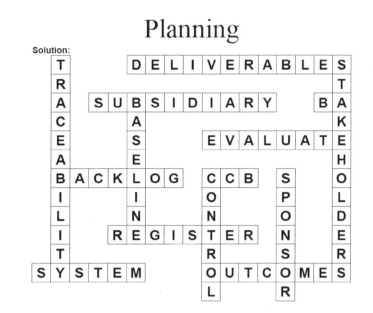

**Planning –
Exercise 4**

Planning Tasks	Mnemonic
1. Determine _Project_ _Context_	P
2. Plan _Requirements_ _Traceability_	T
3. Plan _Requirements_ _Management_	M
4. Plan Requirements Change Control	C
5. Plan _Document_ _Control_	D
6. Define Project Expected Outcomes	E

Planning – Exercise 5

Planning

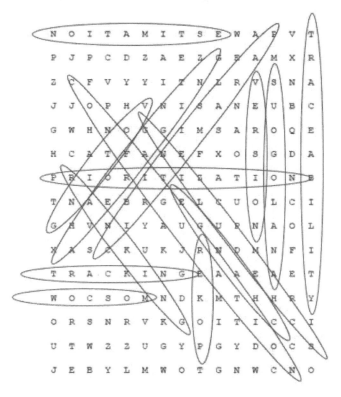

ANALOGOUS	AVERAGING	CHANGE
CONFIGURATION	ESTIMATION	MOSCOW
PARAMETRIC	POKER	PRIORITIZATION
RANKING	SCHEDULING	TRACEABILITY
TRACKING	VERSION	VOTING

PMI-PBA Practice Exam Answers

1. What should be included in the Requirements Management Plan?

   a. Requirements analysis activities, configuration management process, requirements prioritization process, traceability structure

   Correct! *PMBOK® Guide* 5.1.3.2 **Requirements Management Plan.**

   b. Requirements analysis activities, project schedule, project team RACI

   The Requirements Management Plan may feed a piece of the project schedule but the project schedule is not in the Requirements Management Plan. There may be a RACI matrix but it will be specific to the BA activities and not a project-wide RACI.

   c. A Requirements Management Plan is not needed

   A Requirements Management Plan is part of the overall scope planning process.

   d. How activities will be planned, tracked, and reported

   This is just one aspect of the Requirements Management Plan.

2. What are valid elements to include in a Requirements Traceability Matrix?

   a. Priority, status, owner, complexity

   These are attributes that help to define key information about the requirement.

   b. **Business needs, project scope, product development, test scenarios**

   Correct! These capture the main elements of requirements traceability. See *PMBOK® Guide* 5.2.3.2 Requirements Traceability Matrix.

   c. Project team progress

   Project team progress is not part of planning.

   d. Changes to requirements

   Changes are handled via change control.

3. Which of the following best describes planning on an adaptive project?

   a. The degree of formality depends on the needs of the sponsor.

   It tends to be relatively informal, regardless of the sponsor.

   b. It may be informal if the project manager has sufficient experience with the approach.

   Planning on adaptive projects tends to be relatively informal.

   c. There is one level of planning that includes very detailed activities.

   This is descriptive of predictive project planning.

   d. **It includes multiple levels of planning with details developed iteratively.**

   Correct! See *BA Practice Guide, page 50.*

4. Which of the following can be said about a configuration management system?

   a. It includes the configuration control system, which is focused on the specification of the requirements, as well as the change control system, which is focused on identifying, documenting, and controlling changes to the stakeholders' needs.

   This is a made up answer as neither addresses specification of the requirements or stakeholders' needs.

b. It includes the configuration control system, which is focused on the delivery mechanism for the products, as well as the change control system, which is focused on identifying, documenting, and controlling changes to the project and product baselines.	Neither has anything to do with the delivery mechanism for the product.
c. It includes the configuration control system, which is focused on the specification of both the deliverables and the processes, as well as the change control system, which is focused on identifying, documenting, and controlling changes to the project and product baselines.	**Correct! See *PMBOK® Guide* 4.5.**
d. It includes the traceability management system which is focused on the specification of both the deliverables and the processes, as well as the change control system which is focused on identifying, documenting, and controlling changes to the requirements.	This is a made up answer. There is no such thing as a traceability management system. Neither addresses changes to requirements.

5. You are making a case for using a traceability matrix. Which of the following is included in your presentation?

a. It provides metrics for quantifying the business value of each requirement.	Traceability matrices do not provide metrics.
b. It provides a method for confirming cross-functional value of project and product requirements.	This is not true.
c. It provides the method for communicating requirements to stakeholders to manage product expectations.	They do not do this.
d. It helps validate the business value of each requirement.	**Correct! See *PMBOK® Guide* 5.2.3.2.**

6. Organizations may have informal and formal standards for business analysis work, including how they fit into a project. Which of the following statements is the most correct?

a. The approach should be tailored to the needs of a specific initiative.	**Correct! Even where a standard approach exists, it must be tailored to the needs of a specific initiative. Tailoring may be governed by organizational standards that define which approaches are permitted, which elements of those processes may be tailored, general guidelines for selecting a process, and so forth. See *PMBOK® Guide* page 48.**
b. A standard approach must be followed exactly for every project.	Each project is different and therefore must be tailored every time.
c. Review the organization standards and dictate to the stakeholders the best approach.	Reviewing the organization's standards is true. However, the *PMBOK® Guide* doesn't

		prescribe having the BA dictate to the stakeholders.
d.	Organizations don't really have standards and it's always best to follow what all other projects are doing.	Many organizations do, indeed, have standards. Sometimes organizations require that these standards be followed.

7. Which statement best describes how to plan business analysis activities?

a.	**Determine the activities that must be performed, the deliverables that must be produced, and estimate the effort required to perform that work.**	**Correct! The only answer that includes the most complete definition. Other answers describe only part of the definition.**
b.	Determine the activities that must be performed to ensure compliance with stakeholder expectations.	Activities should be more than just to comply with stakeholder expectations.
c.	Identify management tools required to measure the progress of business analysis work.	This statement defines business analysis performance, not planning.
d.	Build the requirements estimates.	Too narrow, only one part of the task.

8. Which of the following is an important tool in defining the scope of work and in developing estimates?

a.	**WBS**	**Correct! A work breakdown structure.** *PMBOK® Guide 5.4.*
b.	RBS	Risk breakdown structure is not used in defining scope.
c.	OBS	Organizational breakdown structure is not used in defining scope.
d.	TBS	This TV station is not used in defining scope.

9. Lydia is planning her business analysis communications with stakeholders on a major new project. Which stakeholder type would she spend the most time with in creating the plan?

a.	Domain SME/End user	They would be involved in reviewing and approving the plan. Their interest is focused on their part of the plan and not the whole thing.
b.	Others on the BA team	Other BAs on a project are not stakeholders in planning business analysis communication.
c.	Sponsor	Their communication needs center around the business requirements, which should not take as much time to plan as other parts of the plan.
d.	**Project manager**	**Correct! Implied in the *PMBOK® Guide* because of the emphasis on integrating the Requirements Management Plan, which includes a communication plan, into the overall project plan.**

10. Which of the following approaches is most likely to use a formal requirements change management system?

a.	Agile	Agile approaches allow for change without a formal change control process.
b.	Scrum	Scrum is an adaptive approach which allows for change without a formal change control process.
c.	**Waterfall**	**Correct! Requirements will be baselined and require a formal approved change request for changes.**
d.	Extreme programming	An adaptive approach which allows for change without a formal change control process.

Summary

The Planning domain describes the tasks and tools and techniques for planning and organizing requirements activities. It emphasizes several planning considerations such as:

- Stakeholders and their roles.

- Business analysis activities and estimating their effort.

- Requirements management plan, and related items like requirements attributes, traceability, and change management.

- Establishes a plan for capturing metrics for solution evaluation.

Here are the themes covered that you should internalize:

- Consider the project approach in place (e.g., predictive or adaptive).

- Understand stakeholders and adjust to their needs (e.g., use RACI).

- Plan processes to control scope and get approval for all changes.

- Plan traceability structure.

 Planning Goal: Plan for the deliverables and activities needed in order to deliver quality requirements and evaluate solution results.

Notes

 PMI-PBA Certification Study Guide

4. Analysis

Overview

The Analysis domain centers on all activities required for good requirements analysis. It starts with requirements elicitation and moves the requirements to a point of "suitable for deployment." In other words, the requirements are such that the project team can satisfy them through product development, test, and implementation. Analysis focuses on requirements that address the product scope identified in Needs Assessment and following the business analysis activities identified in Planning.

 Analysis Goal: Product requirements that are approved, within scope, and suitable for development.

When you are finished with this chapter, you will know:

	Analysis
	The task, tools, and techniques to elicit requirements, determine requirements within scope, and ensure they product development team can act to satisfy

- The eight tasks contained in the Analysis domain.

- The major areas of emphasis in Analysis, including elicitation, decomposition, verification, validation, sign-off, and acceptance criteria.

- Tools and techniques for eliciting requirements.

- Tools and techniques for analyzing and specifying requirements.

Domain Themes

The PMI-PBA exam includes several reoccurring themes. One useful way to use these themes is when you narrow down an exam question to two close answers. If one of the themes suggests one over the other, then go with the theme. The common themes to watch for in Analysis are as follows:

Theme	Comments
Progressive Elaboration	You can see a pattern emerging that more detailed requirements are available through each step as you step through the eight tasks of the Analysis domain. This is called "progressive elaboration" in the *PMBOK® Guide*. This helps to make the point that eliciting is only the first step to analysis and that the requirements are not "suitable for development" until much more analysis activity is completed.
Scope and Value	Many of the techniques used in Needs Assessment in determining product value come into play in this domain as well. This shows how requirements analysis involves understanding the value proposition of each requirement, especially as it relates to the project goals and objectives. The business analyst will facilitate recommendations and decisions on product scope requirements that are needed to satisfy the scope.
Models	Analysis is the domain where you will find all of the requirements model techniques. Requirements models leads to better analysis by providing additional insights to the requirements that lead to finding additional needed requirements and provide better clarity of the requirements. Models also facilitate communication by providing a visual representation of the requirements that many stakeholder will more easily understand.

Figure 4-1: PMI-PBA Exam Themes Applicable to Analysis

This is it! This is the big one! The Analysis domain makes up 35 percent of the PMI-PBA Exam. See *Figure 4-2* below. This is the domain where you will want to focus the largest percentage of your study. It also is the largest chapter of this study guide. Additional review exercises are included in this chapter to help you remember the tasks, concepts, tools, and techniques of analysis. This includes a mid-chapter practice exam.

Domain	Percentage of Items on Test	Approximate number of questions
Domain 1: Needs Assessment	18%	36
Domain 2: Planning	22%	44
Domain 3: Analysis	35%	70
Domain 4: Traceability and Monitoring	15%	30

 PMI-PBA Certification Study Guide

Domain 5: Evaluation	10%	20

Figure 4-2: Analysis Domain
Source: PMI

Domain: High-Level View

Listed below are the eight tasks in the Analysis domain. The tasks in the domain may not be performed sequentially, but it is helpful to learn the tasks and their order as a way to remember what each of them does. PMI® does not provide task titles for each task, but rather a detailed description. See the table below for the tasks as defined by PMI® with a task title developed for this study guide in order to aid learning and remember the tasks.

Task 1
Elicit Requirements

Elicit or identify requirements, using individual and group elicitation techniques in order to discover and capture requirements with supporting details (e.g., origin and rationale).

Task 2
Analyze, Decompose, and Elaborate Requirements

Analyze, decompose, and elaborate requirements using techniques such as dependency analysis, interface analysis, and data and process models in order to collaboratively uncover and clarify product options and capabilities.

Task 3
Evaluate Product Options and Capabilities

Evaluate product options and capabilities by using decision-making and valuation techniques in order to determine which requirements are accepted, deferred, or rejected.

Task 4
Allocate Requirements

Allocate accepted or deferred requirements by balancing scope, schedule, budget, and resource constraints with the value proposition using prioritization, dependency analysis, and decision-making tools and techniques in order to create a Requirements Baseline.

Task 5
Get Requirements Sign-off

Obtain sign-off on Requirements Baseline using decision-making techniques in order to facilitate stakeholder consensus and achieve stakeholder approval.

Mnemonic Tip

EACASSVA: "Everything As Calm As Singing Saints Visualizing Acceptance"

E	**E**licit Requirements
A	**A**nalyze, Decompose, and Elaborate Requirements
C	Evaluate Product Options and **C**apabilities
A	**A**llocate Requirements
S	Get Requirements **S**ignoff
S	Write Requirements **S**pecifications
V	**V**alidate Requirements
A	Elaborate and Specify **A**cceptance Criteria

Task 6

Write Requirements Specifications

Write requirements specifications using process (such as use cases, user stories), data, and interface details in order to communicate requirements that are measurable and actionable (that is, suitable for development).

Task 7

Validate Requirements

Validate requirements using tools and techniques such as documentation review, prototypes, demos, and other validation methods in order to ensure requirements are complete, accurate and aligned with goals, objectives, and value proposition.

Task 8

Elaborate and Specify Acceptance Criteria

Elaborate and specify detailed metrics and acceptance criteria using measurement tools and techniques for use in evaluating whether the solution meets requirements.

To help you remember the tasks, use a mnemonic of "Everything As Calm As Singing Saints Visualizing Acceptance". This mnemonic captures the tasks within Analysis in their given order. The first letter of the mnemonic is highlighted to help you memorize it.

The chapter below presents each of the tasks along with more information on the task descriptions and tools and techniques used to perform each task.

Task Inputs and Outputs

The PMI-PBA exam does not follow a specific "Body of Knowledge" in terms of identifying inputs, tools and techniques, and outputs (ITTOs) for each of the tasks. The table below describes some standard concepts in inputs, tools and techniques, and outputs for each task in order to provide context and greater understanding. The PMI-PBA exam will not test specifically on these ITTOs. ITTOs may be present in test questions as a means to test your understanding of the task.

Input	Task	Tools and Techniques	Output
Requirements Management Plan Solution Scope	1. Elicit or identify requirements, using individual and group elicitation techniques in order to discover and capture requirements with supporting details (e.g., origin and rationale).	Elicitation Business Rule Analysis	Requirements (Elicited)
Requirements (Elicited)	2. Analyze, decompose, and elaborate requirements using techniques such as dependency analysis, interface analysis, and data and process models in order to collaboratively uncover and clarify product options and capabilities.	Analytic Business Rule Analysis Data Analysis Interface Analysis Process Analysis	Requirements (Analyzed)
Requirements (Analyzed) Product Scope	3. Evaluate product options and capabilities by using decision-making and valuation techniques in order to determine which requirements are accepted, deferred, or rejected.	Decision Making Valuation *(covered in Needs Assessment domain)*	Requirements (Accepted, deferred, or rejected)
Requirements (Accepted)	4. Allocate accepted or deferred requirements by balancing scope, schedule, budget, and resource constraints with the value proposition using prioritization, dependency analysis, and decision-making tools and techniques in order to create a Requirements Baseline.	Decision Making Prioritization Valuation *(covered in Needs Assessment domain)*	Requirements (Allocated)

Input	Task	Tools and Techniques	Output
Requirements (Allocated)	5. Obtain sign-off on Requirements Baseline using decision-making techniques in order to facilitate stakeholder consensus and achieve stakeholder approval.	Decision Making	Requirements Baseline (Approved)
Requirements Baseline (Approved)	6. Write requirements specifications using process (such as use cases, user stories), data, and interface details in order to communicate requirements that are measurable and actionable (that is, suitable for development).	Data Analysis Interface Analysis Process Analysis	Requirements Specifications
Business Case Requirements Specifications	7. Validate requirements using tools and techniques such as documentation review, prototypes, demos, and other validation methods in order to ensure requirements are complete, accurate and aligned with goals, objectives, and value proposition.	Verification *(covered in Evaluation domain)* Validation *(covered in Evaluation domain)*	Requirements (Validated)
Business Case Requirements Baseline	8. Elaborate and specify detailed metrics and acceptance criteria using measurement tools and techniques for use in evaluating whether the solution meets requirements.	Measurement Validation *(covered in Evaluation domain)*	Acceptance Criteria (Elaborated)

Figure 4-3: Analysis ITTOs

                       PMI-PBA Certification Study Guide

Part 1 – Analysis Tasks

Task 1 – Elicit Requirements

Elicit or identify requirements, using individual and group elicitation techniques in order to discover and capture requirements with supporting details (e.g., origin and rationale).

<u>E</u>ACASSVA

"Everything As Calm As Singing Saints Visualizing Acceptance"

The elicitation process is more than collecting or gathering requirements. The terminology "collecting" or "gathering" requirements implies that stakeholders already have requirements ready to be collected or gathered. While stakeholders may not have actual requirements, they do often have wants and needs, but may not be able to express them clearly. Part of the BA's job is to help the stakeholders define the problem or opportunity and determine what should be done to address it. *identify*

The goal of elicitation is to "call forth or draw out" requirements from and with stakeholders. There are many tools and techniques available in order to elicit requirements. The actual tools and techniques are in Part 2 of this chapter. This section will provide more general guidance on considerations for eliciting requirements.

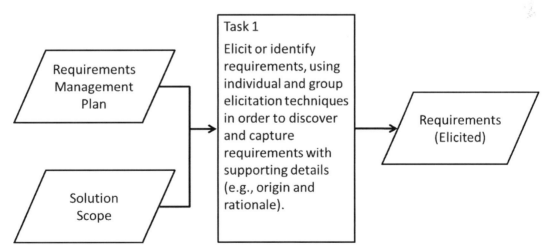

Figure 4-4: Elicit Requirements ITO

Considerations for Elicit Requirements Task

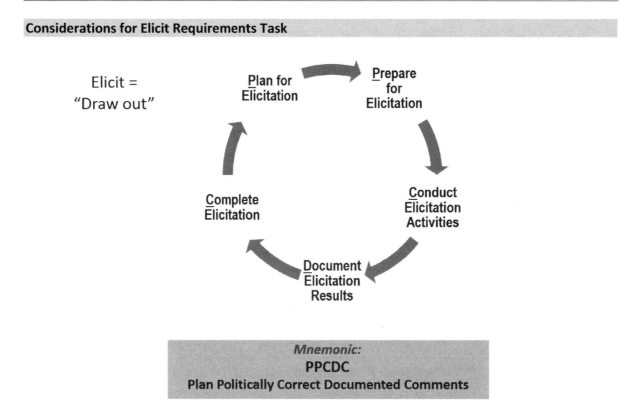

Figure 4-5: Iterative Elicitation Process

Plan

Elicitation plans will be documented in the Requirements Management Plan. However, plans are meant to be iterative and adapted. Start with the identified elicitation plans and refine the plans to specify the information requiring elicitation, where that information can most likely be found, the best method for extracting the information, and the sequence of elicitation activities that will get the best results. You should now have a list of elicitation events to be conducted in order to produce complete requirements for the solution.

Some of the elements in an elicitation plan include:
- What information to elicit
- Where to find that information
- How to obtain the information
- Sequencing the elicitation activities

A well thought out approach to elicitation provides the following benefits:
- Clearer idea of the necessary information to define a problem, affect an improvement, or produce a solution
- Fewer unnecessary elicitation activities
- More valuable results from each elicitation session
- More efficient and predictable use of stakeholder time to elicit the information
- Better overall focus on the elicitation process

Source: *Business Analysis for Practitioners: A Practice Guide*, pages 70-71

Prepare

Preparation for each elicitation event may be formal or informal, and includes organizing and scheduling resources for conducting requirements elicitation. The preparation includes detailed schedules for participants, locations, and other resources.

Participants in elicitation typically include stakeholders, users, and subject matter experts (SMEs) who will be providing their requirements. Multiple complementary techniques for elicitation work the best. Ideally, the techniques would have been selected when planning business analysis activities (see Planning, Plan Requirements Management).

The purpose in preparing for elicitation is to:

- Clarify the objectives and desired results for the given elicitation technique. Gather any supporting materials for it.
- Schedule all the resources for the elicitation, including people, facilities, and equipment.
- Notify appropriate parties of the schedule.
- Well-run event-based elicitations need ground rules.

Preparation notes can be used to measure the progress achieved in a session against what was planned to be achieved and can be used to adjust expectations for future sessions.

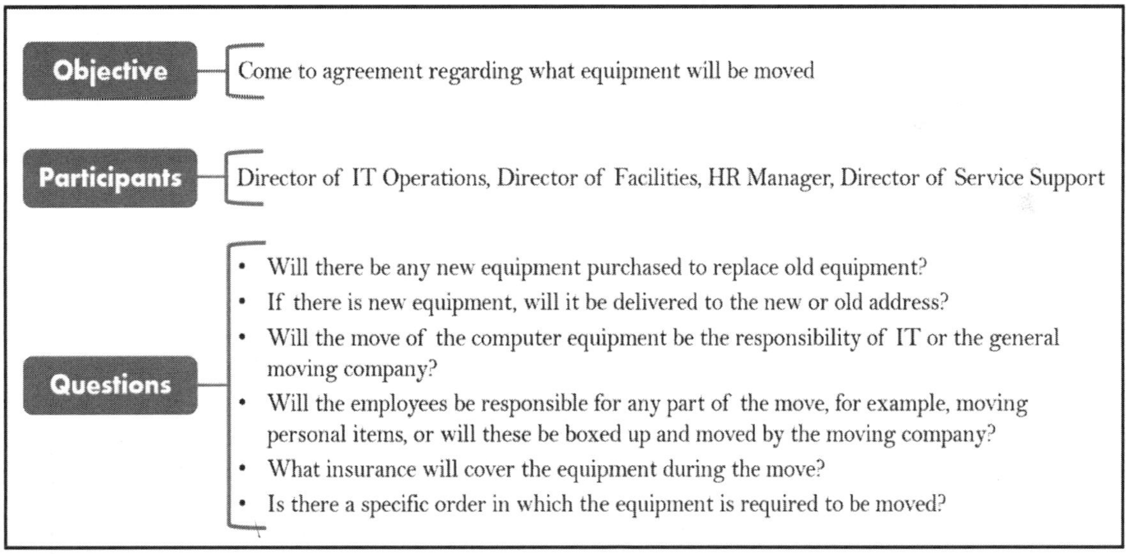

Objective — Come to agreement regarding what equipment will be moved

Participants — Director of IT Operations, Director of Facilities, HR Manager, Director of Service Support

Questions —
- Will there be any new equipment purchased to replace old equipment?
- If there is new equipment, will it be delivered to the new or old address?
- Will the move of the computer equipment be the responsibility of IT or the general moving company?
- Will the employees be responsible for any part of the move, for example, moving personal items, or will these be boxed up and moved by the moving company?
- What insurance will cover the equipment during the move?
- Is there a specific order in which the equipment is required to be moved?

Figure 4-6: Preparation Notes Example

Business analysts must be certain to include all defined stakeholders during elicitation of requirements.

Conduct

Eliciting requirements is highly dependent on:

- The knowledge of the stakeholders
- Their willingness to participate in defining requirements
- The group's ability to reach consensus

Four Stages for Conducting Elicitation Activities

1. **Introduction.** Each elicitation event should begin with an introduction. This is an opportunity to set the tone for the event and build rapport with the stakeholders. Use this time to set expectations by sharing the meeting purpose, objectives, agenda, and processes. Be sure to discuss and agree to the event's ground rules.

> **Ground Rules**
>
> Agreed-upon rules of conduct among the participants of an event-based elicitation. Ground rules help the facilitator enforce discipline and keep the elicitation on track.

2. **Body.** The body is where the questions are asked and the answers are given. There are a number of types of questions you can use in order to elicit requirements from stakeholders.
   - Open-ended – responses to the question are free flowing with limitless possibilities
   - Close-ended – will have a single response from a limited number of choices; may be yes or no or a selection from a set list of possibilities
   - Contextual – response will be related to the topic at hand, namely the solution under development
   - Context-free – question can be on anything, even outside of the context of the solution

   The type of event will drive the mix of question types that will work best to elicit requirements. Interviews work best with open-ended questions to facilitate discussion and discovery, and to help build rapport and trust between the business analyst and the stakeholders. Surveys and questionnaires work best with close-ended questions where the results from respondents can be compiled and quantified.

   It is important that the business analyst effectively facilitate group sessions. Proper facilitation will help to ensure that all stakeholders have an opportunity to participate in the discussion and have their ideas heard without being drowned out by those who have a tendency to over contribute.

> **Event-Based Elicitation**
>
> Elicitation that involves dynamic interaction between participants. These interactions (or events) may take place as: brainstorming, focus groups, interviews, observation, prototypes, requirements workshops.

   Finally, the business analyst must be ready to actively listen to the ideas being presented. This includes confirming that the words and the message received is the intended message. It is also important to pay attention to non-verbal cues as these will help determine if there may be an opportunity to probe for more information or if further discussion is needed to get to consensus.

3. **Close.** The close provides a graceful termination to the particular elicitation session. The session should close with a summary of the results and findings of the event. There should be an opportunity for questions on the results. Next steps should also be discussed to continue setting expectations with stakeholders.

               PMI-PBA Certification Study Guide

4. **Follow-up.** Finally, follow up the event by sending participants the final summary results. Validate stated requirements and concerns to ensure they match stakeholders' understanding. Schedule any additional follow-up with groups or individuals until satisfied that all requirements for the work at hand have been captured.

Document Elicitation Results

Note the details provided by stakeholders from an elicitation event or other techniques (e.g., document analysis) that will be used in requirements analysis. Also record stakeholder concerns.

Different kinds of documentation may be produced from an elicitation event or technique. Specific techniques will dictate the type of documentation produced. For instance, a facilitated requirements workshop may use sticky notes on white boards to elicit a process map. The particular examples worth noting are:

Type	Description	Examples
Written Documents	Describe outcomes form the elicitation.	Interview notes. Notes from observations. Findings from document analysis.
Recordings	Visual or audio recordings of elicitation events.	Video of observation session. Audio recordings from interviews.
Whiteboards	Whether tangible or virtual, they contain notes that will eventually be transferred to another medium, such as written documents.	Sticky notes and drawings of a business process. Notes from a virtual meeting with changes to a prototype.

Figure 4-7: Elicitation Documentation Types

Don't forget to record the elicited requirements in your **Requirements Traceability Matrix.** This will be discussed in great detail in Chapter 4. Supporting documentation from the elicitation event should be referenced or linked to in the Requirements Traceability Matrix for easier access.

Complete Elicitation

When does elicitation end and analysis start? For the **predictive** approach, the iterative process of elicitation and analysis continues until the analysis produces no further questions, or when the risk of problems due to incomplete information is determined to be acceptable.

For the **adaptive** approach, elicitation and analysis occur throughout the project as part of initial backlog definition, grooming the backlog, and then analyzing the details for each iteration.

Elicitation Issues and Challenges

There are a number of difficulties associated with the elicitation, for example:
- Conflicting viewpoints and needs among different types of stakeholders
- Conflicting information and resulting requirements from different business units
- Unstated or assumed information on the part of stakeholders
- Stakeholders who are resistant to change and may fail to cooperate and possibly sabotage the work
- Inability to schedule time for interviewing or elicitation sessions because stakeholders cannot take time away from their work
- Inability of stakeholders to express what they do or what they would like to do
- Inability of stakeholders to refrain from focusing on a solution

Techniques

Techniques – *Elicit Requirements*

Business Rule Analysis Tools and Techniques	Includes:
Tools and techniques used to discover, understand, and articulate business rules that govern the organization, its processes, and its data. Business rules are operating principles or self-imposed constraints that apply across all projects and systems. They constrain, define, or enable the organization to function. They are specific, actionable, and testable (vs. policies, which support goals, but are non-actionable). Business rules are also atomic (i.e., can't be broken down further) and are independent of any one process.	- Decision Table - Decision Tree - Business Rule Catalog
Elicitation Tools and Techniques Tools and techniques used to draw out requirements and assumptions from stakeholders through individual and group settings, and from existing documentation.	**Includes:** - Brainstorming - Document Analysis - Facilitated Workshops - Focus Groups - Interviews - Non-Functional Requirements Analysis - Observation - Prototypes - Research - Surveys and Questionnaires

Outputs

> ### Output: *Requirements (Elicited)*
>
> Requirements (Elicited) is the only output of this task. It's important to note the status of the requirements as they are not yet ready for the team. Requirements should be captured in the Requirements Traceability Matrix with an appropriate status.

PMBOK® Guide References

More information on Elicit Requirements can be found in the *PMBOK® Guide*:

- Section 5.2 – Collect Requirements

Business Analysis for Practitioners: A Practice Guide References

- Sections 4.1 - 4.8

Task 2 – Analyze, Decompose, and Elaborate Requirements

Analyze, decompose, and elaborate requirements using techniques such as dependency analysis, interface analysis, and data and process models in order to collaboratively uncover and clarify product options and capabilities.

E<u>A</u>CASSVA

"Everything As Calm As Singing Saints Visualizing Acceptance"

Requirements that have been elicited are far from being ready for implementation by the project team. This is where analysis begins! It is through this analysis that stakeholder statements of requirements begin to take form to provide a complete list of product requirements that are suitable for development.

The business analyst will be doing a significant amount of work to analyze, elaborate, and decompose the elicited requirements which will result in more requirements that contribute to a more complete picture of the final solution. The business analyst will also be creating models and other artifacts that support and provide additional context to the requirements.

Definitions have been provided below for "decompose" and "elaborate." For "analyze" we let the Microsoft Word synonym finder feature help to provide more context around the meaning of the word.

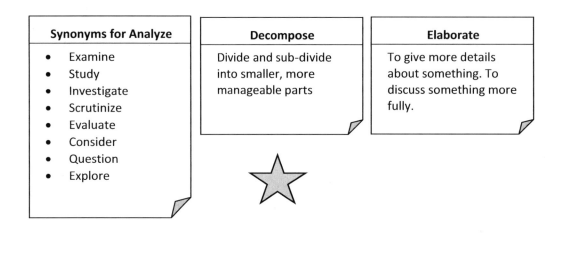

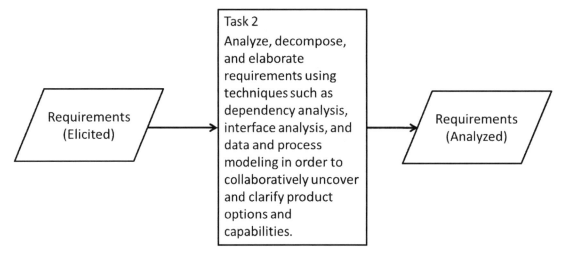

Figure 4-8: Analyze, Decompose, and Elaborate Requirement ITO

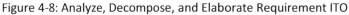

Considerations for Analyze, Decompose, and Elaborate Requirements

Text

Some requirements are best documented with text, such as declarative requirements statements, business rules, and features lists. Any text needs to articulate:

- The capabilities of the solution
- Any conditions that must be met for the requirement to be valid
- Any constraints that may prevent the requirement from being fulfilled

Guidelines for writing text requirements include:

Guidelines for Text Requirements		
Guideline		**Example**
Document one requirement at a time (i.e., no compound requirements)	DO	"The system shall permit incomplete applications to be saved at any point in the application process."
	DON'T	"The system shall permit incomplete applications to be saved at any point in the application process and allow for resuming a saved application."
Use simple wording and avoid complicated conditional clauses	DON'T	"The system shall permit entering a mortgage application through the web site, except when the site is down for maintenance, and only when no other application has been started."
Assume no domain knowledge by the reader	DON'T	"Only fractural mitigators are allowed to pass through the viscous membrane of co-exhibitors."
Use consistent terminology	DON'T	"Customers are allowed to open any number of accounts. Accounts are opened by clients."
Use verbs or verb phrases	DO	"Account holders own one or more accounts."
	DON'T	"Accounts should be owned by account holders."
Use active voice, describing who or what is responsible for fulfilling each requirement	DO	"A mortgage loan officer must approve every preliminary loan application before a rate can be quoted to applicants."
Use familiar terminology for reviewing stakeholders	DON'T	"The LI1003 Index table shall be used as a secondary index to do a SELECT query of the FST2000 table to find temp applications without needing the Application ID."

Figure 4-9: Text Requirement Guidelines

Matrix Documentation

Matrices are used for information that cross-references other information. Traceability is best and most commonly expressed in a matrix, as are requirements attributes, data dictionary items, CRUD matrices, etc.

Simple tables of information are another form of matrix. More complex matrices have relationships between columns of the matrix for the same row of information. For instance, a traceability matrix row will list the requirement and have data that traces back to objectives (one column) and forward to design (another column).

Models

Models are templates of standard symbols to document requirements, which could include the other elements of diagrams, text, and matrices. Graphical models are also called diagrams. Typical models include: process, data, use case, organizational, etc. that look at a business area from different perspectives to give complete coverage. The choice of models depends on the information to be captured and the audience who needs the information. Models help to uncover ambiguities and clarify requirements, and are an important part of analysis.

Notations. Models use standard symbols to represent actions, decisions, hierarchies, and components, as well as their relationships. They may need a key to help interpret them. Specific modeling languages have been developed to provide continuity in model development interpretation throughout common industries. Unified Modeling Language (UML) is a common standard that we cover in our training classes. Other languages include:

- Business Process Modeling Notation (BPMN)

- Requirements Modeling Language (RML)

- System Modeling Language (SysML)

Formal vs. Informal. Formal models use standard symbols as described above. Informal models lack the structure of formal ones, but connect important pieces for the analyst and other stakeholders.

Capture Requirements Attributes

The attributes planned during the Plan Requirements Traceability should be recorded for each requirement. For example, the author, source, status, priority, etc.

Improvement Opportunities

As requirements are analyzed, business analysts should look for and note business areas that could be improved. Consider and identify opportunities in the following areas:

Opportunity Areas to Consider	
Automate or Simplify Workflow	Simple, repetitive tasks, with decision-making based on firm rules are good candidates for automation.
Improve Access to Information	Provide direct access to information, especially for customer-facing employees, reducing reliance on special lists. Decision-makers need to know meaning/significance of data provided to operational staff.
Reduce Complexity of Interfaces	Reducing the complexity of interfaces makes them easier to use and understand which can also lead to improved workflow.
Increase Consistency of Behavior	Refining and standardizing of processes leads to better customer service and reduced staff frustration.
Eliminate Redundancy	Duplicate work and outputs can be consolidated for different stakeholder groups by using one solution, reducing costs.

Figure 4-10: Opportunity Areas to Consider

Techniques – *Analyze, Decompose, and Elaborate Requirements*

Analytic Tools and Techniques Tools and techniques used to analyze the business and requirements for further understanding of the situation and solution requirements.	**Includes:** - Decomposition - Dependency Analysis - Gap Analysis - Impact Analysis - Progressive Elaboration - Risk Analysis
Business Rule Tools and Techniques Tools and techniques used to discover, understand, and articulate business rules that govern the organization, its processes, and its data.	**Includes:** - Business Rule Catalog - Decision Table - Decision Tree
Data Analysis Tools and Techniques Tools and techniques used to discover, understand, and articulate data requirements for a solution.	**Includes:** - Data Dictionary - Data Flow Diagram - Data Models - State Diagrams and Tables
Interface Analysis Tools and Techniques Interface analysis helps defines boundaries of a system by defining the other systems that provide functionality, inputs, and outputs. This is an important tenet of systems theory, which the PMI-PBA exam may test you on. A practical outcome of this technique is that interactions between systems are better defined and smoother interactions result.	**Includes:** - Interoperability - Prototypes - Report Table - Storyboarding - System Interface Table - User Interface Flow - Wireframes and Display-Action-Response
Process Analysis Tools and Techniques Tools and techniques used to understand and document processes in order to elicit and capture process related requirements.	**Includes:** - CRUD Matrix - Data Flow Diagrams - Dependency Graphs - Events - Process Models - Sequence Diagrams - Use Cases - User Stories

> ### Output: *Requirements (Analyzed)*
>
> The analyzed, modeled, and elaborated requirements for a project. They may be in the form of text, matrices, diagrams, or models. The Requirements Traceability Matrix should updated to match requirements and supporting documentation referenced.

PMBOK® Guide References

More information on Analyze, Decompose, and Elaborate Requirements can be found in the *PMBOK® Guide*:

- Section 5.2 – Collect Requirements

Business Analysis for Practitioners: A Practice Guide References

- Section 4.9 – Analyze Requirements

- Section 4.10 – Model and Refine Requirements

Analysis – Exercise 1

Write the mnemonic letters for the eight tasks of Analysis, and then complete the missing words for each task in the blanks provided below. This exercise will be repeated throughout the section. Partial task name answers have been provided only for those tasks not yet covered in this chapter. Hint: Think of something calming.

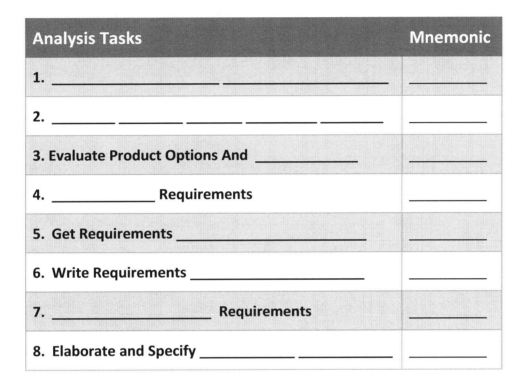

Analysis Tasks	Mnemonic
1. _____ _____	_____
2. _____ _____ _____ _____ _____	_____
3. Evaluate Product Options And _____	_____
4. _____ Requirements	_____
5. Get Requirements _____	_____
6. Write Requirements _____	_____
7. _____ Requirements	_____
8. Elaborate and Specify _____ _____	_____

Task 3 – Evaluate Product Options and Capabilities

Evaluate product options and capabilities by using decision-making and valuation techniques in order to determine which requirements are accepted, deferred, or rejected.

EA<u>C</u>ASSVA

"Everything As Calm As Singing Saints Visualizing Acceptance"

Before additional time is spent on requirements, the business analyst must first determine the requirements that are in scope. Making this determination early helps to avoid spending time on requirements that will not be approved for further development. Often a requirement may sound like a great idea, but when compared to the purpose and scope of the project, it does not contribute to addressing the original business need. These requirements should be considered as out of scope early in the process. Having a clear product scope as defined in Needs Assessment will make this an easy task for the business analyst.

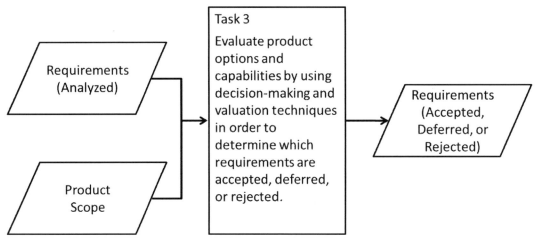

Figure 4-11: Compare Requirements to Product Scope ITO

Considerations for Evaluate Product Options and Capabilities

Product Scope

Decisions were made during Needs Assessment to determine the features, functions, and capabilities needed in order to satisfy the business need that the project was undertaken to address. The business analyst will need to continually go back to this scope in order to make recommendations on features and requirements that support the objectives of the project. A clearly defined and articulated product scope is the best defense against scope creep. Staying focused on scope greatly heightens the probably of project success.

Accepted Requirements

Requirements are accepted when it has been determined that the condition or capability is truly needed in order for the solution to address the original business need. The cost of implementing the requirement does not exceed the value it will bring to the successful implementation of the solution.

Deferred Requirements

> **Scope Creep**
>
> "The uncontrolled expansion to product or project scope without adjustment to time, cost, and resources." PMBOK® Guide
>
> Scope creep is a major contributor to project challenges by adding work without adding time or resources to support the work. Often this added work does not add value to the product or contribute to project success factors.

Requirements may be deferred to a later release when immediate implementation is not required. It may be that the requirement is seen as adding value in addressing the business need, but the cost of implementing cannot be justified. A requirement may also be deferred for a later project phase planned to address specific features or functionalities after the initial project release.

Rejected Requirements

A requirement may be rejected when it does not align with product scope and does not contribute to solving the business need that the current project was meant to address. Rejected requirements may be resurrected for new business cases to support future projects.

Status

All requirements should be captured in the Requirements Traceability Matrix and noted with the appropriate status. Including deferred and rejected requirements in the matrix will better support the business analyst if the requirement or a related requirement is brought up in the future. Further, tracking deferred and rejected requirements enhances communication and stakeholder engagement by providing transparency into the requirement decision making process.

Techniques – *Evaluate Product Options and Capabilities*	
Decision Making Tools and Techniques Tools and techniques to facilitate a group in order to understand options and agree upon a selected course of action.	**Includes:** - Consensus Building - Delphi Technique - Multi-Voting - Nominal Group Technique - Options Analysis - Weighted Criteria
Valuation Tools and Techniques *(covered in Evaluation domain)* Tools and techniques used to determine the value of the potential solution to the organization.	**Includes:** - Cost-Benefit Analysis - Force Field Analysis - Kano Model - Net Promoter Score - Purpose Alignment Model - SWOT Analysis - Value Stream Map

Output: *Requirements (Accepted, Deferred, or Rejected)*
Requirements that are accepted for the project. Requirements may also be deferred or rejected. The Requirements Traceability Matrix should be updated to include requirements status for all allocated, deferred, or rejected requirements.

PMBOK® Guide References

More information on Compare Requirements to Product Scope can be found in the *PMBOK® Guide*:

- Section 5.5 – Validate Scope

- Section 5.6 – Control Scope

Task 4 – Allocate Requirements

Allocate accepted or deferred requirements by balancing scope, schedule, budget, and resource constraints with the value proposition using prioritization, dependency analysis, and decision-making tools and techniques in order to create a Requirements Baseline.

EAC**A**SSVA

"Everything As Calm As Singing Saints Visualizing Acceptance"

Now that requirements have been determined to be in scope, including requirements deferred for later phases, further analysis is needed to prioritize and allocate the requirements. The goal is to recommend a Requirements Baseline to represent the proposed final set of requirements to be developed and implemented within the current project. The proposed baseline will include the recommended allocation of requirements by solution components or release phase for implementation. The baseline will not be set until after sign-off, as described in the next task.

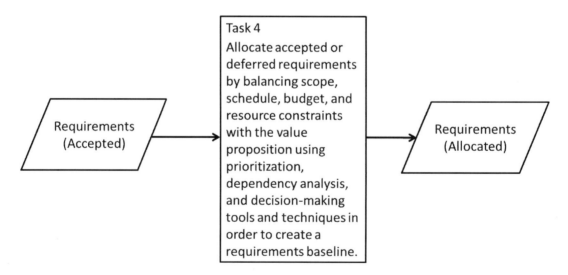

Figure 4-12: Allocate Requirements ITO

Considerations for Allocate Requirements

Prioritize

To focus on the most important and critical requirements, and to determine which should be analyzed and implemented first, prioritization must be done. It is a process of ranking requirements relative to each other, using criteria of importance to stakeholders, such as:

- Value
- Cost

- Difficulty of implementation
- Regulatory
- Risk

All requirements are not created equal. Therefore, the business analyst, with the assistance of the project manager and project sponsor, should determine the criteria by which each requirement will be reviewed in relationship to its value to the business and its importance to the stakeholder.

A number of important criteria that are frequently used for prioritizing requirements are:

Basis for Prioritization	
Business Value	Uses a cost-benefit analysis to judge a requirement's value and therefore its priority. High-value requirements may be addressed first to get financial or other value sooner.
Cost	Prioritizes requirements based on financial or opportunity costs.
Difficulty	Prioritizes requirements based on difficulty of fulfilling them. Requirements that are easiest to implement may be prioritized in order to learn about the product at a lower risk.
Regulatory	Used when compliance issues or demands are placed on an organization. These may rank higher than internal priorities, often because of potential financial penalties, or because the corporate image may be at stake.
Risk	Selects requirements based on the highest project risks to focus on them first. This helps ensure that if the risks materialize, they are discovered early, usually at a lower cost.

Figure 4-13: Requirements Prioritization Criteria

These are often challenged in facilitating a requirement prioritization:

- **Non-negotiable demands** – stakeholders who rank everything a high priority or who have trouble making choices, and those who may not realize the importance of making tradeoffs.
- **Unrealistic tradeoffs** – overestimates by the solution builders of the complexity or difficulty of implementing may unduly influence prioritization.

The plan for prioritization should be addressed in the Requirements Management Plan and include information on who will be included and has a say in requirements prioritization. The business analyst will lead the effort to get resolution to requirements prioritization issues. Focusing on the project objectives and scope can often offer resolution. Continued conflicts in requirements priority should be escalated to the project sponsor. Keep the discussion with the project sponsor at high-level requirements.

Dependencies

Record any dependencies and inter-relationships between requirements. This helps to plan the order of analyzing and developing a solution and to allocate requirements effectively. For example, assume a mortgage company is creating a new web-based application process. The company requires applicants to have a login and password to be able to save and retrieve their application. All of the online application requirements are then dependent on the login function and its related requirements. Understanding this relationship will ensure that the requirements get allocated in a way that supports product development.

Common requirements relationships are provided in *Figure 4-21* in the tool description in part 2 of this chapter.

Allocated Requirements

Requirements may be allocated to a solution component, a specific release (or phase), or a combination of both.

A component is a segment or part of a solution and it may be technical or non-technical. Since typical solutions include multiple components each having several requirements, the allocation process implies costs for implementing them.

Considerations for allocating requirements and making tradeoffs are:

- **Available Resources**. Cost and people constraints will limit what can be produced and will influence allocation.
- **Constraints on the Solution**. Other constraints, such as government regulation or business policies may dictate allocation or priority of requirements.
- **Dependencies between Requirements**. Some components may need to be implemented first to enable others. Example: a secure login capability to permit online banking transactions.

Release planning facilitates the decision-making involved in allocating requirements. Factors that guide release planning include:

- Overall project budget
- Time constraints
- Resource constraints
- Training schedule
- Ability for the business to absorb changes in a certain timeframe

Allocation decisions should be captured in the Requirements Traceability Matrix. This will allow for easier management, reporting, and communication of requirements based on solution component and/or release.

Techniques – *Allocate Requirements*

Decision Making Tools and Techniques	Includes:
Tools and techniques to facilitate a group in order to understand options and agree upon a selected course of action.	- Consensus Building - Delphi Technique - Multi-Voting - Nominal Group Technique - Options Analysis - Weighted Criteria
Prioritization Tools and Techniques Tools and techniques used to facilitate determining and documenting the priority (or desirability) of many options.	**Includes:** - High, Medium, Low - MoSCoW - Multi-voting - Weighted Criteria
Valuation Tools and Techniques *(covered in Needs Assessment domain)* Tools and techniques used to determine the value of the potential solution to the organization.	**Includes:** - Cost-Benefit Analysis - Force Field Analysis - Kano Model - Net Promoter Score - Purpose Alignment Model - SWOT Analysis - Value Stream Map

Output: *Requirements (Allocated)*

Requirements that are allocated to solution components and/or project phases for release. The allocation information should be included in the Requirements Traceability Matrix.

PMBOK® Guide References

More information on the Allocate Requirements can be found in the *PMBOK® Guide*:

- Section 5.5 – Validate Scope

- Section 5.6 – Control Scope

Analysis – Exercise 2

Write the mnemonic letters for the eight tasks of Analysis, and then complete the missing words for each task in the blanks provided below.

Analysis Tasks	Mnemonic
1. _____ _____	_____
2. _____ _____ _____ _____ _____	_____
3. _____ _____ _____ __ _____	_____
4. _____ _____	_____
5. Get Requirements _____	_____
6. Write Requirements _____	_____
7. _____ Requirements	_____
8. Elaborate and Specify _____ _____	_____

Analysis – Exercise 3

Match the requirements state (status) with the description provided below.

A. Elicited

B. Analyzed

C. Prioritized

D. Accepted

E. Deferred

F. Rejected

G. Allocated

___ 1. Mary has just prepared a final list of requirements that she will present for sign-off.

___ 2. Bert just completed reviewing the system manual for the legacy system and documented several requirements that he found in the process.

___ 3. Aaron has finished compiling scores from the weighted criteria matrix that key stakeholders completed.

___ 4. Kendra has communicated to Joe that his requirement will not be included in this project. He should consider making a business case for a new project if he wishes to pursue it.

___ 5. Jeff has created a report indicating requirements that will be addressed in Release 2 of the solution.

___ 6. Crystal has completed data models and process models for the requirements related to opening an account.

___ 7. Kelly has confirmed that the requirements elicited in the focus group are within the scope of the solution.

Task 5 – Get Requirements Sign-off

Obtain sign-off on Requirements Baseline using decision-making techniques in order to facilitate stakeholder consensus and achieve stakeholder approval.

EACASSVA

"Everything As Calm As Singing Saints Visualizing Acceptance"

The Requirements Baseline is the approved version of requirements for implementation by the project team. Sign-off is needed to indicate this approval. The process and information required to get sign-off is going to vary from project to project. Adaptive (agile) projects utilize the product backlog to indicate approved, prioritized user stories. The process and people included for sign-off should be addressed in the Requirements Management Plan.

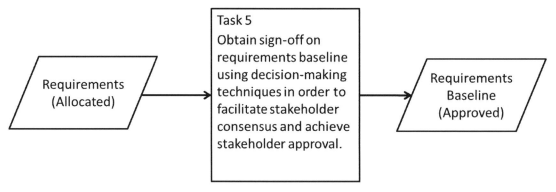

Figure 4-14: Get Requirements Sign-off ITO

Considerations for Get Requirements Sign-off

Stakeholder Approval

The process of signing off is a formal way for authorized stakeholders to approve requirements. It signifies that requirements are complete, accurate, and understandable. Stakeholder approval levels should be available in the Stakeholder Register and Requirements Management Plan. Organizational standards may dictate the sign-off format and documentation. Normally sign-offs are done in person with the authorized decision-maker(s). Approvals can be verbal, written, or electronic, according to organizational standards and preferences.

Note that stakeholders may have specific authority over specific requirements, and not the complete package. In that case, the requirements package should include a list of the requirements the stakeholder is authorized to approve. A companion list of non-authorized requirements is a good practice. Whether approved by one person or several, all requirements need sign-off before they are considered approved and finished.

Requirements Conflicts

Stakeholders may have concerns that need be resolved before the requirements can be approved. The business analyst is responsible for resolving requirements conflicts. This may include facilitating consensus amongst stakeholders using negotiation skills. Often this requires being able to understand the source of the conflict and helping stakeholders focus on the project objectives and goals. The project sponsor will have ultimate authority for requirements sign-off and should be consulted if resolution cannot be attained through consensus building activities. The business analyst should always be prepared with a recommendation that supports the project's objectives and goals when escalating issues.

Techniques – *Get Requirements Sign-off*	
Decision Making Tools and Techniques Tools and techniques to facilitate a group in order to understand options and agree upon a selected course of action.	**Includes:** - Consensus Building - Delphi Technique - Multi-Voting - Nominal Group Technique - Options Analysis - Weighted Criteria

Output: *Requirements Baseline (Approved)*
Requirements approved by stakeholders via a sign-off, ready for additional use in analysis or development work. The collection of approved requirements makes up the Requirements Baseline. The approval information should be included in the Requirements Traceability Matrix.

PMBOK® Guide References

More information on the Get Requirements Sign-off can be found in the *PMBOK® Guide*:

- Section 5.5 – Validate Scope

- Section 13.3 – Manage Stakeholder Engagement

- Section 13.4 – Control Stakeholder Engagement

Task 6 – Write Requirements Specifications

Write requirements specifications using process (such as use cases, user stories), data, and interface details in order to communicate requirements that are measurable and actionable (that is, suitable for development).

EACAS̲VA

"Everything As Calm As Singing Saints Visualizing Acceptance"

The approved requirements in the Requirements Baseline may not yet be "suitable for use" by the development team. More work is needed to progressively elaborate on the requirements and provide more specificity. Many of the tools and techniques used in analyzing requirements will help to further specify requirements.

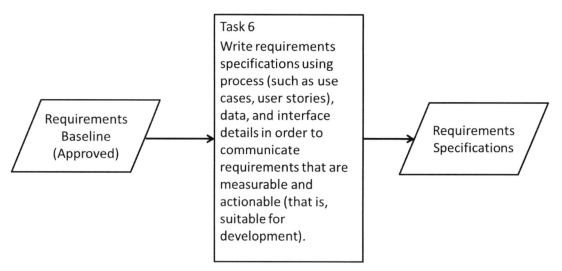

Figure 4-15: Write Requirements Specifications ITO

Considerations for Write Requirements Specifications

User Interactions

Requirements specifications often take the form of user interaction specifications as they provide requirements that are "measurable and actionable." They provide a level of detail so that a solution can be designed, coded, and tested to ensure the solution meets the requirement. A tester will need to observe the expected behavior of the system in order to confirm the requirement has been met. Specifications should focus on the interaction of the solution with the user and the transformation of data throughout a process. Use cases provide a great foundation for understanding and articulating these interactions. Data models and user interface diagrams complement the use cases to provide a holistic view of the expected system behavior.

Project Approach

An adaptive (agile) project will rely on user stories to document stakeholder requirements. The specifications for those requirements will be developed in the iteration in which the user story has been selected for development. The specification process will often be less formal and include the entire project team. The self-organizing project team will determine the level of specificity needed to develop and test the user story. This will often be accomplished in a Joint Application Design (JAD) session. The team will decide the documentation needed to support development throughout the sprint.

Techniques – *Write Requirements Specifications*

Data Analysis Tools and Techniques	Includes:
Tools and techniques used to discover, understand, and articulate data requirements for a solution.	- Data Dictionary - Data Flow Diagram - Data Models - State Diagrams and Tables
Interface Analysis Tools and Techniques Helps define boundaries of a system by defining the other systems that provide functionality, inputs, and outputs. This is an important tenet of systems theory, which the PMI-PBA exam may test you on. A practical outcome of this technique is that interactions between systems are better defined and smoother interactions result.	**Includes:** - Interoperability - Prototypes - Report Table - Storyboarding - System Interface Table - Wireframes and Display-Action-Response
Process Analysis Tools and Techniques Tools and techniques used to understand and document processes in order to elicit and capture process related requirements.	**Includes:** - CRUD Matrix - Data Flow Diagrams - Dependency Graphs - Events - Process Models - Sequence Diagrams - Use Cases - User Stories

Output: *Requirements Specifications*

Requirements have sufficient detail and supporting information that the solution development team can design, develop, and test to confirm requirements have been satisfied.

PMBOK® Guide References

More information on the Write Requirements Specifications can be found in the *PMBOK® Guide*:

- Section 5.2 – Collect Requirements

Analysis – Exercise 4

Let's try something a little bit different this time. The crossword puzzle below contains words from Analysis tasks. See if you can fill in the blanks. You may find it helpful to first write out the task names with the aid of the mnemonic provided at the beginning of this chapter. The solution is available towards the end of this chapter.

Analysis Tasks

ACROSS

1 Get Requirements _____ (task 5)
7 _____ Requirements (task 2)
8 _____ Requirements (task 1)
9 _____ Requirements (task 2)

DOWN

1 Write Requirements _____ (task 6)
2 _____ Requirements (task 4)
3 _____ Requirements (task 7)
4 _____ Requirements to Product Scope (task 3)
5 Specify _____ Criteria (task 8)
6 _____ Requirements (task 2)

Task 7 - Validate Requirements

Validate requirements using tools and techniques such as documentation review, prototypes, demos, and other validation methods in order to ensure requirements are complete, accurate and aligned with goals, objectives, and value proposition.

EACASS<u>V</u>A

"Everything As Calm As Singing Saints Visualizing Acceptance"

Validating requirements is done to make sure that a product, service, or result meets the needs of the stakeholders.

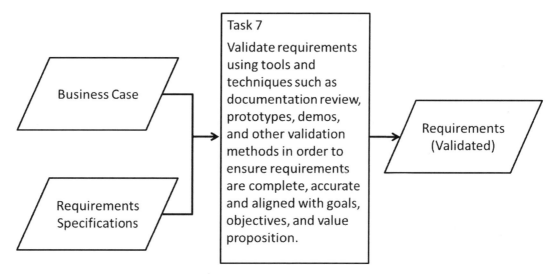

Figure 4-16: Validate Requirements ITO

Considerations for Validate Requirements

Identify Assumptions

Part of validating requirements is to align them with the business needs to ensure they provide business value. It may be necessary to make assumptions about the proposed value and benefits of a solution. Those assumptions may be a risk and should be managed as such.

Define Measurable Evaluation Criteria

If the criteria to measure benefits of a solution were not included in the business case, they will need defining to enable measurement of the benefits of implementing the solution. Stakeholders need to feel confident that what they are validating will have benefit and that it can be measured.

Determine Business Value

Individual requirements can be assessed for their potential value as an aid to validating them. Stakeholders will likely not validate requirements if they don't produce value, unless other requirements that will deliver value are dependent on them. Value can be either objective (like cost or time savings) or subjective (like increased morale).

Determine Dependencies for Benefits Realization

As stated above, some requirements are necessary because they enable others. Value can be assigned by virtue of the relationship of one requirement to another.

Evaluate Alignment with Business Case and Opportunity Cost

If requirements are valuable, but not aligned with a given business case, they should be considered for removal from the solution. They could also be justified in a separate business case. All requirements should be traceable back to the business case for a given project, and should minimize the opportunity cost of implementing a solution. Opportunity cost is the value of an option that was *not* selected in order to do something else. When considering requirements, opportunity cost refers to the value that would have been achieved by implementing requirements that were not selected in order to implement others.

For example, given a choice between Requirement A which is expected to provide $50,000 in value to the organization, and Requirement B which is expected to provide $35,000 in value to the organization, the opportunity cost of choosing Requirement A is $35,000, and the opportunity cost of choosing Requirement B is $50,000. That is, Requirement B has a higher opportunity cost.

Techniques – *Validate Requirements*	
Validation Tools and Techniques *(covered in Evaluation domain)* Tools and techniques used to validate the effectiveness of a solution.	**Includes:** - Day-in-the Life (DITL) Testing - Exploratory Testing - Given-When-Then - Integration Testing - User Acceptance Testing
Verification Tools and Techniques *(covered in Evaluation domain)* Tools and techniques used to verify the work product.	**Includes:** - Desk checking - Inspection - Peer Review - Test - Walk-through

        PMI-PBA Certification Study Guide

Output: Requirements (Validated)
Validated requirements are those that are valuable to stakeholders and support organization goals and objectives. They can be traced back to the goals and objectives they support and are in scope for a project.

PMBOK® Guide References

More information on the Validate Requirements can be found in the *PMBOK® Guide*:

- Section 5.5 – Validate Scope

- Section 5.6 – Control Scope

Task 8 – Elaborate and Specify Acceptance Criteria

Elaborate and specify detailed metrics and acceptance criteria using measurement tools and techniques for use in evaluating whether the solution meets requirements.

EACASSV**A**

"Everything As Calm As Singing Saints Visualizing Acceptance"

This task is about being able to answer the question "is the solution ready for deployment?" You may think that the solution is ready when every in-scope requirement has been satisfied. Perhaps the requirements have technically been satisfied, yet something is missing. Or, perhaps some requirements have not been satisfied. This does not necessarily mean that the solution cannot be deployed. Specifying acceptance criteria means identifying and articulating how stakeholders will determine that the solution is ready for use. This task is <u>not</u> how to evaluate the project (processes, schedule, and budget).

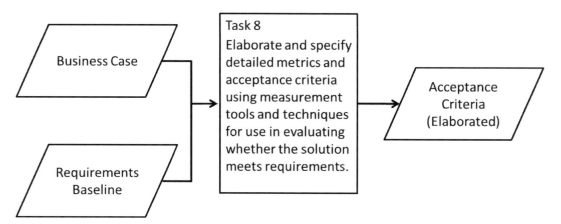

Figure 4-17: Specify Acceptance Criteria ITO

Considerations for Elaborate and Specify Acceptance Criteria

Factors for Acceptance

Acceptance criteria is a set of conditions that must be met before the deliverables are accepted. The decision about whether to "accept" a deliverable and the criteria represent the minimum level a solution must meet. For instance, a new order entry system must be capable of adding a new order, and adding items to the order.

Acceptance criteria likely is already evident in existing project documentation. Look to the project's objectives and goals, including Key Performance Indicators (KPI) which are metrics used to evaluate how well an organization is meeting its objectives as identified in the business case and project charter. How can these be used to determine solution readiness? You can also look to the project and quality requirements for the project. These requirements may directly serve as acceptance criteria. Additional criteria may be found in the use cases or user stories for the solution.

Tools and techniques related to acceptance criteria include Planguage and Service Level Agreements (SLAs). These are discussed in more detail in the second part of this chapter. What these two have in common is that they provide specific expected measures of product expectations such as availability, response time, and support expectations.

Acceptance criteria is for the acceptance of the solution. In other words, it is overall acceptance that the solution is ready for implementation and the business can anticipate that the solution will meet expected outcomes. It is not about specific requirements or defects. A system may be implemented with known issues and still meet the objectives of the project. It is not about the project metrics. A solution may be implemented on time and on budget, yet not be ready to meet the objectives of the project. Establishing acceptance criteria for solution readiness helps to keep focus on achieving business results, the primary purpose for the project.

The acceptance criteria established here will be instrumental in the Evaluation domain, Task 2 – Analyze Solution Gaps.

Techniques – *Elaborate and Specify Acceptance Criteria*	
Measurement Tools and Techniques Tools and techniques used to measure solution performance after implementation.	**Includes:** - Metrics such as Key Performance Indicators (KPIs) - Service Level Agreement (SLA) - Planguage
Validation Tools and Techniques *(covered in Evaluation domain)* Tools and techniques used to validate the effectiveness of a solution.	**Includes:** - Day-in-the Life (DITL) Testing - Exploratory Testing - Given-When-Then - Integration Testing - User Acceptance Testing

Output: *Acceptance Criteria (Elaborated)*
Criteria that will be used to determine the readiness of the solution for implementation.

PMBOK® Guide References

More information on the Elaborate and Specify Acceptance Criteria can be found in the *PMBOK® Guide*:

- Section 4.6 – Close Project or Phase

- Section 5.5 – Validate Scope

Analysis – Exercise 5

Okay, last time! Can you name the tasks of the Analysis domain in order? Let's see if you can do it without any hints.

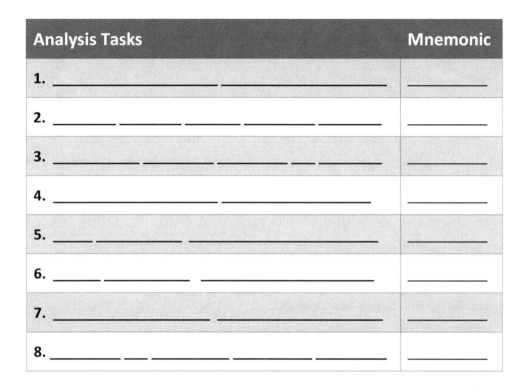

Analysis Tasks	Mnemonic
1. _____ _____	_____
2. _____ _____ _____ _____	_____
3. _____ _____	_____
4. _____ _____	_____
5. ___ _____ _____ ____	_____
6. ___ _____ _____ ___	_____
7. _____ _____	_____
8. _____ __ _____ _____	_____

Test Tip: PMI® has not published a formal list of Inputs, Tools and Techniques, and Outputs (ITTO's) for the tasks outlined in the *PMI-PBA Examination Content Outline*. Also, they have not published short task names for each. The test will not specifically test you on the ITTO's provided within this guide. Learning these tasks and their tools and techniques WILL help you in answering situational questions.

Example

Won't see: What are the tools and techniques of the Get Requirements Sign-off task?

Will see: Sally has elicited, analyzed, decomposed, and verified the requirements to be in scope. What else must she do before getting stakeholder sign-off?

PMI-PBA Practice Exam (Part 1)

This is the first practice exam for the Analysis domain. Due the amount of information and the weight of the Analysis domain on the PMI-PBA exam, we have extended the practice exam to 20 questions in two separate parts of this chapter to help you practice taking the PMI-PBA exam questions. Part 1 focuses on the tasks and concept of Analysis. Answers are listed at the end of the chapter.

1. What are the different types of requirements?
    a. Business, stakeholder, functional, non-functional and transition
    b. Business, stakeholder, solution requirements, transition, project, and quality
    c. Optional, important, critical
    d. Sponsor, stakeholder, functional, non-functional, transition, project, and quality

2. Considerations when collecting requirements include which of the following?
    a. Project charter and stakeholder register
    b. Project charter and WBS
    c. Stakeholder register and scope statement
    d. Scope statement and WBS

3. Which of the following statements about conflict is most true?
    a. Conflict should be avoided as higher performing teams are collaborative in nature.
    b. The project manager should stay out of conflicts between team members and let them work it out.
    c. Conflict can lead to increased creativity and better decision-making.
    d. The project manager should first try "smoothing" as a conflict resolution strategy.

4. The ability to influence others is a critical interpersonal skill required of business analysts and includes which of the following?
    a. The ability to get others to see the inconsistencies in their perspectives.
    b. A relentless passion and unyielding commitment to one's perspectives.
    c. The ability to understand various stakeholders' perspectives.
    d. The willingness to subordinate your goals to others' goals.

5. A requirement is best defined as:
    a. A need or want of the business to solve a problem or achieve an objective.
    b. A condition or capability that is required to be present in a product, service, or result to satisfy a contract or other formally imposed specification.
    c. A condition or capability of a product or solution that documents a problem or objective of the business.
    d. A need or necessary feature of a system that could be sensed from a position anywhere within the system.

6. The BA serving as facilitator encounters a situation such as this during a requirements workshop with a client: A 'scribe' is assigned to keep track of important discussion points and action items. Several times during the morning session, issues are deferred to a 'Parking Lot.' The scribe makes no visible gesture that the issue has been noted. What should the facilitator do?
    a. Mention to the scribe's supervisor that the scribe should be excluded from future workshops.
    b. Indicate to the scribe during the meeting that 'Parking Lot' issues should be acknowledged, and suggest writing them on a white board or flip chart.
    c. Wait until after the workshop has ended for the day, and out of the client's presence to provide coaching to the scribe with respect to meeting procedures and artifacts.
    d. Start tracking 'Parking Lot' issues independently so that they are not lost.

7. Which of the following best describes what is needed in order to prioritize requirements?
    a. Assessment of the proposed solution
    b. Allocated requirements
    c. Validated solution
    d. Requirements Management Plan

8. How are transition requirements defined?
    a. Communication with technical operational teams
    b. The same way all requirements are defined
    c. Through a transition decision matrix
    d. Through requirements validation

9. Eliana is a business analyst working on the requirements for a new marketing system. When she mentions to her manager that the stakeholders already have a commercial software package in mind, her manager tells her that they should plan to build custom software. She explains the situation to the subject matter experts, who at first express concern. Eliana explains something that puts their mind at rest. What does Eliana explain to them?
    a. That the decision will not be made until the requirements are captured and understood. At that time she will recommend the purchase of the commercial software to the project manager and sponsor.
    b. That the decision will not be made until the requirements are captured and understood. At that time she will compare multiple proposed solutions to see which best meets the requirements.
    c. That she will ensure that the vendor discusses the situation with her manager to emphasize the benefits of buying a package and the disadvantages of custom solutions.
    d. That she will ensure that the vendor discusses the situation with the sponsor to emphasize the benefits of buying a package and the disadvantages of custom solutions.

10. As the lead BA you are analyzing requirements collected by another BA on a big project. You run across a requirement that states "The system shall be easy for new team members to learn." What should you suggest to the BA regarding this requirement?
    a. Ask the BA to work with the stakeholder to prioritize the requirement.
    b. Tell the BA "good job."
    c. Suggest that the BA discuss the requirement with the stakeholder to get specific criteria on what is "easy to learn."
    d. Ask the BA to restate the requirement with specific criteria on what is "easy to learn."

Part 2 – Techniques for Analysis

The tools and techniques below are those that may be most helpful in the Analysis domain. Importantly, the tools and techniques are not domain or task specific; they may be used for more than one task and in more than one domain. It will be necessary for the person doing the business analysis work to determine which tools to use and when.

Category	Technique
Analytic Tools and Techniques	
Tools and techniques used to analyze the business and requirements for further understanding of the situation and solution requirements.	
	Decomposition
	Dependency Analysis
	Gap Analysis
	Impact Analysis
	Progressive Elaboration
	Risk Analysis
Business Rule Analysis Tools and Techniques	
Tools and techniques used to discover, understand, and articulate business rules that govern the organization, its processes, and its data.	
	Business Rule Catalog
	Decision Table
	Decision Tree
Data Analysis Tools and Techniques	
Tools and techniques used to discover, understand, and articulate data requirements for a solution.	
	Data Dictionary and Glossary
	Data Flow Diagram
	Data Models
	State Diagrams and Tables
Decision Making Tools and Techniques	
Tools and techniques to facilitate a group in order to understand options and agree upon a selected course of action.	
	Consensus Building
	Delphi Technique
	Multi-Voting
	Nominal Group Technique
	Options Analysis
	Weighted Criteria (aka Multi-criteria Decision Analysis)
Elicitation Tools and Techniques	
Tools and techniques used to draw out requirements and assumptions from stakeholders through individual and group settings and from existing documentation.	
	Brainstorming
	Document Analysis
	Facilitated Workshops

Category	Technique
	Focus Groups
	Interviews
	Non-Functional Requirements Analysis
	Observation
	Prototypes
	Research
	Survey / Questionnaire
Interface Analysis *Interface analysis helps defines boundaries of a system by defining the other systems that provide functionality, inputs, and outputs.*	
	Interoperability
	Prototypes
	Report Table
	Storyboarding
	System Interface Table
	User Interface Flow
	Wireframes and Display-Action-Response
Measurement Tools and Techniques *Tools and techniques used to measure solution performance after implementation.*	
	Key Performance Indicators
	Organizational Readiness
	Planguage
	Service Level Agreement (SLA)
Prioritization Tools and Techniques *Tools and techniques used to facilitate determining and documenting the priority (or desirability) of many options.*	
	High, Medium, Low
	MoSCoW
	Voting
Process Analysis Tools and Techniques *Tools and techniques used to understand and document processes in order to elicit and capture process-related requirements.*	
	CRUD Matrix
	Data Flow Diagrams *(see Data Analysis tools)*
	Dependency Graphs
	Events (business event analysis)
	Process Models
	Sequence Diagrams
	Use Cases
	User Stories
Scope Models Tools and Techniques *(covered in Needs Assessment domain)*	
	Context Diagram

                                       PMI-PBA Certification Study Guide

Category	Technique
	Ecosystem Map
	Feature Model
	Goal Model and Business Objective Model
	Use Case Diagram
Validation Tools and Techniques *(covered in Evaluation domain)*	
	Day-in-the Life (DITL) Testing
	Exploratory Testing
	Given-Then-When
	Integration Testing
	User Acceptance Testing
Valuation Tools and Techniques *(covered in Needs Assessment domain)*	
	Cost-Benefit Analysis
	Feasibility Analysis
	Force Field Analysis
	Kano Model
	Net Promoter Score
	Purpose Alignment Model
	SWOT Analysis
	Value Stream Map
Verification Tools and Techniques *(covered in Evaluation domain)*	
	Desk Checking
	Inspection
	Peer Review
	Test
	Walk-through

Figure 4-18: Tools and Techniques for Analysis

The following pages provide additional details about the tools and techniques that may be most helpful in this domain. (Details for some techniques may be covered in a different domain as noted above.) Not all tools and techniques will be discussed at a great level of detail. The amount of information provided relates to the priority of the tool or technique on the exam. Each technique has been rated with a priority level of low, moderate, or high to help in prioritizing study. Items marked as low may appear in your certification exam; items marked moderate are likely to show up in one or two questions, and items marked high may have multiple questions relating to their use.

Analytic Tools and Techniques

Tools and techniques used to analyze the business and requirements for further understanding of the situation and solution requirements.

Analytic Tools and Techniques
Decomposition
Dependency Analysis
Gap Analysis
Impact Analysis
Progressive Elaboration
Risk Analysis

Decomposition   Priority: High

Decomposition breaks down something that is higher-level – such as functional areas, their processes, or project deliverables – into simpler subsets for the purpose of studying or analyzing it. This technique is often presented using graphical models, such as a decomposition diagram as shown below.

> **Decomposition**
>
> Breaking down something higher-level into subsets to study or analyze.

Decomposition	
Description	Decomposition is a common technique in business analysis and project management. Solution scope, organizational units, processes, and functions are examples of things that may be decomposed, or broken into smaller components to aid in analysis or understanding.
Characteristics	• Document the high-level object that needs decomposing (e.g., business functions, goals, objectives, requirements, scope) • Visually show the hierarchy representing the object being broken down (e.g., subsets or features of a deliverable) • Decompose until "sufficient" detail is reached (e.g., for a Work Breakdown Structure [WBS], decompose until activities or tasks can be estimated and tracked)

Figure 4-19: Decomposition Overview

Example

A new commission system (a solution) might be broken into data capture, reporting, and maintenance components. The data capture is decomposed into sales and invoicing, expense tracking, matching, and exceptions. Sales and invoicing is broken down into data feeds from various billing systems, and so on. See *Figure 4-20* for a visual.

> **WBS**
>
> **Work Breakdown Structure**
> A project planning technique that hierarchically breaks down deliverables and/or tasks of a project into manageable pieces.

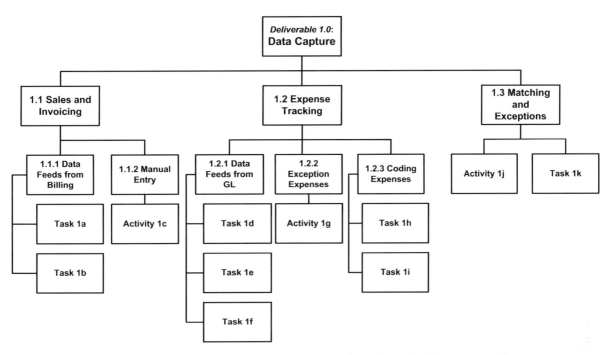

Figure 4-20: Example of a Work Breakdown Structure (WBS) used to decompose solution scope

Dependency Analysis   Priority: High

A technique used to identify and clearly articulate dependencies between two or more requirements. Common requirements dependencies are outlined below.

Relationship	Description
Subsets	A requirement may be a subset of another requirement. For example, a bank may have customers, and subsets or subtypes could include personal and commercial. They may have data and processes that are common to both, and there may be data and processes unique to each.
Implementation Dependency	Some requirements cannot be implemented until another requirement is implemented, i.e., they are dependent on the implementation of another requirement. For example, a retail organization may want to generate a report based on customers' accumulated purchases, but until the additional functional requirements to capture accumulated purchases are implemented, the report requirements cannot be addressed.
Benefit or Value Dependency	The benefit of some requirements may not be realized until other requirements are first implemented. For example, based on customer feedback, a bank may want to improve its customers' ATM experience by adding a customizable interface to reduce the number of buttons pushed, but that feature won't be available until the ATM software is upgraded.

Figure 4-21: Requirements Relationships

Gap Analysis   Priority: High

As with much business analysis work, knowing the current state can help understand how far apart that state is from the desired state or objectives. Here the specific new capabilities to meet the business need are identified. Like the current state, models may need to be developed to depict the desired future state.

Gaps are the differences between the current and future states. Gap analysis compares the states to identify differences between them. It can then be determined whether the organization has the capability to address the business need, or whether a project is needed to add the capability.

> **Gap Analysis**
>
> Comparing the current and future states of an organization to identify changes needed to meet business needs.

Example. Our example of automating a commission process is part of a corporate strategy of efficiency and cost containment.

Current state: extensive manual processing, with heavy use of spreadsheets and human interpretation, subject to bias and error.

Future state: 1) automated processing of all routine commissions, 2) fewer exceptions, and 3) no delays in processing routine commissions to resolve exceptions.

Gap: automated and "cleaner" inputs to decrease exceptions, automated calculations using programmed algorithms, workflow that separates exceptions from routine processing, new accounting policy to process all routine commissions and isolate the exceptions.

Impact Analysis   Priority: High

Changes to requirements are much easier to analyze if the impact of the change is known. Tracing to related requirements and development components permits a quick review of potentially affected changes to understand the impact.

Progressive Elaboration   Priority: High

This approach to planning accounts for the iterative nature of planning; it allows for more detailed planning to be done as more becomes known. For example, requirements tend to be very high-level early in the life of a project. As more information becomes available and more is known, requirements are able to be more specific and detailed, i.e., progressively elaborated.

Risk Analysis   Priority: High

Risks are uncertain events or conditions that will have an impact, positive or negative, on one or more project objectives. This technique is usually done in planning.

Risk Analysis	
Description	Process of identifying and analyzing risks related to a program, project, or process to understand the impacts and develop appropriate responses. May be positive or negative.
Characteristics	Responses for negative risk events: • Accept – no change to plan • Transfer – give to third party • Avoid – change probability to 0% • Mitigate – lessen probability and/or impact Responses for positive risk events: • Accept – no change to plan • Share – split some of benefit • Exploit – change probability to 100% • Enhance – increase probability and/or impact

Business Rule Analysis Tools and Techniques

Business rules are important internal regulations to understand since they affect one or more processes, and requirements must support and not contradict them. In practice, business rules are often mixed in with requirements for a project, but business rules are independent concepts that apply across all projects.

Business rules are operating principles or self-imposed constraints that apply across all projects and systems. They constrain, define, or enable the organization to function. They are specific, actionable, and testable (vs. policies, which support goals, but are non-actionable). Business rules are also atomic (i.e., can't be broken down further) and are independent of any one process. They should be uniquely identified and documented independently of their enforcement. They are maintained to allow change and adaptation as the business changes.

Business Rule Analysis Tools and Techniques
Business Rule Catalog
Decision Table
Decision Tree

Business Rule Catalog   Priority: High

A document containing a complete list of business rules. The list may include the rule description, examples, related rules, references, notes, and assumptions for each.

Decision Table   Priority: High

A tool used to document business rules in a tabular format. The table provides an easy way to document all factors that may impact the processing of a decision. For example, age, residency, and military service all are contributing factors to determine the cost of a hunting or fishing recreational license in the state of Washington. The decision table simplifies the processing of these business rules to determine the correct license price.

Decision Tree   Priority: High

A decision tree is useful in documenting complex business rules graphically in a hierarchical structure. This may be used in conjunction with a decision table to analyze and document complex business rules.

Data Analysis Tools and Techniques

Tools and techniques used to discover, understand, and articulate data requirements for a solution.

Data Analysis Tools and Techniques
Data Dictionary and Glossary
Data Flow Diagram
Data Models
State Diagrams and Tables

Data Dictionary and Glossary   Priority: High

Data dictionaries are a type of requirements documentation that catalogs the attributes of specific data objects. They may be recorded using simple tools like word processors, or more elaborate tools for generating models. In general, they are used to foster communication between the business and project team. Data dictionaries are typically refined into more detailed data models when used for supplemental data documentation (covered later).

Data Dictionary and Glossary	
Description	Key items are formally recorded to identify **terminology** and corresponding **definitions** used by the organization. Also defines the **data used** or needed by an organization, including both high-level and more complex data definitions. **Goal**: Gain stakeholder consensus about the data needed and the terminology used for an organization.
	• **Glossary** Contains terms and unique, formal definitions for them, plus any synonyms or aliases. Once recorded and agreed upon, the glossary brings stakeholders into consensus about the terminology for a project and beyond. o *Example*: **Customer** – a person or business who inquires about our products or makes a purchase. <u>Alias</u>: Client • **Data Dictionary** Formal definitions of individual data items and groups. Includes meanings and ranges of permissible values (i.e., constraints).

Figure 4-22: Data Dictionary and Glossary Overview

Data Flow Diagram   Priority: Moderate

Data Flow Diagrams (DFDs) are described as "data centric" although they also have a heavy process component. The processes are shown in context of the data that flows into and out of the process, and is stored by the system. Like process maps and data models, these diagrams were created to show what the business does with its processes and data, and to document requirements for a system.

Data Flow Diagrams	
Description	Data Flow Diagrams (DFDs) combine processes, systems, and data to show how data flows through a solution. They show the relationships between systems, and actors, and the data that is exchanged and manipulated over the course of one or many processes. It is a model that can be used after business data diagrams, process flows, and an ecosystem map have been created. (Business Analysis for Practitioners: A Practice Guide, PMI.)
Characteristics	1. **External Entities** (also called 'external agents' or just 'actors') are people or other systems that interact with the system. Shown on a DFD as a square. 2. **Data Process** or the processes within the system. Shown as circles or rounded rectangles. 3. **Data Flows** show data flowing into and out of the processes. Shown by single lines with arrows indicating direction of the flow. 4. **Data Stores** show where and when the information is stored in the system. Shown as open rectangles with labels. o *Example*: See *Figure 4-24* below.

Figure 4-23: Data Flow Diagrams Overview

Example Data Flow Diagram

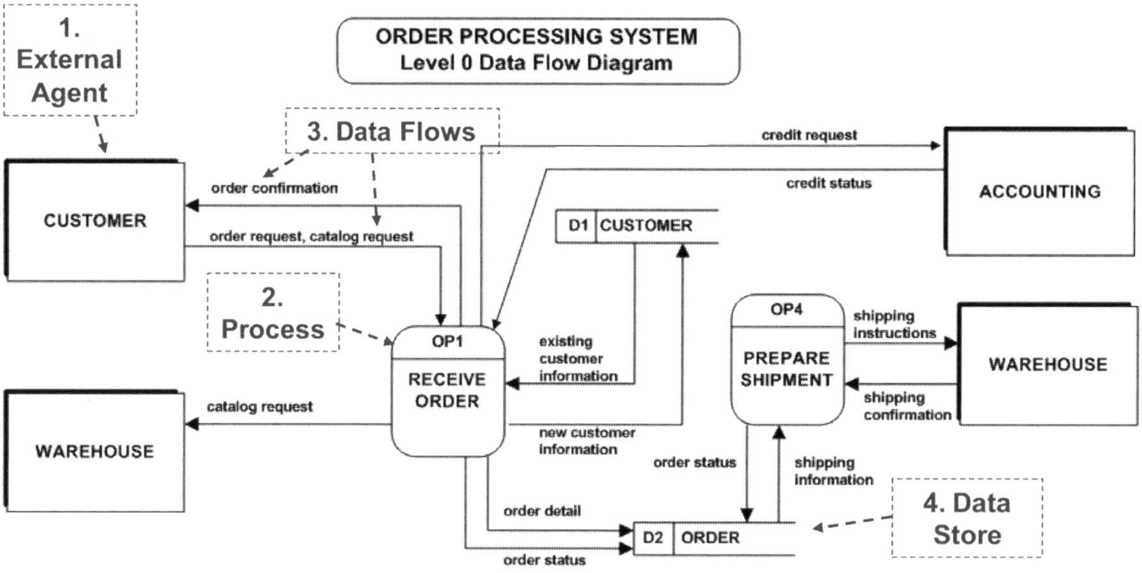

Figure 4-24: Data Flow Diagram Example

Note: Numbers correspond to elements in *Figure 4-23*: Data Flow Diagrams Overview

Data Models   **Priority: High**

Data models document data used in a process or system and its life cycle. Data models use standard diagramming techniques to illustrate the relationship between data and the relationship to processes. They are used to extract requirements and business rules.

Assuming you are working with a receptive and trained customer, data models can be used to validate data requirements with users. They are even more effective for communicating and collaborating on the logical and physical data models with the project and development teams.

Because of the visual nature of ERDs, it is typical for supplemental data documentation to be done in the form of text business rules and data dictionaries as previously described.

> **Data Model**
>
> A diagram used to show the relationship between data and how data is related to processes. Entity Relationship Diagrams (ERDs) are a primary type of data model.

Data Models	
Description	Document the data used in a process or system and its life cycle. They are used to illustrate relationships between data, how data is related to processes, and to help identify requirements and business rules. An Entity Relationship Diagram (ERD) is a typical type of data model.
Characteristics	• **Entity** is the term for either an entity in an ERD or a class in a class diagram. These are the basic structures of a data model, representing a person, place, thing, process, or event. Entities contain attributes, one set of which uniquely identifies each instance of them. • **Attributes** are the individual facts of interest about an entity. A data model usually includes additional information about attributes, such as allowable values, ranges of data, optionality, etc. 　○ **Name**: unique name of the attribute, including any synonyms 　○ **Value/Meanings**: any constraints on the attribute's values, such as numerical ranges, lists of allowable values, codes, etc. 　○ **Description**: definition of the attribute • **Relationships** are significant business connections between entities. They represent two business rules between entities and appear on diagrams with "cardinality" symbols 　○ **Example**: See *Figure 4-26* below.

> **Entity**
>
> The term for business data objects or pieces of information of interest. They are not references to exact objects in a database; rather, they represent the people, places, things, and concepts that are of concern to the business.

> **Attribute**
>
> An individual fact about an entity, and assigned to a specific entity.

> **Relationship**
>
> A significant business connection between entities.

Data Models	
Characteristics	• **Metadata** is "data about data" and may be constraints on attributes, volumes of instances or relationships, or other data that helps define the context of how the data will be used. • Example: See *Figure 4-26* below.

Cardinality

The degree of a relationship between entities, expressed usually as one or many on an ERD or class diagram.
Also called "multiplicity."

Figure 4-25: Data Model Overview

Example Data Models

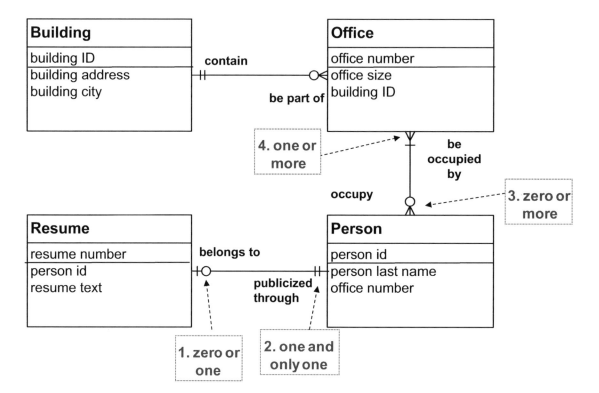

Figure 4-26: Entity Relationship Diagram Example
Note: The boxes marked 1-4 and texts are for illustration only.

                PMI-PBA Certification Study Guide

Entity Relationship Diagram Components

Like their name implies, ERDs contain three major components as shown in the example above:

Entities represent business subjects and can be people, places, things, processes, or events relevant to the business. Examples above include Building, Office, Person, and Resume.

Relationships represent significant connections between the entities. There are four types of relationships: 1) zero-to-one, 2) one and only one, 3) zero-to-many, and 4) one or more. The example shows a Building can be part of zero to many Offices. A Person is publicized through zero or one Resume. A Resume belongs to only one Person. Relationship names such as "contain" and "belongs to" in the example are optional.

Attributes are data characteristics assigned to entities, such as "building city," "office number," and "resume text" in the example above. The unique identifier attributes are special and are shown in their own area, e.g., "building ID" and person ID."

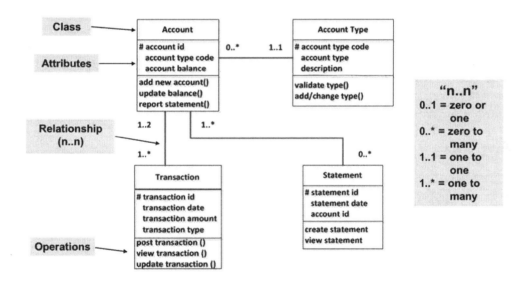

Figure 4-27: Class Model Example

Class Model Components

Classes are similar to entities and are shown by boxes.

Attributes are listed in the box as for entities, and are the facts about the class.

Operations are processes that can operate on/for the class and optionally can be listed below attributes.

Relationships are shown as lines between classes, with the symbols adjoining the lines representing the degree of each relationship. The format for relationships is $x..y$, where x is the minimum degree, and y is the maximum degree of the relationship as follows:

1..1 = A class can have one and only one association, such as an Account can have only one Account Type.

0..* = A class can have "zero to many" associations, such as an Account can have any number of statements, including none. "*" means no upper limit to the relationship.

1..* = A class has at least one association, and possibly several, like a Statement that has at least one and potentially many Accounts on it.

0..1 = means "zero or one," and is the other type of relationship possible, but is not shown in this example.

State Diagrams and Tables   **Priority: High**

State diagrams depict the various states which an entity or class flows through during its lifetime (i.e., from creation to deletion). It also shows the events or triggers that prompt the flow from one state to another, and formally labels the transitions. This type of analysis technique applies to complex entities with multiple states or "life cycles." State diagrams can help discover missing data attributes and processes involved in the various transitions.

State

Discreet condition or status that an entity/class can occupy. An object of a class has one and only one current state. Business rules dictate the states.

State Diagrams and Tables	
Description	A diagram that depicts the various "states" that an entity/class goes through during its lifetime. Transitions move an entity from state to state based on events or other triggers. Alternatively, a table may be used to note the states with transitions and triggers.
Characteristics	<ul><li>**States.** Discreet conditions or statuses that an entity/object of a class can occupy. An object has one and only one current state. States are defined by the business and become sources for requirements and rules for entering and leaving the various states.<ul><li>*Example*: A Customer may have states of New, Provisional, Regular, Preferred, Delinquent, and Former. What makes a regular customer a Preferred one is dictated by a business rule.</li></ul></li></ul>

Transition

An event or other trigger that causes an entity to move from one state to another. Business rules dictate which transitions are valid for which states.

State Diagrams and Tables
• **Transitions**. An event or other trigger that causes an entity to move from one state to another. Again, business rules dictate which transitions are valid for which states.

Figure 4-28: State Diagrams Overview

Example State Diagram

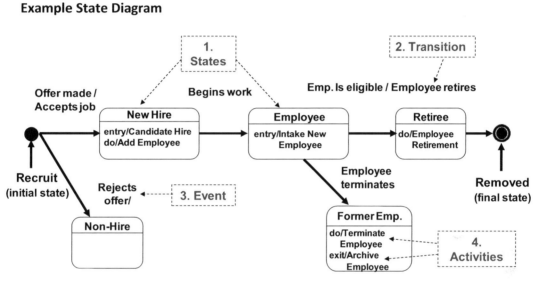

Figure 4-29: State Diagram Example

Initial State	Event / Transition	New State	Activities
Recruit	Accept job	New Hire	Candidate Hire, Add Employee
Recruit	Rejects Offer	Non-Hire	
New Hire	Begins Work	Employee	Intake New Employee
Employee	Terminates	Former Employee	Terminate Employee, Archive Employee
Employee	Retires	Retiree	Employee Retirement

Figure 4-30: State Table Example

> **State Diagrams and Tables** contain the following major components:
>
> 1. **State** – the given states to which an entity can transition.
> 2. **Transition** – the process that moves the entity to a new state.
> 3. **Event** – a trigger or pre-condition that initiates the transition.
> 4. **Activity** –an activity that occurs when the entity is in the state (Entry/, Do/, *event*/, Exit/).

Decision Making Tools and Techniques

Tools and techniques to facilitate a group in order to understand options and agree upon a selected course of action.

Decision Making Tools and Techniques
Consensus Building
Delphi Technique
Multi-Voting
Nominal Group Technique
Options Analysis
Weighted Criteria (aka Multi-criteria Decision Analysis)

> **Decision Making Mnemonic**
>
> **C**rafty **D**eals **M**ake **N**ew **O**ptions **W**orthy

Consensus Building   Priority: High

Although Consensus Building is called out as a specific tool or technique in the Decision Making category in the *PMI-PBA Examination Content Outline*, this is really a general term for getting a group to generally agree. Consensus building (also known as collaborative problem-solving or collaboration) is a conflict-resolution process used mainly to settle complex, multiparty disputes. Many specific techniques (further described in Decision Making) may help lead to group consensus.

Delphi Technique   Priority: High

The Delphi Technique provides a way to gain consensus using expert opinion. Experts are asked to provide their opinions independently through a facilitator. The facilitator will coordinate anonymous feedback to responses until agreement is achieved. This is commonly used for creating estimates or getting a recommendation on a decision to be made.

Multi-Voting   Priority: High

Multi-Voting involves giving participants multiple votes for applying to a variety of options on a specific issue. The facilitator will assign a number of votes to each participant and then provide guidelines on how to use the votes. The instructions may be one vote per preferred item, or participants may be instructed that they may use multiple votes for a single item in order to give more weight to preferred selections.

Nominal Group Technique   **Priority: Low**

The Nominal Group Technique is a process that includes brainstorming to generate ideas. Voting or multi-voting is then used to rank the ideas in order to identify the most desirable options.

Options Analysis   **Priority: High**

This technique is basically analyzing various options to understand the benefits, risks, and consequences of each in order to make a selection that will bring the greatest value to the project.

Weighted Criteria   **Priority: High**

Weighted Criteria (aka multi-criteria decision analysis) is a tool used to score various options against pre-selected criteria. This technique can be used in decision making to determine the best option for moving forward, or in prioritization rank options against a quantifiable score.

Weighted Criteria (aka Multi-Criteria Decision Analysis)	
Description	Uses weighted criteria of variables for judging how alternatives accomplish the objectives. The variables used as the basis for choosing are assigned weights, such as from 1 to 100 or a percentage. The alternatives are judged on how well they support each objective, and relative weighted scores are used to calculate the best alternative.
Characteristics	Criteria - elements of importance in which to score options (e.g., cost, ease of use, speed of implementation) Weight - Each criterion identified may have different weights to be used in scoring (e.g., cost is most important and will be given twice the weight) Options - Each option under evaluation Score - Multiply the score by the weight for each criteria of each option. Sum the total weighted score of each option to determine a ranking of options in priority order.

Figure 4-31: Weighted Criteria Overview

	Usability (50%)	Cost (30%)	Speed (20%)	Weighted Score	Final Rank
Accounting Pro	4	2	5	3.6	1
GL Plus	2	5	4	3.3	2
Lawson	3	3	4	3.2	3
SAP	5	1	1	3.0	4

Figure 4-32: Weighted Criteria Example

Analysis – Exercise 6

Write the mnemonic and name for each of the **DECISION MAKING** tools and techniques in the spaces below.

Mnemonic	Tools and Techniques

Elicitation Tools and Techniques

Tools and techniques used to elicit requirements, assumptions, and constraints. Most tools relate to eliciting requirements, assumptions, and constraints from stakeholders, but they can also be elicited from existing documents.

 PMI-PBA Certification Study Guide

Elicitation Tools and Techniques
Brainstorming
Document Analysis
Facilitated **W**orkshops
Focus Groups
Interviews
Non-Functional Requirements Analysis
Observation
Prototypes (see Interface Analysis tools)
Research (aka Benchmarking) (see Problem Solving tools in Needs Assessment domain)
Survey / Questionnaire

Try this Mnemonic to aid in remembering all the Elicitation Techniques:
NO, PROm Date **IS B**ad **For W**anda

Non-Functional
Prototypes
Research
Observation
Document Analysis
Interviews
Survey
Brainstorming
Focus Group
Workshops

Brainstorming	**Priority: High**

This is a technique that promotes **divergent thinking**. Divergent refers to activities that produce a broad or diverse set of options. It works best by focusing on one problem or issue. It then uses the creative powers of a group to generate many ideas quickly to help solve the problem or resolve the issue. By contrast, convergent thinking narrows down possibilities to select the best idea or option.

Brainstorming is used extensively in requirements activities, ranging from analyzing root causes of business problems, to initial product concept, to recommended solutions. A skilled facilitator is needed to guide the group through the technique, to avoid a chaotic free-for-all of ideas. Done well, brainstorming can be a fun and engaging way to involve participants and to produce solutions quickly.

Brainstorming	
Description	A data gathering and creativity technique used to collect a variety of ideas around product and project requirements, identify risks, or solutions to issues using a group of team members or subject matter experts. Best applied in a group as it draws on the experience and creativity of all members. May include voting when used in conjunction with other group-creativity techniques.
Characteristics	Team-based approach, usually with experts with different perspectives and areas of expertise. Often includes those outside the team. Typically lead by a facilitator and may be free-form or done using a structured approach.

Figure 4-33: Brainstorming Overview

Document Analysis   Priority: High

A technique that collects requirements for an existing ("as is") system by studying and summarizing available documentation. This technique gathers details of a current system in two broad categories:

1. **Business documentation** - business plans, market studies, contracts, procedures, training guides, problem reports, suggestion logs, etc.

2. **System documentation** - process flows, data entities/attributes, business rules, reports, etc.

Document analysis can compensate for a lack of qualified Subject Matter Experts (SMEs), assuming the documentation is current. It is limited to studying an existing system and only when current documentation exists for it.

Document Analysis	
Description	Elicitation technique in which existing documentation is analyzed and information relevant to requirements is identified. Also known as current systems analysis.
Characteristics	Types of documents that may be analyzed include business plans, marketing materials, contracts or agreements, procurement documents, current process flows, logical data models, business rules repositories, software documentation, use cases, issue logs, policy and procedure documentation, and others.

Figure 4-34: Document Analysis Overview

Facilitated Workshops   Priority: High

Useful for several requirements-related purposes, facilitated workshops are a commonly accepted elicitation technique. There are widely-varying uses such as to scope, discover, define, review, prioritize, and reach closure on requirements for the solution.

Well-run workshops are one of the most effective ways to discover and define high quality requirements quickly. This general goal is also central to specific elicitation methodologies such as Joint Application Design, or JAD for short.

The need for a skilled and neutral facilitator is critical to a productive workshop, and is also one of the PMI-PBA themes. The facilitator keeps the group focused on the session objectives, and enforces discipline if needed. Agendas are especially important to rely on when meetings become emotional. The scribe role is also mentioned as a critical role for capturing the requirements generated.

Facilitated Workshops	
Description	An elicitation technique for defining product requirements in which key cross-functional stakeholders are brought together in a focused session. Structured, collaborative session is led by skilled, neutral facilitator. Carefully selected participants explore and evaluate product requirements. A primary technique for defining cross-functional requirements quickly and reconciling differences among diverse stakeholders.
Characteristics	Sometimes called joint application design/development (JAD) in software development. They bring subject matter experts (SMEs) and the development team together to improve the development process. In the manufacturing industry, quality function deployment (QFD) is another type of facilitated workshop that helps identify the most important characteristics for a new product. It starts with collecting the customer needs, referred to as the voice of the customer (VOC). Those needs are sorted, prioritized, and goals are set for achieving them. Key roles in a facilitated workshop include the facilitator and the scribe. Good facilitators: • Maintain neutrality • Keep the group on track • Ensure that all participants are able to contribute • Use techniques to help the group achieve its goal Good scribes: • Document requirements or pertinent information in the agreed-upon format • Help keep track of issues or items deferred during the session

Figure 4-35: Facilited Workshop Overview

Focus Groups   Priority: High

A facilitated workshop setting where participants are selected to provide their thoughts and attitudes about the potential solution.

Focus Group	
Description	A group of pre-qualified individuals meeting to elicit ideas and attitudes about a specific product, services, or opportunity in an interactive group environment.
Characteristics	Requires a trained moderator who prepares a handful of questions (usually 5-6) that are thrown out to the group to gauge their response. The purpose is to get insight into the diversity of ideas or expectations. It is intended to be interactive and more conversational in tone.

Figure 4-36: Focus Group Overview

Interviews involve systematic questioning of stakeholders to learn about their problems, the root causes, and the stakeholders' requirements. Interviews may be formal or informal, structured or unstructured (see below), and by individual (most common) or by group.

There are several factors that lead to successful interviews, such as:

- The knowledge of the "domain" (interview subject) by the interviewer
- Experience of the interviewer in conducting and documenting interviews
- Rapport of the interviewer with the interviewee
- The willingness of the interviewee to provide relevant information
- The interviewee's ability to understand their own requirements and what the business wants from a new system

Expect a few questions on your exam pertaining to interviews.

Open-Ended Questions

Designed to open a dialog to explore a topic or provide multiple answers. Used to elaborate and probe.

Closed-Ended Questions

Intended to elicit a single answer, such as yes/no, quantities, durations, choices, etc. Used to confirm.

Interviews	
Description	A systematic approach designed to elicit information from a person or group of people in an informal or formal setting by talking to an interviewee, asking relevant questions and documenting the responses. Successful interviews depend upon understanding the domain, experience of interviewer, skill in documenting discussion, readiness of interviewee to provide information, degree of understanding of business requirements, rapport.
Characteristics	May be **structured** with pre-defined and specific questions, or **unstructured** with ad hoc, open-ended questions. Interviews allow for full discussions and follow-up questions, as well as privacy for discussing sensitive issues.

Figure 4-37: Interview Overview

Non-Functional Requirements Analysis   Priority: *See note*

Note: Non-functional requirements analysis is not called out as a tool or technique in the PMBOK® Guide, PMI-PBA Examination Content Outline, or the Business Analysis for Practitioners: A Practice Guide. However, we feel it is important to understand this aspect of analysis to better prepare you to answer possible questions related to non-Functional requirements that are sure to appear in the exam.

Non-functional requirements document environmental conditions or qualities under which the solution must remain effective. They supplement the behavior or functionality of the solution, and so they complement the functional requirements. Examples of non-functional requirements are response time, data retention, reliability, scalability, etc.

Note: the concept of non-functional requirements applies mainly to software development. Many of the categories may also apply to non-software projects and are often expressed as Service Level Agreements (SLAs). For example, any product has "learnability" and "maintainability" components to it. Another synonymous term that may apply to these cases is "quality of service" requirements.

> **Non-functional Requirements**
>
> Environmental conditions or qualities under which the solution must remain effective. They complement the behavior or functionality of the solution.

Non-Functional Requirements Analysis	
Description	Non-functional requirements are environmental conditions or qualities under which the solution must remain effective. They supplement the functional requirements. Examples of non-functional requirements are response time, data retention, reliability, scalability, etc.
Characteristics	Examples of non-functional requirements include: • **Reliability**: Defines whether the system or software is available when needed. This category also includes **recoverability,** or the ability to recover from errors or system crashes. • **Security**: Protection of the application from unauthorized use. Covers **privacy** and **confidentiality, integrity** of data, ability to monitor application actions ("**auditability**"), and **authentication** of users. • **Performance**: Specifies the level of performance needed for the application or system. • **Data Retention**: Specifies how long the data should be kept, where, and in what format. • **Capacity**: Specifies how much traffic the system needs to be able to handle. • **Maintainability**: Defines how well the application can be changed or enhanced to meet future needs. Also covers being able to make **component changes** independently of others and without causing unexpected failures, **reusability** of components, and **testability** (including problem diagnosis). • **Transferability**: Requirements for being able to install and use an application in **multiple environments**. Covers the ease of **installing/uninstalling** software and for migrating it, plus the kinds of different environments an application can run in.

Figure 4-38: Non-functional Requirements Analysis Overview

Observation   **Priority: High**

Observation is a common elicitation technique that is used to watch people in their natural work environment. This technique is sometimes called "job shadowing" and is useful as an adjunct to other elicitation methods. For instance, it is frequently used to help fill in gaps in processes and related requirements based on what people describe verbally in interviews and requirements workshops.

> **Job Shadowing**
>
> An informal term for the observation technique. Shadowing implies a passive observer, but observation may also involve active participation.

It is also valuable when stakeholders are unwilling or unable to articulate their work or their processes. A business analyst may need to do observation to conduct basic discovery work when more routine methods prove fruitless. For example, observing SMEs on the job starts to reveal some of the exceptions they face, but can't articulate in an interview.

Depending on the situation, it may be helpful to actively participate in the job being observed. This is sometimes referred to as "participant observation." This kind of observation gives a "hands-on feel" for the work being observed, should be limited to non-expert work, and should minimally impact the business.

Observation	
Description	A means of eliciting requirements by studying people perform their jobs in their work environment. It is a means of understanding how someone does something when it is difficult for them to explain their process or they are reticent to articulate their requirements.
Characteristics	Four types: • Passive – involves just observing without interrupting the person doing the work. • Active – involves interrupting the person doing the work to ask questions or get clarification. • Participatory observation – involves the observer actually performing the work to experience a process and uncover potential hidden requirements. • Simulation – involves observation of simulated work that is created using a tool that recreates the activities, operations, or processes of a process worker.

Figure 4-39: Observation Overview

Survey/Questionnaire   Priority: High

A survey allows for collecting a large amount of both qualitative and quantitative information from people in a fairly short amount of time. Surveys or questionnaires are best used when a large number of responses to a limited set of questions are needed quickly.

> **Survey/Questionnaire**
>
> A means to elicit information and requirements from many people in a relatively short time.

The project team determines the data that needs collecting, formulates the questions, then collects and analyzes the responses. A key part of the process is determining the sample population to be surveyed, and finding a representative group of respondents to measure.

Survey / Questionnaire	
Description	A written set of questions designed to gather information from a large number of respondents in a short period of time. Includes the distribution of questions designed to elicit requirements.
Characteristics	Questions may be open- or closed-ended. **Closed-Ended** – Limited choice of answers, including "Yes/No." Because possible answers are known and limited, limited choice questions are easier to quantify and analyze than open-ended ones. **Open-Ended** – Respondents are able to answer in any way or degree they wish. Open-ended answers can provide more substance than closed-ended ones, but are more difficult and time-consuming to analyze.

Figure 4-40: Survey/Questionnaire Overview

Analysis – Exercise 7

Match the Elicitation Techniques to Examples

Examples

Elicitation Techniques

A. Brainstorming

   __ 1. Barbara has just watched Geoff complete an order.

B. Focus groups

   __ 2. Jose has drafted several questions that will be made available through the company website for customers to respond to.

C. Interviews

D. Facilitated workshop

   __ 3. Susan has asked each of the account managers to name three preferred customers to be invited to a discussion regarding the company's products.

E. Observation

   __ 4. Kent has scheduled a meeting with the chief architect to discuss potential requirements for the project.

F. Document analysis

G. Research (benchmarking)

   __ 5. Hannah has spent the afternoon visiting competitors' websites to understand the functionality they offer.

H. Surveys and questionnaires

   __ 6. Rae Lyn has completed review of system documentation for the legacy system and was able to note a number of requirements for the current project.

I. Nominal group technique

   __ 7. Martin has asked each meeting participant to write their ideas on a sticky note and post to the meeting room wall.

J. Multi-criteria decision analysis

   __ 8. Lynn has asked each participant to score each requirement for each category indicated on the score sheet provided.

   __ 9. Thomas has brought together customer service SMEs to elicit requirements.

   __ 10. Teri has handed each meeting participate five "dots" to use to vote on the requirements presented throughout the meeting.

Interface Analysis Tools and Techniques

Interface analysis helps define boundaries of a system by defining the other systems that provide functionality, inputs, and outputs. This is an important tenet of systems theory, which the PMI-PBA exam may test you on. A practical outcome of this technique is that interactions between systems are better defined and smoother interactions result.

Interface Analysis Tools and Techniques
Interoperability
Prototypes
Report Table
Storyboarding
System Interface Table
User Interface Flow
Wireframes and Display-Action-Response

Interoperability   Priority: High

Analysis to understand how applications communicate and collaborate with each other to exchange data, or complete a workflow or process.

For example, it might include analysis of the ability of a computer system to run application programs from different vendors, and to interact with other computers across local or wide-area networks regardless of their physical architecture and operating systems. Interoperability is feasible through hardware and software components that conform to open standards such as those used for the internet.

Prototypes   Priority: High

Prototypes are viewed as both an elicitation and an interface analysis technique. When used for elicitation, prototypes facilitate discovery of interfaces and related requirements, such as data and navigation. Prototypes are valuable because they produce quick and early feedback for defining requirements. They are also valuable because they emulate the end user's work environment which can stimulate participation and discussion.

> **Prototype**
>
> "Mock ups" of screens or report layouts for a proposed system in order to elicit requirements for it. Can be paper/pencil or electronic.

Prototypes can be "horizontal" or "vertical." Horizontal prototypes are shallow and don't contain much detail, but are intended to cover a wide view of a solution's functionality. Think of these as models for navigation requirements. Vertical prototypes go deeper into a narrower range of interfaces, and can be used to elicit detailed interface or data requirements.

Prototypes	
Description	A method of getting feedback on requirements early on by providing stakeholders with a working model of a product before actual construction or building. Key to prototypes is iteration: Prototypes are built and reviewed; feedback is gathered; the prototype is modified, and then reviewed again.

Characteristics	Two categorizations:
	Low-Fidelity – Pen or computer aided sketch of the user interface undergoing analysis
	High-Fidelity – A representation of a final finished product, usually completed with the same development tool that will be used to develop the solution. Although usable, they are limited in data and functionality. Types of high-fidelity prototypes include:
	   • "Throw-away" (paper and pencil)
	   • "Evolutionary" or functional (electronic) prototypes
	
	Related tools/terms:
	Wireframes – A drawing or schematic of a user interface
	Storyboarding – See description in Interface Analysis tools

Figure 4-41: Prototypes Overview

Report Table   Priority: Low

A tabular listing of requirements relating to development of a single report. May include:
- Name
- Description
- Decisions facilitated by
- Objectives
- Audience
- Trigger
- Data fields
- Data volume
- Display format
- Calculations

Storyboards   Priority: High

Storyboarding is very much like prototyping. Storyboarding will be done using low-tech techniques such as pen and paper or Visio drawing to provide a concept of a user interface early in the project lifecycle. The focus is on gaining understanding of requirements for a process based on a potential user interface.

System Interface Table   Priority: Low

A system interface table is a model of attributes that captures all of the detailed level requirements for a single system interface. A tabular listing of requirements relating to development of a system interface may include:
- Source system
- Target system
- Volume of data
- Security or other rules
- Data passed

User Interface Flow   Priority: Low

A graphical representation of pages or screens that map user navigation of the screens based on various triggers.

A user interface flow displays specific pages or screens within a functional design and plots out how to navigate the screens according to various triggers. The boxes in the diagram are the main screens in the user interface. The line show the flows allowed between screens.

Wireframes and Display-Action-Response   Priority: Low

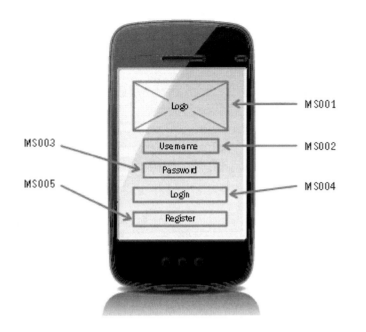

The display-action-response model is used in conjunction with wireframes or screen mockups to identify page elements in the functions. The display-action-response model details displays and interactions in a single user interface element based on wireframes (see prototype) using a tabular format, and may include:

- ID

- Description

- Display conditions (upon screen entry, upon entering information, upon saving information)

- Behaviors (upon entry, upon exit)

Figure 4-42: Wireframe Example

UI Element: Password Field

UI Element Description		
ID	MS003	
Description	A field for the user to enter their password	

UI Element Displays		
Precondition	Display	
On login screen	Display field	
No text entered	Grayed out password	
Text entered	Privacy dots are displayed per character	

UI Element Behaviors		
Precondition	Action	Response
On login screen	Select field	Keyboard appears
Text entered	Enter additional text	Privacy dots per character appear

Figure 4-43: Display-Action-Response Model

Picture Source: *Business Analysis for Practitioners: A Practice Guide*, pages 117

Display-action-response models are traced directly to wireframes, user stories, user interface flows, and data dictionaries. These models contain user interface requirements and do not need further specification.

Measurement Tools and Techniques

Tools and techniques used to measure solution performance after implementation.

Measurement Tools and Techniques
Metrics such as Key Performance Indicators (KPIs)
Organizational Readiness
Planguage
Service Level Agreement (SLA)

Metrics such as Key Performance Indicators (KPIs)   Priority: High

Metrics can be used to measure business performance. Commonly used metrics for measuring business performance are **Key Performance Indicators**, or KPIs. KPIs measure progress on strategic goals. The measures can be many things in an organization, and for BA work, it mainly involves the performance of a solution or its components. **Monitoring** is used to track a solution's performance over time.

In this technique, the benefits of a business case are compared to relevant performance metrics to assess and manage actual results. It also includes possible changes to measures to ensure they align with desired results.

Metric
A standard of measurement, often associated with a goal or the performance or progress of something.

Key Performance Indicators
Measures of progress towards strategic goals and performance.

Key Performance Indicators (KPI's)	
Description	Metrics typically defined by an organization's executives that evaluate how well an organization is doing in achieving its objectives or goals. The benefits of a business case are compared to performance metrics to assess and manage actual results. Includes possible changes to measures to ensure they align with desired results.
Characteristics	Categories may include finance, customer, employee, sustainability, etc. Most goals address more than one category.

Figure 4-44: Key Performance Indicators (KPI's) Overview

Example: A new commission system might include metrics such as the cost of producing commission reports, the speed of producing commissions, and commission error rates.

| Organizational Readiness | Priority: High |

Organizations may be assessed regarding how open they are to a new solution. This may include acceptance of and preparedness to use new technology or tools effectively, as well as openness to changes in processes.

| Planguage | Priority: High |

"Planguage" is short for Planning Language. Planguage is specifically listed as a measurement technique in the *PMI-PBA Examination Content Outline*. This is a relatively new tool in the industry and the details below will help to recognize Planguage if it does appear on your exam.

Planguage	
Description	A set of closely defined identifiers ("tags") to describe and quantify specific elements of the requirements.
Characteristics	Sample tags: - Gist - Scale - Must - Wish - Past - Plan - Meter

| Service Level Agreement (SLA) | Priority: High |

Service level agreements (SLAs) are commonly used in contract negotiations as a tool to establish terms and conditions for services to be provided. The SLA may also be used within organizations to articulate a promise to the business on the service levels to expect in relation to the product.

Service Level Agreement (SLA)	
Description	An agreement detailing the nature, quality, and scope of service to be provided.
Characteristics	May include: - Service Name - Description - Specifications - Availability period - Maintenance window - Availability percent - Restrictions - Performance thresholds

Figure 4-45: Service Level Agreement (SLA) Overview

Prioritization Tools and Techniques

Tools and techniques used to facilitate determining and documenting the priority (or desirability) of many options.

Prioritization Tools and Techniques
High, Medium, Low
MoSCoW
Multi-Voting (see Decision Making tools)
Voting
Weighted Criteria (see Decision Making tools)

High, Medium, Low   Priority: Moderate

Priority is identified as high, medium, or low. This is the most subjective prioritization technique available as each stakeholder can have a different threshold for "high". This can be mitigated by establishing clear criteria on what constitutes a high, medium, or low priority in the context of requirements.

MoSCoW   Priority: High

MoSCoW is a prioritization technique used to rate requirements or features using ratings of "**M**ust have," "**S**hould have," "**C**ould have," and "**W**on't have" as it relates to project or release scope. The business analyst can use this technique to facilitate meaningful priority setting with stakeholders by phrasing a question as it relates to the next release. For example, "You have rated this requirement as 'must,' so that means that implementation of the solution should be delayed if this requirement is not yet satisfied." The requirement can be downgraded to "should" if it does not impact the product implementation.

Voting   **Priority: Moderate**

Ideas are voted on by stakeholders to identify the preferred ranking of ideas.

Process Analysis Tools and Techniques

Tools and techniques used to understand and document processes in order to elicit and capture process related requirements.

Process Analysis Tools and Techniques
CRUD Matrix
Data Flow Diagrams (see Data Analysis tools)
Dependency Graphs
Events (business event analysis)
Process Models
Sequence Diagrams
Use Cases
User Stories

CRUD Matrix   **Priority: Low**

A CRUD Matrix (create, read, update, delete) matrix is used to cross check data and processes to ensure that a process is in place to create, read, update, and delete every entity. The matrix helps spot gaps. It is also helpful in documenting user permissions in a system.

Dependency Graphs   **Priority: High**

A dependency graph visually depicts dependencies in system requirements, functions, or components. There is not a single method or process for developing the graph.

Events (business event analysis)   **Priority: High**

The process of analyzing business events in order to determine organizational responses needed to support the business. Events may be:
- External
- Internal
- Time-based

Process Models   Priority: High

This is a technique for visually documenting work performed in an organization, including who does it and how they collaborate. Process models can be used to discover requirements, document inputs and outputs, document the business analysis approach, and uncover stakeholders.

A **process** is a series of business steps performed to accomplish a goal, done in response to a trigger, which transforms inputs to outputs. Triggers are events, which can be requests, actions, or even time (such as month-end).

Process
A series of business steps performed to accomplish a goal, done in response to a trigger that transforms inputs to outputs.

Process models can be at different stages and levels:

- **High-level** for an "As Is" view of a current process.
- **Medium-level** to understand stakeholders and handoffs between them.
- **Detailed-level** for a "To Be" view of future needs.

Process Models
A technique for visually documenting work performed in an organization, including who does it and how they collaborate. Useful for many aspects of analysis.

Process Models	
Description	A technique for visually documenting work performed in an organization, including who does it and how they collaborate. Useful for many aspects of business analysis.
Characteristics	<ul><li>**Notation Elements**<ul><li>**Activities**: Steps or tasks done to accomplish the goal of the process. Activities can be hierarchical and may be broken down into lower-level sub-processes as needed to manage the detail.</li><li>**Decisions:** Variations in the process flow that deviate and optionally come back together. Variations can have mutually exclusive or parallel flows (see forks/joins below).</li><li>**Events**: Actions, requests, or time passages outside of a process that can initiate, interrupt, or terminate the process.<ul><li>**Flow**: The direction or path of a process. Flow documents the primary (normal) and alternate paths of a process, which can split and later merge together.</li><li>**Roles**: Type of person, group, or system that participates in a process. See *Organizational Modeling* for more on roles.</li><li>**Swimlanes**: Swimlanes are segregated bands on a diagram that show which roles perform which parts of a process. Flows that cross boundaries indicate the passage of work to another role, and usually involve a "handoff" (input or output).</li></ul></li></ul></li><li>**Terminal Points:** Process models need to clearly show a beginning and end point. Often associated with events.</li><li>**Process Improvement.** A general name (often abbreviated **BPI**) for a discipline that seeks to improve process efficiency and effectiveness. Six Sigma and Lean are two process improvement approaches.</li></ul>

Figure 4-46: Process Model Overview

Activity Diagrams

The five main parts of an activity diagram are described below, with examples following:

- **Activity steps** (process) – steps in a process, indicated with rounded rectangles.
- **Control flows** – an arrow that depicts the directional flow of the activities. Also called "transitions" in earlier versions of UML.
- **Forks and joins** – used to show where concurrent or parallel processing can occur.
- **Decision points** – shows where decisions are made using an empty diamond.
- **Guard conditions** – a condition from a decision that will return either a "true" or "false." A decision can have many guard conditions, but will have only one guard condition that is "true."

Example Activity Steps

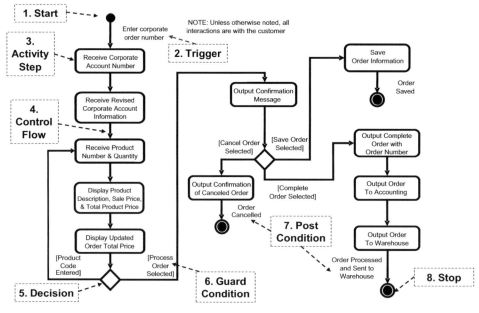

Figure 4-47: Activity Diagram Example

Example Fork and Join

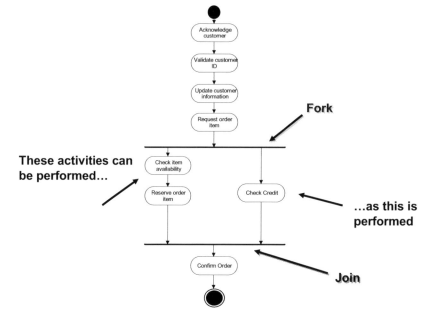

Figure 4-48: Activity Diagram with Fork and Join Example

Example Swimlane Flowchart

The main parts of a swimlane flowchart include:

- **Terminal points** – start and end positions shown by ovals.
- **Activities** and **flows** – the processes or sub-processes shown by rectangles are activities and the lines with arrows between them are flows.
- **Swimlanes** and **roles**– the horizontal bands in this case show four swimlanes for each of the roles or "actors."
- **Decisions** – diamonds show the decision; flowcharts have "Yes/No" answers.

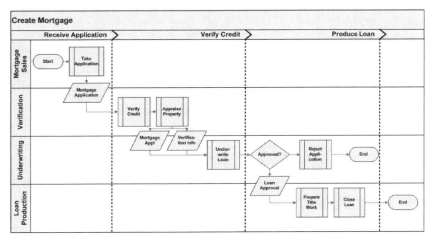

Figure 4-49: Swimlane Flowchart Example

Sequence Diagrams   **Priority: Low**

Sequence diagrams are UML (Unified Modeling Language) diagrams that show the interactions between objects in a system. An object is a specific instance of a class. The diagram name derives from the sequence of logic and message flow (i.e., interaction) that occurs to carry out a scenario. They don't show how the objects structurally relate to each other, which is done through class diagrams. Along with activity diagrams, sequence diagrams are useful to visually model use cases and scenarios.

Another use of sequence diagrams is to provide design-like details for how user interface or software elements should work (such as navigation components or messages). Designers and developers are prime users of sequence diagrams.

> **Object**
>
> An instance or example of a UML class, much more often used in design work and programming than in business analysis.

Sequence Diagrams	
Description	UML (Unified Modeling Language) diagrams that show the interactions between objects in a system. Along with activity diagrams, they are useful to visually model use cases and scenarios.
Characteristics	Sequence diagrams show object names across the top, which are derived from classes on the class diagram. They have a time sequence from left to right to show the order of actions, not specific timing. The lines flowing between objects are messages that are outputs of one object, and inputs to others. UML calls the receipt of a message by an object an event.

Figure 4-50: Sequence Diagrams Overview

                PMI-PBA Certification Study Guide

Example Sequence Diagram

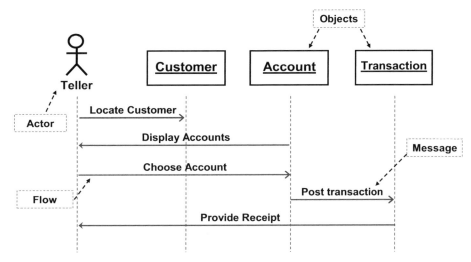

Figure 4-51: Sequence Diagram Example

Use Cases	Priority: High

Use cases describe how "actors" interact with a "system" to accomplish a business goal or respond to events. Use case models contain a visual overview component and detailed written narratives. They can be readily verified with business clients, and will effectively communicate requirements to development teams.

Scenarios are often used interchangeably with the term "use case." However, scenarios are actually just one aspect of a use case narrative, namely a primary or alternate path through the use case. A use case can be thought of as a group of related scenarios.

Primary (normal) path scenarios are the main or simplest path through the use case for the actor to reach their goal.
Alternate path scenarios are deviations from the primary path, whether they are variations, errors, or exceptions. They may reconnect with the primary path or have their own ending to the use case.

> **Use Case Model**
>
> A model that combines 1) a graphical system overview showing actors, use cases, and their interfaces, and 2) written narratives that detail the interactions between actors and the system.

> **Scenario**
>
> One instance of a use case, whether it is a primary or alternate path (or flow) through the use case.

Use Cases	
Description	Use cases describe how "actors" interact with a "system" to accomplish a business goal or respond to events. They contain "scenarios," which are primary and alternate paths through the use case for accomplishing the desired goal.

Use Cases	
Characteristics	• **Name.** Each use case and scenario needs a unique name. It should describe the process being performed using a verb-noun combination. *Examples:* Locate Customer, Add Product, Balance Ledger • **Actors**. The roles that people, groups, events, and time play in a system as they interact with use cases. Actors need unique names that match their role. *Examples:* Customer Service Representative, Accounting • **Preconditions.** A condition, state, or event that must be true for a use case to begin. *Examples:* "CSR logged in to system," "Daily transactions received" • **Post-conditions.** A condition, state, or event that will be true when a use case ends. Primary and alternate post-conditions are possible. *Examples*: "Customer located," "Ledger balanced" • **Flow of events.** The steps detailing the interaction between an actor and the system. Usually contains a **primary flow**, related **alternate flows** for variations and error handling, and **exceptions** for when a use case needs to be terminated. *Examples:* <u>Primary</u>-'Customer Located,' <u>Alternate</u>-'Customer Not Found,' <u>Exception</u>-'Locate Cancelled'

Figure 4-52: Scenario and Use Case Overview

Use Case Diagram Examples

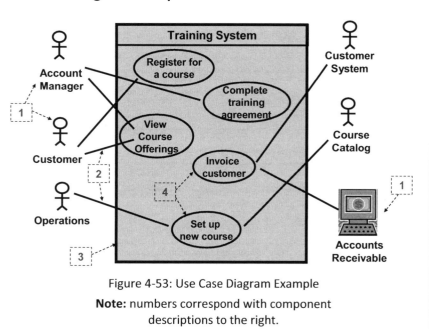

Figure 4-53: Use Case Diagram Example

Note: numbers correspond with component descriptions to the right.

Use Case Diagrams contain the following components:

1. **Actors** – must be connected to at least one use case, and may be connected to several.
2. **Association** – (interface) lines linking actors and use cases.
3. **Boundary box** – represents the system boundary; all use cases within the box are considered "in scope."
4. **Use Case** - with Generalization, Extend, and Include relationships (note the example does not show any of these relationships).

Use Case Description Example

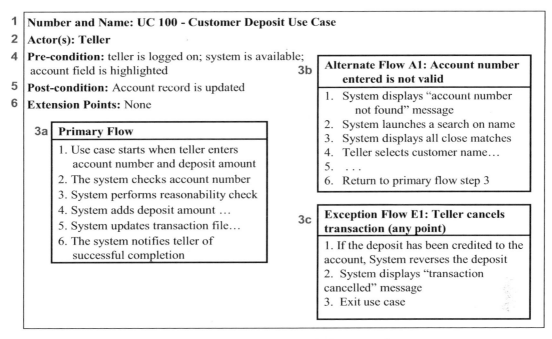

Figure 4-54: Use Case Description Example
Note: Numbers correspond with component descriptions below.

Use case descriptions contain these major components:

1. **Name** – The use case name, which should be formed like processes with a verb and noun, such as Take Order. A number is optional.

2. **Actor(s)** – The humans, systems, or events that interact in the use case.

3. **Flow of events** – The steps involved in the use case, including the Primary Flow, Alternate Flow(s) and Exception Flow(s).

4. **Pre-conditions** – The beginning state for the use case to begin.

5. **Post-conditions** – The new state that is true when a use case ends.

6. **Extension points** – Optionally, the pre-defined points in a use case for extensions or enhancements to take place. (used with the "Extend" relationship.)

| User Stories | Priority: High |

User stories are brief text statements that describe functional requirements at a high, narrative level that are generally used in adaptive (agile) projects. They focus on behavior requirements, as opposed to data or interface requirements. Their hallmark is that they are written by users to establish ownership over requirements, to facilitate communication, and to encourage participation.

Index cards are often used to record user stories, but any suitable medium could be used. Each story represents a different user need and should be "atomic" (i.e., low-level) enough to be implementable in a short time, such as 2-3 weeks. When building the system to support the user story, additional requirements need to be gathered, such as data, interface, and navigation requirements.

User Stories	
Description	Text descriptions that document functional requirements at a high, narrative level, focusing primarily on behavior. They are written by users with the intent of establishing user ownership of requirements, and the trade-off is a "light" set of requirements documentation.
Characteristics	User stories are brief descriptions of who a user is (their **role**), what the user wants to accomplish (their **goal**), and why they want to accomplish it (the **motivation** or benefit). A minimum of detail is included – only enough to reduce risk of misunderstanding by developers. A user story typically includes these components: • **Actor:** The stakeholder role who will benefit from or use the story. • **Description:** A short text description of what the user wants the system to do. • **Benefit:** The motivation or business value the story provides. **Note:** Acceptance and evaluation criteria should be defined for each user story, usually on the "back of the card" in the context of "I know this is done when…"

Figure 4-55: User Stories Overview

Example User Story

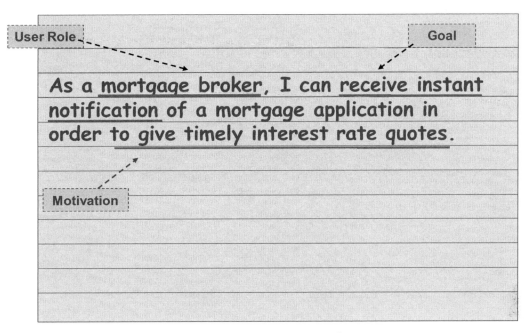

Figure 4-56: User Story Example

Analysis – Exercise 8

How many words related to high priority analysis techniques can you find in the grid below?   Write the word, category of technique, and a brief description in the space below for each word that you find.

Analysis Techniques

```
E  D  O  Y  N  Q  P  V  Q  N  X  O  H  S  P
F  U  V  A  O  O  Z  R  C  L  O  C  S  R  O
L  S  W  S  K  O  I  Q  O  D  D  E  S  I  H
W  E  U  K  K  M  H  T  W  T  C  M  L  N  S
H  R  D  X  S  R  L  Q  A  O  O  E  A  F  K
C  S  T  T  Y  O  Z  U  R  V  D  T  O  Y  R
A  T  R  Z  M  T  G  P  X  O  R  B  Y  Q  O
N  O  I  T  I  S  O  P  M  O  C  E  D  P  W
D  R  O  M  G  N  A  A  C  K  V  A  S  V  E
J  Y  D  S  Z  I  T  U  F  L  Q  G  T  B  M
P  I  W  C  U  A  D  E  T  H  G  I  E  W  O
B  O  O  X  D  R  U  S  E  C  A  S  E  D  S
F  L  F  P  P  B  V  X  B  Q  G  X  T  G  C
I  N  T  E  R  V  I  E  W  G  R  E  V  F  O
Y  L  F  D  E  D  U  I  Y  I  W  L  C  F  W
```

Word	Category	Description
1.		
2.		
3.		
4.		
5.		
6.		
7.		
8.		
9.		
10.		
11.		
12.		
13.		

PMI-PBA Practice Exam (Part 2)

This is the second practice for the Analysis domain. Due the amount of information and the weight of the Analysis domain on the PMI-PBA exam, we provided two 10-question exams to help you practice taking the PMI-PBA exam questions. Part 2 focuses on the tools and techniques used in Analysis. Answers are listed at the end of the chapter.

1. What prioritization method is typically used on an agile project?
   a. Multi-voting
   b. High, medium, low
   c. MoSCoW
   d. Stack ranked

2. A prototype that is continuously modified and updated is known as what?
   a. Exploratory prototype
   b. Evolutionary prototype
   c. A mockup
   d. Horizontal prototype

3. You are starting to recruit your participants for your focus group. You are looking for a very diverse group of people. The participants you are looking for would be categorized as what?
   a. Homogeneous
   b. Heterogeneous
   c. Esoteric
   d. Homogenized

4. You are in the middle of doing an unstructured interview. You ask the question "How many days are counted for the member's activity in the program per month?" Your stakeholder replies "I don't know." This is an example of what type of question?
   a. Open-ended
   b. Calculation
   c. Closed-ended
   d. Unstructured

5. You are in the process of selecting people to participate in a particular requirements elicitation event. Among your considerations are whether the type of questions will be open-ended or closed-ended. You are also considering the best mode of distribution. What technique are you likely to be planning?
   a. Survey/Questionnaire
   b. Focus group
   c. JAD workshop
   d. Interview

6. The following process step is NOT recommended in the interviewing process:
    a. Contact potential interviewees and explain why their assistance is needed.
    b. Organize questions in a logical order or an order of significance based on the interviewee's knowledge or subject of the interview.
    c. Use a standard set of interview questions for all interviewees in order to facilitate scoring each question.
    d. Send summary notes of the interview to the interviewee for review.

7. Allison has been going through hundreds of difficult scenarios that the business needs to understand. All of the scenarios are rules-based. What is the best document for Allison to use to represent these difficult scenarios?
    a. Decision table
    b. Hierarchy table
    c. Multiplication table
    d. Rules table

8. You are walking your stakeholders through a diagram that shows the life cycle of a class. What type of diagram are you using?
    a. Context level data flow diagram
    b. Sequence diagram
    c. State diagram
    d. Functional decomposition diagram

9. Business value, implementation difficulty, and urgency are all basis for:
    a. Requirements allocation
    b. Requirements prioritization
    c. Requirements planning
    d. Requirements status

10. Which of the following tools would be used in the Collect Requirements process?
    a. Facilitated workshops and focus groups
    b. Facilitated workshops and variance analysis
    c. Focus groups and inspection
    d. Decomposition and prototypes

Exercise Answers

Exercises 1, 2, and 5

Analysis Tasks	Mnemonic
1. Elicit Requirements	E
2. Analyze, Decompose, and Elaborate Requirements	A
3. Compare Requirements to Product Scope	C
4. Allocate Requirements	A
5. Get Requirements Sign-off	S
6. Write Requirements Specifications	S
7. Validate Requirements	V
8. Elaborate and Specify Acceptance Criteria	A

Exercise 3

A. Elicited

B. Analyzed

C. Prioritized

D. Accepted

E. Deferred

F. Rejected

G. Allocated

___ 1. Mary has just prepared a final list of requirements that she will present for sign-off **(G)**

___ 2. Bert just completed reviewing the system manual for the legacy system and documented several requirements that he found in the process. **(A)**

___ 3. Aaron has finished compiling scores from the weighted criteria matrix that key stakeholders completed. **(C)**

___ 4. Kindra has communicated to Joe that his requirement will not be included in this project. He should consider making a business case for a new project if he wishes to pursue it. **(F)**

         PMI-PBA Certification Study Guide

_____ 5. Jeff has created a report indicating requirements that will be addressed in Release 2 of the solution. **(E)**

_____ 6. Crystal has completed data models and process models for the requirements related to opening an account. **(B)**

_____ 7. Kelly has confirmed that the requirements elicited in the focus group are within the scope of the solution. **(D)**

Exercise 4

Analysis Tasks

Solution:

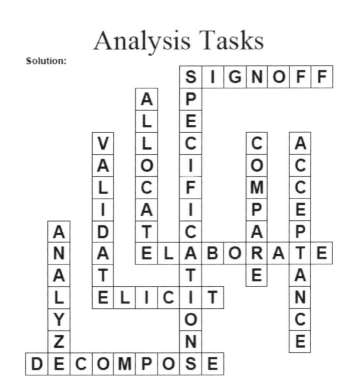

Exercise 6

Decision Making Tools and Techniques
Consensus Building
Delphi Technique
Multi-Voting
Nominal Group Technique
Options Analysis
Weighted Criteria (aka Multi-criteria Decision Analysis)
Mnemonic: Crafty **D**eals **M**ake **N**ew **O**ptions **W**orthy

Exercise 7

Elicitation Techniques

A. Brainstorming

B. Focus Groups

C. Interviews

D. Facilitated workshop

E. Observation

F. Document analysis

G. Research (benchmarking)

H. Surveys and questionnaires

I. Nominal group technique

J. Multi-criteria decision analysis

Examples

1. Barbara has just watched Geoff complete an order. **(E)**

2. Jose has drafted several questions that will be made available through the company website for customers to respond to. **(H)**

3. Susan has asked each of the account managers to name three preferred customers to be invited to a discussion regarding the company's products. **(B)**

4. Kent has scheduled a meeting with the chief architect to discuss potential requirements for the project. **(C)**

5. Hannah has spent the afternoon visiting competitors' websites to understand the functionality they offer. **(G)**

6. Rae Lyn has completed review of system documentation for the legacy system and was able to note a number of requirements for the current project. **(F)**

7. Martin has asked each meeting participant to write their ideas on a sticky note and post to the meeting room wall. **(A)**

8. Lynn has asked each participant to score each requirement for each category indicated on the score sheet provided. **(J)**

9. Thomas has brought together customer service SMEs to elicit requirements. **(D)**

10. Teri has handed each meeting participate five "dots" to use to vote on the requirements presented throughout the meeting. **(I)**

            PMI-PBA Certification Study Guide

Exercise 8

Analysis Techniques

```
E   D   O   Y   N   Q   P   V   Q   N   X   O   H   S   P
F   U   V   A   O   O   Z   R   C   L   O   C   S   R   O
L   S   W   S   K   O   I   Q   O   D   D   E   S   I   H
W   E   U   K   K   M   R   T   W   T   C   M   L   N   S
H   R   D   X   S   R   L   Q   A   O   O   E   A   F   K
C   S   T   T   Y   O   Z   U   R   V   D   T   O   Y   R
A   T   R   Z   M   T   G   P   X   Q   R   B   Y   Q   O
N   O   I   T   I   S   O   P   M   O   C   E   D   P   W
D   R   O   M   G   N   A   A   C   K   V   A   S   V   E
J   Y   D   S   Z   I   T   U   F   L   Q   G   T   B   M
P   I   W   C   U   A   D   E   T   H   G   I   E   W   O
B   O   O   X   D   R   U   S   E   C   A   S   E   D   S
F   L   F   P   P   B   V   X   B   Q   G   X   T   G   C
    I   N   T   E   R   V   I   E   W   G   R   E   V   F   O
    Y   L   F   D   E   D   U   I   Y   I   W   L   C   F   W
```

Word	Category	Description
1. **Brainstorm**	Elicitation	To gather a list ideas (features, requirements, stakeholders, etc.) quickly in a group setting, usually at the direction of a facilitator.
2. **Data Model**	Data	Represents data structures, relationships between structures, and the detailed data attributes or facts within the structures.
3. **Decomposition**	Analytic	Decomposition breaks down something that is higher-level – such as functional areas, their processes, or project deliverables – into simpler subsets for the purpose of studying or analyzing it.
4. **Interview**	Elicitation	A systematic approach designed to elicit information from a person or group of people in an informal or formal setting by talking to an interviewee, asking relevant questions and documenting the responses.
5. **MoSCoW**	Prioritization	A prioritization technique used to rate requirements or features using ratings of "must have", "should have", "could have", "won't have" as it relates to project or release scope.
6. **Observation**	Elicitation	A means of eliciting requirements by observing the stakeholders completing activities within their work environment.
7. **Process (model)**	Process	A technique for visually documenting work performed in an organization, including who does it and how they collaborate.
8. **Prototype**	Interface (may also be used for elicitation)	Prototypes detail user interface requirements and integrates them with other requirements such as use cases, scenarios, and data and business rules.
9. **Survey**	Elicitation	A means of eliciting information from many people, sometimes anonymously, in a relatively short period of time by preparing and sending a set list of questions for response.
10. **Use Case**	Process	A textual model detailing the interactions between system users (actors) and the solution undergoing development.

Word	Category	Description
11. User Story	Process	A brief description of functionality that users need from a solution to meet a business objective. The user story is stated with the specific format of "as a <actor>, I want to <function>, so that I can <benefit>. These serve as stakeholder requirements on adaptive projects.
12. Weighted (criteria)	Decision Making (may also be used for prioritization)	Uses weighted rankings of variables for judging how alternatives accomplish the objectives.
13. Workshop (facilitated)	Elicitation	A structured way to capture requirements. A workshop may be used to scope, discover, define, prioritize and reach closure on requirements for the target system.

PMI-PBA Practice Exam Answers (Part 1)

1. What are the different types of requirements?

a. Business, stakeholder, functional, non-functional and transition	Some use these categories for requirements, but they are not the types identified in the *PMBOK® Guide*.
b. Business, stakeholder, solution requirements, transition, project, and quality	**Correct! Per *PMBOK® Guide*, 5.2 Collect Requirements**
c. Optional, important, critical	These represent potential priorities
d. Sponsor, stakeholder, functional, non-functional, transition, project, and quality	Sponsor is not a classification of requirement. Functional and non-functional requirements are included in Solution requirements.

2. Considerations when collecting requirements include which of the following?

a. Project charter and stakeholder register	**Correct! These are inputs into the Collect Requirements process. *PMBOK® Guide* 5.1.1. Plan Scope Management: Inputs**
b. Project charter and WBS	The WBS is the output of Create WBS which comes after the Collect Requirements process. Note that requirements documentation is an input into Create WBS.
c. Stakeholder register and scope statement	The scope statement is an output of the Define Scope process which comes after the Collect Requirements process. Note that requirements documentation is an input into Define Scope.
d. Scope statement and WBS	These are outputs of Define Scope and Create WBS processes.

3. Which of the following statements about conflict is most true?

a. Conflict should be avoided as higher performing teams are collaborative in nature.

Conflict is inevitable and can actually lead to increased creativity and positive working relationships. It should not be avoided, but it should be managed.

b. The project manager should stay out of conflicts between team members and let them work it out.

Initially, perhaps. However, if team members are not able to resolve conflict themselves, the PM should intervene to ensure that the performance of the team is not compromised.

c. **Conflict can lead to increased creativity and better decision-making.**

Correct! *PMBOK® Guide* 9.4.2.3. **Conflict Management**

d. The project manager should first try "smoothing" as a conflict resolution strategy.

Smoothing is not a particularly effective conflict resolution strategy. It may, however, be appropriate in certain circumstances.

4. The ability to influence others is a critical interpersonal skill required of business analysts and includes which of the following?

a. The ability to get others to see the inconsistencies in their perspectives.

Influence is not about getting others to see how they are wrong.

b. A relentless passion and unyielding commitment to one's perspectives.

This is not likely to be particularly effective in influencing others. It's critical to be able to see things from others' perspectives.

c. **The ability to understand various stakeholders' perspectives.**

Correct!

d. The willingness to subordinate your goals to others' goals.

You need to be able to understand other perspectives, but that doesn't mean your goals should made less important.

5. A requirement is best defined as:

a. A need or want of the business to solve a problem or achieve an objective.

Needs or wants don't solve problems - they are the problem/opportunity.

b. **A condition or capability that is required to be present in a product, service, or result to satisfy a contract or other formally imposed specification.**

Correct! *PMBOK® Guide* **Glossary, p. 558.**

c. A condition or capability of a product or solution that documents a problem or objective of the business.

Documentation that represents a condition or capability is a requirement, but not documentation of the problem or objective.

d. A need or necessary feature of a system that could be sensed from a position anywhere within the system.

This answer is one way to describe a well-formed requirement, not a definition of a requirement.

6. The BA serving as facilitator encounters a situation such as this during a requirements workshop with a client: A 'scribe' is assigned to keep track of important discussion points and action items. Several times during the morning session, issues are deferred to a 'Parking Lot'. The scribe makes no visible gesture that the issue has been noted. What should the facilitator do?

a. Mention to the scribe's supervisor that the scribe should be excluded from future workshops.

Too prescriptive an answer and not a good practice in any event.

b. Indicate to the scribe during the meeting that 'Parking Lot' issues should be acknowledged, and suggest writing them on a white board or flip chart.

Correct! It is important for participants in a meeting to see that 'Parking Lot' issues have been captured, and for the roles during the meeting to be carried out professionally. For the facilitator to take any of the other actions, the immediate need would not be satisfied.

c. Wait until after the workshop has ended for the day, and out of the clients' presence to provide coaching to the scribe with respect to meeting procedures and artifacts.

This type of coaching is appropriate, but would not satisfy the immediate need of capturing 'Parking Lot' issues.

d. Start tracking 'Parking Lot' issues independently so that they are not lost.

It is the role of the facilitator to ensure that the scribe is appropriately capturing the information of the meeting.

7. Which of the following best describes what is needed in order to prioritize requirements?

a. Assessment of the proposed solution

This happens after prioritizing requirements.

b. Allocated requirements

This happens after prioritizing requirements.

c. Validated solution

This happens after prioritizing requirements.

d. Requirements management plan

Correct! The Requirements Management Plan will include how to prioritize requirements.

8. How are transition requirements defined?

a. Communication with technical operational teams.

This step may be part of the definition, but only one step.

b. The same way all requirements are defined.

Correct! There is no special format for transition requirements.

c. Through a transition decision matrix.

No such matrix.

d. Through requirements validation.

Validation comes after defining requirements.

9. Eliana is a business analyst working on the requirements for a new marketing system. When she mentions to her manager that the stakeholders already have a commercial software package in mind, her manager tells her that they should plan to build custom software. She explains the situation to the subject matter experts, who at first express concern. Eliana explains something that puts their mind at rest. What does Eliana explain to them?

a. That the decision will not be made until the requirements are captured and understood. At that time she will recommend the purchase of the commercial software to the project manager and sponsor.

There are three reasons not to choose this answer. First, at this point in business analysis it is not clear which alternative is better, so the BA should not recommend any solution. Second, the BA should hold off on the decision until alternatives can be analyzed. Third, although PMs need updates on these kinds of situations, they are not the decision-makers. They will need to know the solution once it has been chosen. This answer, however, implies that the PM, as recipient of the recommendation, has some say in the solution.

b. **That the decision will not be made until the requirements are captured and understood. At that time she will compare multiple proposed solutions to see which best meets the requirements.**

Correct!

c. That she will ensure that the vendor discusses the situation with her manager to emphasize the benefits of buying a package and the disadvantages of custom solutions.

Having the vendor talk to the manager may or may not be helpful, but the manager is not the decision-maker in this situation and should not dictate the solution.

d. That she will ensure that the vendor discusses the situation with the sponsor to emphasize the benefits of buying a package and the disadvantages of custom solutions.

It may or may not be appropriate for the vendor to discuss the situation with the sponsor, but that discussion should not influence the business analyst to recommend the right solution, whether it be a commercial or customized solution.

10. As the lead BA you are analyzing requirements collected by another BA on a big project. You run across a requirement that states "The system shall be easy for new team members to learn." What should you suggest to the BA regarding this requirement?

a.	Ask the BA to work with the stakeholder to prioritize the requirement.	The requirement is not complete and ready for prioritization.
b.	Tell the BA "good job."	Not a good job yet!
c.	**Suggest that the BA discuss the requirement with the stakeholder to get specific criteria on what is "easy to learn."**	**Correct! The stakeholder needs to provide the specific criteria of what is "easy to learn."**
d.	Ask the BA to restate the requirement with specific criteria on what is "easy to learn."	This is close, but it is essential the stakeholder own the requirement and articulate the acceptance criteria.

PMI-PBA Practice Exam Answers (Part 2)

1. What prioritization method is typically used on an agile project?

   a. Multi-voting

   Predictive

   b. High, medium, low

   Predictive

   c. MoSCoW

   Predictive

   d. Stack ranked

   Correct! User stories are stack ranked on the product backlog in agile (adaptive approach).

2. A prototype that is continuously modified and updated is known as what?

   a. Exploratory prototype

   This is a throwaway prototype generally used once.

   b. Evolutionary prototype

   Correct!

   c. A mockup

   This is a generic term for a point-in-time view of the prototype.

   d. Horizontal prototype

   This models a shallow and wide view of the functionality. It is a way of categorizing prototypes.

3. You are starting to recruit your participants for your focus group. You are looking for a very diverse group of people. The participants you are looking for would be categorized as what?

   a. Homogeneous

   No. Homogeneous groups are similar.

   b. Heterogeneous

   Correct! Heterogeneous groups are diverse.

   c. Esoteric

   No such group.

   d. Homogenized

   This answer may be true for milk, but not for types of groups! (We invented this "distracter" to illustrate what a test designer might do.)

4. You are in the middle of doing an unstructured interview. You ask the question "How many days are counted for the member's activity in the program per month?" Your stakeholder replies "I don't know." This is an example of what type of question?

a.	Open-ended	The question is asking for a specific number, which is not an open-ended question.
b.	Calculation	There is no such question type.
c.	**Closed-ended**	**Correct! It is asking for a specific answer.**
d.	Unstructured	This is an interview type, not a question type.

5. You are in the process of selecting people to participate in a particular requirements elicitation event. Among your considerations are whether the type of questions will be open-ended or closed-ended. You are also considering the best mode of distribution. What technique are you likely to be planning?

a.	**Survey/Questionnaire**	**Correct! The key to the question is the distribution of the survey. Closed-ended questions are best for questionnaires.**
b.	Focus group	Persons are selected based on background and objectives, not the type of question and distribution.
c.	JAD workshop	Persons are selected based on background and objectives, not the type of question and distribution.
d.	Interview	Distribution is not an issue for the interview, as it is for the questionnaire.

6. The following process step is NOT recommended in the interviewing process:

a.	Contact potential interviewees and explain why their assistance is needed.	This is a good interviewing practice.
b.	Organize questions in a logical order or an order of significance based on the interviewee's knowledge or subject of the interview.	This is a good interviewing practice.
c.	**Use a standard set of interview questions for all interviewees in order to facilitate scoring each question.**	**Correct! May need to custom design the interview based on desired outcome.**
d.	Send summary notes of the interview to the interviewee for review.	This is a good interviewing practice.

7. Allison has been going through hundreds of difficult scenarios that the business needs to understand. All of the scenarios are rules-based. What is the best document for Allison to use to represent these difficult scenarios?

a. Decision table	**Correct! A table can simplify the complexity of the numerous scenarios.**
b. Hierarchy table	An invented answer.
c. Multiplication table	This answer is relevant only to mathematics.
d. Rules table.	A rules table is not a known standard definition, so is not the best choice.

8. You are walking your stakeholders through a diagram that shows the life cycle of a class. What type of diagram are you using?

a. Context level data flow diagram	This diagram shows the scope of the solution.
b. Sequence diagram	This shows interaction of objects and the exchange of messages between them.
c. State diagram	**Correct!**
d. Functional decomposition diagram	This shows the breakdown of processes and functions.

9. Business value, implementation difficulty, and urgency are all basis for:

a. Requirements allocation	Not allocation.
b. Requirements prioritization	**Correct!**
c. Requirements planning	Not urgency.
d. Requirements status	Not status.

10. Which of the following tools would be used in the Collect Requirements process?

    a. **Facilitated workshops and focus groups.**   **Correct!**

    b. Facilitated workshops and variance analysis.   Facilitated workshops would be, but variance analysis would be used to control scope, not collect requirements.

    c. Focus groups and inspection.   Focus groups would be, but inspection would be used to verify scope.

    d. Decomposition and prototypes.   Prototypes would be, but decomposition is used to create the WBS, not collect requirements.

Summary

The Analysis domain describes the tasks, tools, and techniques to support eliciting and documenting quality requirements that provide sufficient detail to support the development, test, and implementation of a solution that will satisfy the requirements and support the project objectives. The tasks outline the process that a requirement goes through from elicitation to final acceptance. Understanding this process will help in answering exam questions in the Analysis domain. Keep in mind that requirements analysis is iterative and ongoing so variations in process may occur to support quality requirements analysis.

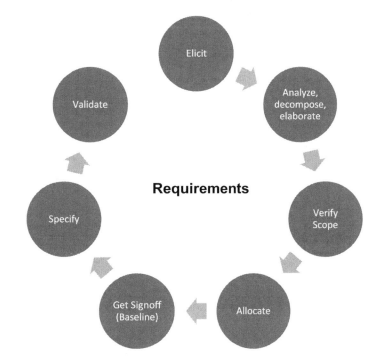

Here are the themes covered that you should internalize:

- Consider the lifecycle approach in place.

- Follow the Requirements Management Plan for making refinements as necessary.

- Use the Requirements Traceability Matrix for recording and tracking.

- Requirements specifications should only be created for requirements that are determined to be in scope and approved by stakeholders.

- Control scope by verifying requirements support project goals and objectives.

 Analysis Goal: Product requirements that are approved, within scope, and suitable for development.

Notes

5. Traceability and Monitoring

Overview

Traceability is at the heart of organizing and managing requirements. Much of this aspect has been covered in the Planning domain and referenced in the Analysis domain. This chapter will provide more practice applying traceability concepts and take a deeper dive into some aspects of traceability.

Traceability and Monitoring is a significant theme within the PMI-PBA exam in part because it crosses multiple domains. The Traceability and Monitoring domain focuses on the execution of the requirement traceability plan which includes documentation, management, and communication of requirements through the requirements life cycle.

 Traceability and Monitoring Goal: Document, manage, and communicate requirements, their status, and approved changes.

When you are finished with this chapter, you will know:

- How to define Traceability and Monitoring.

- The five tasks contained in Traceability and Monitoring.

- The major areas of emphasis in Traceability and Monitoring – documentation, management, change control, communication of requirements and status.

> **Traceability and Monitoring**
>
> The tasks and outputs for documenting, managing, controlling change, and reporting requirements and their status.

Domain Themes

The PMI-PBA exam includes several reoccurring themes. One useful way to use these themes is when you narrow down an exam question to two close answers. If one of the themes suggests one over the other, then go with the theme. The common themes to watch for in Traceability and Monitoring are as follows:

Theme	Comments
Consider the Lifecycle Approach	Consider the approach in place, predictive or adaptive, when making decisions about things like tasks, techniques, or risks.
Traceability	The Requirements Traceability Matrix is the single most important tool in requirements management. It is with the traceability matrix that requirements are documented, managed, and communicated throughout the requirements life cycle.

Figure 5-1: PMI-PBA Themes Related to Traceability and Monitoring

The questions for Traceability and Monitoring domain represent 15 percent of all the exam questions. Don't let this fool you. The themes of Traceability and Monitoring will appear in questions directly attributed to other domains such as Planning and Analysis. See *Figure 5-2* below.

Domain	Percentage of Items on Test	Approximate number of questions
Domain 1: Needs Assessment	18%	36
Domain 2: Planning	22%	44
Domain 3: Analysis	35%	70
Domain 4: Traceability and Monitoring	15%	30
Domain 5: Evaluation	10%	20

Figure 5-2: Traceability and Monitoring Domain
Source: PMI®

Domain: High-Level View

The five tasks in Traceability and Monitoring are listed below. The tasks in the domain may not be performed sequentially, but it is helpful to learn the tasks and their order as a way to remember what each of them does. PMI® does not provide task titles for each task, but rather a detailed description. See the table below for the tasks as defined by PMI® with a task title developed for this guide in order to aid learning and remember the tasks.

                   PMI-PBA Certification Study Guide

Task 1
Trace Requirements

Trace requirements using a traceability artifact or tool, capturing the requirements' status, sources, and relationships (including dependencies) in order to provide evidence that the requirements are delivered as stated.

Task 2
Monitor Requirements Status

Monitor requirements throughout their lifecycles using a traceability artifact or tool in order to ensure the appropriate supporting requirements artifacts (such as models, documentation, and test cases) are produced, reviewed, and approved at each point in the lifecycle.

Task 3
Update Requirements Status

Update a requirement's status as it moves through its lifecycle states by communicating with appropriate stakeholders and recording changes in the traceability artifact or tool in order to track requirements towards closure.

Task 4
Communicate Requirements Status

Communicate requirements status to the project manager and other stakeholders using communication methods in order to keep them informed of requirements issues, conflicts, changes, risks, and overall status.

Task 5
Manage Changes to Requirements

Manage changes to requirements by assessing impacts, dependencies, and risks in accordance with the Change Control Plan, and comparing to the requirements baseline in order to maintain the integrity of the requirements and associated artifacts.

> **Mnemonic Tip**
>
> **TMUCC:** "Too Many Undertones Cause Confusion"
> **T**   **T**race Requirements
> **M** **M**onitor Requirements' Status
> **U**   **U**pdate Requirements' Status
> **C**   **C**ommunicate Requirements
> **C**   Manage **C**hanges to Requirements

To help you remember the tasks, use a mnemonic of "Too Many Undertones Cause Confusion." This acronym captures the tasks within Traceability and Monitoring in their given order. The first letter of the mnemonic is highlighted to help you memorize it.

> The chapter below presents each of the tasks along with more information on the task descriptions and tools and techniques used to perform each task.

Task Inputs, Tools and Techniques, and Outputs

Following is a summary of the ITTOs (Inputs-Tasks-Techniques-Outputs) for Traceability and Monitoring.

Input	Task	Tools and Techniques	Output
Requirements Management Plan Requirements	1. Trace requirements using a traceability artifact or tool, capturing the requirements' status, sources and relationships (including dependencies), in order to provide evidence that the requirements are delivered as stated.	Traceability	Requirements Traceability Matrix (updated)
Requirements Management Plan Requirements	2. Monitor requirements throughout their lifecycles using a traceability artifact or tool in order to ensure the appropriate supporting requirements artifacts (such as models, documentation, and test cases) are produced, reviewed, and approved at each point in the lifecycle.	Traceability	Requirements Traceability Matrix (updated)
Requirements Management Plan Requirements	3. Update a requirement's status as it moves through its lifecycle states by communicating with appropriate stakeholders and recording changes in the traceability artifact or tool in order to track requirements towards closure.	Traceability	Requirements Traceability Matrix (updated)

                    PMI-PBA Certification Study Guide

Input	Task	Tools and Techniques	Output
Requirements Management Plan Requirements	4. Communicate requirements status to the project manager and other stakeholders using communication methods in order to keep them informed of requirements issues, conflicts, changes, risks, and overall status.	Traceability	Requirements Communication
Change Requests Requirements Management Plan	5. Manage changes to requirements by assessing impacts, dependencies, and risks in accordance with the Change Control Plan, and comparing to the requirements baseline in order to maintain the integrity of the requirements and associated artifacts.	Change Control Traceability Version Control	Requirements Traceability Matrix (updated) Requirements Baseline (updated)

Figure 5-3: Traceability and Monitoring ITTOs

Part 1 – Traceability and Monitoring Tasks

Task 1 – Trace Requirements

Trace requirements using a traceability artifact or tool, capturing the requirements' status, sources, and relationships (including dependencies) in order to provide evidence that the requirements are delivered as stated.

<u>T</u>MUCC

"Too Many Undertones Cause Confusion"

Traceability Review

A useful way to view traceability is discovering and maintaining relationships between important facets of requirements, such as:

- Relation to business objectives
- Relation or dependency to other requirements
- Relation to team deliverables, such as use cases and test cases
- Relation to solution components, such as design documents and development modules

Being able to "trace" a requirement means the ability to trace a requirement's main relationships as listed above through the development life cycle. Traceability should be bi-directional, which means being able to trace requirements <u>back</u> to the business need for them and <u>forward</u> through design and implementation (called "**allocation**"). Relationships to other requirements should also be traced.

Requirements Traceability
The ability to trace a requirement's relationships through the development life cycle. It should be bi-directional, to trace requirements back to the business need for them, and forward through design and implementation.

Benefits. Traceability helps manage scope by connecting requirements to the business need behind an initiative. It also assists in making sure that the implemented solution "conforms to requirements," and in turn supports the business need. Traceability can also support other project management areas such as risk management, cost management, and communication management. It can also help identify missing functionality in the proposed or completed solution. Conversely, it can guard against "rogue" requirements and functionality being added that do not support business objectives.

Derivation
Identifies the "lineage" of a requirement by tracing back to the business need.

Allocation
Traces a requirement through development, testing, and implementation.

Level. Traceability can be done at the individual requirement level, at a group level, or at the feature or function level. The factors for choosing are not mentioned, but we would suggest that the amount of time available, the kind of product being developed, plus any associated regulations, and the organization's preferences, are some factors for selecting the level to trace requirements.

Interrelationships. Requirements typically have relationships to other requirements and deliverables. Documenting these relationships provide the following advantages:

Impact Analysis	Changes to requirements are much easier to analyze if the impact of the change is known. Tracing to related requirements and development components permits a quick review of potentially affected changes to understand the impact.
Requirements Coverage	Decomposing of business and project objectives into detailed requirements identifies how they will be addressed. Each objective can be traced to appropriate aspects of detailed requirements, such as use cases, data models, etc. to ensure it has been analyzed.
Requirements Allocation	Will help ensure that requirements that are related or with other dependencies will be allocated in a way that supports cohesive development of the solution.

Figure 5-4: Need for Requirements Relationships

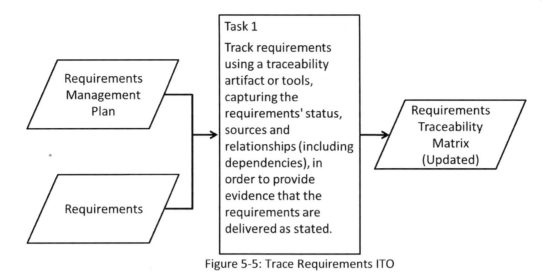

Figure 5-5: Trace Requirements ITO

Considerations for Trace Requirements

Relationships

Record any dependencies and inter-relationships between requirements. This helps to plan the order of analyzing and developing a solution. For example, assume a mortgage company is creating a new web-based application process. The company requires applicants to have a login ID and password to be able to save and retrieve their application. All of the online application requirements are then dependent on the login function and its related requirements.

See the following list of some of the more common requirements relationships and dependencies, which were also described in the Analytic Tools and Techniques section in the Analysis chapter of this Study Guide:

Relationship	Description
Subsets	One requirement may be a decomposed subset of another. For example, a "password reminder question" is a subset of the login requirement.
Implementation Dependency	A requirement may be dependent on the implementation of another requirement. For example, requirements pertaining to a new project history report may be dependent on other requirements that provide the interface for capturing project data.
Benefit or Value Dependency	The value of a requirement may not be recognized until another requirement is implemented. For example, a requirement to use a new, simpler form may have an expected benefit of faster loan approval. However, that benefit may not be recognized until another requirement regarding modifications to the loan application online interface is implemented.

Figure 5-6: Requirements Relationships

Requirements Management Tools

When large numbers of requirements need to be traced, then requirements management tools are useful to manage the details. Requirements management tools are specially designed relational databases that allow for easier recording of requirements with the ability to relate requirements to each other and to other items (e.g., use cases, user stories, goals, objective, design documents, test cases). Requirements management tools provide an added advantage with the ability to configure and customize the input of requirements information and a rich set of out-of-the-box reports. These tools can be customized to make requirements communication a breeze. Some tools may also include diagramming and wireframe tools to capture requirements analysis within the tool.

Many organizations rely on their office productivity software (e.g., Word and Excel) for traceability in the absence of a specially designed requirements management tool.

Adaptive (Agile) Project Approaches

A formal Requirements Traceability Matrix may not be used on an agile project. Instead, stakeholder level requirements will be traced and maintained via the product backlog. The product backlog contains a stack ranked, prioritized list of user stories representing stakeholder requirements. User stories will be decomposed by the project team and recorded in the least formal way that will support their development within the iteration the story was selected for development.

Techniques

Tools and techniques related to tracing requirements.

Techniques – *Trace Requirements*	
Traceability Tools and Techniques	**Includes:**
Tools and techniques used to aid in the recording, management, update, and communication of requirements and their status.	- Backlog Management - Issue (Problem) Tracking - Requirements Traceability Matrix

Outputs

Output: *Requirements Traceability Matrix (Updated)*

All requirements should be documented in the Requirements Traceability Matrix and include information such as dependencies and other attributes needed in order to effectively manage and communicate requirements and their status. The tools, process, and items to include should come from the Requirements Management Plan.

More information on the Requirements Traceability Matrix can be found in the PMBOK® Guide:

- Section 5.2.3.2 – Requirements Traceability Matrix

Task 2 – Monitor Requirement Status

Monitor requirements throughout their lifecycles using a traceability artifact or tool in order to ensure the appropriate supporting requirements artifacts (such as models, documentation, and test cases) are produced, reviewed, and approved at each point in the lifecycle.

TM̲UCC

"Too Many Undertones Cause Confusion"

Actively monitoring and updating the Requirements Traceability Matrix is key to effective traceability and quality requirements. The business analyst is responsible for ensuring that the Requirements Traceability Matrix contains the information needed to support the requirements and the information necessary to understand the status of the requirements throughout the requirements and project life cycle.

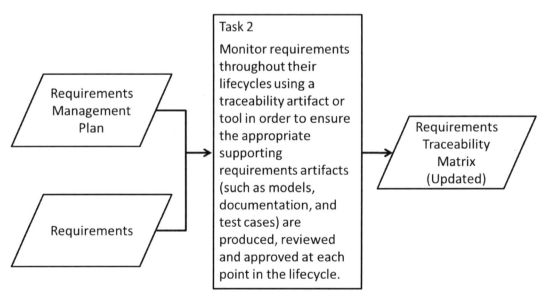

Figure 5-7: Monitor Requirements ITO

                    PMI-PBA Certification Study Guide

Considerations for Monitor Requirements

Progressive Elaboration

As requirements move through the Analysis activities in its life cycle, additional, more detailed requirements may emerge. It is essential that these emerging requirements are captured in the Requirements Traceability Matrix with reference to their dependencies. Requirements and specifications that emerge in support of approved requirements are considered a support detail rather than a new requirement.

Business Analysis Work Product

Conducting analysis on requirements results in a work product that supports the analysis and the requirement. References to this work product should be captured in the Requirements Traceability Matrix to facilitate finding and tracking supporting documentation. Tracking this work product may also highlight if a requirement (or set of requirements) has not been further analyzed when no work product references are found.

Team Deliverables

Referencing team deliverables in the Requirements Traceability Matrix is just one way to help monitor the status of a requirement. Include reference to design documents, code developed, and test scripts with status to quickly identify the overall status of product development.

Issue and Problem Tracking

There will often be requirements that are not yet "suitable for development." There may be conflicts in the requirements, unconfirmed assumptions to be resolved, or simply questions to be resolved by business stakeholders. The Requirements Traceability Matrix should clearly provide information on requirements that have outstanding issues and information on those issues and their resolution. The issue tracking may occur within the Requirements Traceability Matrix itself, or there may be a supplemental log with appropriate reference made in the Requirements Traceability Matrix.

Techniques

Tools and techniques related to tracing requirements.

Techniques – *Monitor Requirements Status*	
Traceability Tools and Techniques	**Includes:**
Tools and techniques used to aid in the recording, management, update, and communication of requirements and their status.	- Backlog Management - Issue (Problem) Tracking - Requirements Traceability Matrix

Outputs

Output: *Requirements Traceability Matrix (updated)*

All requirements should be documented in the Requirements Traceability Matrix with reference to related requirements, business analysis work products, project team deliverables, and information on outstanding issues.

PMBOK® Guide References

More information on the Requirements Traceability Matrix can be found in the *PMBOK® Guide*:

- Section 5.2.3.2 – Requirements Traceability Matrix

Task 3 – Update Requirement Status

Update a requirement's status as it moves through its lifecycle states by communicating with appropriate stakeholders and recording changes in the traceability artifact or tool in order to trace requirements towards closure.

TM<u>U</u>CC

"Too Many Undertones Cause Confusion"

This task is one of the more straight-forward of the exam – keep the requirements status up-to-date throughout the requirements life cycle. One element of keeping the requirements current is being proactive in working with the project team and stakeholders to monitor the status so updates can be made in a timely manner.

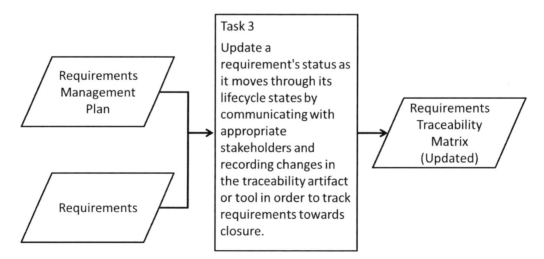

Figure 5-8: Update Requirements Status ITO

Considerations for Update Requirements Status

Requirements Status

Traceability can facilitate understanding of requirement status or state. The statuses that will be used for tracking requirements should be outlined in the Requirements Management Plan. There is no PMI®-established standard for requirements status throughout the requirements life cycle. An example is offered in the *Business Analysis for Practitioners: A Practice Guide*. Exam questions are mostly likely to look for evidence of status being defined in the Requirements Management Plan but they may follow this example in general terms. You should not need to memorize the details of this example to answer questions on the exam.

Open Statuses	Closed Statuses
• Proposed	• Rejected
• Approved	• Cancelled
• In Progress	• Deferred
• Completed	• Implemented

ID	Requirement	Status	Priority	Phase	Objectives	Owner	Author	Design Ref	Test Ref	Comments
1	The CSR must be able to view customer call history online	Approved	Must	Ph 1	PO1	G. Anderson	D. Kelley	DS 12.1	TC 25.3	
2	The system must include the ability to log a call including date, time, subject, comments for each customer	Approved	Must	Ph 1	PO1	G. Anderson	D. Kelley	DS 12.1	TC 25.3	
3	The system shall include the ability to upload a recording of each telephone call	Issue	Should	Ph 1	PO1	G. Anderson	D. Kelley			What is the file type and size for recordings?
4	The system must include a function to mine customer call data to identify trends	Deferred	Must	Ph 2	PO2	D. Morris	D. Kelley			
5	The system must send an automated email to survey customer satisfaction with 48 hours of contact	Deferred	Must	Ph 3	PO2	L. Wilson	D. Kelley			

Figure 5-9: Example Traceability Matrix

In the example above we can see that requirements 1 and 2 have been designed and test cases developed. We also see that requirement 3 has an issue associated with it. These are just a few examples of how traceability can facilitate understanding of requirement status. As mentioned in the previous task, it can also help identify a requirement that has not been sufficiently analyzed when no supporting detail is referenced in the matrix.

Requirements Life Cycle State Diagram

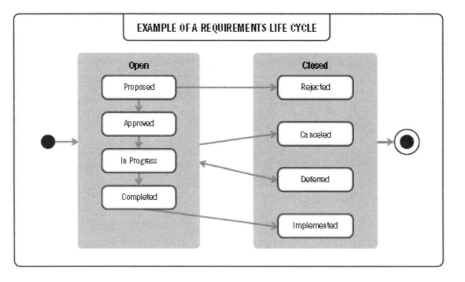

Figure 5-10: Example of a Requirements Life Cycle Diagram

The example above is a state diagram that provides an example of some common requirement states and the life cycle that may be followed. The requirement state is used when reporting requirement status to project stakeholders. For example, the state is required in order to report how many requirements are documented and how many are approved, deferred, or rejected in order to provide a fuller understanding of the conditions of the requirements on the project at any given point in the life cycle.

Source: *Business Analysis for Practitioners: A Practice Guide,* page 149-150

Techniques

Tools and techniques related to tracing requirements.

Techniques – *Update Requirements Status*	
Traceability Tools and Techniques Tools and techniques used to aid in the documentation, management, update, and communication of requirements and their status.	**Includes:** - Backlog Management - Issue (Problem) Tracking - Requirements Traceability Matrix

                    PMI-PBA Certification Study Guide

Outputs

Output: *Requirements Traceability Matrix (updated)*

All requirements should be documented in the Requirements Traceability Matrix with status and include reference to related requirements, business analysis work products, project team deliverables, and information on outstanding issues.

PMBOK® Guide References

More information on the Requirements Traceability Matrix can be found in the *PMBOK® Guide*:

- Section 5.2.3.2 – Requirements Traceability Matrix

Task 4 - Communicate Requirements Status

Communicate requirements status to the project manager and other stakeholders using communication methods in order to keep them informed of requirements issues, conflicts, changes, risks, and overall status.

TMU<u>C</u>C

"Too Many Undertones Cause Confusion"

Proactively communicating requirements status will ultimately make the job of the business analyst easier. Keeping stakeholders apprised of issues, conflicts, and risks provides them the opportunity to help facilitate resolution. It also helps to manage expectations by providing early notification of potential requirements-related project risks. A well-designed and current Requirements Traceability Matrix will provide great insights into the solution development status.

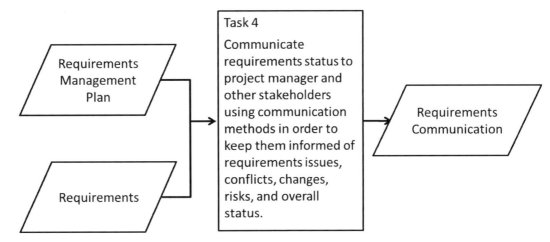

Figure 5-11: Communicate Requirements Status ITO

Considerations for Communicate Requirements Status

Communication Plan

The Communication Plan portion of the Requirements Management Plan should provide detailed information on who, what, and how for communicating requirements status. Use this as a starting point to determine communication needs and adapt for any new project or stakeholder communication needs.

For adaptive or some iterative approaches, a requirements package is not created. Instead, an informal work product may be created. The BA should work in close connection with the project manager for any format, template, or organization standards. In addition, the BA must select the optimal format which communicates the information to the specific audience and which meets the technology constraints by reviewers. To this end, the BA will identify stakeholder presentation preferences such as the level of detail, language, and formality that is appropriate for each type of stakeholder. They must also determine what information is important to communicate. Always remember that the primary goal of a requirements package it to convey information clearly and in an understandable manner so it can be reviewed and approved.

Communication by Role

Not all stakeholders require full detail of all requirements. In fact, providing too much unnecessary detail to a stakeholder may be a barrier to them reading and engaging in the information provided. One benefit of a well-designed Requirements Traceability Matrix is the ability to filter, sort, and organize the requirements to facilitate communicating the needed information to the appropriate people. The Communication Plan in the Requirements Management Plan should address these specific needs. Here are a few examples of communication strategies that may be employed to ensure the right stakeholders get the right information.

What	Who	How	Why
Broker stakeholder requirements	Broker SMEs	Filter on broker features, requirement type "stakeholder"	Provide insight to requirements affecting the broker functionality at a high level of detail
Detailed home page requirements / specification	Development team	Filter on home page features	Provide sufficient detail to support feature design and development
Requirements issues	Project manager, project team, project sponsors	Filter on requirement status "issue"	Communicate current issues to facilitate resolution
Backlog	Project manager	Filter on requirements without reference to appropriate BA or team deliverables (e.g., no design reference)	Provide a list of requirements that have not been addressed at a given point in the project life cycle

> **Backlog**
>
> Planned work that is not yet completed.

Figure 5-12: Requirements Communication Strategy Example

Below are some common project roles with communication needs to consider when planning and disseminating communications regarding requirements.

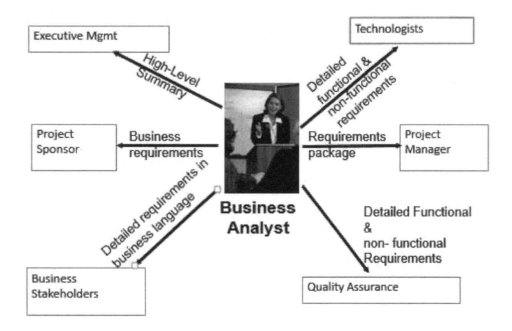

Figure 5-13: Common project roles with requirements needs

The business analyst is responsible for disseminating requirements information to all key stakeholders. Each stakeholder group may need different information. For example:

Executive Management and Executive Sponsors: These stakeholders will probably want to see a requirements summary and high level requirements. Their purpose is to understand the requirements in regards to their business plans.

Project Sponsor: The type of communication the sponsor needs often depends on the organizational level of the sponsor. A sponsor who is more hands-on may want more detailed information. A sponsor who is at a higher level in the organization or a sponsor who has a more hands-off approach may only want a summary or high level version of the information.

Business Stakeholders: Stakeholders who represent the customer and business normally like to see detailed requirements presented in their business language.

Quality Assurance: QA analysts will need to understand the detailed functional and non-functional requirements to make sure they understand what each requirement will deliver so they can develop test cases and test scripts.

Project Manager: Although the project manager usually will not need a separate requirements package, they will still want to see the requirements. It is best to work with the project manager to determine what requirements documentation they will need on the project.

Subject Matter Experts (SME)/Technologists: SMEs/Technologists could include developers, architects, database administrators, web designers, capacity planners, etc. Most technologists will need the detailed functional, non-functional and technical requirements so they can develop their design plans and the solution.

Techniques – *Update Requirements Status*	
Traceability Tools and Techniques Tools and techniques used to aid in the recording, management, update, and communication of requirements and their status.	**Includes:** - Backlog Management - Issue (Problem) Tracking - Requirements Traceability Matrix

Outputs

Output: *Requirements Communication*
Communications regarding requirements including status, issues, risks, and conflicts disseminated to appropriate stakeholders at the appropriate level of detail as determined in the Requirements Management Plan plus any needed adaptations to those plans.

PMBOK® Guide References

More information on the Requirements Traceability Matrix and stakeholder communication can be found in the *PMBOK® Guide*:

- Section 5.2.3.2 – Requirements Traceability Matrix

- Section 10.2 – Manage Communications

- Section 10.3 – Control Communications

- Section 13.3 – Manage Stakeholder Engagement

Task 5 – Manage Changes to Requirements

Manage changes to requirements by assessing impacts, dependencies, and risks in accordance with the Change Control Plan, and comparing to the requirements baseline in order to maintain the integrity of the requirements and associated artifacts.

TMUC<u>C</u>

"Too Many Undertones Cause Confusion"

Once requirements are baselined, changes to requirements should be made and recorded using a change control process. Changes in the business are one trigger for a change in scope and would be subject to the same change control process. Such changes could affect previously approved requirements. Adaptive (agile) approaches do not typically use formal change control. At the beginning of iterations, which are typically short, both old and new requirements are prioritized. Once selected for implementation, requirements are not allowed to change.

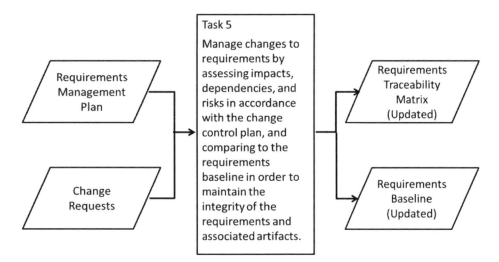

Figure 5-14: Manage Changes to Requirements ITO

Change Control Plan

The business analyst works to ensure change is managed according to the Change Control Plan within the Requirements Management Plan as outlined in task 4 of the Planning domain. Following the plan is the first defense against scope creep and will limit risk to the project. The business analyst has responsibility to manage product scope while the project manager has responsibility for the project scope and processes. Overall change control is a coordinated effort with team members responsible for the portions of the process as outlined in the plan.

In order to reduce conflict related to change control roles and responsibilities, it is useful to create a change control RACI.

	CCB	PM	BA	Dev/ Design	Test
Verify Business Value/Scope	I	C	R	I	I
Determine impact to requirements	I	C	R	I	I
Determine impact to design/dev	I	A	C	R	I
Estimate level of effort to address	I	A	C	R	R
Identify project impacts (cost/schedule)	I	A, R	C	I	I
Prepare recommendation for CCB	I	A, C	R	I	I
Approve or Reject Change	A, R	C	C	I	I
Rebaseline project plan	I	A, R	I	I	I
Rebaseline requirements	I	A	R	C	C
Update tech documents	I	A	C	R	R

Figure 5-15: Change Control RACI

- **Change Control Board (CCB):** Reviews impact analysis from the project team including recommendations based on cost-benefit provided by the business analyst; approves or rejects the change.

- **Project Manager (PM):** Ensures the change control process is followed, facilitates information gathering and analysis from team, determines overall project impacts for consideration along with the benefit(s) of the change, and updates project plans as necessary if approved.

- **Business Analyst (BA):** Determines the business impact and value of the change, determines cost-benefit (or overall value) of the change to the project, identifies additional impacted requirements, provides information to aid the team in identification of additional impacts, prepares recommendation, updates requirements baseline if approved.

- **Technical Team (Dev/Design & Test):** Analyzes impacts to their work, develops cost and time estimates to support the change, updates necessary documents if change is approved, and implements the change.

Impact Analysis

To assess the impact of a change, analysis should be done to determine the resulting effects. Traceability is one tool for analyzing impacts, which involves examining related requirements that will be affected by a change to another requirement. The related requirements may also need to change accordingly. In turn, the related requirements that need to change can be traced to yet other requirements that will also need to change, and so on. Impact analysis provides valuable input to the requirements change approval process.

It is important to recognize that this analysis goes well beyond the specific requirements or features identified in the change request. The Requirements Traceability Matrix will aid in this assessment. Here are a few specific examples of how:

- Identifies dependent and related requirements that may also be impacted
- Identifies features, use cases, or user stories that may identify additional requirements impacted by the change
- References business analysis work products such as diagrams, models, and matrices that may identify additional requirements impacted by the change

As per the Change Control Plan, the project manager will facilitate the analysis of impacts to the project schedule, budget, and risks. The project manager and business analyst work together to propose a recommendation once all of the analysis has been coordinated and completed.

Requirements Updates

The Requirements Traceability Matrix should be updated with the outcome of change requests, including changes to other impacted requirements, in a timely manner and made available to project stakeholders. Possible outcomes include approved, deferred, rejected, or more information required. Supporting requirements documentation may also require updates to provide the most current information to project stakeholders. Utilize version control tools and techniques to ensure project stakeholders know they have the most current version of requirements documentation.

Techniques – *Manage Changes to Requirements*	
Traceability Tools and Techniques Tools and techniques used to aid in the documentation, management, update, and communication of requirements and their status.	Includes: - Backlog Management - Issue (Problem) Tracking - Requirements Traceability Matrix
Change Control Tools and Techniques Tools and techniques that facilitate modifications to documents, deliverables, or baselines associated with the project are identified, documented, approved, or rejected. There are many automated tools on the market to facilitate	Includes: - Configuration Management System (CMS)

Techniques – *Manage Changes to Requirements*

this, however, the system may also be a manual process or set of processes.	
Version Control Tools and Techniques Tools and techniques used to manage and control versions of a work product, including revisions. There are many automated tools on the market to facilitate this, however, the system may also be a manual process or set of processes.	**Includes:** - Version Control System (VCS)

Outputs

Output: *Requirements Traceability Matrix (updated)*

The Requirements Traceability Matrix will be updated with all outcomes of all change requests. Version information will help the project team ensure they have the most current version of the requirements and supporting documentation.

Output: *Requirements Baseline (updated)*

The Requirements Baseline will be updated with approved change requests that modify the baseline. Change control will help the project team ensure that only approved changes get incorporated into an updated baseline.

PMBOK® Guide References

More information on the Requirements Traceability Matrix and change control can be found in the *PMBOK® Guide*:

- Section 4.5 – Perform Integrated Change Control

- Section 5.2.3.2 – Requirements Traceability Matrix

Traceability and Monitoring – Exercise 1

Write the mnemonic letters for the five tasks of Traceability and Monitoring domain, and then complete the missing words for each task in the blanks provided below.

Traceability and Monitoring Tasks	Mnemonic
1. _____ Requirements	_____
2. _____ Requirements Status	_____
3. _____ Requirements Status	_____
4. _____ Requirements Status	_____
5. Manage _____ to Requirements	_____

Part 2 – Techniques for Traceability and Monitoring

The tools and techniques below are those that may be most helpful in the Traceability and Monitoring domain. Importantly, the tools and techniques are not domain or task specific; they may be used for more than one task and in more than one domain. It will be necessary for the person doing the business analysis work to determine which tools to use and when.

Category	Technique
Change Control Tools and Techniques *Tools and techniques that facilitate modifications to documents, deliverables, or baselines associated with the project are identified, documented, approved, or rejected.*	
	Configuration Management System
Traceability Tools and Techniques *Tools and techniques used to aid in the documentation, management, update, and communication of requirements and their status.*	
	Backlog Management
	Issue (Problem) Tracking
	Requirements Traceability Matrix
Version Control Tools and Techniques *Tools and techniques used to manage and control versions of a work product, including revisions.*	
	Version Control System

Figure 5-16: Tools and Techniques for Traceability and Monitoring

The following pages provide additional details about the tools and techniques that may be most helpful in this domain. (Details for some techniques may be covered in a different domain as noted above.) Not all tools and techniques will be discussed at a great level of detail. The amount of information provided relates to the priority of the tool or technique on the exam. Each technique has been rated with a priority level of low, moderate, or high to help in prioritizing study. Items marked as low may appear in your certification exam; items marked moderate are likely to show up in one or two questions, and items marked high may have multiple questions relating to their use.

Change Control Tools and Techniques

> Tools and techniques that facilitate modifications to documents, deliverables, or baselines associated with the project are identified, documented, approved, or rejected. There are many automated tools on the market to facilitate this; however, the system may also be a manual process or set of processes.

Change Control Tools and Techniques
Configuration Management System

Configuration Management System   Priority: High

> A system used to ensure a solution conforms to approved requirements by documenting, tracking, and defining change control approval levels. The system should ensure that

requirements related articles are accessible yet are safeguarded for loss or unapproved change.

The "system" may be a set of formally documented procedures and manual tools used to manage changes or may be a sophisticated tool that allows for capture, management, and reporting through an integrated automated system.

Traceability Tools and Techniques

Traceability Tools and Techniques
Backlog Management
Issue (Problem) Tracking
Requirements Traceability Matrix

Backlog Management   Priority: High

The tools and techniques used to manage and maintain backlog work to be completed. In adaptive (agile) projects this relates to the product backlog. The product backlog is a prioritized list of user stories with the high priority stories at the top. The product backlog is maintained by the product owner, meaning user stories are added, moved, or deleted as needed to adapt to the current project/solution needs.

"Backlog" may apply to any list of features, requirements, or components that are not completed.

Issue (Problem) Tracking   Priority: High

One aspect of requirements management and traceability is tracking, monitoring, and understanding which requirements have issues. Issues can range from conflicts with other requirements that need resolution, uncertainty of the specifics of a requirement, defects, or unconfirmed assumptions. Issue (problem) tracking helps to prevent project barriers and slowdowns by facilitating timely resolution of requirements before they are handed off to the project team for implementation.

Issue (Problem) Tracking	
Description	An organized approach to tracking, management, and resolution of defects, issues, problems, and risks throughout the requirements life cycle.
Characteristics	Helps to monitor who is working on a particular issue and any timelines regarding resolution. Details captured may include a description, date discovered, impact, priority, date needed by, owner, status, who implementing the response, date closed, etc.

Requirements Traceability Matrix   **Priority: High**

We cannot stress enough the important of understanding the Requirements Traceability Matrix in preparing for the PMI-PBA exam. The Requirements Traceability Matrix provides many advantages to the business analyst in requirements management such as:

- Ensures requirements align with project and organization goals and objectives.

- Provides for requirements to be traced back to the business or project objectives to validate they will solve the problem being addressed, and forward through design and to the finished product.

- Links requirements that are related and/or dependent on each other for easier identification of impacts resulting from change requests.

- Provides a means to record other information regarding requirements.

- Organizes requirements in a meaningful way that will facilitate communication with project stakeholders.

- Helps manage scope creep.

- Tracks the status of requirements and satisfaction of them through to the team deliverables.

Requirements Traceability Matrix	
Description	A matrix used to link product requirements from the business goals to the deliverables that support them. The matrix will include additional attributes useful to tracking and managing each requirement.
Characteristics	Examples of what may be included: - Unique identifier - Short description - Business requirements - Product development stage (design, build, test...) - WBS cross reference - Status - Rationale - Priority - Owner - Source - Version - Date completed - Stakeholder satisfaction - Stability - Complexity - Acceptance criteria

Version Control Tools and Techniques

Version Control Tools and Techniques
Version Control System

Version Control System	Priority: High

Tools and techniques to manage and control versions of the work product. This includes tracking revisions and information regarding those decisions. There are automated tools to aid in this and some software packages include versioning as a standard. Version control may be handled without an automated system with techniques such as creating a revision table that document authors maintain manually.

The "system" may be a set of procedures and manual tools used to manage document changes or it may be a sophisticated tool that allows for capture, update, and communication of document versions through an integrated automated system.

Traceability and Monitoring – Exercise 2

Use the clues to complete the crossword puzzle below for terms used in Traceability and Monitoring.

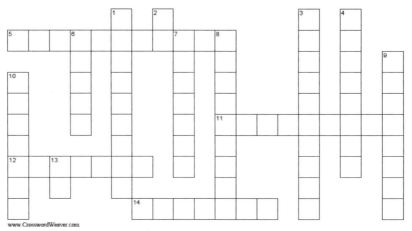

Traceability and Monitoring

www.CrosswordWeaver.com

ACROSS

5 Work created to supply needed information
11 A requirement should trace up to this
12 A Requirements Traceability Matrix helps to identify these
14 A well designed Requirements Traceabiilty Matrix can promote communicating the right information by use of these.

DOWN

1 A requirement relationship where one requirement is essential to the other
2 Responsible for product scope (abbr.)
3 Work that is not authorized
4 Approved version of a work product
6 A concern or question regarding a requirement may get tracked as this
7 Planned work that has not been done
8 To progressively provide more detail
9 A requirement that has been postponed to a later release may have a status of this.
10 Different instance of a work product
13 Responsible for project scope (abbr.)

PMI-PBA Practice Exam

Here are sample questions on Traceability and Monitoring to help you practice answering PMI-PBA exam questions. Answers are listed at the end of the chapter.

1. You have received an approved change request from the project manager and have updated the baseline requirements with the changes and published a new version of the document. This is an example of:
    a. Change control.
    b. Configuration management.
    c. Re-baselining.
    d. Requirements management.

2. The following statements demonstrate how requirements traceability benefits scope management EXCEPT for:
    a. A stakeholder requirement must be traced to solution requirements to prevent a gap in fulfilling customer needs.
    b. A high priority requirement must be traced to a test condition or test case.
    c. A design function must be traced to a functional requirement to prevent scope creep.
    d. A functional requirement must be traced to a business requirement to ensure all requirements belong within the scope of the project.

3. Which of the following can help guard against scope creep?
    a. A strong stakeholder leader
    b. Brainstorming
    c. Problem management
    d. Requirements traceability

4. Requirements must be _____ to be managed, as stakeholders cannot consent to requirements they are not aware of.
    a. Defined
    b. Elicited
    c. Documented
    d. Communicated

5. Traceability of requirements means:
    a. Requirements can be traced forward through design and to the finished product and are tested to ensure they work.
    b. Requirements can be traced back to the business or project objectives, and who provided them, to validate they will solve the problem being addressed.
    c. Requirements can be traced back to the business or project objectives to validate they will solve the problem being addressed, and forward through design and to the finished product.
    d. Requirements adhere to an organization template to ensure they help support strategic direction of the organization.

6. When communicating requirements, which of the following roles typically wants to have high-level summaries to help them understand the impact of the requirements?
   a. SME
   b. Regulator
   c. Sponsor
   d. Tester

7. Which of the following examples demonstrates the "effort" relationship:
   a. For an online mortgage application, the online application is not wanted without adequate login functionality.
   b. Once the login is implemented, it makes it easy to add other secure features like accessing loan information after the loan is created.
   c. The login requirement includes the user id, password, and password reminder requirements.
   d. The 'password reminder' requirement increases in desirability when the login functionality is implemented.

8. Quint was assigned as the BA/QA for his next project. After requirements were completed several months later, management learned that there were over 2,000 requirements for the project. The requirements were completed on time but Quint's estimate for traceability, quality assurance, and defect resolution due to the large number of requirements made it clear that the project deadline would need to be delayed if they wanted the project to move forward. In order to speed things up in the future, Quint likely recommended which of the following:
   a. Mercury automated testing tool
   b. Configuration management system
   c. Requirements management tool
   d. Outsource the effort

9. Which statement about conflict is true?
   a. Conflicts that affect the requirements must be resolved before formal approval is given.
   b. Sign-off can occur provisionally if the parties agree that not resolving the conflict does not present a risk to the business analysis effort.
   c. Conflicts do not need to be resolved when using a change-driven approach and no formal approval is required.
   d. When conflicts occur that jeopardize the effort, the business domain subject matter expert will resolve the conflict.

10. It is the role of the BA to analyze change requests by performing each of the following tasks EXCEPT for which one:
    a. Ensure that each change request is traceable back to the source.
    b. Determine the timeline in order to achieve the appropriate design solution for the problem to be solved.
    c. Ensure that the request is understood by key stakeholders.
    d. Determine the impact of executing the change on external processes, people or systems.

Exercise Answers

Exercise 1

Traceability and Monitoring Tasks	Mnemonic
1. **Trace** Requirements	**T**
2. **Monitor** Requirements Status	**M**
3. **Update** Requirements Status	**U**
4. **Communicate** Requirements Status	**C**
5. Manage **Changes** to Requirements	**C**

Exercise 2

Traceability and Monitoring

Solution:

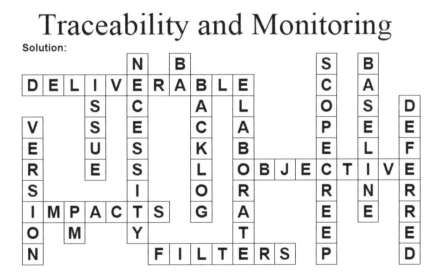

PMI-PBA Practice Exam Answers

1. You have received an approved change request from the project manager and have updated the baseline requirements with the changes and published a new version of the document. This is an example of:

   a. Change control

   > The question speaks to what the 'new version of the document' is an example of. The overall process is change control. The versioning of the document is configuration management.

   b. Configuration management

   > **Correct!** *PMBOK® Guide* 5.6.1.1 Project management plan / configuration management plan.

   c. Rebaselining

   > Made up answer.

   d. Requirements management

   > Too broad.

2. The following statements demonstrate how requirements traceability benefits scope management EXCEPT for:

   a. A stakeholder requirement must be traced to solution requirements to prevent a gap in fulfilling customer needs.

   > This benefits scope management, so does not answer the question.

   b. A high priority requirement must be traced to a test condition or test case.

   > **Correct! Traceability aids risk-based testing, but whether or not a requirement is high-priority does necessarily relate to scope management.**

   c. A design function must be traced to a functional requirement to prevent scope creep.

   > This benefits scope management, so does not answer the question.

   d. A functional requirement must be traced to a business requirement to ensure all requirements belong within the scope of the project

   > This benefits scope management, so does not answer the question.

3. Which of the following can help guard against scope creep?

   a. A strong stakeholder leader.

   > Not applicable.

   b. Brainstorming.

   > This could actually lead to scope creep unless other things are done.

   c. Problem management.

   > Not applicable.

   d. Requirements traceability.

   > **Correct!** *PMBOK® Guide* 5.2.

4. Requirements must be _____ to be managed, as stakeholders cannot consent to requirements they are not aware of.

    a. Defined.

    > Just because a requirement is defined does not mean the stakeholders are aware of it.

    b. Elicited.

    > Elicitation of requirements is the drawing out of requirements from stakeholders.

    c. Documented.

    > In an adaptive approach, all requirements are not formally documented.

    d. Communicated.

    > **Correct!** *PMBOK® Guide* **10.1.2.1**

5. Traceability of requirements means:

    a. Requirements can be traced forward through design and to the finished product and are tested to ensure they work.

    > Only part of the meaning of traceability (forward).

    b. Requirements can be traced back to the business or project objectives, and who provided them, to validate they will solve the problem being addressed.

    > Only part of the meaning of traceability (backward).

    c. Requirements can be traced back to the business or project objectives to validate they will solve the problem being addressed and forward through design and to the finished product.

    > **Correct! Traceability is bi-directional. Trace back to the business/project objectives, and forward into the development/testing.**

    d. Requirements adhere to an organization template to ensure they help support strategic direction of the organization.

    > An invented answer.

6. When communicating requirements, which of the following roles typically wants to have high-level summaries to help them understand the impact of the requirements?

    a. SME.

    > They will typically have to understand each requirement at a detailed level, not just a summary.

    b. Regulator.

    > If involved, they will likely need detailed requirements information, not summaries.

    c. Sponsor.

    > **Correct! Sponsors will often want summaries and high-level requirements.**

    d. Tester.

    > It is true that testers should have an understanding of how a solution meets business needs. They also need detailed requirements to help build test cases.

7. Which of the following examples demonstrates the "effort" relationship:

    a. For an online mortgage application, the online application is not wanted without adequate login functionality.

        This is an example of the 'necessity' relationship.

    b. Once the login is implemented, it makes it easy to add other secure features like accessing loan information after the loan is created.

        Correct! It will be less effort to implement one requirement once the other has been met.

    c. The login requirement includes the user id, password, and password reminder requirements.

        This is an example of the 'cover' relationship.

    d. The 'password reminder' requirement increases in desirability when the login functionality is implemented.

        This is an example of the 'value' relationship.

8. Quint was assigned as the BA/QA for his next project. After requirements were completed several months later, management learned that there were over 2,000 requirements for the project. The requirements were completed on time but Quint's estimate for traceability, quality assurance and defect resolution due to the large number of requirements made it clear that the project deadline would need to be delayed if they wanted the project to move forward. In order to speed things up in the future, Quint likely recommended which of the following:

    a. Mercury automated testing tool.

        A software testing tool.

    b. Configuration management system.

        Correct! *PMBOK® Guide* 4.5.

    c. Requirements management tool.

        Useful to manage the requirements details, not issues.

    d. Outsource the effort.

        Increases risk.

9. Which statement about conflict is true?
    a. **Conflicts that affect the requirements must be resolved before formal approval is given.'**   Correct!

    b. Sign-off can occur provisionally if the parties agree that not resolving the conflict does not present a risk to the business analysis effort.'   No, conflicts and issues related to requirements must be resolved before sign-off.

    c. Conflicts do not need to be resolved when using a change-driven approach and no formal approval is required.'   No, conflicts and issues related to requirements must be resolved before sign-off.

    d. When conflicts occur that jeopardize the effort, the business domain subject matter expert will resolve the conflict.'   Possibly, but not necessarily. The authority levels should dictate who resolves conflicts.

10. It is the role of the BA to analyze change requests by performing each of the following tasks EXCEPT for which one:
    a. Ensure that each change request is traceable back to the source.   *PMBOK® Guide* 5.2.

    b. **Determine the timeline in order to achieve the appropriate design solution for the problem to be solved.**   Correct! The timeline is something a project manager would determine.

    c. Ensure that the request is understood by key stakeholders.   *PMBOK® Guide* 4.5 and 5.2.

    d. Determine the impact of executing the change on external processes, people or systems.   *PMBOK® Guide* 4.5 and 5.2.

Summary

The Traceability and Monitoring domain describes the tasks and outputs documenting, managing, controlling changes, and communicating requirements including status. It emphasizes several traceability considerations such as:

- Continuous monitoring and updating of requirements including status.

- Communicating requirements and their status to stakeholders.

- Leveraging the Requirements Traceability Matrix to aid in impact analysis and communication of requirements.

Here are the themes covered that you should internalize:

- Use planned processes to control scope and get approval for all changes.

- Use planned traceability structure to help manage and communicate requirements.

 Traceability Monitoring Goal: Document, manage, and communicate requirements, their status, and approved changes.

                    PMI-PBA Certification Study Guide

6. Evaluation

Overview

Before implementing a product or solution, the solution must be assessed to confirm that the requirements have been satisfied and that the solution is a success. It is important to note that the business analyst is assessing quality control results rather than performing quality control activities. The final task of the Evaluation domain is to assess a "deployed" solution to assess how well it is meeting the business need.

Tasks in this domain are devoted to BA activities to evaluate a solution, facilitate an implementation go/no-go decision, and finally to evaluate performance after the solution is deployed.

 Evaluation Goal: Assess the solution's ability to satisfy requirements and meet the business need.

When you are finished with this chapter, you will know:

- How to define Evaluation.

- The four tasks contained in the Evaluation domain.

- The major areas of emphasis in evaluation, including assessing test and implementation results.

Evaluation
The tasks, tools, and techniques used to determine that the solution satisfies the requirements and meets the business need.

Domain Themes

The PMI-PBA exam includes several reoccurring themes. One useful way to use these themes is when you narrow down an exam question to two close answers. If one of the themes suggests one over the other, then go with the theme. The common themes to watch for in Evaluation are as follows:

Theme	Comments
Quality control	Understanding quality control concepts is essential to assessing solution test results.
Deployed solution	Task 4 is specific to evaluating a "deployed" solution, meaning that the solution has been implemented and in use, and the

Theme	Comments
	business can measure performance of the solution.
Evaluate early and often	• Treat requirements analysis, traceability, testing, and evaluation as complementary activities. • Many of the techniques used during Evaluation activities may be also used during analysis, testing, or needs assessment. • There is some overlap between evaluation techniques and traceability.

Figure 6-1: PMI-PBA Themes applicable to the Evaluation domain

Evaluation is the smallest domain with only 10 percent of questions. See below.

Domain	Percentage of items on test	Approximate number of questions
Domain 1: Needs Assessment	18%	36
Domain 2: Planning	22%	44
Domain 3: Analysis	35%	70
Domain 4: Traceability and Monitoring	15%	30
Domain 5: Evaluation	10%	20

Figure 6-2: Evaluation Domain
Source: PMI®

Domain: High-Level View

The four tasks in the Evaluation domain are listed below. The tasks in the domain may not be performed sequentially, but it is helpful to learn the tasks and their order as a way to remember what each of them does. PMI® does not provide task titles for each task, but rather a detailed description. See the table below for the tasks as defined by PMI® with a task title developed for this guide in order to aid learning and remember the tasks.

PMI-PBA Certification Study Guide

Task 1
Validate Test Results

Validate the solution's test results, reports, and other test evidence against the requirements acceptance criteria in order to determine whether the solution satisfies the requirements.

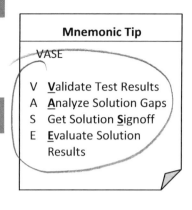

Mnemonic Tip

VASE

V **V**alidate Test Results
A **A**nalyze Solution Gaps
S Get Solution **S**ignoff
E **E**valuate Solution Results

Task 2
Analyze Solution Gaps

Analyze and communicate the solution's identified gaps and deltas using quality assurance tools and methods in order to enable stakeholders to resolve discrepancies between solution scope, requirements, and developed solution.

Task 3
Get Solution Sign-off

Obtain stakeholder sign-off on the developed solution using decision-making techniques in order to proceed with deployment.

Task 4
Evaluate Solution Results

Evaluate the deployed solution using valuation techniques in order to determine how well the solution meets the business case and value proposition.

To help you remember the tasks, use a mnemonic of "VASE." This nonsense acronym captures the tasks within Evaluation in their given order. The first letter of the mnemonic is highlighted to help you memorize it.

The chapter below presents each of the tasks along with more information on the task descriptions and tools and techniques used to perform each task.

Task, Tools, Techniques, and Outputs

The PMI-PBA exam does not follow a specific "Body of Knowledge" in terms of identifying inputs, tools and techniques, and outputs (ITTOs) for each of the tasks. The table below describes some standard concepts in inputs, tools and techniques, and outputs for each task in order to provide context and greater understanding. The PMI-PBA exam will not test specifically on these ITTOs. ITTOs may be present in test questions as a means to test your understanding of the task.

Input	Task	Tools and Techniques	Output
Acceptance Criteria Constructed Solution Test Results	1. Validate the solution's test results, reports, and other test evidence against the requirements acceptance criteria in order to determine whether the solution satisfies the requirements.	Validation Verification	Test Results (validated)
Solution Scope Developed Solution Requirements Test Results (validated)	2. Analyze and communicate the solution's identified gaps and deltas using quality assurance tools and methods in order to enable stakeholders to resolve discrepancies between solution scope, requirements, and developed solution.	Analytic *(covered in Analysis domain)* Quality Management	Gap Analysis Resolved Discrepancies
Gap Analysis Resolved Discrepancies	3. Obtain stakeholder sign-off on the developed solution using decision-making techniques in order to proceed with deployment.	Decision Making *(covered in Analysis domain)*	Solution Sign-off
Business Case Deployed Solution	4. Evaluate the deployed solution using valuation techniques in order to determine how well the solution meets the business case and value proposition.	Evaluation Measurement *(covered in Analysis domain)* Valuation *(covered in Needs Assessment domain)*	Solution Assessment

Figure 6-3: Evaluation Monitoring ITTOs

                      PMI-PBA Certification Study Guide

Part 1 – Evaluation Tasks

Task 1 – Validate Test Results

Validate the solution's test results, reports, and other test evidence against the requirements acceptance criteria in order to determine whether the solution satisfies the requirements.

<u>V</u>ASE

While solution testing itself is not a business analysis activity, validating the test results is a large responsibility of the business analyst. The business analyst works closely with the quality assurance team to ensure all requirements are adequately tested, support the test efforts by providing information and clarification as needed, and reviewing the test results. This begins with review and feedback of the test plan and test cases. The Requirements Traceability Matrix provides a foundation for the validation. While the quality assurance function will test each requirement, the business analyst is responsible for evaluating whether the solution will be usable, adds value to the business, and is meeting project goals and objectives.

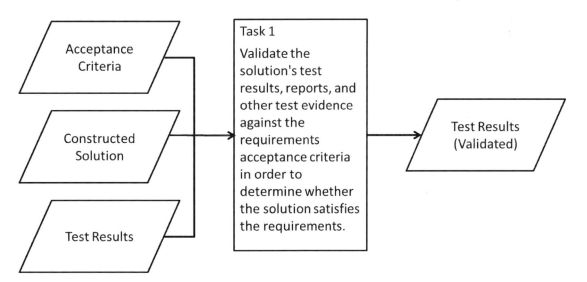

Figure 6-4: Validate Test Results ITO

Considerations for Validate Test Results

Roles & Responsibilities

The lines between business analysis and quality assurance activities can be pretty unclear. This task explicitly states **"validate the solution's test results."** This implies that the actual testing is occurring outside of the business analysis role. Often-times business analysts may be asked to assist with testing activities. In this case, they have shifted from business analysis into quality assurance. The roles and responsibilities should be addressed in the Requirements Management Plan, specifically in a RACI matrix. Below are some typical delineators between the business analyst and the quality assurance team.

Activities / Deliverables	Business Analyst	Quality Assurance
Test Plans	Consulted	Responsible
Test Cases	Consulted	Responsible
QA Support	Responsible	Consulted
Test Execution	Informed	Responsible
Defect Tracking	Consulted	Responsible
Prioritize Defects	Responsible	Consulted
Determine Solution Readiness	Responsible	Consulted

Figure 6-5: Quality Assurance Activities RACI

Plan for Evaluation of Solution

The business analyst should confirm that test plans cover all needed aspects of solution validation while balancing the cost-benefit of the testing activities. Some considerations in the test plan review are:
- Do the test activities align and support the project goals and objectives?
- Does the cost of conducting the test activity provide sufficient benefit to justify the activity?
- Does the planned solution include the infrastructure and data needed to support the test plan?
- Has adequate consideration been given to:
  - End-to-end integrated testing
  - Data and data migration testing
  - Testing for appropriate access given user roles and permission
  - Reporting and tracking of identified defects

        PMI-PBA Certification Study Guide

Cost of Quality

The "Cost of Quality" includes all costs to a solution throughout its life. This cost should be factored into the overall cost-benefit of the project. The *PMBOK® Guide* identifies the following as elements of the cost of quality.

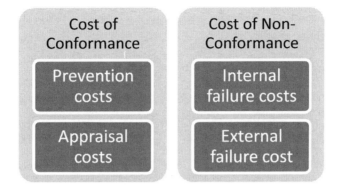

Figure 6-6: Cost of Quality (COQ)
Source: *PMBOK® Guide-Fifth Edition*

- **Cost of Conformance** – Money spent to ensure compliance to requirements
    - o **Prevention costs** – Building a quality product
        - ▪ Training
        - ▪ Process documentation
        - ▪ Equipment
        - ▪ Time to do it right
    - o **Appraisal costs** – Assessing the quality
        - ▪ Testing
        - ▪ Destructive testing loss
        - ▪ Inspections
        - ▪ Training
        - ▪ Process documentation
        - ▪ Equipment
        - ▪ Time to do it right
- **Cost of Non-Conformance** – Money spent because of failure to comply with requirements
    - o **Internal failure costs** – Failures found by the project
        - ▪ Rework
        - ▪ Scrap
    - o **External failure costs** – Failures found by the customer
        - ▪ Liabilities
        - ▪ Warranty work
        - ▪ Lost business

Requirements Traceability

The Requirements Traceability Matrix should be leveraged in validating the test results in two ways:

1. Verify all requirements will be tested by tracing test documentation references.

2. Track changes in requirements status as tests are executed.

When to Validate Test Results

- For a predictive project life-cycle, validate the solution at the end of the project life cycle either immediately before a release or at an agreed-upon time after a release.

- For an iterative or adaptive project life cycle, validation is performed at the end of every iteration, sprint, or release, when the team provided production-ready functionality for the stakeholders to evaluate.

    Source: *Business Analysis for Practitioners: A Practice Guide*, pages 164-168

Techniques

There are several techniques that can help in validating test results. These techniques fall into two categories – **Validation Tools and Techniques** and **Verification Tools and Techniques**. A summary of the categories are provided below. Details on each technique will follow in the final section of the Evaluation chapter.

Techniques – *Validate Test Results*	
Validation Tools and Techniques Tools and techniques used to validate the effectiveness of a solution.	Includes: - Day-in-the Life (DITL) Testing - Exploratory Testing - Given-When-Then - Integration Testing - User Acceptance Testing
Verification Tools and Techniques Tools and techniques used to verify work product.	Includes: - Desk Checking - Inspection - Peer Review - Test - Walk-through

Outputs

Output: *Test Results (Validated)*

Test results that have been confirmed to support adequate testing of all solution requirements and verification of the reported test results. The Requirements Traceability Matrix should be updated to indicate requirement status based on the validated results.

PMBOK® Guide References

More information on test validation can be found in the *PMBOK® Guide*:

- 8.1 – Plan Quality Management

- 8.3 – Control Quality

Task 2 – Analyze Solution Gaps

Analyze and communicate the solution's identified gaps and deltas using quality assurance tools and methods in order to enable stakeholders to resolve discrepancies between solution scope, requirements, and developed solution.

VASE

This next step in the Evaluation domain focuses on the analysis of test results to determine the level of conformance with the solution scope and requirements. Quality control techniques are used here to better understand the causes, impacts, and overall effects of solution defects. The information gathered through this analysis will be communicated to project stakeholders to aid in making a decision as to whether or not the solution is ready for implementation.

Defect
A flaw in a deliverable that either lessens its quality, or causes it to vary from its preferred characteristics.   Example: defective requirements include: incorrect, incomplete, missing, etc.

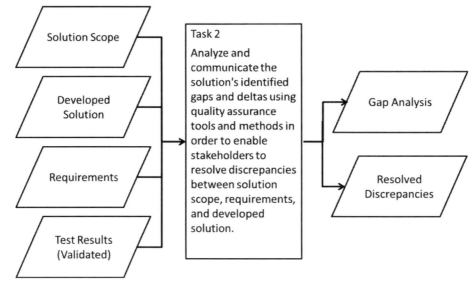

Figure 6-7: Analyze Solution Gaps ITO

Considerations for Analyze Solution Gaps

Solution Gaps

Solution gaps are gaps between the stated required functionality and performance and the results from the developed solution. The following describes potential gaps to be noted and addressed:

- Features or functions that do not meet acceptance criteria.
- Solution requirements that are not satisfied.
- Barriers to the solution meeting project objectives.

Not all gaps are created equal. The analysis of each gap should include understanding of the overall impact to the project goals and objectives. Business analysts may be called upon to help identify which defects must be *resolved*, which could be *moderated* through "workarounds" or other solutions, and which can be *accepted* until work can be done to repair them. Those defects that will not have a significant impact to the business value may be determined acceptable for implementation. This is especially true if the impact of the defect is insignificant and/or of the likelihood of the defect being experienced is low. The table below provides one example of how gaps and defects may be prioritized by the business analyst.

Impact of Defect			
	Low	Medium	High
Low	Level 4	Level 3	Level 2
Medium	Level 3	Level 2	Level 1
High	Level 2	Level 1	Critical

(Left side vertical label: Likelihood of Occurrence)

Figure 6-8: Defect Probability and Impact Matrix

Quality Management

Quality management tools help to identify trends in defects that are pertinent to understanding the overall causes and effects of solution quality. Quality control is a team effort, but the business analyst is the one making the determination that the solution is ready for implementation or not. Quality analysis will help identify project and team strategies needed to improve the overall solution quality. The specific aspects of these tools are discussed in Part 2 of this chapter. Here are few examples how the use of the tools contribute to analysis and understanding:

- **Checksheet** – Identify and count the main contributing factor to each defect. Is it because of ambiguous requirements, misstated requirements, or an error in the code? Identify the causes to help identify patterns.
- **Pareto Diagram** – Use the information from the checksheet to identify the greatest contributing causes to defects. Identifying and addressing these causes first will help bring the overall quality of the solution up faster.
- **Root Cause Analysis** – Use the Cause and Effect Diagram in conjunction with Five Whys to better understand the root cause and identify corrective action that will have the biggest impact on quality improvement.
- **Control Charts** – Use to provide big picture on variances in quality measures for better understanding of the impact to the solution.

Techniques – *Analyze Solution Gaps*	
Analytic Tools and Techniques (*covered in Analysis domain*) Tools and techniques used to analyze the business and requirements for further understanding of the situation and solution requirements.	**Includes:** - Decomposition - Dependency Analysis - Gap Analysis - Impact Analysis - Progressive Elaboration - Risk Analysis
Quality Management Tools and Techniques Tools and techniques used to measure the quality of work product or deliverables.	**Includes:** - Activity Network Diagram - Affinity Diagram - Cause and Effect Diagram - Checksheets - Control Charts - Flow Chart - Histogram - Interrelationship Diagram - Matrix Diagrams - Pareto Diagram - Process Decision Program Chart (PDPC) - Statistical Sampling - Tree Diagrams

Communicating

Communications should provide stakeholders with a clear picture of the solution gaps and the overall impact to achieving project goals and objectives. As with all communications, special attention needs to be given to providing the right level of information to stakeholders so that they can make an informed decision without extraneous information that may cloud or confuse judgment. Use the RACI matrix and the communication portion of the Requirements Management Plan to determine information to communicate and to whom. Be candid about known defects and the impact to the solution and anticipated impact to the overall business. Be prepared with specifics to aid in decision-making. These specifics will also need to be shared with product users upon implementation to set expectations and avoid surprises.

Outputs

Output: *Gap Analysis*

An analysis documenting the variances in the planned scope, features, and requirements within the developed solution.

Output: *Resolved Discrepancies*

Provide a recommendation as to whether or not the developed solution is ready for implementation. Include rationale for the recommendation and potential impacts if the recommendation is not accepted.

PMBOK® Guide References

More information on test validation can be found in the *PMBOK® Guide*:

- 4.6 – Close Project or Phase

- 8.3 – Control Quality

Task 3 – Get Solution Sign-off

Obtain stakeholder sign-off on the developed solution using decision-making techniques in order to proceed with deployment.

VA<u>S</u>E

Formal sign-off is required before a solution can be implemented for use. Approval will be required from those stakeholders identified in the Requirements Management Plan and RACI matrix. The business analyst will facilitate approval and sign-off based on the results of the gap analysis and resulting recommendation.

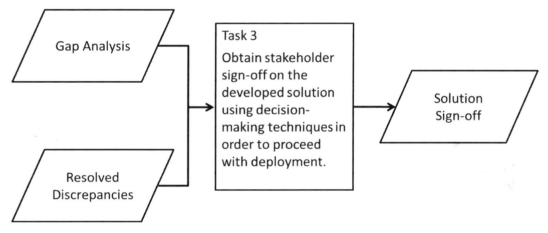

Figure 6-9: Get Solution Sign-off ITO

Considerations for Get Solution Sign-off

Go/No-Go Decision

The business analyst will facilitate a go/no-go decision for solution implementation from the stakeholders who have been identified as approvers using decision-making tools and techniques. Considerations for this decision include:

- Identified solution gaps and impacts to project goals and objectives.
- Business analyst recommendation for go/no-go with rationale and anticipated impacts of not following the recommendation.
- Stakeholder expectations and needs.
- External project constraints.
- Alternatives including:
    - Implement the solution.
    - Implement with planned corrective action (subsequent maintenance release or new transition requirements).
    - Delay solution implementation.
    - Cancel project, do not implement.

One aspect of the decision needs to be an understanding of the cost of implementing versus not implementing. This is where it is important to recognize the concept of **"sunk cost."** Sunk costs cannot be recovered. In looking at whether or not to implement a solution, the evaluation needs to be based on the additional cost to complete the project compared to the value to be achieved. To use an old cliché, "don't throw good money after bad." If the solution cannot achieve the project goals and objectives, don't spend time, effort, and money implementing, transitioning to, and maintaining the solution. The bad investment will only be compounded.

Sunk Cost
The cost already invested in a project or solution. Sunk costs often unduly influence stakeholders to proceed with solution implementation in order to not "waste" the investment.

Sign-off

Sign-off should be facilitated and captured according to the Requirements Management Plan. The level of formality for sign-off will vary by project. Complex, far-reaching projects are likely to require more formal sign-off processes and include storage and retention of approvals. Sign-off may be indicated by a "wet signature" (handwritten signature), electronic signature, official email, or through electronic voting.

Techniques – *Get Solution Sign-off*	
Decision Making Tools and Techniques *(covered in Analysis domain)* Tools and techniques to facilitate a group in order to understand options and agree upon a selected course of action.	**Includes:** - Consensus Building - Delphi Technique - Multi-Voting - Nominal Group Technique - Options Analysis - Weighted Criteria

Outputs

Output: *Solution Sign-off*
Official, documented approval for implementing the solution or other course of action as determined by those with approval authority.

PMBOK® Guide References

More information on test validation can be found in the *PMBOK® Guide*:

- 4.6 – Close Project or Phase

Task 4 – Evaluate Solution Results

Evaluate the deployed solution using valuation techniques in order to determine how well the solution meets the business case and value proposition.

VAS**E**

One often neglected aspect of business analysis for projects is an evaluation to determine if the solution is successful. This evaluation happens after the solution is implemented, the users have effectively transitioned, and the business has had the opportunity measure the impacts. The project goals, objectives, and solution acceptance criteria serve as a basis for the evaluation. The results of this evaluation will help to make better informed decisions regarding the product. A residual benefit is gaining insights that can be applied to future projects.

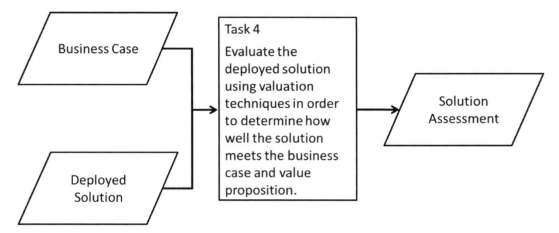

Figure 6-10: Evaluate Solution Results ITO

Considerations for Evaluate Solution Results

The extent to which a project or project deliverable met its objectives cannot be measured until the solution has been deployed and the end-users have been using the solution for a sufficient amount of time. The term "deployed solution" may be on the PMI-PBA exam.

Measuring Results

Evaluating a deployed solution means to conduct an assessment after the project is closed and the project team is dispersed. This task will often fall to a Project Management Office or Portfolio Staff. The original business analyst may be consulted or asked to perform the assessment or the task may be completed by someone else.

The key performance indicators (KPIs) and acceptance criteria identified in Analysis, Task 8 (Elaborate and Specify Acceptance Criteria), serves as the basis for the evaluation. The metrics selected in analysis should be supported given the organization's infrastructure and available data. Long-term analysis will require capturing individual and cumulative metrics over time in order to identify trends that will inform future product and project decisions.

Understanding Solution Options

The result of evaluating solution results is knowing how well the solution meets or does not meet the project objectives and the value it brings to the organization overall. This information can be used to facilitate future decisions regarding the product. Likely outcomes include:

- Continue maintenance and operation of the solution as implemented.
- Enhance the solution with additional investment in features, functions, or service (business case for a new technology project).
- Update business processes to address deficiencies (business case for a process improvement project).
- Solution replacement or phase out the solution.

Future Projects

A benefit of evaluating the deployed solution results is gaining knowledge and information to support future projects. The results add to the organizational process assets and can be used in future business cases and project planning. This information provides historical knowledge of the types of projects that have resulted in the most value to the organization, and the projects that will provide clues to the most effective requirements and project management practices that can be leveraged in future projects.

Techniques – *Evaluate Solution Results*

	Includes:
Evaluation Tools and Techniques Evaluation tools and techniques are techniques used to evaluate the effectiveness of a project, team, or solution.	- Lessons Learned - Retrospectives
Measurement Tools and Techniques *(covered in Analysis domain)* Tools and techniques used to measure solution performance after implementation.	- Metrics such as Key Performance Indicators (KPIs) - Service Level Agreement (SLA) - Planguage
Valuation Tools and Techniques *(covered in Needs Assessment domain)* Tools and techniques used to determine the value of the potential solution to the organization.	- Cost-Benefit Analysis - Force Field Analysis - Kano Model - Net Promoter Score - Purpose Alignment Model - SWOT Analysis - Value Stream Map

Outputs

Output: *Solution Assessment*

An assessment of how well the solution is meeting the project goals and objectives. May include recommendations for specific actions to increase overall value to the organization, including potential enhancements or a recommendation to replace or phase out the solution.

PMBOK® Guide References

More information on the Evaluate Solution Results can be found in the *PMBOK® Guide*:

- 4.6 – Close Project or Phase

Evaluation – Exercise 1

Write the mnemonic letters for the four tasks of the Evaluation domain and then complete the missing words for each task in the blanks provided below.

Evaluation Tasks	Mnemonic
1. _____ _____ Results	_____
2. _____ Solution _____	_____
3. Get _____ _____	_____
4. _____ Solution Results	_____

Evaluation – Exercise 2

Use the clues below to complete the crossword puzzle.

Evaluation

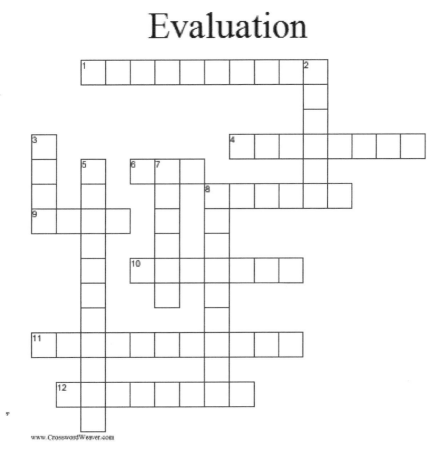

www.CrosswordWeaver.com

ACROSS

1 A way to accomplish a task that is different than originally intended

4 A defect is _____ if a decision is made to implement it as-is

6 Contains information on how to get solution signoff (abbr.)

8 The name associated with the 80-20 rule

9 Investment dollars that are already spent and cannot be recovered are referred to as this

10 Indication of approval

11 Responsible, _____, Consulted, Informed

12 Status of solution that is used daily by end users in the business

DOWN

2 Does not conform to requirements

3 The differences between desired and actual state

5 A solution that is developed and available for quality assurance activities

7 A document that ensures requirements align to business goals and objectives

8 Uses tags to define acceptance criteria

Part 2 – Techniques for Evaluation

The tools and techniques below are those that may be most helpful in the Evaluation domain. Importantly, the tools and techniques are not domain or task specific; they may be used for more than one task and in more than one domain. It will be necessary for the person doing the business analysis work to determine which tools to use and when.

Category	Technique
Analytic Tools and Techniques *(covered in Analysis domain)*	
	Decomposition
	Dependency Analysis
	Gap Analysis
	Impact Analysis
	Progressive Elaboration
	Risk Analysis
Decision Making Tools and Techniques *(covered in Analysis domain)*	
	Consensus Building
	Delphi Technique
	Multi-Voting
	Nominal Group Technique
	Options Analysis
	Weighted Criteria
Evaluation Tools and Techniques *Evaluation Tools and techniques are techniques used to evaluate the effectiveness of a project, team, or solution.*	
	Lessons Learned
	Retrospectives
Measurement Tools and Techniques *(covered in the Analysis domain)*	
	Metrics such as Key Performance Indicators (KPIs)
	Organizational Readiness
	Planguage
	Service Level Agreement (SLA)
Quality Management Tools and Techniques *Tools and techniques used to measure and analyze the quality of work product or deliverables.*	
	Activity Network Diagram *(see Scheduling Tools in Planning domain)*
	Affinity Diagram *(see Facilitation tools in Competencies)*
	Cause and Effect Diagram *(see Root Cause Tools in Needs Assessment domain)*
	Checksheet
	Control Chart
	Flow Charts
	Histograms
	Interrelationship Diagrams *(see Root Cause Tools in Needs Assessment domain)*
	Matrix Diagram
	Pareto Diagrams

Category	Technique
	Process Decision Program Chart (PDPC)
	Statistical Sampling
	Tree Diagrams *(see Decomposition in Analytic Tools in Analysis domain)*
Validation Tools and Techniques *Tools and techniques used to validate the effectiveness of a solution.*	
	Day-in-the Life (DITL) Testing
	Exploratory Testing
	Given-When-Then
	Integration Testing
	User Acceptance Testing
Valuation Tools and Techniques *(covered in Needs Assessment domain)*	
	Cost-Benefit Analysis
	Feasibility Analysis
	Force Field Analysis
	Kano Model
	Net Promoter Score
	Purpose Alignment Model
	SWOT Analysis
	Value Stream Map
Verification Tools and Techniques *Tools and techniques used to verify work product.*	
	Desk Checking
	Inspection
	Peer Review
	Test
	Walk-through

Figure 6-11: Tools and Techniques for Needs Assessment

The following pages provide additional details about the tools and techniques that may be most helpful in this domain. (Details for some techniques may be covered in a different domain as noted above.) Not all tools and techniques will be discussed at a great level of detail. The amount of information provided relates to the priority of the tool or technique on the exam. Each technique has been rated with a priority level of low, moderate, or high to help in prioritizing study. Items marked as low may appear in your certification exam; items marked moderate are likely to show up in one or two questions, and items marked high may have multiple questions relating to their use.

Evaluation Tools and Techniques

Evaluation tools and techniques are used to evaluate the effectiveness of a project, team, or solution.

Evaluation Tools and Techniques
Lessons Learned
Retrospectives

Lessons Learned   Priority: High

This technique is done by project teams and key stakeholders to reflect on and capture project successes and areas that could be improved for the future. There is no standard way of conducting these and the stakeholders' preferences often dictate how they are run. When celebrations are done in conjunction with a lessons learned session, it can encourage participation and emphasize the positive outcomes from a project or project phase/iteration.

Lessons Learned	
Description	Discuss and compile what went well, and what could be improved on projects or project phases. Done to improve future performance.
Characteristics	Review and compile project items such as: • Project deliverables and final product delivered • Things that went well on the project • BA activities performed • Stakeholder concerns or issues • Performance and variances from plan • Root causes of variances • Corrective or preventive actions

Figure 6-12: Lessons Learned Overview

Example

After conducting a project to create an automated sales commission system, the team holds a lessons learned session. They combine it with a celebration because the project was difficult to do in conjunction with daily operational duties. The lessons learned discovered some missed requirements. The team discovered late in the project the need to include Accounting Control as a stakeholder, as well as the main Accounts Payable stakeholder group.

> **Lessons Learned**
>
> What went well and what could be improved on future projects or project phases. Done to improve future performance.

Retrospectives   **Priority: High**

Retrospectives are more than just a fancy way of saying "lessons learned." There are many differences. In particular, lessons learned typically happen at the end of a project or major project phase. This means the review may happen long after the project action. In contrast, a retrospective occurs at the end of each iteration. Agile iterations are typically one to four weeks. This means that the team is never more than four weeks away from the work of the iteration being reviewed. The retrospective identifies what is working well, what needs to be improved, and what should be discontinued in order for the team to be most effective. When this review happens at regular, short intervals, the improvement discussion occurs close to when the processes occur. This allows the team to do away with bad practices and increase productively quickly.

Retrospectives	
Description	Retrospectives are typically used in agile projects to review iterations. Team members meet to identify and discuss the results of the latest iteration, what is working well, and identify opportunities and actions for improvement.
Characteristics	• Set the stage – why we are here • Gather data – what has happened • Generate insights – what can we learn • Decide what to do – what action(s) will bring the greatest improvement • Close the retrospective – summary and action Source: Adapted from *Agile Retrospectives: Making Good Teams Great* (Derby, Larson 2006)

Figure 6-13: Retrospectives Overview

Quality Management Tools and Techniques

Tools and techniques used to measure and analyze the quality of work product or deliverables.

Quality Management Tools and Techniques
Activity Network Diagram (see Scheduling Tools in Planning domain)
Affinity Diagram (see Facilitation Tools in Competencies)
Cause and Effect Diagram (see Root Cause Tools in Needs Assessment domain)
Checksheet
Control Chart
Design of Experiments
Flow Charts
Histograms
Interrelationship Diagrams (see Root Cause Tools in Needs Assessment domain)
Matrix Diagram
Pareto Diagrams
Process Decision Program Chart (PDPC)
Scatter Diagram
Statistical Sampling
Tree Diagrams (see Decomposition in Analytic Tools in Analysis domain)

Checksheets

Priority: Moderate

Checksheets often are used to collect sampling results information about defects which then may be further analyzed using a Pareto Diagram.

Software Defects	
Categories	Occurrences
A	II
B	~~IIII~~ ~~IIII~~ ~~IIII~~ I
C	I
D	IIII ~~IIII~~ ~~IIII IIII IIII~~ III
E	IIII
F	~~IIII IIII IIII IIII IIII IIII~~ ~~IIII IIII IIII IIII IIII~~ III
G	II

Figure 6-14: Checksheet Example

A control chart's purpose is to determine whether or not a process is stable or has predictable performance (typically) over time by measuring output variables representing repetitive activities. Control charts can be used for both project and product life cycle processes.

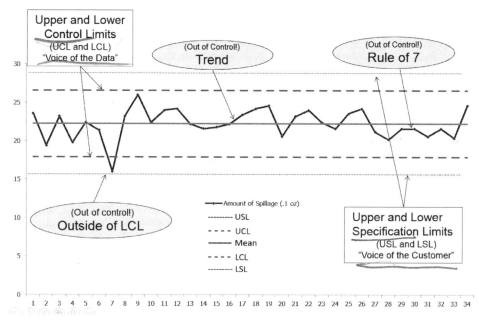

Figure 6-15: Control Chart Example

Key Concepts

- The middle line represents the mean or average of the data.

- The upper and lower control limits are usually set at +/- 3 sigma ("voice of the data"). Data points are plotted and then analyzed to determine if the process is "out of control" (unstable) or "in control" (stable). There are eight rules for "out of control" or <u>special cause</u> conditions – the exam will focus on the following four:

    - One point more than 3 sigma from the center line (outside of control limits).

    - Seven points in a row on same side of the center line (Rule of 7).

    - Six points in a row, all increasing or decreasing (trend).

    - Fourteen points in a row, alternating up and down.

- "Normal" variation (data points falling within control limits that do not follow the above-stated rules) is also called <u>common</u> or <u>random cause</u> variation.

- The upper and lower specification limits (USL, LSL) represent the "voice of the customer"; in other words, what is acceptable to the customer. The USL and LSL may be inside or outside of the UCLs and LCLs.

Design of Experiments   **Priority: Low**

Using statistical "what-if" scenarios to determine which combination of variables produce the best or desired quality outcome. Design of experiments, unlike other quality techniques, provides a tool for modifying multiple factors at the same time rather than just one at a time. It is more typically used on the product of the project, rather than the project itself.

Figure 6-16: Design of Experiments Cartoon

Flow Chart   Priority: Moderate

Graphically depict how the process flows from beginning to end to illuminate how components of the system are related. Flowcharting also helps to analyze how problems occur and highlight inefficiencies.

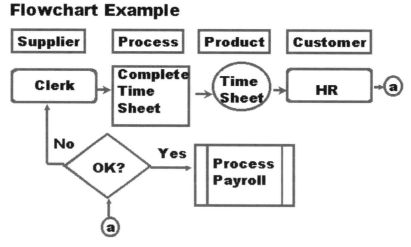

Figure 6-17: Flowchart Example

Histograms   Priority: Moderate

Histograms are bar charts showing how often something occurs. The height of each column represents the frequency of the data. Histograms help identify the cause of problems by the shape and width of the distribution. The columns of data may be unordered as shown above, or ordered as shown in the Pareto chart. Histograms typically don't include the element of time and how variations occur over time, although a Run Chart can be displayed as a Histogram as shown on the next page.

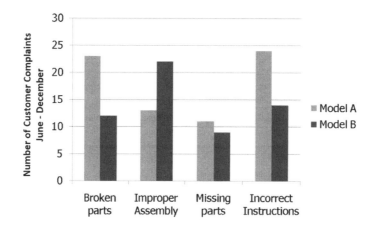

Figure 6-18: Histogram Example

Matrix Diagram   Priority: Low

Matrix diagrams use a series of columns and rows in order to map factors, causes, and objectives that are related.

Pareto Diagram   Priority: High

In 1906, Vilfredo Pareto inspired the 80/20 Principle, which states that 80 percent of problems are due to 20 percent of the causes.

The Pareto diagram shows how many results were generated by type or category of identified causes. It identifies the "vital few" causes of most quality problems. If those few problems are eliminated, about 75 to 80 percent of the problems will be eliminated. For example, if most of the problems in the Call Center are due to network issues, resolving those issues will eliminate most of the calls.

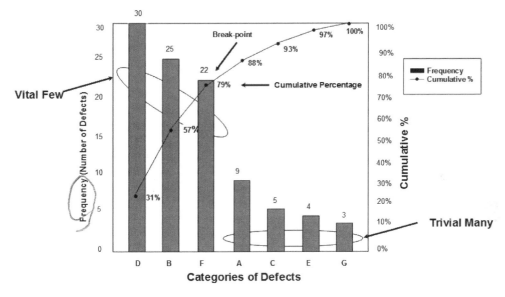

Figure 6-19: Pareto Diagram Example

Common Pareto Terminology *(It is unlikely you will be tested on this)*
- *Before and After Measures* – New Pareto bars can be drawn side by side with the original Pareto showing the effect of the change.
- *Breakpoint* – This is where the Pareto principle visibly takes effect on the chart.
- *Categories* of Contributors – These are the groups or clusters of problem categories.
- *Cumulative Percentage* –- This is the ongoing total percentage of contribution each problem contributes when added together.
- *Magnitude of Contribution* – This is how much each individual problem contributes to the total sum of all the problems added together.
- *Major Cause Breakdown* – This is the tallest bar on the graph.
- *Trivial Many* – These are other contributors to the problem that could be studied at a later time.
- *Vital Few* – These are the contributors that make up most of the problem.

Process Decision Program Chart (PDPC)   Priority: Low

A PDPC is a tool where process steps are identified and mapped in order to identify any potential issues and needed contingency plan.

Scatter Diagram   Priority: Moderate

A scatter diagram shows relationships or correlations between independent ("X" axis) and dependent ("Y" axis) variables. Independent variables are also known as "inputs" or "potential causes." Dependent variables are also known as "outputs" or "effects."

While scatter diagrams do show correlation, they DO NOT show cause and effect (further analysis is needed).

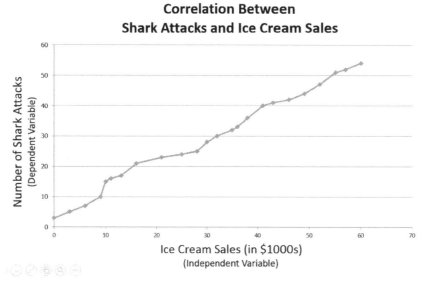

Figure 6-20: Scatter Diagram Example

The closer the points are to a diagonal line, the more closely they are positively (/) or negatively (\ ) correlated.

Statistical Sampling   Priority: Moderate

Statistical sampling is a technique where a small number of items representing a sample of the entire quantity are chosen for inspection. This is used to reduce the cost of quality rather than inspecting every item.

- **Attribute sampling** – The result is rated by whether or not the product conforms.
- **Variable sampling** – The result is rated by the degree of conformity.

Validation Tools and Techniques

Tools and techniques used to validate the effectiveness of a solution.

Validation Tools and Techniques
Day-in-the Life (DITL) Testing
Exploratory Testing
Given-When-Then
Integration Testing
User Acceptance Testing

Day-in-the Life (DITL) Testing   Priority: Low

DITL is testing conducted by someone knowledgeable in the business that focuses specific scenarios in order to verify the expected results are realized.

Exploratory Testing   Priority: Low

Exploratory testing is conducted by someone with knowledge of the business and testing without a script. This provides testing of some "out of the box" scenarios for expanded test coverage. This supplements formal testing methods but should not be done in place of them.

Given-When-Then   Priority: High

Given-When-Then is a tool used to articulate acceptance criteria. Statements are produced with:
- Given (some context)
- When (some action is carried out)
- Then (a particular set of observable consequences should obtain)

Example:

- Given my bank account is in credit, and I made no withdrawals recently
- When I attempt to withdraw an amount less than my card's limit
- Then the withdrawal should complete without errors or warnings

Integration Testing   Priority: Moderate

Testing conducted to ensure that requirements for the complete business process have been satisfied. This testing focuses on end-to-end business and includes all of the systems and interaction points within scope of the solution.

User Acceptance Testing	Priority: High

Testing conducted by someone with in-depth business knowledge at the direction of the project business analyst and quality professionals in order to validate that the solution meets the defined acceptance criteria. Testing is often scripted and observed by the project BA and/or quality team to ensure full coverage and to observe questions and issues first hand.

Verification Tools and Techniques

Verification Tools and Techniques
Desk Checking
Inspection
Peer Review
Test
Walk-through

Desk Checking	Priority: High

Desk checking involves the person who creates the deliverable reviewing their own work prior to presenting it for formal quality control review.

Inspection	Priority: High

Inspections are a rigorous form of peer review done by those who contributed to the creation and documentation of the requirements and are the recipients of the requirements document. It allows the business to make sure that the requirements are acceptable in their current form.

Peer Review	Priority: High

A review process (either formal or informal) involving peers of the business analyst in order to ensure that the documented business analysis deliverables comply with the standards of the organization and general principles of requirements writing.

Typical participants in a peer review may include practitioners from:
- Business Analysis Center of Excellence
- Quality assurance
- Quality testing

Formal peer reviews are also called walk-throughs. They support the verification and validation efforts in the project. The purpose of peer reviews or walk-throughs is to catch errors, oversights, and incorrect assumptions early in the project. The costs of capturing the errors and oversights are much lower at the beginning of the project than toward the end of the project. The first reviews are often informal and conducted with the key stakeholders. Peer reviews are conducted with other project team members or other business analysts. The requirements and models (requirements package) are then subjected to a more formal and final review.

The key concept in walk-throughs or review is that people can't always edit their own work and see their own mistakes. If the business analyst is conducting a formal review during a stage gate process, then they may work with the project manager and technologists to determine whether the cost and time is sufficient to build the product and achieve the project objectives. The project manager will then ask for approval to move the project forward. *See also Walk-through.*

Test   Priority: High

The examination of a work product or deliverable in order to determine the level of quality.

Test tip: "Test" and "inspection" are very similar in definition. Recognizing that both are verification techniques should be sufficient for answering questions on the PMI-PBA exam. Don't worry too much about the finite differences between the two.

Walk-through   Priority: High

Walk-throughs are for the purpose of reviewing requirements with stakeholders to confirm that requirements are valid as stated. Participants may be asked to review materials ahead of the session and come prepared to provide feedback.

It is one of the final opportunities for stakeholders to weigh in on the requirements. It also provides an opportunity for the business analyst to address issues before obtaining final approval for the requirements.

Walk-through	
Description	Formal sessions designed to "communicate, verify, and validate requirements." Also referred to as "requirements reviews."

Characteristics	• **Prerequisites**
	• **Process**
	   a. Review scope
	   b. Organize and schedule review
	   c. Conduct the review
	   d. Compile notes and results of the review
	   e. Re-review if necessary.
	• **Rules** to be Followed During the Review
	
	Note: Details of these characteristics are shown following this table.

Figure 6-21: Walk-through Overview

Example

After creating a use case description for an automated mortgage project, the project team does a walk-through of the main application entry use case with stakeholders. The intent is to get the use case approved so the sponsor or delegate will need to be present to give approval.

Prerequisites

A complete requirements package

Prior to scheduling a review, the requirements package or document should be complete. The walk-through could include one document, several, or the entire package.

A list of appropriate reviewers

You need to know who is reviewing, and reviewers should be authorized. They may include project stakeholders, such as SMEs or end-users, other business analysts, and other team members.

There also needs to be reviewers who can approve the requirements – either the sponsor or their delegate.

A meeting vehicle

Reviews need to be held in a place amenable to doing a walk-through, such as a conference room or virtually, using electronic tools to collaborate.

Process

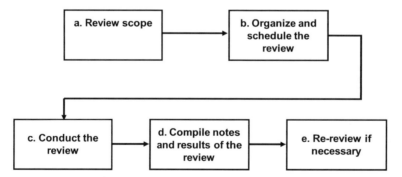

Figure 6-22: Structured Walk-through Process

Review scope

In advance, provide participants with a list of problem items the review should address, such as requirements out of scope or requirements describing how to implement a solution.

Organize and schedule review

Provide the objective of the review, which in general is to find and eliminate requirements that are unclear, inconsistent, and/or incorrect. Ask participants to preview the requirements package in advance of the formal review. That means it must be sent out far enough in advance to give people enough time to read it. For approving requirements, schedule stakeholders with sufficient authority.

Conduct the review

Consider the following roles for conducting a structured walk-through:

Role	Who Performs	Required?	Notes
Author	The person(s) who documented the requirements, typically the business analyst.	Y	• Answers questions. • Listens to comments and suggestions. • Changes requirements after session.
Scribe	Any team member who will record notes from the review. May be the author.	Y	Documents all comments, suggestions, issues, etc. raised in the session.
Moderator	Neutral facilitator (ideally). Best if moderator is not the author to maintain objectivity. May be another team member.	Y	• Facilitates session, maintains focus/discipline, encourages participation. • Verifies participants reviewed the document before session.
Peer	Typically other BAs with experience preparing similar documents.	N	Reviews documents for adherence to good documentation standards.
Reviewer	Any stakeholder.	Y	• Reads document prior to session. • Presents and discusses comments, questions, and suggested changes with the group.
Approver	Not in list, but mentioned elsewhere. Stakeholder(s) with approval authority.	Preferred	Approves requirements during or after the session.

Figure 6-23: Roles in Structured Walkthroughs

A typical walk-through meeting agenda is provided below:

- Introductions

- Purpose for the review

- Objectives of the review

- Project background (if required)

- Review – walk through the deliverable

- Agree on actions and changes needed

- Review the status of the deliverable

Compile notes and results of the review

Participants should agree as to whether or not the requirements document needs modification and if additional participants needs to be involved in the review or approval.

Re-review if necessary

For deliverables not accepted, the team will make a decision about whether to re-review the requirement(s) or not.

Rules to be followed during the review

A proper structured walk-through should follow common practices for conducting them. The facilitator is responsible for enforcing the following ground rules:

- **"Leave titles at the door."** Frequently, if managers or supervisors attend the same review as their staff, staff may feel constrained and contribute less. The responses are usually more guarded, and if too much deference is paid to the manager, it will curtail honest and valuable feedback.

- **"Disagree with ideas and not people."** Comments should be directed to the content, not the author or provider of the requirement.

- **"Come Prepared."** Review all documents before the session.

Output of a review:

List of questions, comments, concerns, and suggestions concerning reviewed requirements.

Evaluation – Exercise 3

Identify the quality tools by their pictures below. The answers are provided toward the end of this chapter.

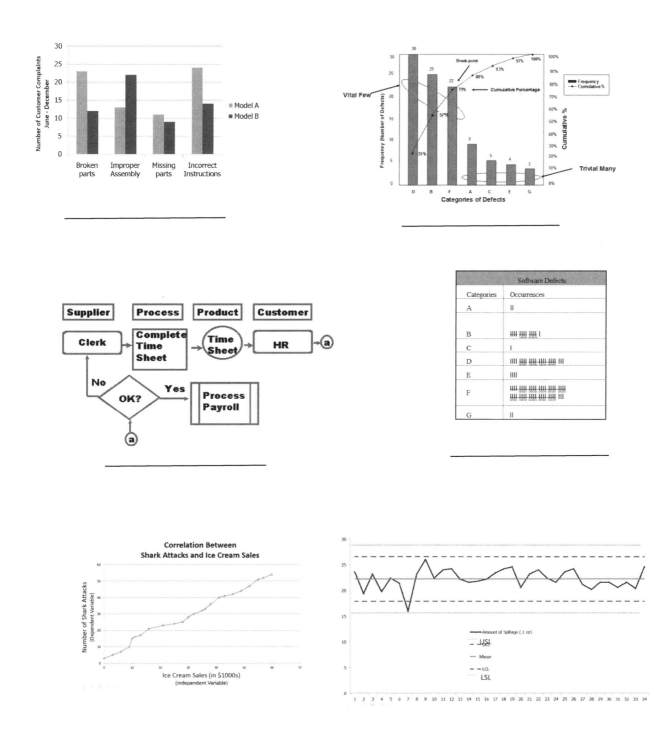

PMI-PBA Practice Exam

Here are sample questions on the Evaluation domain to help you practice taking PMI-PBA exam questions. Answers are listed at the end of the chapter.

1. Evaluation includes the business analysis activities done to validate what?
   a. The team's performance
   b. The hardware components of a solution
   c. A full solution or a solution segment
   d. The requirements documentation

2. What are the validation tools and techniques you can use in evaluation?
   a. DITL testing, UAT, exploratory testing
   b. Inspection, peer review, desk checking
   c. Control charts, scatter diagram, histogram
   d. Force field analysis, net promoter score, planguage

3. How do business analysts typically participate in testing of a solution?
   a. Perform testing if there is no formal testing group to do it.
   b. Ensure requirements are testable.
   c. Execute the test plan.
   d. Track defects and problems.

4. During a team meeting, you suggest using a Pareto chart. What might be the problem you are trying to address?
   a. Team members need to know whether or not a process is in control.
   b. Team members need to know which type of defects are causing the most problems and on which they should focus.
   c. Team members need to know whether or not a process has improved since making changes.
   d. Team members have identified two key variables and want to know if there is any cause and effect relationship between them.

5. What type of analysis is used to ensure the underlying reason for a defect has been identified?
   a. Problem tracking
   b. Defect tracking
   c. Root cause analysis
   d. Business analyst performance metrics

© 2015-2016, Elizabeth Larson and Richard Larson   PMI-PBA Certification Study Guide

6. Which of the following can be said about statistical sampling?
    a. It is rarely used for highly complex, heterogeneous populations.
    b. It requires identification of the key sub-populations and then choosing equal numbers from each.
    c. Various techniques can be used to ensure that the sample selected is representative of the population.
    d. Any method for randomization in the selection process works equally well for any population.

7. Sunk cost is:
    a. A recommendation on whether the developed solution is ready for implementation.
    b. Cost already invested in a project or solution.
    c. An evaluation of the costs of a deployed solution.
    d. Cost needed to replace or phase out a solution.

8. When validating a solution and its potential defects, an identified defect is best described as:
    a. Known problem with a requirement.
    b. Known problem with the project.
    c. Known problem with the requirements approach.
    d. Known problem that exists in a solution.

9. The business analyst should conduct a post-implementation assessment to evaluate the performance of the solution. Which of the following items is NOT an input to this process:
    a. Technical design
    b. Business requirements
    c. Identified defects
    d. Solution performance metrics

10. The solution was delivered a month prior when you receive a phone call from a stakeholder who showed little interest in the project. She states that the product is of poor quality as a number of the features she was expecting were not included. You review the scope and baseline requirements and find that her requirements were determined to be out of scope. What is her real complaint?
    a. The project delivered a low quality product.
    b. Poor communication and stakeholder engagement throughout the project.
    c. You have an unreasonable stakeholder.
    d. The project meets quality requirements. Her issue is with the grade of the product based on the approved scope.

Exercise Answers

Evaluation – Exercise 1

Evaluation Tasks	Mnemonic
1. <u>Validate</u> <u>Test</u> Results	_____ V _____
2. <u>Analyze</u> Solution <u>Gaps</u>	_____ A _____
3. Get <u>Solution Sign-off</u>	_____ S _____
4. ___<u>Evaluate</u>___ Solution Results	_____ E _____

Evaluation – Exercise 2

Evaluation - Exercise 3

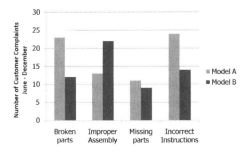

Histogram

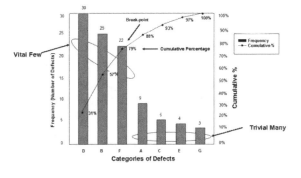

Pareto Diagram

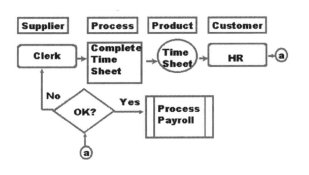

Flowchart

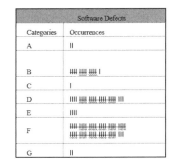

Checksheet

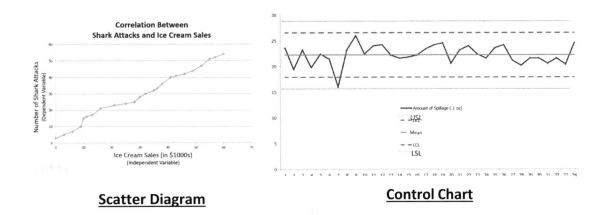

Scatter Diagram   **Control Chart**

PBA-PBA® Practice Exam Answers

1. Evaluation includes the business analysis activities done to validate what?

   a. The team's performance.

   This domain is not about validating the team's performance.

   b. The hardware components of a solution.

   Validating hardware components is not included in this domain.

   c. A full solution or a solution segment.

   Correct! Evaluation is validating a solution or solution segment that is about to be or has already been implemented.

   d. The requirements documentation.

   This domain is not about validating documentation.

2. What are the validation tools and techniques you can use in evaluation?

   a. DITL testing, UAT, exploratory testing

   Correct!

   b. Inspection, peer review, desk checking

   These are verification tools and techniques.

   c. Control charts, scatter diagram, histogram

   These are quality management tools and techniques.

   d. Force field analysis, net promoter score, planguage

   These are valuation tools and techniques for use in Needs Assessment and are measurement tools and techniques.

3. How do business analysts typically participate in testing of a solution?

   a. Perform testing if there is no formal testing group to do it.

   This may be the norm at some organizations, but is not a prescribed practice.

   b. Ensure requirements are testable.

   Correct! Business analysis and testing are two very different functions. Testability is an element of acceptance/evaluation criteria. Business analysts may facilitate user acceptance testing but testing itself is not a business analyst task.

   c. Execute the test plan.

   This is a testing function and not part of business analysis.

   d. Track defects and problems.

   This is a testing function and not part of business analysis. Business analysts evaluate the tracked defects in evaluating the solution.

4. During a team meeting, you suggest using a Pareto chart. What might be the problem you are trying to address?

   a. Team members need to know whether or not a process is in control.

   A control chart would be good for this.

   b. Team members need to know which type of defects are causing the most problems and on which they should focus.

   Correct! *PMBOK® Guide* 8.1.2.3.

   c. Team members need to know whether or not a process has improved since making changes.

   A run chart would be good for this.

   d. Team members have identified two key variables and want to know if there is any cause-and-effect relationship between them.

   A scatter diagram would work for this.

5. What type of analysis is used to ensure that the underlying reason for a defect has been identified?

   a. Problem tracking

   Done to ensure problems are resolved.

   b. Defect tracking

   Tracking won't lead to understanding underlying reasons for a defect.

   c. Root cause analysis

   Correct! Use for finding underlying causes to any problems, including solution defects.

   d. Business analyst performance metrics

   Focused on overall business analyst performance, not just defects. And, reasons for defects may not involve metrics.

6. Which of the following can be said about statistical sampling?

   a. It is rarely used for highly complex, heterogeneous populations.

   This is not true.

   b. It requires identification of the key sub-populations and then choosing equal numbers from each.

   This is not true.

   c. Various techniques can be used to ensure that the sample selected is representative of the population.

   Correct!

   d. Any method for randomization in the selection process works equally well for any population.

   This is a made up answer.

7. Sunk cost is:

    a. A recommendation on whether the developed solution is ready for implementation.   This is not sunk cost.

    b. **Cost already invested in a project or solution.**   **Correct!**

    c. An evaluation of the costs of a deployed solution.   This is not sunk cost

    d. Cost needed to replace or phase out a solution.   This is not sunk cost

8. When validating a solution and its potential defects, an identified defect is best described as:

    a. Known problem with a requirement.   This answer describes a requirement defect, not a solution defect.

    b. Known problem with the project.   This answer describes a project defect, not a solution defect.

    c. Known problem with the requirements approach.   This answer describes a business analysis defect, not a solution defect.

    d. **Known problem that exists in a solution.**   **Correct! When dealing with solution, an identified defect pertains to the solution.**

9. The business analyst should conduct a post-implementation assessment to evaluate the performance of the solution. Which of the following items is NOT an input to this process:

    a. **Technical design**   **Correct! The business analyst evaluates against the requirements, not the design.**

    b. Business requirements   This is an input to evaluating solution performance, so is not the correct answer.

    c. Identified defects   This is an input to evaluating solution performance, so is not the correct answer.

    d. Solution performance metrics   This is an input to evaluating solution performance, so is not the correct answer.

          PMI-PBA Certification Study Guide

10. The solution was delivered a month prior when you receive a phone call from a stakeholder who showed little interest in the project. She states that the product is of poor quality as a number of the features she was expecting were not included. You review the scope and baseline requirements and find that her requirements were determined out of scope. What is her real complaint?

a.	The project delivered a low quality product.	No statement has been made about the conformance of the product to the approved requirements. This is not a quality issue.
b.	Poor communication and stakeholder engagement throughout the project.	This is true and she has a hand in the communication breakdown. However, her stated concern is regarding the grade of the solution.
c.	You have an unreasonable stakeholder.	This may be true however the question asks "what is her complaint." She should not be calling to complain about herself.
d.	**The project meets quality requirements. Her issue is with the grade of the product based on the approved scope.**	**Correct! Grade refers to the richness of the product scope. Think of a 1-star hotel that has zero amenities but is clean, quiet, and well maintained.**

Summary

The Evaluation domain describes the tasks, tools, and techniques required to ensure the delivered solution meets project goals and objectives and delivers value to the organization.

Here are the themes covered that you should internalize:

- The business analyst is responsible for evaluating test results and not for executing the tests.

- Quality management tools will help understand the big picture of the solution quality and identify any trends that are contributing to poor quality.

- Evaluation does not end with the project. Evaluate how well a deployed solution that is used by the end-users is meeting project goals and objectives.

 Evaluation Goal: Assess the solution's ability to satisfy requirements and meet the business need.

7. Competencies

Overview

A great business analyst has more than the technical know-how described in the first six chapters. A great business analyst needs to have exceptional competencies. They are called out with the Skills and Knowledge section of the *PMI-PBA Examination Content Outline*. It is also important to remember that by applying for the PMI-PBA exam you have signed a Code of Ethics and Professional Conduct. This chapter will provide additional insights and information to help you navigate those tough "competency" questions that will be on the PMI-PBA exam.

Collaboration

Communication

Conflict Management

Negotiation

Facilitation Skills

Leadership

Political/Cultural Awareness

Systems Thinking

Competencies Goal: Utilize soft skill competencies in order to work effectively with others.

When you are finished with this chapter, you will know:

- The critical competencies required of a PMI-PBA®

- The importance of the competencies and how they can impact a PMI-PBA's business analysis practice

- How to apply an understanding of competencies to help answer exam questions

                          PMI-PBA Certification Study Guide

Competencies Skills and Knowledge

Collaboration

Collaboration is working together to achieve a common goal. Business analysts collaborate with the business team to elicit requirements, and get buy-in and sign-off for the final product. The business analyst also collaborates with the project team to ensure the requirements can and will be met.

Below are five tips for effective collaboration:

1. **Keep communications open** – Effective collaboration requires trust. Being open with communication will help build that trust and will ensure that everyone has the same information to support the project moving forward.

2. **Work toward a shared vision** – A shared vision helps to keep collaborators focused and work in support of that vision. On a project, successful solution delivery should be the vision all are working towards. Be prepared to revisit the vision as needed. Consider creating a poster that embodies the vision as a constant reminder.

3. **Value diverse ideas** – Quite often the best ideas come from the most unlikely places. Give team members the opportunity to express their ideas. Give due consideration to these ideas by asking questions and working together do understand the benefits, drawbacks, and refine as needed. Remember, you are working toward a shared vision.

4. **Be respectful** – Common courtesy goes a long way to building rapport and improving collaboration. Simple things such as showing up on time, keeping commitments, preparing for meetings and events, removing distractions (cell phone and laptops), and actively listening and participating in discussions demonstrate respect of your team members which will results in better team results.

5. **Acknowledge contributions** – Recognize individual and team contributions and successes. Team members will feel that their contribution is valued and will be more inclined to continue to supporting you and the team.

Tools, techniques, concepts, and models

The following model is often referenced in relation to collaboration and teamwork. You can expect to see a question or two on this.

The Tuckman Model, Stages of Team Development, was developed in 1965 by Bruce Tuckman. It describes the stages that all teams experience when they are formed, and also when changes occur within the team. Adding one new team member starts the cycle over again, although the length of the stages may shorten.

Stages of Team Development – Tuckman Model

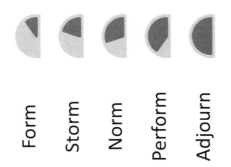

Figure 7-1: Tuckman Model Graphic

Form: Team members meet and learn about the project and their roles and responsibilities.

Storm: The team begins to address the project work, technical decisions, and the project approach. The work environment may cause friction or even conflict as team members learn each other's styles and perspectives.

Norm: Team members begin to work together and adjust their work habits and behaviors to support the team.

Perform: Teams function as a well-organized unit. They are interdependent and work through issues smoothly and effectively.

Adjourn (aka Mourn): The team completes the works and moves on from the project. This stage may also be referred to as "mourn" in some literature.

PMBOK® Guide References

More information on Collaboration can be found can be found in the *PMBOK® Guide*:

- Section 9.3 – Develop Project Team

Communication

It should be no surprise to see Communication as a top knowledge or skill needed for business analysts as it is such a huge part of what we do day-to-day. The *PMBOK® Guide* dedicates a whole knowledge area to this skill set.

Communication takes on many dimensions that may affect the form and timing of the actual communication. The *PMBOK® Guide* summarizes these as:

Internal	External
Within the project team	Outside of the project team
Formal	Informal
Reports, minutes, briefings	Emails, memos, ad-hoc discussions
Vertical	Horizontal
Up or down the organization hierarchy	With peers
Official	Unofficial
Newsletters, reports	Off the record
Written	Oral
Verbal	Non-Verbal
With voice inflection	Body language

Figure 7-2: Dimensions of Communication

Source: *PMBOK® Guide*

The urgency and nature of the message will factor into the decision of how to communicate. Communication technologies available and common within the organization will also play a role in determining the specific medium in which to communicate.

Interactive communication

Two or more people exchanging information (meetings, phone calls, instant messaging, video conferencing).

Push communication

Sent to specific recipients who need the information (letters, memos, reports, emails, faxes, voice mails, blogs, press releases).

Pull communication

Recipients must access the communication content at their own discretion (intranet site, e-learning, database, knowledge repository).

Consider these aspects when planning for communication (Task 3 of the Planning domain) and adjust as necessary to keep communications effective and open.

Tools, techniques, concepts, and models

There are communication models that are included in the *PMBOK® Guide* that you can expect to see a couple of questions for on the exam.

Basic Communication Model

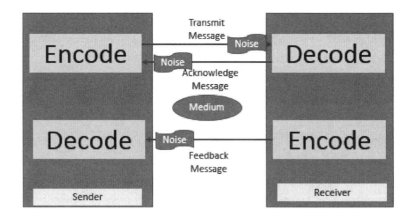

Figure 7-3: Basic Communication Model

- **Encode:** Thoughts or ideas are translated (encoded) by the sender.
- **Transmit Message:** Information is sent using a chosen communication channel (medium).
- **Decode:** The receiver translates the message into meaningful thoughts or ideas.
- **Acknowledge:** The receiver acknowledges receipt of the message, although does not necessarily agree.
- **Feedback / Response:** The receiver encodes thoughts and ideas and transmits the response back to the original sender.

Things such as distance, unfamiliar technology, inadequate infrastructure, cultural differences, or a lack of background or context create "noise" and cause the message to be altered as it is received.

Working with Virtual Teams

Communicating with virtual team members, that is, team members who are not face-to-face, is another dimension of communication that requires additional thought and effort in order to be effective. Virtual team members are often not only in different time zones, but they are often in different countries with different languages and cultures.

The following are a few best practices when working with virtual teams to mitigate the problems of disengagement, low morale, and lack of accountability that can occur with virtual teams:

- **Confirm Understanding:** Request clarification or elaboration when on conference calls to ensure understanding.

- **Be Ultra Responsive:** Respond promptly to at least acknowledge a message when working in a virtual team environment.
- **Listen for Ideas:** Pay attention to the gist of the message; hear beyond what's stated.
- **Communicate 1-on-1:** Augment group conference and video calls with individual voice or video calls.
- **Encourage Social Interaction:** Use ice-breakers and ask people to share personal stories or news before online meetings to allow people to get to know each other.
- **Notify Team Members of Availability:** Make sure all team members know other team members' work hours to set expectations for response timing and availability.

Communication Complexity

The more people that are involved on a project, the larger the number of communication channels there are. The number of communication channels increases dramatically with each new person involved. The formula for the number of communication channels is **n (n - 1) / 2** where **n = number of people**.

Each time a resource is added, the communication's complexity increases exponentially. *Figure 7-4* illustrates how adding people to any form of communication increases the complexity. For example, if there are three people involved, there are three channels: 3 (3-1) / 2 = 3. Increasing the number of people on a project to four expands the number of channels to six: 4 (4-1) / 2 = 6.

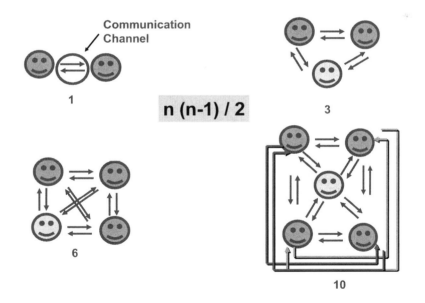

Figure 7-4: Communications Complexity Illustrated

PMBOK® Guide References

More information on communication can be found in the *PMBOK® Guide*:

- Chapter 10 – Project Communications Management

Conflict Management

Conflicts often arise on projects. There can be conflicts in the projects goals and objectives, product scope, the priority of solution requirements, or go/no-go decisions for solution implementation. Conflict is not always a bad thing. Conflict is what helps us to understand differences and discuss various aspects in order to decide on the best course of action. The business analyst plays a key role in managing and resolving these conflicts to enable the project to continue to move forward and be successful. There are different strategies that may be used to get to conflict resolution. Successful conflict management is:

- Being able to understand the root cause of the conflict.
- Being able to draw out and understand differing points of view.
- Staying focused on what is in the best interest of the project.

Tools, techniques, concepts, and models

The *PMBOK® Guide* identifies the following strategies for resolving conflict:

Strategy	Description	Example
Withdraw / Avoid	Ignore or postpone addressing a conflict	Sally does not feel this is a battle worth fighting so she concedes to Don's point.
Smooth / Accommodate	Focus on the area of agreement or concede to maintain harmony	Haleigh drops the issue because she doesn't want to upset things and understands Joe's point of wanting to get the solution implemented on time.
Compromise / Reconcile	Look for an opportunity that somewhat satisfies all parties	David agrees to give Julie an additional week, instead of the two requested to complete requirements.
Force / Direct	Impose ones viewpoint	Scott tells the team that the feature will be cut to make the project schedule.
Collaborate / Problem Solve	Discuss the various viewpoints, focus on the shared vision, come to a mutually agreeable resolution	Srini and Tracy had a discussion about their different perspectives and together they found a new solution that they both liked.

Figure 7-5: Conflict Resolution Strategies

Generally, collaborating and problem solving is the best strategy for conflict resolution as it focuses on finding a mutually agreeable solution. Someone will lose something in each of the other strategies. However, the specific strategy selected to resolve a conflict may vary depending on things such as importance or intensity of the conflict, time constraints, and stakeholders and their stand on the issue along with their influence.

PMBOK® Guide References

More information on Conflict Management and Resolution can be found can be found in the *PMBOK® Guide*:

- Section 9.4.2.3 – Conflict Management

Negotiation

Negotiation is listed in the Knowledge and Skills section of the *PMI-PBA Examination Content Outline*. The *PMBOK® Guide* defines negotiation as "the process and activities to resolving disputes through consultations between involved parties." Conflict resolution combined with facilitation covers the knowledge needed in regards to negotiation. Here are some specific principles for negotiating.

Basic Negotiation Principles
(From *Getting to Yes*, by Roger Fisher and William Ury):
• Don't bargain over positions at the cost of a relationship.
• Separate people from the problem.
• Focus on interests, not positions.
• Invent options for mutual gain.
• Use objective criteria.
• Develop a fallback plan in advance in case negotiation fails.

Tools, techniques, concepts, and models

No specific tools, techniques, concepts or models can be found in either the *PMBOK® Guide* or the *Business Analysis for Practitioners: A Practice Guide*.

PMBOK® Guide References

The *PMBOK® Guide* glossary, page 547, includes the definition of negotiation and the use of negotiation during procurement.

- Section 12.2.2.7 Procurement Negotiations

Facilitation

Business analysts will be required to moderate and guide discussions regarding business analysis planning, product scope, requirements, and go/no-go decisions. Good facilitation means:

- Ensuring that participants in a discussion correctly understand one another's positions.

- Using meeting management skills and tools (including agendas and meeting minutes to keep discussions focused and organized).

- Preventing discussions from being sidetracked.

- Identifying common areas of agreement.

- Effectively using different negotiation styles.

- Having the ability to identify important issues.

- Understanding and considering all parties' interests, motivations, and objectives.

- Encouraging stakeholders to reach win-win outcomes on a regular basis.

Tools, techniques, concepts, and models

The *PMBOK® Guide* identifies the following as techniques that are often used to facilitate group creativity. These techniques have been described previously in this guide as indicated.

- Brainstorming – See Elicitation Techniques in the Analysis domain
- Nominal Group Technique – See Decision Making Techniques in the Analysis domain
- Weighted Criteria – See Decision Making Techniques in the Analysis domain

It is also important to understand the various methods for reaching group decisions. These include:

- Unanimity – Everyone agrees on a single course of action.
- Majority – More than 50 percent of the group agrees to a course of action.
- Plurality - The course of action that gets the highest percentage of votes. This is typically used when there are more than two options.
- Dictatorship - One individual makes the decision.

Category	Technique
Facilitation Tools and Techniques	
Affinity Diagram	
Mind Mapping	

Figure 7-6: Tools and Techniques for Facilitation

Affinity Diagram   Priority: Low

A diagram used to classify and group like ideas (from brainstorming) in order to facilitate further review and analysis.

Mind Mapping   Priority: Low

A visual representation of ideas and the relationships between them. The mind map starts with a central theme in mind. A team (or person) brainstorms related items to populate the map.

PMBOK® Guide References

Some information on Facilitation can be found can be found in the *PMBOK® Guide*:

- Section 4.1.2.2– Facilitation Techniques

- Section 5.2.2.3 – Facilitated Workshops

- Section 5.2.2.4 – Group Creativity Techniques

- Section 5.2.2.5 – Group Decision-Making Techniques

-

Leadership

The business analyst role is inherently a leadership one due to its "change agent" nature. This is true whether anyone reports to the business analyst or not. Here are a few leadership success factors:

Figure 7-7: Leadership Success Factors

- Developing a vision of a positive future state that will engage people to want to reach it.
- Motivating others to act cooperatively to achieve a shared goal and objectives.
- Understanding individual needs and abilities of team members, and channeling them to reach the needed goal.
- Reducing resistance to necessary changes.
- Willingness to set aside personal objectives for the sake of the team when necessary.
- Articulating a clear and inspiring vision of a desired future state.

Tools, techniques, concepts, and models

Being a great leader entails understanding what motivates people. Maslow's Hierarchy of Needs is the most common model of human motivation. You can expect to see a question or two on the test about the needs hierarchy. This model was originally developed by Abraham Maslow in 1943 and has become the top referenced model regarding motivation. The theory is that unsatisfied needs drive motivation. It goes on to say that lower-level needs must be met before the next level will be a motivator (e.g., the needs for safety must be met before the person will be motivated by love and belonging).

> **Motivation: Maslow's Hierarchy of Needs**
>
> **P.S.L.E.S.**
> - **P**hysiological
> - **S**afety
> - **L**ove and Belonging
> - **E**steem
> - **S**elf-Actualization

Figure 7-8: Maslow's Hierarchy of Needs

PMBOK® Guide References

Some information on Leadership can be found can be found in the *PMBOK® Guide*:

- Section 9.4.2.4 – Interpersonal Skills

Political / Cultural Awareness

Having awareness of the political and cultural environment is a fundamental competency. This awareness provides information that will enable you to make better decisions in how you collaborate, communicate, and lead project stakeholders. This goes well beyond government politics and ethnic cultures.

Factors such as age, nationality, and department and organizational culture all play a role in determining how individuals work, participate, contribute in decision-making, interpret body language, interact with authority, and view their role on the team. The group will take on its own culture as it moves through the stages of team development to become a high performing organization.

Political awareness refers to understanding how things get done within the organization context. It focuses on the relationships and where the power and authority exist. Often those with power are not those with formal authority but those who have gained great influence within the organization through other means. The culture of the organization may lend itself to a political climate that mirrors that of a military chain of command, or perhaps a much less formal and personal approach works best in order to get things done.

Tools, techniques, concepts, and models

No specific tools, techniques, concepts or models can be found in either the *PMBOK® Guide* or the *Business Analysis for Practitioners: A Practice Guide*.

PMBOK® Guide References

Information on cultural awareness can be found in the *PMBOK® Guide*.

- Section 2.1.1 – Organizational Culture and Styles

- Section 2.3.1 – Composition of Project Teams

- Section 9.3 – Develop Project Team (introduction)

- Section 10.1 – Plan Communications Management (introduction)

Systems Thinking

Systems thinking means to view the organization (whole or in part) as a system, with inter-relationships and patterns. System extends beyond the technical solution. It includes the people, interactions, external forces, and anything that contributes to accomplishing organizational objectives. Systems thinking allows the business analyst to understand the impact that one change has throughout the organization, internally and externally.

Tools, techniques, concepts, and models

No specific tools, techniques, concepts or models can be found in either the *PMBOK® Guide* or the *Business Analysis for Practitioners: A Practice Guide*.

PMBOK® Guide References

The *PMBOK® Guide* does not include any reference to Systems Thinking.

Systems Thinking

(Adapted from Wikipedia.com)

- "Systems" are a dynamic and complex whole, interacting as a structured functional unit.
- Information flows between the different elements that compose the system.
- Information flows from and to the surrounding environment via definite boundaries.
- Improvements should focus on systems and not people.

PMI-PBA Certification Study Guide

Competencies – Exercise

Match the competency from the left to the definition on the right by indicating the appropriate letter in the space provided.

A. Collaboration	___ 1. The exchange of information and ideas.
B. Communication	
C. Conflict Management	___ 2. The ability to get the support of others in pursuit of a goal.
D. Negotiation	
E. Facilitation Skills	___ 3. Understanding how decisions are made.
F. Leadership	
G. Political / Cultural Awareness	___ 4. Working as a team.
H. Systems Thinking	
	___ 5. Discuss in order to make an agreement
	___ 6. Understanding the likely effect to a process if a new tool is implemented.
	___ 7. Understanding and leveraging differences in ideas.
	___ 8. Providing an opportunity for all ideas to be heard and discussed.

PMI-PBA Practice Exam

Here are sample questions on Competencies to help you practice taking PMI-PBA exam questions. Answers are listed at the end of the chapter.

1. Team members come to you with a disagreement about a technical problem. One person wants to modify the software but not the hardware except under specific circumstances pending the software changes. The other person wants to upgrade the hardware but not make changes to the software except under specific circumstances pending the hardware upgrade. You facilitate a meeting in which all the alternatives are explored for solving the problem and a solution is developed. What technique have you used?
   a. Forcing
   b. Compromising
   c. Collaborating
   d. Smoothing

2. When requirements conflicts occur, the BA should:
   a. Escalate to the project manager.
   b. Escalate to the implementation manager.
   c. Facilitate the conflict by meeting with the PM and sponsor.
   d. Facilitate communication between the stakeholders who are in conflict.

3. Some of your project stakeholders disagree about which requirements to include in the project. Your project manager asks you to negotiate. He is asking you to:
   a. Consistently produce key results expected by stakeholders.
   b. Confer with the stakeholders to come to terms.
   c. Influence behavior to get the stakeholders to do what they would not otherwise do.
   d. Just solve the problem.

4. As a senior business analyst, you are preparing the requirements package for a significant process improvement initiative that would be strategically important to the future of the company. It involves implementing an IT initiative to establish a Business Rules Management system across the enterprise. However, you have met with resistance from one particular stakeholder who seems to be loading unnecessary requirements and expectations into the go/no-go criteria. What would be your approach before submitting the requirements package?
   a. Call a meeting with the project sponsor and the SME in question and lay out your assessment of the situation.
   b. If you believe the stakeholder will be disruptive to the decision-making process, dis-invite the stakeholder from the decision package review meeting.
   c. Facilitate a brainstorming session among executive team members to deal with the SME's expectations.
   d. Seek a meeting with the SME to listen carefully to his concerns and be able to reflect them back to the stakeholder. Then engage the stakeholder in suggestions for how to mitigate the particular issues. Consider next steps after thoroughly understanding the concerns from the stakeholder's perspective.

5. You are planning an elicitation workshop with a group of users with similar roles. You are hoping to get a jump start on requirements with some group creativity. What activities might you plan?
    a. Brainstorming, nominal group technique, affinity diagram, mind mapping.
    b. Focus group, facilitated workshop, brainstorming, majority.
    c. Unanimity, majority, plurality, dictatorship.
    d. Focus group, facilitated workshop, prototypes, survey.

6. Sally is the director of marketing in your organization. She has been very interested in your project and has asked to be kept in the loop. You have heard that she has the ear of the CEO and can make things happen in the organization. What is your engagement strategy for Sally?
    a. Respond to Sally's questions in a timely manner.
    b. Initiate conversations with Sally and keep an open door policy.
    c. Provide status reports on a regular basis.
    d. Ask the project sponsor to meet with Sally on a regular basis.

7. Jorge from marketing has been reluctant to participate in requirements workshops. He indicates that his marketing strategies are highly sensitive and exposure could result in a major competitor beating us to market. How will you get marketing's requirements?
    a. Explain to Jorge that requirements will be kept confidential within the project team and stakeholders.
    b. Ask someone else from marketing who is not as paranoid.
    c. Escalate to the project sponsor to require Jorge to participate.
    d. Ask to meet with Jorge one-on-one to discuss marketing's requirements.

8. Which method of conflict management brings some degree of satisfaction to all parties?
    a. Compromising
    b. Smoothing
    c. Withdrawing
    d. Collaborating

9. A disagreement has come up on your project, splitting the team members into two groups at odds over a technical decision that needs to be made. What is the ideal approach to addressing this problem?
    a. Come up with a resolution that incorporates some ideas from both sides and bring everyone together for a vote.
    b. Focus on the areas of agreement and just keep everyone distracted until the issues resolves itself.
    c. Make time and space available to get everyone involved in identifying the issues and coming up with a resolution that addresses everyone's concerns.
    d. Evaluate the cost of the decision, choose which is best for the project and inform the team of your decision.

10. Performance reports are typically distributed using which method?
    a. Interactive
    b. Face-to-face
    c. Pull
    d. Push

Exercise Answers

A. Collaboration

B. Communication

C. Conflict
    Management

D. Negotiation

E. Facilitation Skills

F. Leadership

G. Political / Cultural
    Awareness

H. Systems Thinking

___ 1. The exchange of information and ideas. (B)

___ 2. The ability to get the support of others in pursuit of a goal. (F)

___ 3. Understanding how decisions are made. (G)

___ 4. Working as a team. (A)

___ 5. Discuss in order to make an agreement (D)

___ 6. Understanding the likely effect to a process if a new tool is implemented. (H)

___ 7. Understanding and leveraging differences in ideas.(C)

___ 8. Providing an opportunity for all ideas to be heard and discussed. (E)

PMI-PBA Practice Exam Answers

1. Team members come to you with a disagreement about a technical problem. One person wants to modify the software but not the hardware except under specific circumstances pending the software changes. The other person wants to upgrade the hardware but not make changes to the software except under specific circumstances pending the hardware upgrade. You facilitate a meeting in which all the alternatives are explored for solving the problem and a solution is developed. What technique have you used?

a. Forcing	If you have told them what to do without considering their input, you would have used this technique.
b. Compromising	If you had decided to upgrade both the hardware and the software, that would be a compromise since they both get what they want and what they don't want.
c. Collaborating	**Correct! Collaborating or problem solving treats the conflict as a problem to be solved.**
d. Smoothing	If you had tried to appease them by focusing on areas of agreement, that would have been smoothing.

2. When requirements conflicts occur, the BA should:

a. Escalate to the project manager.	This may be needed in severe cases, but is not the best answer.
b. Escalate to the implementation manager.	Not necessarily true.
c. Facilitate the conflict by meeting with the PM and sponsor.	The BA needs to facilitate communication between the stakeholders in conflict.
d. Facilitate communication between the stakeholders who are in conflict.	**Correct! See the *PMI-PBA Examination Content Outline*.**

3. Some of your project stakeholders disagree about which requirements to include in the project. Your project manager asks you to negotiate. He is asking you to:

a. Consistently produce key results expected by stakeholders.	This sounds like a good thing, but it is not the definition of negotiate.
b. Confer with the stakeholders to come to terms.	**Correct! *PMBOK® Guide*, Glossary p. 547.**
c. Influence behavior to get the stakeholders to do what they would not otherwise do.	This is a definition of Power.
d. Just solve the problem.	This is not a definition of negotiate.

4. As a senior business analyst, you are preparing the requirements package for a significant process improvement initiative that would be strategically important to the future of the

company. It involves implementing an IT initiative to establish a Business Rules Management system across the enterprise. However, you have met with resistance from one particular stakeholder who seems to be loading unnecessary requirements and expectations into the go/no-go criteria. What would be your approach before submitting the requirements package?

a. Call a meeting with the project sponsor and the SME in question and lay out your assessment of the situation.

It is possible that this approach will become confrontational.

b. If you believe the stakeholder will be disruptive to the decision-making process, dis-invite the stakeholder from the decision package review meeting.

This will avoid understanding the issue and it will probably come back later in the project. You will have less trust in your relationship than before.

c. Facilitate a brainstorming session among executive team members to deal with the SME's expectations.

Executives are not likely to brainstorm for a leadership issue.

d. Seek a meeting with the SME to listen carefully to his concerns and be able to reflect them back to the stakeholder. Then engage the stakeholder in suggestions for how to mitigate the particular issues. Consider next steps after thoroughly understanding the concerns from the stakeholder's perspective.

Correct! This is an example of problem-solving, which is an effective way to resolve conflict. A significant ingredient in problem-solving is listening, which helps SMEs explain their views. It may help uncover underlying issues not related to his expectations or requirements.

5. You are planning an elicitation workshop with a group of users with similar roles. You are hoping to get a jump start on requirements with some group creativity. What activities might you plan?

a. Brainstorming, nominal group technique, affinity diagram, mind mapping.

Correct! See PMBOK® Guide 5.2.2.4.

b. Focus group, facilitated workshop, brainstorming, majority.

Brainstorming is the only group creativity technique in this list.

c. Unanimity, majority, plurality, dictatorship.

These are group decision-making techniques.

d. Focus group, facilitated workshop, prototypes, survey.

These are techniques for collect requirements but they are not specific to group creativity techniques.

6. Sally is the director of marketing in your organization. She has been very interested in your project and has asked to be kept in the loop. You have heard that she has the ear of the CEO and can make things happen in the organization. What is your engagement strategy for Sally?

a. Respond to Sally's questions in a timely manner.

You should do this with all stakeholders.

b. Initiate conversations with Sally and keep an open door policy.

Correct! The higher the interest and the higher the influence the more closely you want to manage the relationship by being proactive and building trust.

c. Provide status reports on a regular basis.

It's likely Sally is not concerned with your status reports.

d. Ask the project sponsor to meet with Sally on a regular basis.

You need to communicate directly with Sally in order to develop a relationship.

7. Jorge from marketing has been reluctant to participate in requirements workshops. He indicates that his marketing strategies are highly sensitive and exposure could result in a major competitor beating us to market. How will you get marketing's requirements?

a. Explain to Jorge that requirements will be kept confidential within the project team and stakeholders.

This would be part of your ground rules and code of ethics.

b. Ask someone else from marketing who is not as paranoid.

You need to work directly with Jorge to build trust.

c. Escalate to the project sponsor to require Jorge to participate.

This would be a trust buster!

d. Ask to meet with Jorge one-on-one to discuss marketing's requirements.

Correct! Interviews are a technique that works well in situations where there may be confidential information. This will further allow you to negotiate with Jorge on what can be shared, how, and with whom.

8. Which method of conflict management brings some degree of satisfaction to all parties?

a. Compromising

Correct! *PMBOK® Guide* 9.4.2.3.

b. Smoothing

Emphasizes areas of agreement and minimizes differences. Parties may or may not be particularly satisfied. It is only a temporary resolution.

c. Withdrawing

Avoiding a conflict only provides a temporary resolution and likely results in little satisfaction for any party.

d. Collaborating

Collaborating and problem-solving results in satisfaction of all parties by exploring all alternative and together choosing which will work best.

9. A disagreement has come up on your project, splitting the team members into two groups at odds over a technical decision that needs to be made. What is the ideal approach to addressing this problem?

a. Come up with a resolution that incorporates some ideas from both sides and bring everyone together for a vote.

You'd be better off letting the team come up with a resolution that incorporates their ideas.

b. Focus on the areas of agreement and just keep everyone distracted until the issues resolves itself.

This does not address the problem and will likely make things worse for the team in the long run.

c. Make time and space available to get everyone involved in identifying the issues and coming up with a resolution

Correct! Healthy team environments are characterized by a collaborative approach to problem solving. *PMBOK® Guide* 9.3.2.3.

that addresses everyone's concerns.

d. Evaluate the cost of the decision, choose which is best for the project and inform the team of your decision.

Forcing is always an option, but it isn't likely to have the best results in this instance. You're better off involving team members.

10. Performance reports are typically distributed using which method?

a. Interactive

This format is generally used when there is a need to make sure everyone has the same understanding about something, which is typically not a need with performance reports. Also, this would not provide a record of the information.

b. Face-to-face

Face-to-face would not be efficient and it would not provide a record of the information.

c. Pull

This is typically used for very large volumes of information or very large audiences that require the recipients to access the information at their convenience.

d. Push

Correct! *PMBOK® Guide* **10.1.2.4.**

Summary

Competencies are every bit as important to good business analysis as the technical skills. A business analyst needs to be able to lead and facilitate teams, communicate information, and resolve conflicts in order to effectively elicit and manage solution requirements. Some themes to keep in mind include:

- The business analyst is a "change-agent," a facilitator of change.

- Candid and timely communication is essential to build trust and ensure all have needed information to make decisions that best support the project.

- Working effectively with others requires understanding the political culture of the organization and the attitudes and preferences of the individuals.

Competencies Goal: Utilize soft skill competencies in order to work effectively with others.

Notes

8. Final Tips

Overview

Congratulations! You have made it through the *PMI-PBA Examination Content Outline* study materials. Now you have a good idea of what to expect on the examination. You may be a bit apprehensive about the amount of terms, concepts, tools, and techniques that you may be tested on. It is at this point that you should be detailing your preparation and test exam testing plan. This chapter will give you practical advice on how to prepare for success on the first try.

 Final Tips Goal: Develop a study and test taking strategy to pass the PMI-PBA exam on the first try.

When you are finished with this chapter, you will know:

- The specific steps that will best prepare you for the exam

- How to best leverage practice exams

- Test-taking strategies for exam day

Preparing to Succeed

Test Preparation Roadmap

Are you feeling overwhelmed by the amount of material needed to learn for the exam? The truth is that very few will be prepared for the exam after a first reading of this guide. Never fear! In this section we will help you to develop a test preparation action plan specific for you.

We know that different people have different styles of learning. Your specific learning style will provide some keys on activities that will best help you prepare.

You learn best with	Study mode ideas
• Lots of detail • Time to analyze Your color is **Blue**	• Re-Read *PMBOK® Guide* sections • Writing notes • Practice exams • Review notes
• Bullet points • Experience Your color is **Red**	• Practice exams • Re-read study guides
• Working with others • Interactive activities Your color is **Yellow**	• Find a "study buddy" • Practice exams
• Activities that reinforce learning Your color is **Green**	• Write notes • Practice exams • Review notes

Figure 8-1: Insights Learning Strategies:
Adapted from Doug Upchurch (copyright 2000 published with permission). Insights was created by Andrew Lothian, Insights, **www.insights.com.**

Re-Read the *PMBOK® Guide* Sections

PMBOK® Guide references have been provided throughout this guide. Detail oriented people will find reading the PMBOK® Guide on those areas will provide greater and supporting detail that will help reinforce learning. There are some areas where the PMBOK® Guide guidance is very light and will not provide much additional detail. Don't get too frustrated by this. This study guide will provide you the basics that you need to know.

Learning

"We Learn . . .
    10% of what we read
    20% of what we hear
    30% of what we see
    50% of what we see and hear
    70% of what we discuss
    80% of what we experience
    95% of what we teach others."
        William Glasser

Writing / Review Notes

Educators know that students learn best when they have an opportunity to experience the learning. One of the easiest ways to experience the knowledge you learn is to take notes. The act of note writing will increase recall of information. Writing notes helps to maintain focus and increase comprehension, as well as organize the thoughts in a way that is meaningful and helpful to the individual. Practice writing notes as you study, especially in those otherwise tough to learn areas. Don't forget to use your notes as you continue your study.

Practice Exams

Taking practice exams helps to prepare for the real deal in two ways. First, it gives you experience with the format, difficulty level, and challenges in answering the tough questions. It also gives you data on your strengths and weaknesses to better focus additional study. There's more on practice exams in the next section.

Re-Read the Study Guide

Continue to review this study guide as you need to get more comfortable with the information. Focus on one section at a time and work to truly understand the material. Re-do the exercises using scratch paper and without referring to the book. Skip those areas that you are not concerned about.

Find a Study Buddy

Many people find having a partner in study greatly improves their study habits and learning. A study buddy can help in drills, discuss concepts, and help keep you accountable for your study plan. Reach out to your local PMI® chapter or find a group online (there are a couple of such groups on LinkedIn).

Additional Resources

You may be seeking additional resources that will help you in learning the material needed to pass the PMI-PBA exam. Below are a few recommended resources. Be deliberate in deciding to use additional study material and what material to use. Information overload can be as detrimental as not having enough information. As a rule of thumb, don't use additional material that leaves you with more questions regarding the material.

- *Business Analysis for Practitioners: A Practice Guide*, Author: Project Management Institute
This practice guide was developed by PMI® as a direct result of the PMI-PBA credential program. It roughly follows the *PMI-PBA Examination Content Outline* but does not provide comprehensive information for all domains, tasks, tools, and techniques. The authors of this study guide were contributors to the *Business Analysis for Practitioners: A Practice Guide*. All contributors of that guide each wrote a number of questions for the actual PMI-PBA exam.

- *A Practitioner's Guide to Requirements Management – Defining and Managing Requirements Using Agile, Waterfall or Hybrid Life Cycles,* Author: Elizabeth Larson and Richard Larson

Another publication by this guide's authors, this book pre-dates the PMI-PBA credential program. The information in this book directly aligns with the Planning and Traceability and Monitoring domains of the exam.

- *Business Analysis Techniques: 72 Essential Tools for Success,* Author: James Cadle, Paul Turner, and Debra Paul
  This book is provided as reference material by PMI® for the PMI-PBA exam. It focuses on tools and techniques used by business analysts. You will find additional information on many of the tools and techniques referenced throughout this guide. This is a good place to start if you are having trouble with a particular tool or technique. This book is available in the PMI® eReads and Reference, unabridged online books.

Additional PMI® referenced material can be found online at
http://www.pmi.org/~/media/PDF/Certifications/PBA_Reference_list_v1.ashx

eReads and Reference

PMI® members have the benefit of access to PMI®'s eReads and Reference online library. This library contains full, unabridged text to over 250 publications. The library is easy to search and provides results by relevance. Use this to find specific books or to browse for books on a given topic.

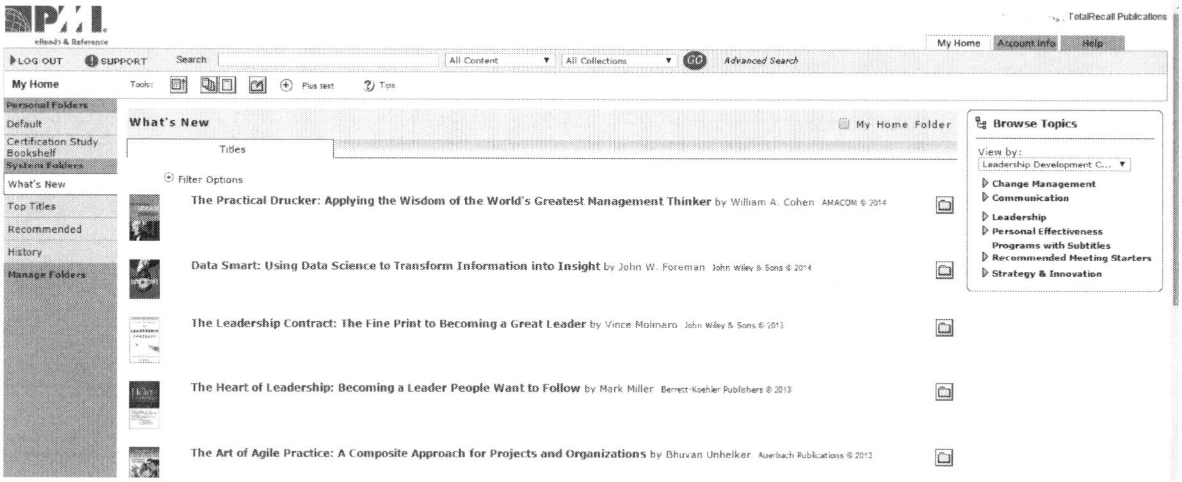

Figure 8-2: eReads and Reference Home Page
(**http://pmi.books24x7.com/bookshelf.asp**)

PMI-PBA Preparation Courses

Some people are comfortable taking the PMI-PBA exam after using our materials independently to study for the exam. Others may find that a preparation course will give them additional confidence needed to be comfortable in sitting for the exam. Watermark Learning provides two options for taking advantage of our PMI-PBA Preparation Course.

Live Instruction

PMI-PBA Preparation Courses are available on a regular basis. These courses are often offered virtually and always led by a live instructor who is PMI-PBA certified. This is an opportunity to work through the material with someone who knows what it takes for exam success and to network with other aspiring for the PMI-PBA certification.

Anytime Learning

Through our Anytime Learning you get the advantage of observing a previous live course. You'll hear the instructor, the students' questions, and group discussions via a recording of a previous session that you can view at any time. An instructor will be available to answer any questions you may have has you work through the course and the material.

Visit **www.watermarklearning.com** or call 952.921.0900 for more information on our courses.

Roadmap

Below is the roadmap from the Foundations chapter as a review of the study strategies to prepare for the PMI-PBA exam.

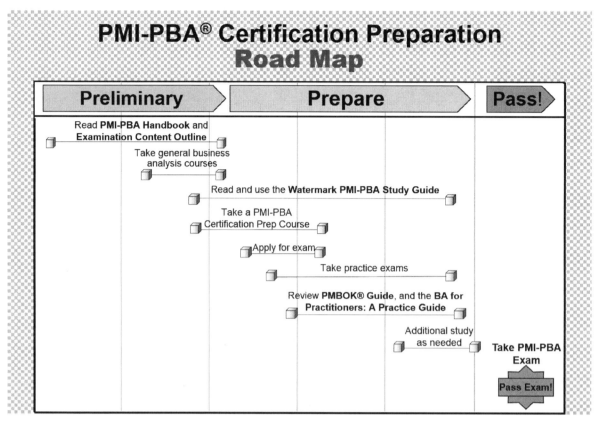

Figure 8-3: PMI-PBA Study Roadmap

Final Tips – Exercise

Use the table below to create your PMI-PBA Preparation Plan. Enter your target test date at the bottom of the page. There are no right on or wrong answers on this exercise.

Activity	Completion Target Date	Status

Activity	Completion Target Date	Status

I will sit for the PMI-PBA exam by: _____

Practice Exams

Practice exams are a valuable tool in your study for the PMI-PBA exam. But it is a tool that should not be abused. Here we will provide some guidance on effective use of practice exams. Be sure to read **Top Ten PMI-PBA Exam Taking Tips and Types of Exam Questions** in the following section for help on answering the questions.

Practice exams have been included for each domain throughout this study guide. A final practice exam follows this chapter. These are helpful in understanding your learning and retention as you work through the *Business Analysis for Practitioners: A Practice Guide*. We recommend always recording your answers on a separate piece of paper so there is no residual hint in subsequences practice rounds.

Purchasing this book entitles you to a trial subscription of our PMI-PBA Online Study Exam. The online study exam mimics the functionality of the actual examination with the ability to flag, skip, and go back to questions. We have provided different exam modes so you can decide to do a drill on one or more domains, or to do a simulation. Depending on the mode, you can select to review the answers with detailed explanations following each question or to wait until exam completion. There are over 750 questions in the simulator to make your test experience unique each time.

Here is our advice for effective use of practice exams:

1. Complete a simulation early in your study program to determine your overall readiness. Passing point of the actual exam is somewhere around 70 percent. We recommend that you aim to get around 80 percent on practice exams before sitting for the exam. Don't be surprised or discouraged if you get a lower percentage the first time through.
2. Use the results of this first run through to re-plan your study approach by prioritizing your additional study by domain. Use a combination of your lowest percentage score and the percentage of items on the exam to determine which domains require the most attention.
3. Re-read and rework the study guide for the first domain you have identified. Review the *PMBOK® Guide* section referenced for additional context. Determine if you need to find and study other materials to help with comprehension.
4. Take a practice drill for the domain to determine your readiness. Repeat steps 3 and 4 until you have achieved a score that you are satisfied with.
5. Move on to the next domain, repeating steps 3 and 4.
6. Re-take a simulation once you are satisfied with results of individual domains.

If all is going well you have now scored near 80 percent on the simulation. You are ready to take the exam! If you score between 70 and 80 percent you are probably in good shape but may want to continue to study weak areas. If you score under 70 percent, you may not be ready. Review your study strategies and determine if there are other tactics you can take to better prepare. Consider rescheduling if your exam is already scheduled and you feel you need more time. These percentages are rough estimates. Use your own discretion when deciding on your additional study needs.

During the Exam

It's exam day. Now what? Here we will discuss what to expect on test day. Knowing what to expect should help relieve the stress of the exam. The experience is the same for all PMI® credentials so if achieved another credential in recent years you already know what to expect.

Exam Logistics

The examination is proctored by Prometric. **https://www.prometric.com.**

The following scenario is intended to help you visualize what to expect in getting seated for the exam.

> Test day is here and Heidi is nervous and excited all at the same time. She is feeling pretty good after getting a score an 82 percent on her final simulation two days ago. She managed to get a good night's sleep and had a healthy breakfast to help fuel her mind. She has packed a couple of healthy snacks and water to help keep her energy up throughout the exam.
>
> Heidi arrived at the test center early and proceeds to check in. As it turns out, they have a computer station available so she can start right away. She is provided a locker and pointed to a shelf where she can keep her snacks. She is informed that the only thing she should have on her person when ready to take the exam is her identification and test notice. She will not be able to access her locker during the exam. She guesses they are worried that she is going to sneak in some critical notes. Oh well, at least her belongings are safe. She locks her items up, puts her water and snacks on the indicated shelf and then makes a final trip to the restroom.
>
> Heidi is now ready to find her computer station. She brings her identification and test notice to the proctor. The proctor asks her to empty her pockets and roll up her sleeves and pant legs to make sure she's not sneaking in any notes. The proctor has her sign the log and marks the time. She is led to a computer station in a room with about 10 other stations and provided 4 blank sheets of paper and a pencil. Some of the stations have people taking various tests already.
>
> Heidi is seated at a station that has been prepared for her test. She notices that there is a practice test and she has been given 15 minutes to use this to learn the test system. The questions on this practice exam are ridiculously easy with questions such as, "What color is an orange?" She answers just a couple of question to get a feel for the test software. She uses the rest of the 15 minutes to do a "brain dump" of some of the things memorized to recall for the examination.
>
> Heidi selects to start the actual examination and the first question is displayed. There is a button to open a calculator if needed and an option to "flag" a question. She notices navigation options to go to next question, first skipped question, or first flagged question. She begins to answer questions, skipping those she's not quite sure about yet. She notices that it got bit easier once she was about 20 questions in. She realizes her anxiety level has decreased which probably explains why it seems slightly easier. She makes it through the first round, answering 143 of 200 questions. She decides a quick break is in order as she has plenty of time.

The proctor has Heidi log out of the room. She grabs a snack, takes a sip of water and takes a quick walk around the test center. She was out of the room maybe 10 minutes but feels refreshed and ready to go back for more.

Heidi has to wait just a couple of minutes as the proctor checks in a new test taker. The proctor has her roll up her sleeves and pant legs again, sign in the log, and verifies her identification before she goes back in.

Heidi starts at the beginning of the exam to answer the questions she had previously skipped. She finds she is spending a bit more time to thoroughly analyze each question and potential answers but limits herself to about two minutes per question. She doesn't want to spend too much time on a single question. She finds she can usually get down to two viable answers and does her best to guess on several. She has "flagged" a few questions along the way that she just isn't sure about. She gets to the end of the test, all questions now answered. She uses the navigation option to take a look at the few questions she had flagged. For the most part she leaves the answers as is.

Heidi notices she has about 30 minutes left in the four-hour test time. With all questions answered she contemplates using the time to do a quick review of her answers. She looks at a couple of the answers and realizes that she has done her best. What if she changes a correct answer to a wrong answer? She'll never know if she is actually hurting her chances of passing. She contemplates this a few minutes and decides it's time to submit the test.

Heidi's heart does a little stop as she hovers over the submit button. She finally clicks it and then… "ARG! A survey!" Apparently she has to answer a Prometric survey before she can get her test score. "Seriously!?" She answers the survey. She thinks she feels her heart stop as the software scores her exam. In about 30 seconds she gets a message on screen "Congratulations, you have passed!" She does a little happy dance on her way out of the test room to check out with the proctor. The proctor provides a certified notice of test results and congratulates her.

Several weeks later she gets a certificate in the mail from PMI®.

This scenario is based on the actual experience of Vicki James, one of the study guide contributors. It is important to note that each Prometric site will have different processes and policies. For example, one test center may hand out paper and pencil while another provides a small white board and dry erase marker. You can read more on Prometric test policies at **https://www.prometric.com/en-us/for-test-takers/prepare-for-test-day/frequently-asked-questions/pages/testing-center-regulations.aspx**.

Top Ten PMI-PBA Exam Taking Tips

The PMI-PBA exam was written to test not only your ability to recall concepts, tools, and techniques, but also the ability to apply this knowledge in real situations. The strategy to test application of knowledge is to require the test taker to work a little harder to understand the question and the potential answers in order to select the BEST answer. This is why many find answering questions tricky. Remember these top 10 tips for taking the exam from Chapter 1:

Tactic	Notes
1. Rest	Get plenty of rest the night before you take the exam. Part of successful test-taking involves problem-solving and logical elimination, so a well-rested mind and body will help you much more than last-minute, anxiety-laced cramming.
2. "Brain Dump"	Because of the length, some people find it useful to start the exam by noting a few key mnemonics and definitions. If nothing else, this "brain dump" helps alleviate a little test anxiety that many people feel in a high-stakes exam.
3. Read each question carefully	A common reason people fail an exam is due to not reading each question thoroughly enough. There may be one word or phrase that affects the entire answer and it will be easy to miss those if you read the question too quickly.
4. Don't dwell	Don't dwell on questions that seem difficult or complicated. Leave them blank and go on to the next question. Chances are it will seem easier later in the exam. You will also save time and energy this way. You can go back any time to review and answer past unanswered questions.
5. 1st pass: skip hard questions	Skip hard questions until you get one you feel confident about. By first answering as many of the 150 questions as you can, you will increase your confidence, learn how the question-makers think, and may even discover hints in one question that helps you in another. One of the authors found this to be true for more than one question and benefited from it.
6. 2nd pass: review skipped questions	After your first pass, go back to the beginning and review questions you skipped. You may have learned from other questions, or even answers, that may trigger a thought that leads to the correct answer. If you are unsure of any question, skip it as described previously and do a 3rd pass through the questions.
7. Don't second-guess yourself!	DO NOT SECOND GUESS questions you have already answered. Chances are you will second guess a correct answer into an incorrect one! If you're unsure, don't answer it.
8. Get down to two viable answers	For tough questions on exams, there are generally two weaker possible answers and two that are stronger. Start by eliminating the weaker answers, then work on determining the correct one from the pair remaining.
9. Watch for "distracters"	Wrong answers are known as "distracters" and are meant to distract you from the correct one. They may have an oxymoronic term, such as "requirements design" or may have a term that clearly doesn't belong in a "list of lists" (see that topic later in this section).
10. Guess if you must	If time is short and you have unanswered questions, you have one of two options: 1) Make your best guess or 2) Mark down answer "B" for each unanswered question. We don't necessarily recommend the latter, but enough urban legends exist about this being the most common answer on exams, that it's worth considering. You are not downgraded for wrong answers, so an educated guess is better than a random one.

Figure 8-4: Top 10 Exam Taking Tips

Types of Exam Questions

Types of exam questions were discussed in Chapter 1. Review these types and strategies for each type.

Type	Explanation	Example	Strategy
Definitions	You are expected to know key business analysis definitions, so be prepared to answer several of these.	You might see a question like "a model that depicts domain information is…" with a correct answer of "Use Case Diagram."	These are pretty straight forward. Rule out any terms or definitions that you don't recognize as they are likely distractors.
Sequences	To test your knowledge of the order of tasks, not just their content, these questions can be challenging. We cover sequences and orders of tasks in the individual chapters of this book on the domain.	In general, be prepared for questions that start with "what is the first thing you do…"	Look at the possible answers and determine their sequence process. Now review the question and determine the next step in the situation.
Scenarios	These are included to test your application of business analysis knowledge and skills. A project-related situation is presented and you are asked to solve a problem, synthesize variables, interpret a diagram, etc.	For example, "given a situation in which stakeholders are spread out over a wide geographic area, and are not coming to consensus about their requirements, which of the following would you do" with a possible answer of "hold a requirements workshop."	These questions will often have extraneous information. Re-read the question to determine what the question is really asking. Now determine what information in the question is relevant. Remember soft skills when you see these types of questions as they may hold a clue to the correct answer.
List of Lists	To test your knowledge of terms and groupings of details, there are several questions to choose the correct grouping of like terms.	You may be asked, "Which group of modeling tools is used to document business processes?" and the correct answer might be "Flowcharts, Process Maps, and Activity Diagrams." These questions are tricky, in that an alternative incorrect answer might be "Flowcharts, Sequence Maps, and Activity Diagrams."	Review each answer's list independently and determine if there is an item in the list that is not like the others. It may be a list of tools with a task thrown it, or perhaps a new nonsensical term. Rule these answers out. Compare the lists of the remaining lists to determine which best fits the question.

Figure 8-5: PMI-PBA Exam Question Types

 PMI-PBA Certification Study Guide

Summary

Taking the PMI-PBA exam is a stressful event. Adequate preparation and knowing what to expect can alleviate some of that stress. General tips to consider include:

- Know your learning style and plan your preparation accordingly.

- Understand how to read and analyze questions for the best possible answer. Use practice exams to improve your question answering skills.

- Be prepared for the Prometric regulations and processes.

 Final Tips Goal: Develop a study and test taking strategy to pass the PMI-PBA exam on the first try.

Notes

        © 2015-2016, Elizabeth Larson and Richard Larson   PMI-PBA Certification Study Guide

9. Appendix A – Glossary Terms

Accuracy

Assessment of correctness.

Agile

An adaptive project approach that focuses on small pieces of a solution for analysis, design, development, and testing that allows for frequent, small releases of solution functionality based on feature priority.

Analogous Estimating

A technique using past projects that are similar to forecast hours and/or costs. It is typically used in the early stages of a project when there may not be a great deal of information available.

Assessment

A generic term to describe evaluating, analyzing, or estimating the quality or ability of someone or something.

Three-Point Estimates

PERT or a simple average of three estimates (optimistic, most likely, pessimistic) can be used to provide an estimate that reveals the range of uncertainty about activity duration or cost.

The three-point formula used depends on what the distribution of the values might be. For a triangular distribution, the three-point average is used. For a beta distribution, the traditional PERT approach is used.

Baseline

An established boundary of approved requirements against which requirements changes are compared. Each time requirements are approved, they are baselined.

Benchmarking (aka Research)

To compare organizational practices against the best-in-class practices that exist within competitor enterprises in government or industry.

To determine how companies achieve their superior performance levels and use that information to design projects to improve operations of the enterprise. Focused on strategies, operations, and processes.

Bottom-Up Estimating

Method of estimating duration or cost for the lowest-level components of the WBS and then aggregating or "rolling up" the individual estimates into higher levels.

Business Analysis

The evaluation of an organization's needs—followed by the identification and management of requirements—to realize a solution. In short, it is the discipline of working with stakeholders to define an organization's requirements in order to shape the output of projects and ensure that expected business benefits are delivered. Source: PMI-PBA FAQ

Business Analyst

A person who conducts business analysis activities regardless of their job title or role.

Business Case

A document that describes the necessary information from a business standpoint to determine whether or not the project is worth the investment.

Business Opportunity

Describes an opportunity that will add value to the business.

Business Problem

Describes a situation that is hindering a business from achieving maximum value.

Business Requirement

Describes the higher-level needs of the organization and provides the rationale for a new project, including business:

- Goals and objectives
- Problems to be solved
- Opportunities to be exploited

Business Rule Catalog

A document containing a complete list of business rules and related attributes. The catalog can be used as reference for related requirements.

Cause and Effect Diagram (aka Fishbone or Ishikawa diagram)

A type of flowchart that helps organize thinking about a problem and diagnose cause and effect to discover root cause. Can be used in conjunction with the "Five Whys" tool.

Checksheet

Used to collect sampling results information about defects which then may be further analyzed using a Pareto diagram.

Communication Plan

A component of the project, program, or portfolio management plan that describes how, when, and by whom information about the project will be administered and disseminated.

Consensus Building

A general term for getting a group to generally agree. Many specific techniques (further described in Decision Making) may help lead to group consensus.

Context Diagram

A diagram that allows the business analyst to clearly show the boundary of the system, the users (both human and other systems), and the high-level data provided by the system and to the system. A context diagram is only a high-level view, but when supported by detailed data definitions, it is an excellent tool for communicating part of the project scope to stakeholders.

Contingency Planning

The outcome of analyzing the risks to a product and the planned response if the risk becomes a reality. May also result in schedule and budget reserves by determining the likelihood and impact of a risk occurring. The likelihood (%) is multiplied by the impact ($) to determine an appropriate reserve amount.

Control Chart

A chart used to determine whether or not a process is stable or has predictable performance (typically) over time by measuring output variables representing repetitive activities. Control charts can be used for both project and product life cycle processes.

Cost-Benefit Analysis

The study of the cost versus the benefits that an organization will receive for a particular solution. This is useful in selecting projects for investment that will yield the greatest financial benefit for the organization.

CRUD Matrix

A matrix used to cross check the data and processes to ensure a process is in place to create, read, update, and delete every entity. The matrix helps spot gaps. Is also helpful in documenting user permissions in a system.

Data Dictionary & Glossary

A document containing key items that are formally recorded to identify terminology and corresponding definitions used by the organization. Also defines the data used or needed by an organization, including both high-level and more complex data definitions.

Data Modeling

A model representing data structures, relationships between structures, and the detailed data attributes or facts within the structures. They are used to document and communicate data requirements, typically using either an Entity Relationship Diagram (ERD) or Class Diagram (in UML or Unified Modeling Language).

Day-in-the Life (DITL) Testing

Testing conducted by someone knowledgeable in the business that focuses on specific scenarios in order to verify that the expected results are realized.

Decision Table

A tool used to document business rules in a tabular format with a series of decisions and the outcomes. The table provides an easy way to document all factors that may impact the processing of a decision. For example, age, residency, and military service all are contributing factors to determine the cost of a hunting or fishing recreational license in the state of Washington. The decision table simplifies the processing of these business rules to determine the correct license price by clearly representing the effects of each pricing factor.

Decision Tree

Used to document complex business rules graphically in a hierarchical structure. This may be used in conjunction with a decision table to analyze and document complex business rules. Decision trees work best when decision points have limited responses such as yes or no.

Decomposition

Breaking down something that is higher-level – such as functional areas, their processes, or project deliverables – into simpler subsets for the purpose of studying or analyzing it. This technique is often presented using graphical models, such as a Work Breakdown Structure diagram.

Delphi Technique

A way to gain consensus using expert opinion. Experts are asked to provide their opinions independently through a facilitator. The facilitator will coordinate anonymous feedback through a questionnaire for responses until agreement is achieved. This is commonly used for creating estimates or getting a recommendation on a decision to be made.

Dependency Analysis

A technique used to identify and clearly articulate dependencies between two or more objects (e.g., requirements).

Dependency Graph

A graph that visually depicts dependencies in system requirements, functions, or components. There is not a single method or process for developing the graph.

Design of Experiments

Using statistical "what-if" scenarios to determine which combination of variables produce the best or desired quality outcome. Design of experiments, unlike other quality techniques, provides a tool for modifying multiple factors at the same time rather than just one at a time. It is more typically used on the product of the project, rather than the project itself.

Desk Checking

This is where the person who creates the deliverable reviews their own work prior to presenting it for formal quality control review.

Document Analysis

To elicit requirements by studying available documentation on existing and comparable solutions and identifying relevant information.

Estimation Poker (aka Planning Poker)

A technique primarily used by agile teams to estimate the effort for each user story. User stories are estimated in relation to each other and not assigned a time estimate. T-shirt sizing (S, M, L, and XL) or Fibonacci sequence (0, 1, 2, 3, 5, 8, 13, and 20) are typical estimation values used.

Evaluation Criteria (aka Acceptance & Evaluation Criteria)

Defined criteria that will be used for determining when a requirement, feature, or solution is acceptable for use.

Events

The process of analyzing business events in order to determine organizational responses needed to support the business. Events may be:

- External
- Internal
- Time-based

Exploratory Testing

Testing conducted by someone knowledgeable of the business and without a script. This provides testing of some "out of the box" scenarios for expanded test coverage. This supplements formal testing methods, but should not be done in place of them.

Facilitated Workshops

A structured way to capture requirements. A workshop may be used to scope, discover, define, prioritize, and reach closure on requirements for the target system.

Feasibility Analysis

An initial study to develop a recommendation on if a solution is viable to accomplish a desired outcome, whether it's to solve a problem or seize an opportunity. May be used to compare multiple options to determine the most feasible.

Five Whys

A technique where the analyst asks "why is the problem occurring?" up to five times to get to the root cause.

Flowcharts

Graphically depict how the process flows from beginning to end to illustrate how components of the system are related. Flowcharting also helps to analyze how problems occur and highlights inefficiencies.

Force Field Analysis

Analyzes the forces for and against a change, to help form a decision and communicate the reasoning behind the decision.

Gap Analysis

A technique that businesses use to determine what steps need to be taken in order to move from its current state to its desired, future state. Also called needs-gap analysis, needs analysis, and needs assessment.

Given-Then-When

A tool used to articulate acceptance criteria. Statements are produced with:

- Given (some context)
- When (some action is carried out)
- Then (a particular set of observable consequences should obtain)

Goal

An observable and measurable end result having one or more objectives to be achieved within a more or less fixed timeframe.

Grade

In quality, category or rank used to distinguish items that have the same functional use but do not share the same quality requirements.

Histograms

Bar charts showing how often something occurs.

Impact Analysis

Analysis of potential requirements or requirements changes to determine impacts to other requirements, the product, or the project.

Incremental

A hybrid of predictive and adaptive project approaches where a solution is developed and features released in increments or phases.

Inspection

Examination or measurement of a deliverable in order to verify it meets requirements specifications.

Integration Testing

Testing conducted to ensure that requirements for the complete business processes have been satisfied. This testing focuses on the end-to-end business and includes all of the systems and interaction points within scope of the solution.

Interoperability

Analysis to understand how applications communicate and collaborate with each other to complete a workflow or process.

Interview

A systematic approach designed to elicit information from a person or group of people in an informal or formal setting by talking to an interviewee, asking relevant questions, and documenting the responses.

Iterative

A common agile approach where release cycles are time-boxed in small time frames. Each iteration may introduce new features, rework of previously released features, or a combination of both.

Job Analysis

Review of job information for potential stakeholders in order to understand how the stakeholder roles and responsibilities fit within the organization in order to develop stakeholder management plans.

Key Performance Indicators (KPIs)

Metrics that are defined to be used in evaluating progress towards meeting objectives or goals. A metric is a quantifiable level of an indicator that an organization uses to measure progress at a specific point in time (e.g., sales in January). An indicator identifies a specific numerical measurement (sales) that represents the degree of progress toward achieving a goal (industry leader).

Lean

A project approach that seeks to optimize efficiency by eliminating waste from activities and operations.

Lessons Learned

Documenting knowledge gained during a project by facilitating team discussion of project successes, opportunities for improvement, failures, and recommendations for improving the performance of future projects or project phases.

Maslow's Hierarchy of Needs

"A Theory of Human Motivation" describes Abraham Maslow's ideas on human motivation as a hierarchy of needs. We are motivated to seek the next level of satisfaction once each level of the hierarchy has been met.

MoSCoW

A prioritization technique used to rate requirements or features using ratings of "must have," "should have," "could have," and "won't have" as it relates to project or release scope.

Multi-Voting

A prioritization technique where participants are given multiple votes for a variety of options on a specific issue. Participants may use one vote per option or multiple votes for a single item for added weight.

Nominal Group Technique

A process that includes brainstorming to generate ideas. Voting or multi-voting is then used to rank the ideas in order to identify the most desirable options.

Non-Functional Requirements

Describe the required qualities of a system, such as its usability and performance characteristics. Important to user and development community.

Objective

Something to which work is to be directed in order for a strategic position to be attained, a purpose to be achieved, a result to be obtained, a product to be produced, or a service to be performed.

Observation

A means of eliciting requirements by observing stakeholders completing activities within their work environment.

Opportunity Analysis

Analysis of a potential opportunity to fully understand the feasibility and potential benefit.

Options Analysis

Analyzing various options to understand the benefits, risks, and consequences of each in order to make a selection that will bring the greatest value to the project. This relates to multi-criteria decision analysis.

Organizational Chart

Describes the roles, responsibilities and reporting structures that exist within an organization and to align those structures with the organization's goals.

Organizational Readiness

Analyzing the organization's readiness to accept and use a new solution. This goes beyond the technical implementation to the acceptance of the solution and organization preparedness to use it effectively.

Parametric Estimating

The use of historical data in formulas or algorithms to extrapolate an estimate for a small amount of work to a large amount of work. For example, if one activity (or series of activities) can be estimated in detail, an algorithm can be developed to determine the total effort for all work involving that activity or series of activities. It's basically using mathematical models to predict time or cost.

Pareto Charts

The Pareto chart shows how many results were generated by type or category of identified cause. It identifies the "vital few" causes of most quality problems. If those few problems are eliminated, about 75-80 percent of the problems will be eliminated. For example, if most of the problems in the Call Center are due to network issues, resolving those issues will eliminate most of the calls.

Peer Review

A review process (either formal or informal) involving peers of the author or creator of the work being inspected in order to verify and improve upon quality.

Personas

A tool used to understand the different user groups of a potential solution by assigning each role a "persona." The persona tells a story about the users of that class including information such as goals, behaviors, motivations, environment, demographics, and skills.

Planguage

A set of closely defined identifiers (tags) to describe and quantify specific elements of the requirements.

Precedence Diagramming Method

A technique used to construct a schedule model in which activities are represented by nodes and graphically linked by one or more logical relationships to show the sequence in which the activities are to be performed.

Precision

A measure of exactness. May not be accurate, but can still be precise.

Process Modeling

A technique for visually documenting work performed in an organization, including who does it and how they collaborate. Useful for many aspects of business analysis.

Types of process models:

- Process map
- Swimlane
- Activity diagram

Product Backlog

A stack ranked prioritized list of user stories used to allocate work to iterations in agile projects.

Progressive Elaboration

The process of analyzing a high level requirement, feature, or estimate to decompose and document additional detail. The *PMBOK® Guide* specifically relates progressive elaboration to estimating, however it may apply in these other uses.

Project Requirement

Describes actions, processes, or other conditions the project needs to meet.

Prototyping

A diagram detailing user interface requirements and integrates them with other requirements such as use cases, scenarios, and data and business rules.

Purpose Alignment Model

A method for aligning business decisions, processes, and feature designs around purpose.

Quadrant Analysis

A generic analysis tool where factors are measured on two axis to determine a "'quadrant" for classification. Examples include the Power/Interest grid in stakeholder management or Likelihood/Penalty of defects when determining if a solution is "fit for use."

Quality

The degree to which a set of inherent characteristics fulfill requirements.

Quality Requirement

Conditions or criteria needed to validate the successful completion of a project deliverable.

Reporting Tools and Techniques

Tools and techniques used to track and report project or activity status and progress.

Requirement

"A condition or capability that is required to be present in a product, service, or result to satisfy a contract or other formally imposed condition." *PMBOK® Guide – Fifth Edition.*

Requirements Baseline

The list of requirements that have been formally approved for continued work. Any changes to the requirements baseline will require formal approval through the change control process.

Requirements Management Plan

A component of the project or program management plan that describes how requirements will be analyzed, documented, and managed.

Requirements Management System

A tool that supports collecting, analyzing, managing, and communicating requirements through a relational database.

Requirements Traceability Matrix

A matrix used to trace requirements up to the supporting project and business goals of the organization and then down to the work product of the project team needed to satisfy the requirements. The matrix includes additional attributes useful to tracking and managing each requirement.

Retrospectives

A review process typically used in agile projects to review each iteration. Team members meet to identify and discuss the results of the latest iteration, what is working well, and identify opportunities and actions for improvement.

Risk Analysis

The process of examining a program, project, or process for risk. Risks may be negative or positive.

Scatter Diagrams

Shows relationship or correlation between independent ("X" axis) and dependent ("Y" axis) variables. Independent variables are also known as "inputs" or "potential causes." Dependent variables are also known as "outputs" or "effects."

Scenario Analysis

Analysis of how the system will be used, and the interactions between users and the system for various situations. Scenario analysis works to capture when variations to the most common situation occur in order to better understand requirements for all scenarios.

Service Level Agreement (SLA)

An agreement detailing the nature, quality, and scope of service to be provided.

Skills Assessment

A study of the skills and competencies of project stakeholders to allow for stakeholder management plans that leverage strengths and can accommodate weaknesses.

Solution Requirement

Requirements that the solution must satisfy, including functional (behaviors of the product) and non-functional (environmental conditions) requirements.

Solution Scope

Describes major features and functions included in the solution and the interactions it will have with people and systems outside its scope.

Solution Scope Statement

A description of the solution scope, major deliverables, assumptions, and constraints.

Stakeholder Register

A document containing information on all identified stakeholders in order. The register includes information that is helpful in determining a stakeholder management strategy and notes on activities relating to the strategy.

Stakeholder Requirement

States needs of stakeholders, specifically how stakeholders or classes of stakeholders will interact with a solution.

State Diagrams and Tables

Either a tabular or visual specification of a sequence of states that an object goes through during its lifetime. Events that cause a transition between those states are also defined. For example, a "PMI-PBA applicant" moves to a state of "PMI-PBA recipient" once they have completed the transition of passing the credential examination.

Statement of Work (SOW)

Narrative description of products, services, or results to be delivered that includes:

- Business Need
- Product Scope Description
- Strategic Plan

Statistical Sampling

A technique where a small number of items representing a sample of the entire quantity are chosen for inspection. This is used to reduce the cost of quality rather than inspecting every item.

Storyboarding

A prototyping technique using images and illustrations to show the sequence or navigation through a series of events. In software development, storyboards show navigation paths through webpages, screens, or interfaces. They are typically low-tech and disposable and are intended to illustrate the experience rather than the look and feel of the system or product.

Strategic

Used during planning to describe long-term plans or goals of what the organization or project strives to accomplish.

Survey/Questionnaire

A means of eliciting information from many people, sometimes anonymously, in a relatively short period of time by preparing and sending a set list of questions for response.

SWOT Analysis

An analysis of the strengths, weaknesses, opportunities, and threats relating to a specific organization, project, or solution option.

Tactical

Used in planning to describe the short term plans or goals that support organization or project strategy. This tends to demonstrate "the how" of how strategies will be achieved.

Test

The examination of a work product or deliverable in order to determine the level of quality.

Time-Boxing

A prioritization method where stakeholders are provided estimates for implementing requirements (or features) and the time available. Stakeholders then select which requirements they choose to include in the "time-box." Time-boxing can be adapted to apply a fixed cost (budget) where stakeholders buy requirements (or features) based on cost and budget available. Play money or poker chips can be used to facilitate prioritization.

Transition Requirement

Temporary capabilities, such as data conversion and training requirements, needed to transition from the "as is" to the "to be" state.

Tuckman Model (Stages of Team Development)

A model of the stages of team development created by Bruce Tuckman. The stages are Form, Storm, Norm, Perform, Adjourn (mourn).

Use Case Diagram

A diagram used to summarize the scope of a solution by illustrating which use cases are in scope and which are out of scope for the system. It identifies the use cases and the actors who directly interact with the solution.

Use Cases

A textual model detailing the interactions between system users (actors) and the solution undergoing development. Each use case focuses on a single user goal (process). Boundaries for the process are stated using pre-conditions and post-conditions. The detailed interaction between the actor and system is described for the normal course of events and extending to alternative or exception paths. Detailing these interactions is useful to uncovering solution functional requirements.

User Acceptance Testing

Testing conducted by future end users of a solution at the direction of the project business analysis and quality professionals in order to gain user acceptance that the solution is ready for implementation. Testing is often scripted and observed by the project BA and/or quality team to ensure full coverage and to observe questions and issues firsthand.

User Journey Map

Documents the customer experience from the users' perspective to understand not only how users interact with the solution, but can also identify improvement opportunities.

User Story

A brief description of functionality that users need from a solution to meet a business objective. The user's story is stated with the specific format of "as a <actor>, I want to <function>, so that I can <benefit>." These serve as stakeholder requirements on adaptive projects.

Value Engineering

An approach used to optimize project life cycle costs, save time, increase profits, improve quality, expand market share, solve problems, and/or use resources more effectively.

Value Proposition

An analysis of the value an organization can expect to achieve as a result of the recommended solution. This is typically stated from the perspective of the customer.

Value Stream Mapping

A lean-management method for analyzing the current state and designing a future state for the series of events which take a product or service from its beginning through to the customer. This is analyzed to identify opportunities for improvement and then used to develop a "future state" map.

Waterfall

A predictive development/project approach where full planning and analysis is conducted early in the project life cycle, prior to any development.

Weighted criteria

An objective method of ranking or prioritizing options. Once options are defined, then criteria for evaluating them are defined and weighted (given a value) for relative importance. Options are then scored against each criterion and the score is multiplied by the weight of the criterion. Scores for each option are totaled, resulting in weighted criteria.

Work Breakdown Structure (WBS)

A hierarchical decomposition of the total scope of work to be carried out by the project team to accomplish the project objectives and create the required deliverables. The WBS provides a graphical view of work that has been decomposed (see decomposition).

10.   Appendix B: Exam Simulation

This section contains a 100-question simulated exam, using the same approximate distribution of domains as provided by PMI® in its "exam blueprint." The questions were originally chosen to provide PMI-PBA candidates with a practice exam.

Your purchase of this book entitles you to a trial subscription to the Watermark Learning PMI-PBA Online Study Exam. This online exam bank provides you with questions that are oriented towards the PMI-PBA exam.

Future editions of this book may contain separate exams if the demand warrants it. Please give us feedback using our online feedback page: **www.watermarklearning.com/Feedback**.

Simulated Exam Questions

1. Which of the following tools are used to analyze defects found in quality control?
    a. Cost-benefit analysis, cost of quality, several basic quality tools, benchmarking, design of experiments, statistical sampling, meetings.
    b. Quality control measurements, validated changes, and verified deliverables.
    c. Checksheets, Pareto diagrams, histograms, control charts, scatter diagrams.
    d. Defect log, impact analysis, customer feedback.

2. The team has agreed to use SharePoint to store the Requirements Traceability Matrix. Updates to the matrix will be saved as a minor version change (e.g., version 1.1) with new baselined requirements being saved with a new version number (e.g., version 2.0). This is part of:
    a. Interactive communications.
    b. A change request.
    c. A baseline management plan.
    d. Configuration management.

3. Requirements are ready for the project team to act upon when they have:
    a. Been prototyped and acceptance criteria is defined.
    b. Been prioritized and approved.
    c. Defined acceptance criteria and the team is not busy.
    d. Been approved and identified as critical.

4. Requirements for agile projects are traditionally captured in which format?
    a. Use cases.
    b. User stories.
    c. Requirements traceability matrix.
    d. Test cases/scenarios.

5. Why is it important determine the appropriate format for requirements?
    a. It assures that the same organizational artifacts are used consistently by all BAs in all situations.
    b. It ensures that each requirement is described in a unique format that respects the title and authority of the highest ranking stakeholder in the audience.
    c. It ensures that requirements are understandable to their particular stakeholders.
    d. It ensures that the presenter has sufficient time to learn new tools to enhance each presentation of requirements to different target audiences.

6. What are engagement level classifications for stakeholders?
    a. Manage closely, keep satisfied, keep informed, monitor.
    b. High, medium, low.
    c. Unaware, resistant, neutral, supportive, leading.
    d. Responsible, accountable, consulted, informed.

7. What are the three features that best describe what a user story must include?
    a. Actor, story, result.
    b. Actor, description, result.
    c. Actor, description, benefit.
    d. Actor, story, requirement.

8. Which statement is most true about approving requirements?
    a. Approving stakeholders need to sign-off on the requirements in writing.
    b. Approval may be obtained from individual stakeholders or as a group.
    c. Once approval is obtained, the decisions surrounding the approval are no longer needed and can be discarded.
    d. Approval decisions need to be traced to the technical design.

9. The Smith & Smith Company is a highly decentralized technology company that focuses on state of the art software solutions for implantable medical devices. The business analyst is currently discussing the relative importance and ranking of the requirements for a new product based on implementation difficulty. What task is the business analyst performing?
    a. Requirements elicitation.
    b. Requirements analysis.
    c. Requirements prioritization.
    d. Requirements risk analysis.

10. To determine if a solution is delivering business value, a business analyst needs which of the following:
    a. Designed solution.
    b. Constructed solution.
    c. Tested solution.
    d. Deployed solution.

11. A business requirement can best be described as:
    a. Higher level statements of goals or objectives.
    b. Specific needs of a class, group, or individual.
    c. They can contain both functional and non-functional aspects.
    d. Capabilities the solution has in the current state but no longer needed in the future state.

12. What format should be used for a requirements package?
    a. A formal presentation, otherwise it is not worth packaging requirements.
    b. One that is appropriate to the needs of the stakeholders.
    c. Minimally they should contain a business requirements specification or equivalent.
    d. Models, diagrams, and documents.

13. The best example of a technical constraint is:
    a. Limitation on the project's flexibility such as budgetary restrictions, time restrictions, limits on the number of resources available, or restrictions based on skills of the project team.
    b. Documentation about things the business analyst believes to be true but is unable to verify.
    c. Expectation concerning the designability, reliability, usability, maintainability, efficiency, human engineering, scalability, and portability of the system.
    d. Any architectural decision that is made, including development language, hardware platform, or applications software that must be used.

14. Which of the following is a weakness when using interface analysis:
    a. The requirements elicitation of an interface's functional requirements early in the project will provide valuable details for project planning.
    b. It does not provide an understanding of the business process.
    c. It is too time consuming to involve the end-to-end resources and SMEs as required.
    d. Knowing the complexity of the interfaces and their testing needs enables more accurate project planning and a potential savings in time and cost.

15. The scope management plan:
    a. Is a formal document.
    b. Is highly detailed.
    c. Is optional.
    d. Is based on the needs of the project.

16. Requirements are validated:
    a. Before they are verified.
    b. Typically after they are verified, although those processes may be done in parallel.
    c. After they have been traced.
    d. When the sponsor signs off on them.

17. The most common approach to forecasting requires a manual, bottom-up calculation of work yet to be done. What problem does this present?
    a. The people doing the work are not typically assigned at that point in the project.
    b. The time it takes to do the manual calculation is typically not included in the budget and it distracts people from working on the project.
    c. Politics tend to interfere with people trying to influence the forecasts.
    d. Project managers seldom get the information fast enough to provide timely forecasts to stakeholders.

18. Barry presented his requirements documentation for approval at the weekly requirements review session. Barry provided the business requirements document, status reports, interview notes with track changes in MS Word, and the issues log. Barry was asked to redo the documentation and to come back the next week for the review. Why?
    a. Barry does not understand the concept of work product and deliverables.
    b. The issues log is inappropriate because it could embarrass people if their name is in the log.
    c. Interview notes are inappropriate to include for a review.
    d. Barry should not have been asked to come back since the documents presented are already appropriate to review for sign-off.

19. Beth is a former project manager and likes to use hierarchical decomposition to break down her business analysis deliverables into activities and tasks. She then adds the hours needed and can give an accurate estimate of the time needed to complete her BA work. What type of estimation does Beth like to use?
    a. Delphi estimation.
    b. Parametric estimation.
    c. Bottom-up estimation.
    d. Historical analysis.

20. Why is change control important?
    a. To stifle project changes.
    b. To deter stakeholders from making requests for changes.
    c. To stop developers from gold-plating.
    d. Provides decision makers with information needed to make informed decisions on potential project changes.

21. Eliciting requirements is a key task in business analysis and serves as a foundation for the solution to the business needs. The business analyst should understand the commonly used techniques to elicit requirements, should be able to select appropriate technique(s) for a given situation, and be knowledgeable of the tasks needed to prepare, execute, and complete each technique. According to the *PMBOK® Guide* what types of requirements are elicited?
    a. Functional, non-functional, customer, stakeholder.
    b. Business, stakeholder, solution, transition, project, and quality.
    c. Focused technical, organizational, external, non-technical.
    d. Isolated, compartmental, validation, verification.

22. Stakeholder lists should be reviewed throughout the life of the project because:
    a. Most projects have a large number of them.
    b. They have the ability to influence the project positively or negatively.
    c. Once identified, their levels of interest and influence can change.
    d. To remember who the important stakeholders are.

23. In a short, 3-month project to implement a commercial-off-the-shelf (COTS) system, the BA determined that a detailed Software Requirements Specification document was not necessary and planned instead to utilize use cases for the analysis technique and documentation format. This is an example of:

    a. An assumption that could become a risk.
    b. Appropriate use of risk mitigation.
    c. A common mistake leading to prescriptive requirements.
    d. Determining appropriate requirements analysis and documentation activities.

24. You have scheduled a focus group to determine the current attitudes towards a new product that your company is developing. Your participants should what?

    a. Be ready to participate.
    b. Have a minimum of five years' experience with the company.
    c. Be pre-qualified.
    d. Only respond to pre-planned questions.

25. Traceability is used to help ensure solution conformance to requirements and to assist in scope and change management. What types of traceability can be performed?

    a. Derivation and allocation, cost and location.
    b. Relationship to other requirements, relationship to sponsorship.
    c. Forwards and backwards, cost and location.
    d. Derivation and allocation, relationship to other requirements.

26. Contingency reserves are used to:

    a. Help reduce the risk of overruns in cost or time to an acceptable level.
    b. Compensate for lack of historical information in quantifying risk.
    c. Address unforeseen work that is within project scope ("unknown unknowns").
    d. Eliminate risk exposure.

27. Which statement about the use case diagram is true?

    a. Is used to show system scope, and typically supported by the user profile.
    b. Must always be supported by the user story.
    c. Is used to show system scope, and associations of actors to use cases.
    d. Must always be supported by the misuse case.

28. The technique of interface analysis is best suited for which of the following:

    a. Allowing an online focus group to include members located remotely while participating by a network connection.
    b. Reaching agreements with stakeholders on what interfaces are needed.
    c. Coordinating the activities used to elicit interface requirements.
    d. Capturing requirements attributes for interfaces.

29. What task needs to occur before a change can be requested?
    a. Determine the cost of the change.
    b. Establish the requirements baseline.
    c. Determine the specific stakeholder who will implement the change.
    d. Analyze the impact(s) of the change.

30. What is the purpose of defining transition requirements?
    a. To ensure the project team will be able to leave the project.
    b. To ensure the organization is ready for change.
    c. To ensure the transition period is short.
    d. To ensure a successful move from the old to new system.

31. You are in the process of ensuring that a delivered solution meets the business need on an ongoing basis. You are confident that the solution meets the business need and have determined the most appropriate response. What form best represents that response?
    a. Verified and approved requirements.
    b. Prioritized requirements and approved requirements.
    c. Identified defects and solution validation assessment.
    d. Mitigating actions and approved requirements.

32. What is one purpose for preparing for requirements elicitation?
    a. Identify problem stakeholders so they can be removed from the project.
    b. Ensure that the project manager is included in the elicitation.
    c. Clarify the objectives and desired results for the given elicitation technique.
    d. Minimize constraints.

33. Which of the following can help you prepare for a requirements workshop?
    a. Conducting pre-workshop interviews.
    b. Eliciting some initial requirements.
    c. Establishing the tone of the meeting.
    d. Enforcing discipline.

34. All of the following are components of the scope management plan EXCEPT:
    a. Process to create WBS.
    b. Process to maintain WBS.
    c. How product deliverables will be accepted.
    d. WBS.

35. Which of the following documents contain key domain terms along with their business definitions?
    a. Requirements analysis plan.
    b. Data modeling.
    c. Glossary.
    d. Requirements package.

36. Which statement best describes the communication with stakeholders in a waterfall approach?
    a. Much of the communication of the actual requirements is verbal.
    b. Communications may be written or verbal.
    c. Informal communication takes precedence over more formal written communication.
    d. Tends to rely on formal communication methods and much of the communications of the actual requirements is in writing.

37. Once requirements are approved, they may be baselined. Future changes to requirements must then follow what process?
    a. Change control.
    b. Traceability.
    c. Manage requirements approval.
    d. Baselining.

38. Which of the following stakeholders plays a key role in validating solutions by identifying defects in solutions?
    a. End user.
    b. SME.
    c. Tester.
    d. Operational support.

39. A business rule is:
    a. An organization-wide, self-imposed constraint on doing business.
    b. A capability or condition needed on a particular project to solve a problem or achieve an objective.
    c. Expressed as a relationship between one entity/business object and another one.
    d. A regulation that an organization must adhere to.

40. Business analysis planning activities include:
    a. Stakeholder engagement, requirements communication, traceability, and document control.
    b. Establishing tools, policies, and procedures for the requirements management plan, requirements traceability, document control, and user acceptance testing.
    c. Creating the WBS, requirements management plan, requirements traceability, document control, and user acceptance testing.
    d. Establishing tools, policies, and procedures for the requirements management plan, requirements traceability, document control, and acceptance criteria.

41. Padma is the business analyst on a project to implement a new financial software package. The solution includes not only the software, but also new business processes and new data to support those processes. A decision has been made to run the current system in parallel with the new system for two months, which will allow comparison over both a month-end and a quarter-end. Padma has captured stakeholder and solution requirements for the 'as-is' and the 'to-be' software and business processes. She knows that in addition she still needs to capture what kind of requirements using which technique:
    a. Transition requirements using data modeling.
    b. Non-functional requirements using interface analysis.
    c. Functional requirements using process modeling and data modeling.
    d. Conversion requirements using data flow diagrams.

42. Internal failure costs are different from external failure costs in that:
    a. Internal costs are typically more expensive than external failure costs.
    b. Internal costs are typically paid by the organization while external costs are typically paid by the customer.
    c. Internal costs are typically found by the project while external costs are typically found by the customer.
    d. Internal costs are the responsibility of the project management team while external costs are the responsibility of the customer.

43. Which type of requirement best describes environmental conditions under which the solution must remain effective or qualities that the systems must have.
    a. Business requirements.
    b. Stakeholder requirements.
    c. Functional requirements.
    d. Non-functional requirements.

44. Omar has been researching a business problem for several days trying to understand why it happened. What is Omar performing?
    a. Decision analysis.
    b. Root cause analysis.
    c. Gap analysis.
    d. Defect analysis.

45. Louis is tracking how well the solution was implemented by collecting data and comparing it to expected results previously defined by the stakeholders. What is Louis doing?
    a. Observation.
    b. Data analysis.
    c. Monitoring.
    d. Shadowing.

46. Jacob was conducting interviews with stakeholders to elicit requirements. The sessions were not going well and he asked you for your help. Stakeholders were confused on the size of the project and why the project was needed. Which of the following would you recommend?

    a. Advise Jacob to make sure the stakeholders are on the approved stakeholders lists and ignore the remaining stakeholders.
    b. Advise Jacob to bring the requirements traceability matrix and supporting materials.
    c. Advise Jacob to work more closely with the project manager and project sponsor to get the stakeholders in line with the project.
    d. Advise Jacob to review the business case/need and solution scope.

47. In managing requirements traceability, the 'value' relationship describes:

    a. A requirement linked to a lower-level requirement.
    b. A requirement is a decomposed outcome of another requirement.
    c. One requirement affects the desirability of another, either positively or negatively.
    d. One requirement is only pertinent when another is included.

48. Your organization has just determined a new system is needed to meet a new market opportunity and you have been asked to evaluate and investigate the underlying rationale. You have been assigned the task to ensure that the widest possible range of alternative solutions are considered. What is the output of your work?

    a. Solution scope.
    b. Business objectives.
    c. Solution approach.
    d. Business need.

49. What is the deliverable that is most likely to include descriptions of the currently identified team roles for a specific project?

    a. Requirements management plan.
    b. RACI matrix.
    c. Table of organization (TO).
    d. Questionnaire to identified stakeholders.

50. You are developing cost and time estimates for the business case break-even point. What technique are you likely to employ?

    a. Estimation.
    b. Organizational breakdown structure.
    c. Financial analysis.
    d. Feature decomposition.

51. During a project planning meeting, consideration of a key stakeholder persuades the project management team to take a different approach to communications on the project. That stakeholder would be characterized as having a high level of what on the project?

    a. Influence.
    b. Impact.
    c. Interest.
    d. Power.

52. Of the following activities, which does a business analyst do to contribute to project initiation?

    a. Determine the most feasible business solution scope.
    b. Set strategy for the organization using techniques such as SWOT analysis (strengths, weaknesses, opportunities, and threats).
    c. Establish strategic goals.
    d. Decide which option of a feasibility study is the option to implement.

53. Which of the following best describes the stakeholders involved with reviewing and approving requirements?

    a. Sponsors, project managers, QA.
    b. Stakeholder lists, roles and responsibilities.
    c. Whomever the sponsor has dictated will sign-off.
    d. Executive sponsor, project manager, quality assurance representative, business analyst, architect or technical lead.

54. One of the easiest facilitation tools to use when problems have a human interaction component is:

    a. What vs. how analysis.
    b. Who, what, where, when, how analysis.
    c. The five whys.
    d. Fishbone diagram.

55. Which of the following statements is NOT a desired business outcome?

    a. Improve revenue by increasing sales or reducing cost.
    b. Upgrade the Customer Relationship Management (CRM) solution.
    c. Increase customer satisfaction.
    d. Improve safety.

56. Conflicts during requirements meetings can be valuable, particularly when?

    a. Conflict situations are in their early stages and emotions are high.
    b. Conflict situations are in their early stages and emotions are low.
    c. Conflict situations are in their late stages and emotions are low.
    d. Multiple conflicts have simultaneously arisen and emotions are high.

57. In order to utilize the Work Breakdown Structure (WBS), the BA will need to understand all but one of the following concepts. Which concept is NOT part of a WBS:
    a. Decomposition.
    b. Expert judgment.
    c. Scope management.
    d. Effort and duration.

58. A table that links requirements to their source and tracks them throughout the life of the project is a:
    a. PMIS table.
    b. Requirements management plan.
    c. Requirements traceability matrix.
    d. Technical requirement source table.

59. Successful interviewing depends on all of the following general factors:
    a. BA's interviewing skills, interviewee's readiness to provide information, interviewee's clarity regarding business expectations from the target system, interviewee's expertise in user interface design, BA and interviewee rapport.
    b. BA's level of understanding programming technologies, BA's interviewing skill, interviewee's readiness to provide information, interviewee's clarity regarding business expectations from the target solution.
    c. BA's level of understanding the business, BA's interviewing skill, interviewee's readiness to provide information, interviewee's clarity regarding business expectations from the target system, BA and interviewee rapport.
    d. BA's level of understanding of organizational behavior, BA's presentation skills, interviewee's readiness to provide information, interviewee's clarity regarding business expectations from the target system, BA and interviewee rapport.

60. In a project with little formal documentation, what would the business analyst rely on?
    a. Email, meeting minutes, whiteboard notes.
    b. User stories, whiteboards, flip charts.
    c. Presentations in requirements workshops and structured walk-throughs.
    d. Verbal discussions with stakeholders.

61. Jon is doing some strategic planning that he hopes will lead to a new initiative. What could Jon do to help his strategic planning?
    a. Perform a SWOT analysis.
    b. Develop the business case.
    c. Perform a feasibility study.
    d. Create a vision statement.

62. Which of the following terms is best described as a simplified representation of a complex reality?

    a. Glossary.
    b. Stakeholder and sponsor diagrams.
    c. Model.
    d. Textual description of requirements relationships.

63. The notation known as 'cardinality' indicates:

    a. The total number of entities associated with each class.
    b. The direction of the logical flow of data into or out from a high-level process in a context diagram.
    c. Minimum and maximum number of occurrences of one entity that may be associated with the other entity.
    d. The presence of a physical data store in a lower-level data flow diagram.

64. The QA team has determined that there is a trend indicating an increase in the number of defects found in software testing. The project manager asks for data that groups the defects by category and in decreasing order of frequency. What type of chart will best provide the result the project manager is looking for?

    a. Pareto diagram.
    b. Scatter diagram.
    c. Control chart.
    d. Checksheet.

65. A requirement is best described by which of the following:

    a. A known deliverable.
    b. A documented representation of a condition or capability.
    c. Whatever the business analyst deems it to be.
    d. A list of items presented to the business analyst on a napkin.

66. A good way to obtain delivery team sign-off is through:

    a. Diagrams.
    b. Traceability.
    c. A presentation.
    d. A feasibility study.

67. Which of the following is true about quality control measurements?

    a. They are defined in the quality management plan.
    b. They are the results of quality control activities.
    c. They are defined in the quality improvement plan.
    d. They are outputs of perform quality assurance.

68. Which of the following LEAST describes the use of an activity diagram?
    a. A model that illustrates complex use cases.
    b. Steps that can be superimposed onto horizontal swimlanes.
    c. Showing the human and non-human roles that interact with the system.
    d. Illustrates the flow of processes.

69. Suppose you discover that stakeholders complain about requirements for a product. They maintain that a set of requirements applied only to a division in Brazil, and did not pertain to those in the U.S. and Europe. You realize that in presenting the requirements you should have:
    a. Told the Brazilian division that their requirements were out-of-scope.
    b. Determined which requirements were relevant to which stakeholder groups and presented those in an appropriate format.
    c. Determined the appropriate stakeholder groups. The Brazilian division had such unique requirements that their requirements should not have been taken into account.
    d. Held separate interviews with each stakeholder group in order to determine the unique requirements.

70. When stakeholders are in disagreement about a requirement to resolve a problem on a project, which method of conflict management will be most effective in that it will likely lead to consensus and commitment?
    a. Compromising.
    b. Smoothing.
    c. Withdrawing.
    d. Collaborating.

71. If no business analysis standards exist in an organization, what is the best approach?
    a. Work with the sponsor to determine the best approach they want to pay for.
    b. Use a change-driven approach.
    c. Follow the PMI-PBA approach.
    d. Work with the stakeholders, project manager, and project team to ensure a suitable approach is determined.

72. Consider a scenario in which a sponsor has initiated an effort to purchase and install a commercial-off-the-shelf (COTS) package. You discover that no other analysis work has been performed. The first thing that typically should be done is to:
    a. Determine the approach to implementing the COTS solution.
    b. Define the scope of the COTS solution.
    c. Determine how the COTS package meets the business need.
    d. Define the business need that the COTS package is intended to address.

73. Which of the following criteria are the basis for prioritization of requirements?
    a. Stakeholder analysis, regulatory compliance, business risk, technical risk.
    b. Urgency, technical risk, enterprise architecture, likelihood of success.
    c. Business value, business risk, regulatory compliance, stakeholder agreement.
    d. Likelihood of success, urgency, business case, business need.

74. Which of the following are valid things to document for data attributes:
    a. Cardinality and relationship.
    b. Optional vs. mandatory and which entity/class it belongs to.
    c. Cardinality and constraints/domains.
    d. Occurrences and which entity/class it belongs to.

75. Which of the following is something you would expect to find in a project communications management plan?
    a. Implementation plans for any new communications infrastructure that will facilitate better project communications.
    b. Methods that will be used for releasing team members from the project when they are no longer needed.
    c. List of stakeholders and their potential influence on the project.
    d. Communication constraints, including regulations, technology, or organizational policies that may limit project communications.

76. Which of the following business rules is really a requirement?
    a. Sales tax is considered part of the total sales price.
    b. Sales taxes must be calculated based on state sales tax laws.
    c. A daily report of collected sales taxes must be produced.
    d. Sales tax for a given order is calculated exclusive of any services provided on that order.

77. What techniques are used in business analysis activity planning?
    a. Assumptions, dependencies, milestones.
    b. Sprint planning, backlog analysis, context diagrams.
    c. Estimation, functional decomposition, risk analysis.
    d. Assumptions, unique numbering, milestones.

78. A lead BA notices that some of the BAs have information about the project requirements, processes, and stakeholders that would be helpful to the entire BA team. Which of the following would the lead BA use to make sure there is shared understanding among all the BAs:
    a. Requirements traceability matrix.
    b. Brainstorming.
    c. Risk management.
    d. Consider project risk, expectations, and standards.

79. You have been asked to facilitate a requirements elicitation activity to prioritize requirements. What techniques might you use?
    a. Risk analysis, MoSCoW analysis, stakeholder analysis.
    b. Decision analysis, risk analysis, estimation.
    c. High-Medium-Low, voting, estimation.
    d. Voting, MoSCoW analysis, High-Medium-Low.

80. Shortly after the launch of a significant project with high impact to the enterprise, the IT Director has decided to introduce the agile approach and would like to use your project as a pilot. Which of the following concerns of the business analyst is LEAST likely to be affected by this decision:
    a. Project management phase strategy.
    b. Degree of testing rigor.
    c. Where the stakeholders are located.
    d. Requirements communications, change management.

81. The principal objective of project stakeholder management is to do what?
    a. Identify all potential users of the project to ensure complete requirement analysis.
    b. Thwart criticism of the project by developing a list of responses to known stakeholder concerns.
    c. Be proactive in managing stakeholder influence on the project to make sure that it is positive.
    d. Build goodwill in the case of schedule and cost overruns.

82. You need to schedule resources for an upcoming requirements workshop and brainstorming session. Which of the following best describes that activity?
    a. Include all participants, locations, and resources required.
    b. Determine materials required for techniques.
    c. Request meeting rooms and participants.
    d. Determine organizational process assets.

83. Which development method or approach places more emphasis on requirements prioritization methods?
    a. Neither waterfall nor agile methods.
    b. Both waterfall and agile methods.
    c. Waterfall.
    d. Agile.

84. Which step typically occurs first when utilizing the survey/questionnaire as a requirements elicitation technique?
    a. Test the survey.
    b. Define the purpose of the survey and select the target survey groups.
    c. Write the survey questions.
    d. Select the distribution and collection methods.

85. How should requirements communications be performed?
    a. Incrementally.
    b. Urgently.
    c. Iteratively.
    d. Sequentially.

86. Juan has been trying to figure out how best to validate the solution scope with his stakeholders, both business and technical. How can Juan best validate the solution scope with his stakeholders?

    a. Conduct a requirements workshop and talk it through with the stakeholders.
    b. Have a brainstorming session with his stakeholders.
    c. Create a use case diagram and schedule a walk-through or review.
    d. Do nothing at all. The architect is responsible for validating solution scope.

87. Which of the following would be considered expectations of reliability, one of the non-functional requirements:

    a. Restrictions on the distribution of personal information without the express or implicit consent of the parties involved.
    b. Safety, security, performance, and trainability.
    c. Ability to recover from errors.
    d. Compatibility with other components.

88. You have worked on a project to implement a new system. When it was first deployed, it seemed to be performing well. However, as transactions increased over a six-month period, the application slowed to a level deemed unacceptable by the end-users. You have been asked to evaluate this performance. In order to do this, you need to have:

    a. Performance metrics of the solution.
    b. Approval to repair any defects found.
    c. Approval to prevent future defects.
    d. An assessment of the solution performance.

89. John is preparing his business case document before a management presentation. He has worked for several days on it, and wants to be sure he has included all essential elements. John brings the document to you and shows you the Table of Contents below and asks for your feedback. How would you respond?

    a. Overview and Business Need.
    b. Gap Analysis
        1. Current Capability Analysis
        2. Assessment of New Capability Requirements
    c. Solution Approach
        1. Alternatives Considered
        2. Alternative Rankings
        3. Recommended Approach
    d. Solution Capabilities Included
        1. Capability Definition
        2. Implementation Approach
        3. Dependencies
    e. Project Justification
        1. Project cost
        2. Risk Assessment
        3. Results Measurement

    a. Great, it looks complete.
    b. It is missing a stakeholder analysis.
    c. It is missing a comparison of benefits to costs.
    d. It is missing the solution scope.

90. When is the precedence diagramming method used?

    a. In developing the schedule of business analysis activities.
    b. In sequencing activities.
    c. Never. This is a project management tool.
    d. In estimating activity duration.

91. What type of stakeholders should be involved in defining assumptions and constraints?

    a. Only those stakeholders who are actively attending the project meetings.
    b. Only business stakeholders.
    c. All stakeholders.
    d. Stakeholders defined in the stakeholder analysis.

92. Which of the following is true about milestones?

    a. They are dummy activities.
    b. They are insignificant events in the project life cycle.
    c. They are measures of achievement for expenditures of money or time.
    d. They are activities with the least duration of all activities in the path.

93. On a project, what needs to be in place before business analysis activities can begin?
    a. Project scope baseline.
    b. Project schedule.
    c. Project activity list.
    d. Charter.

94. All approved changes should be:
    a. Run through Perform Integrated Change Control and reflected in the performance measurement baseline.
    b. Run through Monitor and Control Project Work and reflected in the change management plan.
    c. Run through Monitor and Control Project Work and reflected in the updated deliverables.
    d. Run through Perform Integrated Change Control and reflected in the project management plan.

95. Which of the following can be said of both tolerances and control limits?
    a. Tolerances indicate when a process is not being done satisfactorily, whereas control limits identify the thresholds of stakeholder acceptance.
    b. Tolerances and control limits can be used interchangeably to identify boundaries of when a process is out of control or stakeholder acceptance levels have been exceeded.
    c. Tolerances identify the range of stakeholder acceptance levels, whereas control limits provide boundaries within which a process must perform to be considered in control.
    d. Tolerances are a quality metric used in quality assurance, whereas control limits are used in controlling quality.

96. Consider the following situation: An analyst is called into an effort to build a third website for her company. The site will be used to display and sell merchandise, and will be updated daily with additions and deletions of items, price changes, sales and promotions, etc. In this scenario, which is the project and which is the product?
    a. The project is building the website, and the product is the new website.
    b. The project is building the website, and the product is updating and maintaining the site.
    c. The project is updating and maintaining the site, and the product is the new website.
    d. The project is the new website, and the product is building the website.

97. As soon as you were assigned to a project, you were advised to begin planning for the requirements work to be done. Which do you need before you can begin the requirements management plan?
    a. Business case.
    b. Stakeholder analysis.
    c. Project management plan.
    d. Requirements baseline.

98. Brainstorming would be the most suitable technique for uncovering requirements in which of the following types of activity:

     a. Add detail to the current process flow for work order transmittals through the warehouse.

     b. Identify dependent tasks in the requirements project plan.

     c. Consult with managers from similar functional units across dispersed locations in an attempt to find process improvement opportunities.

     d. Determine the appropriate format for requirements communications to key technical stakeholders.

99. Which of the following statements best describes an agile approach?

     a. Presume that it is difficult to identify all requirements in advance of their implementation and choose requirements from a product backlog.

     b. Capture requirements in a formal document or set of documents which follow standardized templates that are formally approved.

     c. Produce formal documentation before the solution is developed and implemented.

     d. Complete most business analysis work at the beginning of the project or during one specific project phase.

100. Components of a good problem statement include which of the following?

     a. Definition of the problem and who is responsible.

     b. Definition of the problem and who is affected.

     c. How the problem impacts the stakeholders and who will have to pay to address the problem.

     d. How the problem impacts the stakeholders and how much it will cost to address the problem.

Simulated Exam Answers

1. Which of the following tools are used to analyze defects found in quality control?

    a. Cost-benefit analysis, cost of quality, several basic quality tools, benchmarking, design of experiments, statistical sampling, meetings.

    These are the tools and techniques of the plan quality management process.

    b. Quality control measurements, validated changes, and verified deliverables.

    These are some of the outputs of quality control, not tools.

    c. **Checksheets, Pareto diagrams, histograms, control charts, scatter diagrams.**

    Correct! These are all tools used to monitor test results to determine how well the solution is conforming to requirements, and to determine if additional analysis is needed to improve product results. See *PMBOK® Guide* 8.1.2.3.

    d. Defect log, impact analysis, customer feedback.

    These sound good but are not listed in the *PMBOK® Guide* and may not help in understanding full impact or root cause of defects.

2. The team has agreed to use SharePoint to store the Requirements Traceability Matrix. Updates to the matrix will be saved as a minor version change (e.g., version 1.1) with new baselined requirements being saved with a new version number (e.g., version 2.0). This is part of:

    a. Interactive communications.

    No, this is not an interactive communication, and the question is not about communication methods, per se.

    b. A change request.

    Change requests would feed into the configuration management system that manages changes to the RTM, but the question does not pertain to a specific change request.

    c. A baseline management plan.

    Changes to baselines are managed through change control, but there is no baseline management plan, per se.

    d. **Configuration management.**

    Correct! Configuration management is defined as "…documentation, tracking systems, and defined approval levels necessary for authorizing and controlling changes" *PMBOK® Guide-Fifth Edition*, page 532.

3. Requirements are ready for the project team to act upon when they have:

    a. Been prototyped and acceptance criteria is defined.

    Not all requirements require prototyping.

    b. **Been prioritized and approved.**

    Correct! These are two, but not all, of the criteria for requirements to be ready.

    c. Defined acceptance criteria and the team is not busy.

    Whether or not the team is busy is not a consideration for requirements being ready for the team to act upon them.

    d. Been approved and identified as critical.

    Requirements do need to be prioritized and approved, but not identified as critical.

4. Requirements for agile projects are traditionally captured in which format?

a. Use cases.	Use cases are used on predictive (traditional or waterfall) life cycles.
b. User stories.	**Correct! User stories help to articulate user requirements. Acceptance criteria for each use story provides more details on requirements.**
c. Requirements traceability matrix.	The traceability matrix provides a means to track and link requirements.
d. Test cases/scenarios.	Test cases are strictly used for testing.

5. Why is it important determine the appropriate format for requirements?

a. It assures that the same organizational artifacts are used consistently by all BAs in all situations.	This answer suggests only one artifact or format. This is wrong.
b. It ensures that each requirement is described in a unique format that respects the title and authority of the highest ranking stakeholder in the audience.	There is no mention in the *PMBOK® Guide* about title or rank of a stakeholder.
c. It ensures that requirements are understandable to their particular stakeholders.	**Correct! A theme of the *PMBOK® Guide* is to adapt requirements to stakeholder needs. *PMBOK® Guide* Chapter 13.**
d. It ensures that the presenter has sufficient time to learn new tools to enhance each presentation of requirements to different target audiences.	The appropriate format will not ensure sufficient time for anything, much less learning new tools.

6. What are engagement level classifications for stakeholders?

a. Manage closely, keep satisfied, keep informed, monitor.	These are strategies for engaging and influencing stakeholders based on their level of power and interest.
b. High, medium, low.	This is a prioritization technique.
c. Unaware, resistant, neutral, supportive, leading.	**Correct! See *PMBOK® Guide* 13.2.2.3 Analytical techniques.**
d. Responsible, accountable, consulted, informed.	These represent the RACI matrix.

7. What are the three features that best describe what a user story must include?

a. Actor, story, result.	Invented answer.
b. Actor, description, result.	Invented answer.

    c. **Actor, description, benefit.**   Correct! Also called 'role, goal, and motivation.'

    d. Actor, story, requirement.   Invented answer.

8. Which statement is most true about approving requirements?

    a. Approving stakeholders need to sign off on the requirements in writing.   Approval can also be verbal.

    b. **Approval may be obtained from individual stakeholders or as a group.**   Correct! Approval may be obtained from stakeholders individually or as a group.

    c. Once approval is obtained, the decisions surrounding the approval are no longer needed and can be discarded.   Stakeholder approval may be required for the result of other business analysis work, including allocation of requirements, proposed problem resolutions, and other decisions.

    d. Approval decisions need to be traced to the technical design.   Invented answer.

9. The Smith & Smith Company is a highly decentralized technology company that focuses on state of the art software solutions for implantable medical devices. The business analyst is currently discussing the relative importance and ranking of the requirements for a new product based on implementation difficulty. What task is the business analyst performing?

    a. Requirements elicitation.   Requirements have already been elicited.

    b. Requirements analysis.   Requirements have presumably already been analyzed.

    c. **Requirements prioritization.**   **Correct!**

    d. Requirements risk analysis.   No such task in the *PMBOK® Guide*. Risk may enter into prioritization, but it is not the only factor.

10. To determine if a solution is delivering business value, a business analyst needs which of the following:

    a. Designed solution.   A solution must be constructed to be validated.

    b. Constructed solution.   This is a close answer because a constructed solution is needed to validate a solution. The question is asking about business value, not business need, and validate solution determines if a solution meets business needs.

    c. Tested solution.   A solution must be constructed to be validated.

    d. **Deployed solution.**   **Correct! A deployed solution is needed to evaluate solution performance, which works to understand the business value of a solution. The task needs a deployed solution as an input.**

11. A business requirement can best be described as:

    a. **Higher level statements of goals or objectives.**   Correct! *PMBOK® Guide* 5.2.

b. Specific needs of a class, group or individual.

These are stakeholder requirements.

c. They can contain both functional and non-functional aspects.

These are additional types of requirements known as solution requirements.

d. Capabilities the solution has in the current state but no longer needs in the future state.

This description fits a transition requirement.

12. What format should be used for a requirements package?

a. A formal presentation, otherwise it is not worth packaging requirements.

Not all requirements will have a formal presentation.

b. **One that is appropriate to the needs of the stakeholders.**

Correct! *PMBOK® Guide* **13.3.**

c. Minimally they should contain a business requirements specification or equivalent.

This particular document may or may not be chosen in a requirements package.

d. Models, diagrams, and documents.

These are common elements, but not always needed.

13. The best example of a technical constraint is:

a. Limitation on the project's flexibility such as budgetary restrictions, time restrictions, limits on the number of resources available or restrictions based on skills of the project team.

These are examples of business constraints.

b. Documentation about things the business analyst believes to be true but is unable to verify.

This is a definition of an assumption.

c. Expectation concerning the designability, reliability, usability, maintainability, efficiency, human engineering, scalability, and portability of the system.

These elements are examples of non-functional requirements.

d. **Any architectural decision that is made, including development language, hardware platform, or applications software that must be used.**

Correct! Constraints limit choices, and these are all technical constraints.

14. Which of the following is a weakness when using interface analysis:

a. The requirements elicitation of an interface's functional requirements early in the project will provide valuable details for project planning.

This is a strength of interface analysis.

    b. **It does not provide an understanding of the business process.**

Correct! This is a weakness of interface analysis. Interface analysis only identifies inputs, outputs, and key data elements that are related to user or system interfaces.

    c. It is too time consuming to involve the end-to-end resources and SMEs are required.

Not an applicable answer.

    d. Knowing the complexity of the interfaces and their testing needs enables more accurate project planning and a potential savings in time and cost.

This is a strength of interface analysis.

15. The scope management plan:

    a. Is a formal document.

The scope management plan may be informal.

    b. Is highly detailed.

The scope management plan may be broadly framed.

    c. Is optional.

The scope management plan may be informal and broadly framed, but it is not optional.

    d. **Is based on the needs of the project.**

Correct! *PMBOK® Guide* 5.1.

16. Requirements are validated:

    a. Before they are verified.

Validation typically happens after verification.

    b. **Typically after they are verified, although those processes may be done in parallel.**

Correct! *PMBOK® Guide*, 5.5.

    c. After they have been traced.

Made up answer.

    d. When the sponsor signs off on them.

Only verify, not validate.

17. The most common approach to forecasting requires a manual, bottom-up calculation of work yet to be done. What problem does this present?

    a. The people doing the work are not typically assigned at that point in the project.

This is a made-up answer.

    b. **The time it takes to do the manual calculation is typically not included in the budget and it distracts people from working on the project.**

Correct! *PMBOK® Guide* 7.4.2.2.

    c. Politics tend to interfere with people trying to influence the forecasts.

This is a made-up answer.

    d. Project managers seldom get the information fast enough to provide timely forecasts to stakeholders.

This is a made-up answer.

18. Barry presented his requirements documentation for approval at the weekly requirements review session. Barry provided the business requirements document, status reports, interview notes with track changes in MS Word, and the issues log. Barry was asked to redo the documentation and to come back the next week for the review. Why?

a. Barry does not understand the concept of work product and deliverables.	**Correct! His working documents were not appropriate for a formal review.**
b. The issues log is inappropriate because it could embarrass people if their name is in the log.	The issues log is a tool to help manage the requirements process but it is not a requirements deliverable.
c. Interview notes are inappropriate to include for a review.	Interview notes are used to build the requirement that goes in the business requirements document.
d. Barry should not have been asked to come back since the documents presented are already appropriate to review for sign-off.	No, the documents presented were not appropriate for the audience.

19. Beth is a former project manager and likes to use hierarchical decomposition to break down her business analysis deliverables into activities and tasks. She then adds the hours needed and can give an accurate estimate of the time needed to complete her BA work. What type of estimation does Beth like to use?

a. Delphi estimation.	Delphi is not an estimation technique, per se. It is a decision-making technique.
b. Parametric estimation.	This technique relies on a defined parameter for a given deliverable, such as business processes or interfaces. It takes an average amount of time for one deliverable and multiplies it by the number of deliverables. The parameter times the number of deliverables equals total time.
c. Bottom-up estimation.	**Correct! This technique breaks down all deliverables and activities into detailed activities and tasks, then rolls them up to the whole to determine accurate estimates. This describes Beth's preferred estimating method.**
d. Historical analysis.	An important basis for estimating, but not an estimation technique. It relies on past project data and records, and can be used with any of the estimation methods. Chances are Beth used historic analysis to help her do her bottom-up estimates.

20. Why is change control important?

a. To stifle project changes.	Project changes will be needed. Change control is to help make sure decisions regarding changes are based on appropriate information.
b. To deter stakeholders from making requests for changes.	Stakeholder requests may be very important to bringing business value to the project. Change control is not about deterring stakeholders from making the requests.

    c.   To stop developers from gold-plating.

> Unfortunately, this probably would not stop a developer from gold-plating. Change control does provide a mechanism that they can use to request a change in an appropriate manner.

    d.   **Provides decision makers with information needed to make informed decisions on potential project changes**.

> **Correct!**

21. Eliciting requirements is a key task in business analysis and serves as a foundation for the solution to the business needs. The business analyst should understand the commonly used techniques to elicit requirements, should be able to select appropriate technique(s) for a given situation, and be knowledgeable of the tasks needed to prepare, execute, and complete each technique. According to the *PMBOK® Guide* what types of requirements are elicited?

    a.   Functional, non-functional, customer, stakeholder.

> Customer requirements is not a classification.

    b.   **Business, stakeholder, solution, transition, project, and quality.**

> **Correct! *PMBOK® Guide* 5.2.**

    c.   Focused technical, organizational, external, non-technical.

> None of these is a requirements classification.

    d.   Isolated, compartmental, validation, verification.

> Sounds like it should mean something, but is not part of the *PMBOK® Guide*.

22. Stakeholder lists should be reviewed throughout the life of the project because:

    a.   Most projects have a large number of them.

> This is true but not why the list should be reviewed regularly.

    b.   They have the ability to influence the project positively or negatively.

> This is true but not why the list should be reviewed regularly.

    c.   **Once identified, their levels of interest and influence can change.**

> **Correct! Regular review of the stakeholder list is critical because who they are and their characteristics will change over the life of the project. *PMBOK® Guide* 13.1.**

    d.   To remember who the important stakeholders are.

> This is true but not why the list should be reviewed regularly.

23. In a short, 3-month project to implement a commercial-off-the-shelf (COTS) system, the BA determined that a detailed Software Requirements Specification document was not necessary and planned instead to utilize use cases for the analysis technique and documentation format. This is an example of:

    a.   An assumption that could become a risk.

> There is nothing to hint that an assumption or a risk is a consideration in the decision.

    b.   Appropriate use of risk mitigation.

> There is nothing to hint that risk is a consideration in the decision.

    c.   A common mistake leading to

> There are no prescriptive requirements.

prescriptive requirements.

    d. **Determining appropriate requirements analysis and documentation activities.**   **Correct! The BA determines the best techniques to be used on the project regarding the requirements process.**

24. You have scheduled a focus group to determine the current attitudes towards a new product that your company is developing. Your participants should what?

    a. Be ready to participate.   This is true for any elicitation technique.

    b. Have a minimum of five years' experience with the company.   There is no such requirement, and the experience should be with the product being discussed.

    c. **Be Pre-qualified.**   **Correct! Participants should represent a cross-section of experience and have experience with the subject being explored. PMBOK® Guide 5.2.**

    d. Only respond to pre-planned questions.   This would limit the discussion.

25. Traceability is used to help ensure solution conformance to requirements and to assist in scope and change management. What types of traceability can be performed?

    a. Derivation and allocation, cost and location.   Cost and location are not traced unless they are embedded within a requirement.

    b. Relationship to other requirements, relationship to sponsorship.   Relationship to sponsorship is not what is traced. Relationships to business need are traced.

    c. Forwards and backwards, cost and location.   Cost and location are not traced unless they are embedded within a requirement.

    d. **Derivation and allocation, relationship to other requirements.**   **Correct! Derivation and allocation are different terms that basically mean backward and forward, respectively. Relationship to other requirements is part of traceability.**

26. Contingency reserves are used to:

    a. **Help reduce the risk of overruns in cost or time to an acceptable level.**   **Correct! PMBOK® Guide 6.5.2.6 and 7.2.2.6.**

    b. Compensate for lack of historical information in quantifying risk.   This is a made-up answer.

    c. Address unforeseen work that is within project scope ("unknown unknowns").   That is a description of management reserves.

    d. Eliminate risk exposure.   This is a fantasy. All projects have risk.

27. Which statement about the use case diagram is true?

    a. Is used to show system scope, and typically supported by the user profile.   The use case diagram and user profile are unrelated techniques.

    b. Must always be supported by the user   The use case diagram and user story are unrelated techniques.

story.

   c. **Is used to show system scope, and associations of actors to use cases.**   Correct!

   d. Must always be supported by the misuse case.   **The use case diagram and misuse case are unrelated techniques. Note: there really is a term called 'misuse case.'**

28. The technique of interface analysis is best suited for which of the following:

   a. Allowing an online focus group to include members located remotely while participating by a network connection.   This answer describes preparing for an elicitation session.

   b. **Reaching agreements with stakeholders on what interfaces are needed.**   **Correct! This is one purpose for using interface analysis as a requirements elicitation technique.**

   c. Coordinating the activities used to elicit interface requirements.   This pertains to planning and preparing to use the technique of interface analysis.

   d. Capturing requirements attributes for interfaces.   This answer pertains to requirements management and not Interface Analysis.

29. What task needs to occur before a change can be requested?

   a. Determine the cost of the change.   The cost may be determined after the request, so this answer is incorrect.

   b. **Establish the requirements baseline.**   **Correct! This is a predecessor task. You have to have a baseline before you can determine any changes.**

   c. Determine the specific stakeholder who will implement the change.   The implementation person would typically be determined after the request has been approved.

   d. Analyze the impact(s) of the change.   The impact would typically be analyzed after the request.

30. What is the purpose of defining transition requirements?

   a. To ensure the project team will be able to leave the project.   Not the kind of transition that Solution Assessment and Validation deals with.

   b. To ensure the organization is ready for change.   This answer describes assess organizational readiness, a separate task.

   c. To ensure the transition period is short.   Not an applicable factor.

   d. **To ensure a successful move from the old to new system.**   Correct!

31. You are in the process of ensuring that a delivered solution meets the business need on an ongoing basis. You are confident that the solution meets the business need and have determined the most appropriate response. What form best represents that response?

a. Verified and approved requirements.

These would come from earlier tasks, which would happen before a solution is constructed.

b. Prioritized requirements and approved requirements.

These would come from earlier tasks, which would happen before a solution is constructed.

c. **Identified defects and solution validation assessment.**

Correct!

d. Mitigating actions and approved requirements.

Mitigating actions is a valid output, but approved requirements would come from an earlier task.

32. What is one purpose for preparing for requirements elicitation?

a. Identify problem stakeholders so they can be removed from the project.

It is not the BA's job to identify "problem" stakeholders or decide who is on the project.

b. Ensure that the project manager is included in the elicitation.

The PM does not need to be included.

c. **Clarify the objectives and desired results for the given elicitation technique.**

Correct!

d. Minimize constraints.

This does not minimize constraints.

33. Which of the following can help you prepare for a requirements workshop?

a. **Conducting pre-workshop interviews.**

Correct! They focus on ensuring that the purpose of the requirements workshop is understood and aligned with the needs of each attendee, and to ensure that any preparation needed for the session by that attendee is understood.

b. Eliciting some initial requirements.

This is the same as conduct elicitation activity and is not part of the preparation work.

c. Establishing the tone of the meeting.

This is the same as conduct elicitation activity and is not part of the preparation work.

d. Enforcing discipline.

This is the same as conduct elicitation activity and is not part of the preparation work.

34. All of the following are components of the scope management plan EXCEPT:

a. Process to create WBS.

This would be included in the scope management plan, which is an input.

b. Process to maintain WBS.

This would be included in the scope management plan, which is an input.

c. How product deliverables will be accepted.

This would be included in the scope management plan, which is an input.

d. **WBS.**

Correct! The Scope Management Plan provides guidance on how to create the WBS, but the WBS is not part of the scope management plan. PMBOK® Guide 5.1.

35. Which of the following documents contain key domain terms along with their business definitions?

a.	Requirements analysis plan.	There is no such plan.
b.	Data modeling.	Too narrow. Some terms are defined in a data model, but only pertaining to data.
c.	**Glossary.**	**Correct!**
d.	Requirements package.	Too broad an answer because a package contains a wide variety of documents.

36. Which statement best describes the communication with stakeholders in a waterfall approach?

a.	Much of the communication of the actual requirements is verbal.	Describes an agile characteristic.
b.	Communications may be written or verbal.	True, but is too vague to be the best answer.
c.	Informal communication takes precedence over more formal written communication.	Describes an agile characteristic.
d.	**Tends to rely on formal communication methods and much of the communications of the actual requirements is in writing.**	**Correct! Waterfall uses more formal and more written documentation than agile.**

37. Once requirements are approved, they may be baselined. Future changes to requirements must then follow what process?

a.	**Change control.**	**Correct! *PMBOK® Guide* 5.6.**
b.	Traceability.	Traceability will continue, but changes to requirements go through whatever change control process is in place.
c.	Manage requirements approval.	Approvals are a part of the change control process.
d.	Baselining.	This has been completed.

38. Which of the following stakeholders plays a key role in validating solutions by identifying defects in solutions?

a.	End user.	True, end users find many defects, but their primary role is to provide input into acceptance criteria and to use a solution.
b.	SME.	SMEs play a key role in validating requirements and possible defects, but not as a vital role in finding defects in solutions.
c.	**Tester.**	**Correct! The tester role is to find defects, so they play a key role in validating solutions.**

d. Operational support.   They support resolving of defects, not in identifying them.

39. A business rule is:

a. **An organization-wide, self-imposed constraint on doing business.**

Correct! Policies and rules direct and constrain the organization and operation of an organization. A business rule is a specific, actionable, testable directive that is under the control of an organization and that supports a business policy.

b. A capability or condition needed on a particular project to solve a problem or achieve an objective.

This is a definition of a requirement.

c. Expressed as a relationship between one entity/business object and another.

This is one of the ways a business rule can be expressed. There are other methods.

d. A regulation that an organization must adhere to.

This is too narrow of a definition.

40. Business analysis planning activities include:

a. Stakeholder engagement, requirements communication, traceability, and document control.

Stakeholder engagement and requirements communication are not included.

b. Establishing tools, policies, and procedures for the requirements management plan, requirements traceability, document control, and user acceptance testing.

User acceptance testing is incorrect. This should be acceptance criteria.

c. Creating the WBS, requirements management plan, requirements traceability, document control, and user acceptance testing.

Creating the WBS and user acceptance testing are not part of business analysis planning activities.

d. **Establishing tools, policies, and procedures for the requirements management plan, requirements traceability, document control, and acceptance criteria.**

Correct! See the *PMI-PBA Examination Content Outline*.

41. Padma is the business analyst on a project to implement a new financial software package. The solution includes not only the software, but also new business processes and new data to support those processes. A decision has been made to run the current system in parallel with the new system for two months, which will allow comparison over both a month-end and a quarter-end. Padma has captured stakeholder and solution requirements for the 'as-is' and the 'to-be' software and business processes. She knows that in addition she still needs to capture what kind of requirements using which technique:

                       PMI-PBA Certification Study Guide

a. **Transition requirements using data modeling.**

Correct! Data modeling is one technique to discover transition requirements.

b. Non-functional requirements using interface analysis.

Solution requirements, which include non-functional requirements, have already been defined. Interface analysis might or might not help.

c. Functional requirements using process modeling and data modeling.

Solution requirements, which include functional requirements, have already been defined.

d. Conversion requirements using data flow diagrams.

The classification of conversion requirements does not exist. These requirements are referred to as transition requirements.

42. Internal failure costs are different from external failure costs in that:

a. Internal costs are typically more expensive than external failure costs.

This is a made-up answer.

b. Internal costs are typically paid by the organization while external costs are typically paid by the customer.

This is a made-up answer.

c. **Internal costs are typically found by the project while external costs are typically found by the customer.**

Correct! *PMBOK® Guide* 8.1.2.2.

d. Internal costs are the responsibility of the project management team while external costs are the responsibility of the customer.

This is a made-up answer.

43. Which type of requirement best describes environmental conditions under which the solution must remain effective or qualities that the systems must have.

a. Business requirements.

These are high-level requirements concerned with goals, objectives, or needs, and are independent of particular behaviors or information.

b. Stakeholder requirements.

These requirements pertain to how business requirements affect a user group.

c. Functional requirements.

These requirements are about behavior and data, and are independent of environmental conditions.

d. **Non-functional requirements.**

Correct! See the requirements categories - *PMBOK® Guide* 5.2.

44. Omar has been researching a business problem for several days trying to understand why it happened. What is Omar performing?

a. Decision analysis.

Decision analysis supports making decisions, not understanding why problems occurred.

b. **Root cause analysis.**

Correct!

	c. Gap analysis.	Gap analysis identifies the difference between the desired state and current state. Root cause analysis is the better answer for understanding why there is a difference.
	d. Defect analysis.	Made-up answer.

45. Louis is tracking how well the solution was implemented by collecting data and comparing it to expected results previously defined by the stakeholders. What is Louis doing?

	a. Observation.	This technique refers to watching stakeholders work to obtain requirements.
	b. Data analysis.	This is how you analyze data.
	c. Monitoring.	**Correct!** *PMBOK® Guide* **Glossary, page 546.**
	d. Shadowing.	This technique refers to watching stakeholders work to obtain requirements.

46. Jacob was conducting interviews with stakeholders to elicit requirements. The sessions were not going well and he asked you for your help. Stakeholders were confused on the size of the project and why the project was needed. Which of the following would you recommend?

	a. Advise Jacob to make sure the stakeholders are on the approved stakeholders lists and ignore the remaining stakeholders.	The stakeholders need an understanding of why the project was undertaken and its benefit.
	b. Advise Jacob to bring the requirements traceability matrix and supporting materials.	The traceability matrix has not been fully created yet because requirements are still being elicited. Also missing is what the requirements trace to--i.e., the business requirements.
	c. Advise Jacob to work more closely with the project manager and project sponsor to get the stakeholders in line with the project.	This does not directly address the need for clarity of the scope and business need.
	d. Advise Jacob to review the business case/need and solution scope.	**Correct! The 'why the project was needed' would be addressed by the business case. The size is contained in the scope.**

47. In managing requirements traceability, the 'value' relationship describes:

	a. A requirement links to a lower-level requirement.	This answer would be closer to a 'cover' or 'subset' type of relationship.
	b. A requirement is a decomposed outcome of another requirement.	This answer describes a 'subset' relationship.
	c. One requirement affects the desirability of another, either positively or negatively.	**Correct!**
	d. One requirement is only pertinent	This describes a 'necessity' type of relationship.

when another is included.

48. Your organization has just determined a new system is needed to meet a new market opportunity and you have been asked to evaluate and investigate the underlying rationale. You have been assigned the task to ensure that the widest possible range of alternative solutions are considered. What is the output of your work?

a.	Solution scope.	This is another output that would be produced after the underlying rationale is refined into a business need.
b.	Business objectives.	Business goals and objectives usually have to be refined in order to define the business need - so this answer is close.
c.	Solution approach.	This is another output that would be created after the underlying rationale is refined into a business need. It is a close answer, since determining the solution approach involves investigating alternatives.
d.	**Business need.**	**Correct! The key is the question asks about underlying rationale, which is the business need.** *PMBOK® Guide* **4.1.**

49. What is the deliverable that is most likely to include descriptions of the currently identified team roles for a specific project?

a.	Requirements management plan.	The RMP contains approaches and processes of how the business analysis work will be performed.
b.	**RACI matrix.**	**Correct! RACI matrix describes the roles of those involved in business analysis activities.** *PMBOK® Guide* **9.1.2.1.**
c.	Table of organization (TO).	Organizational chart does not describe roles.
d.	Questionnaire to identified stakeholders.	Used to elicit information.

50. You are developing cost and time estimates for the business case break-even point. What technique are you likely to employ?

a.	**Estimation.**	**Correct!**
b.	Organizational breakdown structure.	This will not help estimate time or cost.
c.	Financial analysis.	Cost and time estimates will be inputs to financial analysis.
d.	Feature decomposition.	Not mentioned or implied in the *PMBOK® Guide*. The closest match would be a solution breakdown structure.

51. During a project planning meeting, consideration of a key stakeholder persuades the project management team to take a different approach to communications on the project. That stakeholder would be characterized as having a high level of what on the project?

a.	Influence.	Influence refers to active involvement on the project. *PMBOK® Guide* 13.1.2.1.
b.	**Impact.**	**Correct! Impact refers to having the ability to effect changes to the project's planning or execution.** *PMBOK® Guide* **13.1.2.1.**

c. Interest.

Interest refers to concern regarding the project outcomes. i 13.1.2.1.

d. Power.

Power refers to the level of authority. *PMBOK® Guide* 13.1.2.1.

52. Of the following activities, which does a business analyst do to contribute to project initiation?

a. **Determine the most feasible business solution scope.**

Correct! The business analyst is responsible for the business case that is an input to the project charter in project initiation. PMBOK® Guide 4.1.

b. Set strategy for the organization using techniques such as SWOT analysis (Strengths, Weaknesses, Opportunities, and Threats).

BAs may participate in SWOT, but they don't set strategy for the organization.

c. Establish strategic goals.

Executive management establishes the strategic goals for the organization.

d. Decide which option of a feasibility study is the option to implement.

Executive management, sponsor or an enterprise governance group select the option to implement.

53. Which of the following best describes the stakeholders involved with reviewing and approving requirements?

a. Sponsors, project managers, QA.

This can be true in certain organizations, depending on the organizational processes and methodologies, but should be documented in the stakeholder list with roles and responsibilities.

b. **Stakeholder lists, roles and responsibilities.**

Correct! The stakeholder list and roles and responsibilities will provide information on who will approve requirements.

c. Whomever the sponsor has dictated will sign-off.

This can be true in certain organizations, depending on the organizational processes and methodologies, but should be documented in the stakeholder list with roles and responsibilities.

d. Executive sponsor, project manager, quality assurance representative, business analyst, architect or technical lead.

This can be true in certain organizations, depending on the organizational processes and methodologies, but should be documented in the stakeholder list with roles and responsibilities.

54. One of the easiest facilitation tools to use when problems have a human interaction component is:

a. What vs. how analysis.

Common questioning technique, but not one of the easiest facilitation tools.

b. Who, what, where, when, how analysis.

Common questioning technique, but not one of the easiest facilitation tools.

c. **The five whys.**

Correct! This is one of the simplest facilitation tools to use when problems have a human interaction component.

              PMI-PBA Certification Study Guide

d. Fishbone diagram.

Also one of the techniques in root cause analysis, but not one of the easiest.

55. Which of the following statements is NOT a desired business outcome?

a. Improve revenue by increasing sales or reducing cost.

Increasing revenue is a beneficial and desired outcome.

b. **Upgrade the Customer Relationship Management (CRM) solution.**

Correct! Definition: 'A desired outcome is not a solution. It describes the business benefits that will result from meeting the business need and the end state desired by stakeholders.

c. Increase customer satisfaction.

Increased customer satisfaction is a beneficial and desired outcome.

d. Improve safety.

Improved safety is a beneficial and desired outcome.

56. Conflicts during requirements meetings can be valuable, particularly when?

a. Conflict situations are in their early stages and emotions are high.

When emotions are high, conflicts are not particularly valuable.

b. **Conflict situations are in their early stages and emotions are low.**

Correct!

c. Conflict situations are in their late stages and emotions are low.

Conflicts are best addressed in the early stages.

d. Multiple conflicts have simultaneously arisen and emotions are high.

It's best to deal with one conflict at a time, and when emotions are low.

57. In order to utilize the Work Breakdown Structure (WBS), the BA will need to understand all but one of the following concepts. Which concept is NOT part of a WBS:

a. Decomposition.

Developing a WBS requires the use of decomposition.

b. Expert judgment.

Expert judgment is often used to analyze the information needed to decompose the project deliverables down into smaller component parts in order to create an effective WBS.

c. Scope management.

A WBS is developed as part of managing scope.

d. **Effort and duration.**

Correct! These are estimating techniques and not used in a WBS. A WBS is used to decompose scope, not to estimate effort and duration.

58. A table that links requirements to their source and tracks them throughout the life of the project is a:

a. PMIS table.

This is a made-up answer.

b. Requirements management plan.

The requirements management plan describes how

requirements activities will be planned, tracked, and reported and how changes to the product, service, or result requirements will be initiated.

   c. **Requirements traceability matrix.**   Correct! *PMBOK® Guide* **5.2.3.2.**

   d. Technical requirement source table.   This is a made-up answer.

59. Successful interviewing depends on all of the following general factors:

   a. BA's interviewing skills, interviewee's readiness to provide information, interviewee's clarity regarding business expectations from the target system, interviewee's expertise in user interface design, BA and interviewee rapport.   Interviewee expertise in interface design is not required.

   b. BA's level of understanding programming technologies, BA's interviewing skill, interviewee's readiness to provide information, interviewee's clarity regarding business expectations from the target solution.   Understanding programming technology is not required by the BA.

   c. **BA's level of understanding the business, BA's interviewing skills, interviewee's readiness to provide information, interviewee's clarity regarding business expectations from the target system, BA and interviewee rapport.**   Correct!

   d. BA's level of understanding of organizational behavior, BA's presentation skills, interviewee's readiness to provide information, interviewee's clarity regarding business expectations from the target system, BA and interviewee rapport.   Organizational behavior and presentation skills are not relevant to interviews in general.

60. In a project with little formal documentation, what would the business analyst rely on?

   a. Email, meeting minutes, whiteboard notes.   This would be a logical answer. Answer B is step further toward informality and is acceptable.

   b. **User stories, whiteboards, flip charts.**   Correct! Informal artifacts would serve the purpose.

   c. Presentations in requirements workshops and structured walk-throughs.   This answer would better address communication of requirements, not documentation of them.

   d. Verbal discussions with stakeholders.   This answer would better address communication of requirements, not documentation of them.

61. Jon is doing some strategic planning that he hopes will lead to a new initiative. What could Jon do to help his strategic planning?

   a.   Perform a SWOT analysis.   Correct! SWOT analysis is a framework for strategic planning.

   b.   Develop the business case.   A business case will follow the strategic planning and may include the result of the SWOT analysis.

   c.   Perform a feasibility study.   A feasibility study is a preliminary analysis of solution alternatives or options to determine whether and how each option can provide an expected business benefit to meet the business need. This helps articulate how the solution alternatives support the strategic plan.

   d.   Create a vision statement.   A vision statement is a brief statement of the desired result of the implemented project. It will help drive the strategic planning process and results.

62. Which of the following terms is best described as a simplified representation of a complex reality?

   a.   Glossary.   Glossaries define terms.

   b.   Stakeholder and sponsor diagrams.   No such diagrams.

   c.   Model.   Correct! This is the definition of a model.

   d.   Textual description of requirements relationships.   Made-up answer.

63. The notation known as 'cardinality' indicates:

   a.   The total number of entities associated with each class.   This is not the definition of cardinality, and is something that is unrelated to analyzing data relationships.

   b.   The direction of the logical flow of data into or out from a high-level process in a context diagram.   This is not the definition of cardinality, and is not even valid for a context diagram.

   c.   Minimum and maximum number of occurrences of one entity that may be associated with the other entity.   Correct! Cardinality indicates the number of allowed relationships, such as one or many.

   d.   The presence of a physical data store in a lower-level data flow diagram.   This is not the definition of cardinality, and is not even valid for a data flow diagram.

64. The QA team has determined that there is a trend indicating an increase in the number of defects found in software testing. The project manager asks for data that groups the defects by category and in decreasing order of frequency. What type of chart will best provide the result the project manager is looking for?

   a.   Pareto diagram.   Correct! See *PMBOK® Guide* 8.1.2.3 The project manager

b. Scatter diagram.	A scatter diagram shows relationships or correlations between independent ("X" axis) and dependent ("Y" axis) variables.
c. Control chart.	A control chart's purpose is to determine whether or not a process is stable or has predictable performance (typically) over time by measuring output variables representing repetitive activities.
d. Checksheet.	A checksheet is often used to collect sampling results information about defects which then may be further analyzed using a Pareto Diagram.

65. A requirement is best described by which of the following:

a. A known deliverable.	The deliverable must be explained through multiple requirements.
b. A documented representation of a condition or capability.	**Correct!** *PMBOK® Guide* **5.2.**
c. Whatever the business analyst deems it to be.	The business analyst often knows best but the input must come from the stakeholders.
d. A list of items presented to the business analyst on a napkin.	This is a method of receiving requirements but not what a requirement is.

66. A good way to obtain delivery team sign-off is through:

a. Diagrams.	May be used in a presentation, but not a complete enough answer.
b. Traceability.	Not appropriate.
c. A presentation.	**Correct!**
d. A feasibility study.	Done before a project is launched, and not appropriate for delivery team sign-off.

67. Which of the following is true about quality control measurements?

a. They are defined in the quality management plan.	Measurements are the results of the activities.
b. They are the results of quality control activities.	**Correct!**
c. They are defined in the quality improvement plan.	There is no such document. There is a quality management plan which specifies the format for documenting quality control measurements. *PMBOK® Guide* 8.3.3.1.
d. They are outputs of perform quality assurance.	They are inputs to that process.

 PMI-PBA Certification Study Guide

68. Which of the following LEAST describes the use of an activity diagram?

  a. A model that illustrates complex use cases.

  > Activity diagrams can be used to show complex use case logic, so this is not correct.

  b. Steps that can be superimposed onto horizontal swimlanes.

  > Activity diagrams are a type of process model, so they can be shown using swimlanes. Not the correct answer.

  c. Showing the human and nonhuman roles that interact with the system.

  > **Correct!**

  d. Illustrates the flow of processes.

  > Activity diagrams are a type of process model, and they show the flow of processes. Not the correct answer accordingly.

69. Suppose you discover that stakeholders complain about requirements for a product. They maintain that a set of requirements applied only to a division in Brazil, and did not pertain to those in the U.S. and Europe. You realize that in presenting the requirements you should have:

  a. Told the Brazilian division that their requirements were out-of-scope.

  > This is not the role of a business analyst.

  b. Determined which requirements were relevant to which stakeholder groups and presented those in an appropriate format.

  > **Correct!**

  c. Determined the appropriate stakeholder groups. The Brazilian division had such unique requirements that their requirements should not have been taken into account.

  > Determining appropriate stakeholder groups is appropriate. However, determining that a group's requirements should not be taken into account is not the role of the business analyst.

  d. Held separate interviews with each stakeholder group in order to determine the unique requirements.

  > The question is about presenting the requirements, not eliciting them.

70. When stakeholders are in disagreement about a requirements to resolve a problem on a project, which method of conflict management will be most effective in that it will likely lead to consensus and commitment?

  a. Compromising.

  > This only brings some degree of satisfaction to all parties.

  b. Smoothing.

  > This does not provide a lasting resolution to a conflict.

  c. Withdrawing.

  > Avoiding a conflict only provides a temporary resolution.

  d. Collaborating.

  > **Correct! *PMBOK® Guide* 9.4.2.3.**

71. If no business analysis standards exist in an organization, what is the best approach?

---

a.	Work with the sponsor to determine the best approach they want to pay for.	The sponsor is only one of the stakeholders the BA needs to work with.
b.	Use a change-driven approach.	The approach will be determined by the BA and the stakeholders.
c.	Follow the PMI-PBA approach.	PMI-PBA is a certified person, not an approach.
d.	**Work with the stakeholders, project manager, and project team to ensure a suitable approach is determined.**	**Correct! A theme of the *PMBOK® Guide*, which is to adapt to stakeholder needs.**

72. Consider a scenario in which a sponsor has initiated an effort to purchase and install a commercial-off-the-shelf (COTS) package. You discover that no other analysis work has been performed. The first thing that typically should be done is to:

a.	Determine the approach to implementing the COTS solution.	It may well happen in many cases, but the *PMBOK® Guide* does not advocate jumping into the solution as presented. The business need is an element of the project charter and must be understood and documented before the project can begin.
b.	Define the scope of the COTS solution.	No, the solution scope would be done after the solution approach, and just before developing a business case. It is not the first thing to do.
c.	Determine how the COTS package meets the business need.	The business needs must be defined before you can determine how well the COTS package meets the need.
d.	**Define the business need that the COTS package is intended to address.**	**Correct! When confronted with a change to a system, the first task is to define why the change is warranted by defining the business need. It applies equally to situations where a sponsor has picked out a package as to other less solution-driven cases. *PMBOK® Guide* 4.1.**

73. Which of the following criteria are the basis for prioritization of requirements?

a.	Stakeholder analysis, regulatory compliance, business risk, technical risk.	Stakeholder agreement, not analysis.
b.	Urgency, technical risk, enterprise architecture, likelihood of success.	Enterprise architecture is used earlier, in needs assessment, but is not used for prioritization.
c.	**Business value, business risk, regulatory compliance, stakeholder agreement.**	**Correct! Prioritization can be based on many factors. Business value tops the list.**
d.	Likelihood of success, urgency, business case, business need.	Business case and business need are close, but 'business value' is what is needed.

74. Which of the following are valid things to document for data attributes:

a.	Cardinality and relationship.	Both apply only to relationships.

b. **Optional vs. mandatory and which entity/class it belongs to.**	Correct! Important things about data attributes.
c. Cardinality and constraints/domains.	Only partially true (constraints).
d. Occurrences and which entity/class it belongs to.	Only partially true (entity).

75. Which of the following is something you would expect to find in a project communications management plan?

a. Implementation plans for any new communications infrastructure that will facilitate better project communications.	No, the communications management plan contains information about project communications as it currently exists, not future plans for new communications methods.
b. Methods that will be used for releasing team members from the project when they are no longer needed.	This would be found in a staffing management plan.
c. List of stakeholders and their potential influence on the project.	This would be found in a stakeholder register.
d. **Communication constraints, including regulations, technology, or organizational policies that may limit project communications.**	Correct!

76. Which of the following business rule is really a requirement?

a. Sales tax is considered part of the total sales price.	This is an operative type of business rule, which applies to any application or project.
b. Sales taxes must be calculated based on state sales tax laws.	This is a structural type of business rule, which applies to any application or project.
c. **A daily report of collected sales taxes must be produced.**	Correct! Specifies a requirement for a project deliverable, whereas business rules transcend projects.
d. Sales tax for a given order is calculated exclusive of any services provided on that order.	This is a structural type of business rule, which applies to any application or project.

77. What techniques are used in business analysis activity planning?

a. Assumptions, dependencies, milestones.	Sounds good on the surface, but not as specific as the correct answer. These are not techniques.
b. Sprint planning, backlog analysis, context diagrams.	Sprint planning is too narrow and specific to only one approach. Context diagrams are not a technique.
c. **Estimation, functional decomposition, risk analysis.**	Correct!

d. Assumptions, unique numbering, milestones.

These are not techniques.

78. A lead BA notices that some of the BAs have information about the project requirements, processes, and stakeholders that would be helpful to the entire BA team. Which of the following would the lead BA use to make sure there is shared understanding among all the BAs:

a. **Requirements traceability matrix.**

Correct! A requirements traceability matrix provides a systematic approach to capture, collect, and share tacit knowledge in order for it to become explicit knowledge.

b. Brainstorming.

Brainstorming may be used to identify ways to share information, but it would not cover all types of sharing and learning.

c. Risk management.

More project than business analysis work. Although there is a risk in not having a shared understanding, a risk management plan would capture the risk and an action plan should it occur, but it would not be a key technique to obtain a common understanding between BAs.

d. Consider project risk, expectations and standards.

Sounds good, but project risk isn't a component of business analysis.

79. You have been asked to facilitate a requirements elicitation activity to prioritize requirements. What techniques might you use?

a. Risk analysis, MoSCoW analysis, stakeholder analysis.

Stakeholder analysis is not a prioritization technique.

b. Decision analysis, risk analysis, estimation.

Estimation is not a prioritization technique.

c. High-Medium-Low, voting, estimation.

Estimation is not a prioritization technique.

d. **Voting, MoSCoW analysis, High-Medium-Low.**

Correct! These are all prioritization techniques.

80. Shortly after the launch of a significant project with high impact to the enterprise, the IT Director has decided to introduce the agile approach and would like to use your project as a pilot. Which of the following concerns of the business analyst is LEAST likely to be affected by this decision:

a. Project management phase strategy.

This would have significant impact to milestone dates and deliverables.

b. **Degree of testing rigor.**

Correct! Testing needs to be just as rigorous with an agile approach.

c. Where the stakeholders are located.

Some agile practices will need to be adapted to a virtual environment.

d. Requirements communications, change management.

This would have significant impact to formal requirements sign-offs and managing 'iterations.'

81. The principal objective of project stakeholder management is to do what?

    a. Identify all potential users of the project to ensure complete requirement analysis.

        This is important, but it is not the main objective.

    b. Thwart criticism of the project by developing a list of responses to known stakeholder concerns.

        Developing a list of responses to known stakeholder concerns is not a reason to do stakeholder management.

    c. Be proactive in managing stakeholder influence on the project to make sure that it is positive.

        Correct! Stakeholder management is all about being proactive to improve the chances that stakeholder influences benefit the project.

    d. Build goodwill in the case of schedule and cost overruns.

        This may be an appealing answer, but it is a bit cynical and definitely not consistent with best practices.

82. You need to schedule resources for an upcoming requirements workshop and brainstorming session. Which of the following best describes that activity?

    a. Include all participants, locations, and resources required.

        Correct! Implied in PMBOK® Guide 5.2.

    b. Determine materials required for techniques.

        Not part of scheduling resources.

    c. Request meeting rooms and participants.

        This is a task you may complete once you have identified all participants, their locations, and the necessary resources.

    d. Determine organizational process assets.

        Not part of scheduling resources.

83. Which development method or approach places more emphasis on requirements prioritization methods?

    a. Neither waterfall nor agile methods.

        Agile approaches emphasize prioritization.

    b. Both waterfall and agile methods.

        Key word is 'more.' Can't be both.

    c. Waterfall.

    d. Agile.

        Correct! Agile approaches tend to place a great deal of emphasis on effective requirements prioritization methods. Since time and money are fixed on agile projects, prioritization aids in delivering value to the business as quickly as possible.

84. Which step typically occurs first when utilizing the survey/questionnaire as a requirements elicitation technique?

    a. Test the survey.

        Testing the survey is the last step before distributing the survey to the target group.

    b. Define the purpose of the survey and select the target survey groups.

        Correct! Defining the purpose of the survey and selecting the target survey groups is the first step in developing a survey/questionnaire.

c. Write the survey questions.

Writing survey questions is the second to the last step in the process, just before testing the survey.

d. Select the distribution and collection methods.

Distribution and collection methods are selected after defining the purpose of the survey and selecting the target survey group.

85. How should requirements communication be performed?

a. Incrementally.

An invented answer.

b. Urgently.

Not necessarily.

c. **Iteratively.**

Correct! Requirements should be communicated iteratively as they become documented for more timely feedback and approval.

d. Sequentially.

An invented answer.

86. Juan has been trying to figure out how best to validate the solution scope with his stakeholders, both business and technical. How can Juan best validate the solution scope with his stakeholders?

a. Conduct a requirements workshop and talk it through with the stakeholders.

This technique could be used in conjunction with creating a domain model but the model needs to be created first.

b. Have a brainstorming session with his stakeholders.

This is a technique for idea generation.

c. **Create a use case diagram and schedule a walk-through or review.**

Correct!

d. Do nothing at all. The architect is responsible for validating solution scope.

According to the *PMI-PBA Examination Content Outline*, the business analyst is responsible for this task.

87. Which of the following would be considered expectations of reliability, one of the non-functional requirements:

a. Restrictions on the distribution of personal information without the express or implicit consent of the parties involved.

Privacy is a type of non-functional requirement, but not specifically a 'reliability' expectation.

b. Safety, security, performance, and trainability.

These are overall non-functional requirements, a higher level than the question is asking.

c. **Ability to recover from errors.**

Correct!

d. Compatibility with other components.

One of the non-functional types, but not specifically a 'reliability' expectation.

88. You have worked on a project to implement a new system. When it was first deployed, it seemed to be performing well. However, as transactions increased over a six-month period, the application slowed to a level deemed unacceptable by the end-users. You have been asked to evaluate this performance. In order to do this, you need to have:

a. Performance metrics of the solution.	**Correct! In order to evaluate the solution performance, measures of how the system performs must be present.**
b. Approval to repair any defects found.	An invented answer.
c. Approval to prevent future defects.	An invented answer.
d. An assessment of the solution performance.	The assessment is what you will create from the evaluation results.

89. John is preparing his business case document before a management presentation. He has worked for several days on it, and wants to be sure he has included all essential elements. John brings the document to you and shows you the Table of Contents below and asks for your feedback. How would you respond?

    a. Overview and Business Need.
    b. Gap Analysis
        1. Current Capability Analysis
        2. Assessment of New Capability Requirements
    c. Solution Approach
        1. Alternatives Considered
        2. Alternative Rankings
        3. Recommended Approach
    d. Solution Capabilities Included
        1. Capability Definition
        2. Implementation Approach
        3. Dependencies
    e. Project Justification
        1. Project cost
        2. Risk Assessment
        3. Results Measurement

a. Great, it looks complete.	It is missing a comparison of benefits to costs.
b. It is missing a stakeholder analysis.	This element is not used for creating a business case.
c. It is missing a comparison of benefits to costs.	**Correct! The cost, risk assessment, and results measurement are included in the Table of Contents, but the cost-benefit analysis is missing.**
d. It is missing the solution scope.	This is an input to the business case and is already included with Table of Contents item 'd,' Solution Capabilities.

90. When is the precedence diagramming method used?

a. In developing the schedule of business analysis activities.	Too broad of an answer. We are looking for a specific step in developing the schedule.

      b. **In sequencing activities.**   **Correct!** *PMBOK® Guide* **6.3.2.1.**

      c. Never. This is a project management tool.   Almost true, however it can apply to scheduling business analysis activities as well.

      d. In estimating activity duration.   It does not include the time activities will take, just the relationships between activities.

91. What type of stakeholders should be involved in defining assumptions and constraints?

      a. Only those stakeholders who are actively attending the project meetings.   This would be unwise to limit to meeting attendees.

      b. Only business stakeholders.   This answer ignores implementation SMEs and others.

      c. **All stakeholders.**   **Correct! Assumptions and constraints may be expressed by any stakeholder.**

      d. Stakeholders defined in the stakeholder analysis.   Stakeholders can change or come into play at any given moment for any task.

92. Which of the following is true about milestones?

      a. They are dummy activities.   This is a made-up answer. There are no 'dummy' activities.

      b. They are insignificant events in the project life cycle.   This is a made-up answer. All events in a project life cycle are significant.

      c. **They are measures of achievement for expenditures of money or time.**   **Correct!**

      d. They are activities with the least duration of all activities in the path.   Milestones are events with a duration of zero.

93. On a project, what needs to be in place before business analysis activities can begin?

      a. Project scope baseline.   This will be developed after the business analysis activities.

      b. Project schedule.   This will be developed after the business analysis activities.

      c. Project activity list.   This will be developed after the business analysis activities.

      d. **Charter.**   **Correct!**

94. All approved changes should be:

      a. Run through Perform Integrated Change Control and reflected in the performance measurement baseline.   Yes, but changes should be reflected in all components of the project management plan.

      b. Run through Monitor and Control Project Work and reflected in the change management plan.   Monitor and control project work is a process that involves assessing project performance and health. Changes would not be reflected in the change management plan.

    c. Run through Monitor and Control Project Work and reflected in the updated deliverables.

Monitor and control project work is a process that involves assessing project performance and health.

    d. Run through Perform Integrated Change Control and reflected in the project management plan.

Correct!

95. Which of the following can be said of both tolerances and control limits?

    a. Tolerances indicate when a process is not being done satisfactorily, whereas control limits identify the thresholds of stakeholder acceptance.

Actually, it's the opposite.

    b. Tolerances and control limits can be used interchangeably to identify boundaries of when a process is out of control or stakeholder acceptance levels have been exceeded.

Tolerances identify the range of stakeholder acceptance levels, whereas control limits provide boundaries within which a process must perform to be considered in control.

    c. Tolerances identify the range of stakeholder acceptance levels, whereas control limits provide boundaries within which a process must perform to be considered in control.

Correct! *PMBOK® Guide* 8.3.

    d. Tolerances are a quality metric used in quality assurance, whereas control limits are used in controlling quality.

These concepts are not specific to a particular process. Tolerances are defined in Plan Quality and used in both quality assurance and control.

96. Consider the following situation: An analyst is called into an effort to build a third website for her company. The site will be used to display and sell merchandise and will be updated daily with additions and deletions of items, price changes, sales and promotions, etc. In this scenario, which is the project, and which is the product?

    a. The project is building the website, and the product is the new website.

Correct! *PMBOK® Guide* **distinguishes between the project and product. Projects are temporary endeavors to create something unique, and building a new website fits that. The deliverable of the project is the new website.**

    b. The project is building the website, and the product is updating and maintaining the site.

Projects are temporary endeavors to create something unique, and building a new website fits that. But, the process of updating and maintaining is a process, not a product.

    c. The project is updating and maintaining the site, and the product is the new website.

The process of updating and maintaining is a process, not a project. The deliverable of the project is the new website.

    d. The project is building the website, and

Correct! *PMBOK® Guide* distinguishes between the project and product. Projects are temporary endeavors to create

the product is the new website.

something unique, and building a new website fits that. The deliverable of the project is the new website.

97. As soon as you were assigned to a project, you were advised to begin planning for the requirements work to be done. What do you need before you can begin the requirements management plan?

   a. **Business case**

   Correct! You need an understanding of the context of the project, including the business case, before you can begin planning.

   b. Stakeholder analysis.

   Stakeholder analysis is ongoing and will not be complete prior to planning requirements management.

   c. Project management plan.

   The requirements management plan is a subsidiary of the overall project plan.

   d. Requirements baseline.

   This requirements management plan includes information used in developing the requirements baseline.

98. Brainstorming would be the most suitable technique for uncovering requirements in which of the following types of activity:

   a. Add detail to the current process flow for work order transmittals through the warehouse.

   Detail is best done by interviewing or observing an individual or small group, rather than getting different ideas from a variety of individuals.

   b. Identify dependent tasks in the requirements project plan.

   Not applicable. While determining tasks can be done by brainstorming, it is not the best answer. In addition, there is no such thing as a requirements project plan. There are business analysis plans for each knowledge area.

   c. **Consult with managers from similar functional units across dispersed locations in an attempt to find process improvement opportunities.**

   Correct! This item isn't as specific or detailed as the others. Brainstorming would be appropriate to uncover unknown opportunities.

   d. Determine the appropriate format for requirements communications to key technical stakeholders.

   This is a matter of stakeholder preference and is better done with individual stakeholders.

99. Which of the following statements best describes an agile approach?

   a. **Presume that it is difficult to identify all requirements in advance of their implementation and choose requirements from a product backlog.**

   Correct! A product backlog is one way to implement a process where highest-priority requirements will be taken from the backlog for detailed requirements analysis.

   b. Capture requirements in a formal document or set of documents which follow standardized templates that are formally approved.

   Describes a waterfall approach.

   c. Produce formal documentation before the solution is developed and implemented.

        Describes a waterfall approach.

   d. Complete most business analysis work at the beginning of the project or during one specific project phase.

        Describes a waterfall approach.

100. Components of a good problem statement include which of the following?

   a. Definition of the problem and who is responsible.

        Problem statements are not intended to place blame on anyone or identify responsible people or groups.

   b. Definition of the problem and who is affected.

        Correct!

   c. How the problem impacts the stakeholders and who will have to pay to address the problem.

        Problem statements do not identify solutions or who will pay for the solution to the problem.

   d. How the problem impacts the stakeholders and how much it will cost to address the problem.

        Problem statements do not identify solutions or the cost for a solution to the problem.

11. Index

A

Acceptance criteria · 124, 182
Accepted requirements · 166
Activity diagram · 223
Adaptive life cycle · 103
Affinity Diagram · 345
Allocate requirements · 149, 151, 168
Allocated requirements · 170
Alternate paths · 227
Analogous · 129
Analysis Domain · 17, 147
Analysis Mnemonic · 149
Analysis Tasks · 149, 153
Analysis Techniques · 187
Analysis Themes · 147
Analyze solution gaps · 291, 292, 297
Analyze, decompose, and elaborate requirements · 149, 151, 159
Assumptions · 179
Attitude and influence · 52
Attitude factors · 52
Attributes · 197
Attributes, requirements · 162
Authority levels · 53
Averaging · 130

B

Backlog management · 277
Baseline · 54, 118
Baselining requirements · 118
Benchmarking · 61
Benefits of PMI-PBA® Certification · 6
Bottom-up estimating · 130
Brainstorming · 205
Business analysis activities · 112
Business events · 221
Business objective models · 69
Business opportunity · 40
Business problem · 39
Business rule analysis · 158, 193
Business rules · 193
Business value · 180

C

Cardinality · 197
Cause and effect diagram · 64
CBAP Application Process · 2
Change control · 115, 119, 122, 127, 128, 273, 274

Change Control Board · 117
Change Control Plan · 272
Change request · 116
Checksheet · 299, 313
Class model · 199
Collaboration (competency) · 337
Communicate requirements status · 255, 257, 267
Communication (competency) · 338
Communication Model · 340
Communication Plan · 268
Compare requirements to product scope · 151, 165, 166
Competencies · 17, 335
Competitive analysis · 61
Complexity of Stakeholder Group · 51
Configuration management · 118
Configuration Management System · 118, 276
Conflict management (competency) · 342
Consensus building · 202
Context Diagram · 67
Control chart · 299, 314
Cost of Quality · 295
Cost-Benefit Analysis · 73

D

Data analysis · 163, 177, 194
Data dictionary · 195
Data flow diagrams · 195
Data models · 197
Day-in-the Life (DITL) Testing · 319
Decision making · 167, 171, 175, 202
Decision table · 194
Decision tree · 194
Decomposition · 190
Deferred requirements · 166
Define business need · 35, 36, 38
Define project expected outcomes · 97, 99, 123
Delphi technique · 202
Dependencies · 170
Dependencies for benefits realization · 180
Dependency graph · 221
Design of experiments · 315
Desk checking · 320
Determine project context · 97, 98, 100
Determine stakeholder values · 35, 37, 54
Determine value proposition · 35, 36, 42
Develop project goals · 35, 36, 44
DFD · See Data flow diagram
Display-Action-Response · 217
Document analysis · 206
Document control · 121
Document elicitation results · 157
Domain Mnemonic · 18
Domains · 15

E

Ecosystem Map · 68
Elicit requirements · 149, 151, 153
Elicitation · 56, 59, 204
Elicitation activities · 156
Elicitation issues and challenges · 158
Elicitation results · 157
Entity · 197
Entity relationship diagram · 198
Estimation · 113, 127, 129
Estimation poker · 131
Evaluate Product Options and Capabilities · 149
Evaluate solution results · 291, 292, 303
Evaluation · 305
Evaluation Domain · 17, 289
Evaluation Tasks · 291
Evaluation Techniques · 308
Evaluation Themes · 289
Evalutation Mnemonic · 291
Exam Questions, Types of · 369
Exam taking tips · 368
Exploratory testing · 319

F

Facilitated workshops · 206
Facilitation (competency) · 343
Facilitator · 206
Feasibility analysis · 74
Feature Model · 69
Fishbone / Ishikawa Diagram · 64
Five Whys · 64, 65
Focus groups · 207
Force Field Analysis · 75

G

Gap analysis · 192
General Exam-Taking Tactics · 7
Get requirements sign-off · 149, 152, 173
Get solution sign-off · 291, 292, 301
Given-When-Then · 319
Glossary · 195
Go/No-Go Decision · 302
Goal models · 69

H

High, Medium, Low · 220
Histogram · 316

I

Identify stakeholders · 35, 37, 49, 50
Impact analysis · 192
Incremental approach · 104
Influence factors · 53
Integration Testing · 319
Interactive communication · 339
Interface analysis · 163, 177, 214
Interoperability · 214
Interrelationship Diagram · 66
Interrelationships · 259
Interviewing · 208
Interviews · 208
Issue (problem) tracking · 277
Iterative approach · 104

J

Job Analysis · 70
Job Shadowing · 211

K

Kano Model · 76
Key Performance Indicators · 124, 218
KPI · *See* Key Performance Indicators

L

Leadership (competency) · 345
Lessons Learned · 110, 310

M

Manage requirement changes · 255, 257, 271
Management components · 108
Matrix diagram · 317
Matrix documentation · 161
Measurable evaluation criteria · 179
Measure solution performance · 124
Measurement · 124, 183, 305
Mind Mapping · 345
Models as requirements · 162
Monitor requirements status · 255, 256, 262
MoSCoW · 220
Multi-Voting · 202

N

Needs Assessment Domain · 16, 33

PMI-PBA Certification Study Guide

Needs Assessment Mnemonic · 35
Needs Assessment Tasks · 35
Needs Assessment Techniques · 59
Needs Assessment Themes · 33
Negotiation (competency) · 343
Net Promoter Score · 76
Nominal Group Technique · 203
Non-functional requirements · 209
NPS · *See* Net Promoter Score

O

Object · 226
Observation · 211
Opportunity identification · 41, 60
Options Analysis · 203
Organizational chart · 70

P

Parametric estimating · 132
Pareto diagram · 299, 317
PDM · *See* Precedence Diagramming Method
Peer review · 320
Personas · 71
Plan document control · 97, 99, 121
Plan requirements change control · 97, 99
Plan requirements management · 97, 98, 109
Plan requirements traceability · 97, 98
Planguage · 219
Planning Domain · 17, 95
Planning Mnemonic · 97
Planning Tasks · 97
Planning Techniques · 127
Planning Themes · 95
PMI-PBA® Application Steps · 4
PMI-PBA® Applications · 3
PMI-PBA® Exam Experience · 6
PMI-PBA® Themes · 10
Political / Cultural Awareness (competency) · 347
Precedence Diagramming Method · 133
Predictive life cycle · 102
Primary (normal) path · 227
Prioritization · 112, 127, 168, 171
Problem and opportunity analysis · 39
Problem solving · 41, 59, 60
Process · 222
Process analysis · 163, 177
Process Decision Program Chart · 318
Process models · 66, 222
Product backlog · 277
Product scope · 166
Product scope baseline · 55
Progressive elaboration · 263
Project approach · 113
Project drivers · 40

Project life cycle · 101
Project Life Cycle Approaches · 23
Project management plan · 113
Prototypes · 214
Pull communication · 339
Purpose Alignment Model · 77
Push communication · 339

Q

Quality control · 312
Question Types · 208
Questionnaire · 212

R

RACI · 50, 72
Rejected requirements · 166
Relationships of requirements · 260
Report table · 215
Requirement models · 162
Requirement relationships
    Benefit or value dependency · 191
    Implementation dependency · 191
    Subset · 191
Requirements alignment · 180
Requirements attributes · 162
Requirements baseline · 173
Requirements change control · 115
Requirements Change Control Plan · 119
Requirements conflicts · 174
Requirements dependencies · 191
Requirements Management Plan · 109, 113, 114
Requirements Management Tools · 261
Requirements prioritization · 168
Requirements status · 167
Requirements traceability · 96, 105
Requirements Traceability Matrix · 105, 278, 296
Requirements traceability plan · 109
Retrospectives · 110, 311
Risk analysis · 193
Risk planning · 112
Role definition · 50, 72
Root cause analysis · 41, 59, 64, 299
Rough Order of Magnitude · 129

S

Scatter diagram · 318
Scenario analysis · 62
Scenarios · 227
Scheduling · 113, 127
Scope models · 46, 59, 67
Scope statement · 45
Scribe · 206

Sequence Diagram Example · 227
Sequence diagrams · 226
Service level agreements · 219
Skills assessment · 73
SLA · *See* Service level agreement
SMART objectives · 45
Solution gaps · 298
Specify acceptance criteria · 150, 152, 181
Stages of Team Development · 337
Stakeholder analysis · 54, 60, 70
Stakeholder approval · 174
Stakeholder Identification · 50
Stakeholder register · 54
State diagram · 200
State Diagram Example · 201
Statistical sampling · 318
Storyboards · 216
Survey · 212
SWAG · *See* Rough Order of Magnitude
Swimlane flowchart · 225
SWOT analysis · 78
System interface table · 216
Systems Thinking (competency) · 348

T

Test Preparation Roadmap · 360
Text requirements · 160
Three-Point Estimation · 130
Trace requirements · 255, 256, 258
Traceability · 127, 259
Traceability and Monitoring Domain · 17, 253
Traceability and Monitoring Mnemonic · 255
Traceability and Monitoring Tasks · 254
Traceability and Monitoring Techniques · 276
Traceability and Monitoring Themes · 253
Traceability attributes · 107
Traceability benefits · 259
Traceability components · 107
Traceability levels · 259
Traceability tools and techniques · 261

Tuckman Model · 337
Types of Exam Questions · 8

U

Update requirements status · 255, 256, 264
Use Case Description Example · 229
Use case diagram · 69, 228
Use Case Diagram Examples · 228
Use cases · 227
User acceptance testing · 320
User interactions · 176
User interface flow · 216
User journey map · 62
User stories · 230
User Story Example · 231

V

Validate requirements · 152, 179
Validate test results · 291, 292, 293
Validation · 127, 180, 183, 296
Valuation · 43, 60, 73, 167, 171, 305
Value engineering · 63
Value Stream Map · 79
Verification · 180, 296
Version control · 121
Version Control System · 121, 279

W

Walk-throughs · 321
WBS · *See* Work Breakdown Structure
Weighted Criteria · 203
Wireframes · 217
Work Breakdown Structure · 111, 191
Write requirements specifications · 150, 152, 175

PMI-PBA Certification Study Guide

About the Authors

Elizabeth Larson, CBAP, PMP, PMI-PBA, CSM, and Richard Larson, CBAP, PMP, PMI-PBA are Co-Principals of Watermark Learning (www.watermarklearning.com), a globally recognized Business Analysis, Project Management, Agile, and Business Process Management training company.

For over 30 years, they have used their extensive experience in both business analysis and project management to help thousands of BA, PM, and BPM practitioners develop new skills. They have helped build Watermark's training into a unique combination of industry best practices, an engaging format, and a practical approach. Attendees immediately learn the retainable real-world skills that enable them to produce enduring results.

Between them they have presented workshops, seminars, and training classes on five different continents. Their speaking history includes repeat appearances at Project Management Institute (PMI) North American, European, and Asia-Pacific Congresses, and at the BBC/Business Analysis Forum, and Business Analyst World conferences in North America and India.

Both Elizabeth and Richard are among the world's first Certified Business Analysis Professionals through the International Institute of Business Analysis (IIBA®) and are contributors to all editions of the IIBA® Business Analysis Body of Knowledge (*BABOK® Guide*). Elizabeth was the lead author for the Business Analysis Planning and Monitoring Knowledge Area. Richard was a lead author for version 3.0 of the *BABOK® Guide*. They are also certified Project Management Professionals and are contributors and lead authors to the 4th edition of the Project Management Body of Knowledge (*PMBOK® Guide*). Elizabeth is the content lead for the entire Scope Management Knowledge Area in the 5th edition of the *PMBOK® Guide*. Both Larsons were lead authors for PMI's <u>Business Analysis for Practitioners: A Practice Guide</u>.

The Larsons are proud parents of two children and grandparents of six lively grandsons. They love to travel and have visited over 35 countries around the world.